One Year
to an
Organized Life

One Year
to an
Organized Life

A Week-by-Week Mindful Guide
to Getting Organized for Good

Regina Leeds

hachette
BOOKS

New York

Hachette Go, an imprint of Hachette Books
Hachette Book Group
1290 Avenue of the Americas
New York, NY 10104
HachetteGo.com
Facebook.com/HachetteGo
Instagram.com/HachetteGo

Previously published by Da Capo Lifelong Books: January 2008
First Hachette Go Edition: December 2022

Hachette Books is a division of Hachette Book Group, Inc.
The Hachette Go and Hachette Books name and logos are trademarks of Hachette Book Group, Inc.

The publisher is not responsible for websites (or their content) that are not owned by the publisher.

Library of Congress Cataloging-in-Publication Data

Name: Leeds, Regina, author.
Title: One year to an organized life: a week-by-week mindful guide to getting organized for good / Regina Leeds.
Other titles: 1 year to an organized life
Description: Revised edition. | New York, NY: Hachette Go, 2022. | Revised edition of One Year to an Organized Life, 2010.
Identifiers: LCCN 2022019043 | ISBN 9780306829642 (paperback) | ISBN 9780306829659 (ebook)
Subjects: LCSH: Home economics. | Orderliness. | Storage in the home.
Classification: LCC TX147 .L387 2022 | DDC 640—dc23/eng/20220712
LC record available at https://lccn.loc.gov/2022019043

ISBNs: 9780306829642 (trade paperback); 9780306829659 (ebook)

Printed in the United States of America

LSC-C

Printing 1, 2022

ALSO BY REGINA LEEDS

The Zen of Organizing: Creating Order and Peace in Your Home, Career, and Life (2002)

Sharing a Place Without Losing Your Space: A Couple's Guide to Blending Homes, Lives, and Clutter (2003)

The Complete Idiot's Guide to Decluttering: Win the Turf War with Your Stuff (2007)

One Year to an Organized Work Life: From Your Desk to Your Deadlines, the Week-by-Week Guide to Eliminating Office Stress for Good (2008)

One Year to an Organized Financial Life: From Your Bills to Your Bank Account, Your Home to Your Retirement, the Week-by-Week Guide to Achieving Financial Peace of Mind (2009)

One Year to an Organized Life with Baby: From Pregnancy to Parenthood, the Week-by-Week Guide to Getting Ready for Baby and Keeping Your Family Organized (2011)

The 8-Minute Organizer: Easy Solutions to Simplify Your Life in Your Spare Time (2012)

Rightsize... Right Now! The 8-Week Plan to Organize, Declutter, and Make Any Move Stress-Free (2015)

My life has been graced by an
astonishing array of teachers and mentors.
This book is for all of them with my deep gratitude.
I extend special thanks to my beloved Thakur,
the incomparable Ramakrishna Ananda,
and all my animal companions.

CONTENTS

A MINDFUL APPROACH

Quiet the mind and the Soul will speak.

—MA JAYA

I F YOU PICKED UP THIS BOOK, CHANCES are good that you have a little chaos in your life. I can absolutely help you clear that up. The physical act of getting organized is fun and creative once you move past the negative feelings most people conjure at the very mention of the word. You gain so many advantages when you are organized, such as having a distraction-free environment and an inventory of what you own.

Divide and...Struggle

We human beings excel at creating mental compartments in order to deal with what are daunting demands on our time, our bodies, and our lives. We have families, careers, jobs, social lives, and friends. Many have a Spiritual practice that involves a church, synagogue, or mosque. Things like hobbies and vacations fill more compartments.

Countless families have additional challenges, such as caring for an elderly parent, homeschooling a child (especially during the COVID era), or having grown children return to the nest. The list is endless and unique to each individual. We all need coping mechanisms to deal effectively with the onslaught. It's easy to zone out in front of the TV, binge on junk food, or have a little too much alcohol. Means of escape are as numerous as the challenges they are meant to thwart.

If your goal is to live in a magazine-shoot-ready home, you can skip to the how-to instructions in each section. On the other hand, if you'd like to literally change your life, including your relationship with time, how you treat your body, the goals you dream about fulfilling, and the way you think, I invite you to read every section, complete the written assignments, see which self-care suggestions you like, and do as many of the projects as are pertinent to your life, And, guess what? You will be a different person in one year, a person who just happens to have a magazine-shoot-ready environment. Your home will inspire you to fulfill your life purpose. In truth, that is my ultimate goal for you. At

1

the end of a year you will understand that organizing is a life skill that assists you just like all the other tools presented in this book, including meditation, aromatherapy, and nutrient-dense food to name a few.

The tools I introduce may be foreign to you, but each has old if not ancient roots in the history of mankind. You don't have to adopt everything I offer. Adapt to your life what feels right. Do your own research if something feels inspiring or healing and you have the desire to know more. You can start with a general Google search of the term or plug a few key words in the Amazon book search feature. Be sure to check out the source of the material before you begin reading and trust what you discover. Learning how to research is a lost art for most people today, and I hope this book inspires you to ignite that skill in your life as well as those with whom you live and work to do the same.

For example, Mindfulness is everywhere in the zeitgeist now. You could easily find articles on popular websites in order to deepen the simple practices I suggest here. You would, however, really launch into your new practice by finding renowned experts in the field like Jon Kabat-Zinn and Sharon Salzberg. (I will include websites in the Resources section.) Once you find the teachers you feel you can trust, you have the pleasure of deepening your knowledge through practice, whether it's meditation, working with oils in aromatherapy, learning about food as energy rather than comfort, or organizing.

This book offers steps, plans, tips, and tricks. All organizing books have them. My approach is unique because it shows you how to prepare for your projects and how each one is a metaphor for all of life's demands, projects, and adventures. Zen Organizing™ removes your closet, kitchen, and office files from the isolated category all organizers put them in and allows them to be teachers and places to practice newfound life skills. Zen Organizing™ seeks to free you from the mundane chaos you have unconsciously chosen to wrap yourself in and free you to fulfill your life purpose, that unique contribution that no one else can make.

A Secure Foundation

Have you ever had the opportunity to watch a skyscraper being built? The first step is to clear away the debris on the land and go as deep into the earth as the structure that rises will need for support. You can skimp on this to save money, time, and energy, but we live in a cause-and-effect universe. When the building lists to one side, you will rue the day you cut corners on the foundation. The more carefully planned the foundation is, the more secure the skyscraper will be.

I want to do just that for you: lay a solid foundation for change. I want to shift your focus away from that extra glass of wine and give you stress-relieving tools that will help you soar as a human being. I don't want you to spend your days at a job you hate. I want you to uncover and fulfill your life purpose. When unexpected, gut-wrenching challenges come, as they do to all of us, you will use the tools you employed to organize your home to meet the challenge at hand.

Organization undergirds everything. Yes, it's true. Name something, from losing weight or starting an exercise program to getting a PhD or directing a blockbuster movie, and I will apply the Zen Organizing™ principles you are going to use to organize your closet or your files. Objects change but the modus operandi is universal. This is the essence of my system called Zen Organizing™. Once you understand this concept deep in your DNA, you'll see the time spent organizing your physical space as practice time to help make every aspect of your life easier. Organizing becomes an act of self-love and an expression of high self-esteem, not a waste of time that you could otherwise use to have fun or do "something important."

Organizing is a deeper, richer pursuit than the how-to videos so popular on social media would have you believe. It can in fact be a Mindfulness practice. To be sure, there are skillful ways to fold socks, store toys, and manage paper, but these hacks are the caboose on the Organizing Train. We're going to learn what drives it as well as examine ways to support you when exhaustion and overwhelm threaten to derail your best intentions. I've started a little macro here, so let's home in on the micro of your life and work our way back.

I Know You

Let's see how accurately I can describe some of your personal organizing challenges. You engage in a near-constant quest for your house keys, your eyeglasses, and all the remotes in your home. Invitations, personal notes, and letters are lost in a sea of paper debris on your desk. Secretly you are ashamed that you have over ten thousand unopened emails on your computer, including those for sales that ended a decade ago. You never use a calendar because you store your schedule in your head. The night before an important meeting, you plan the perfect outfit. Finding all the items in your closet, however, is usually impossible. TikTok, Instagram, and YouTube are your drugs of choice. You peruse them for hours convinced that once you find the perfect product or learn the best hack, you will turn into the organizing genius you suspect yourself to be. You want to help your children succeed. Your heart sinks each time you see them frantically search for a lost homework assignment, a note from their teacher, or a favorite toy. This is not the example you meant to set.

Your home is not your castle; it's your prison. Guilt is your frequent companion. You want your life experience to be bigger, richer, but it seems to be forever diminished by an endless series of dramas, all of which have a lack of organization as their source.

Take heart—help is at hand. In fact, it is literally in your hands as you read these words.

HOW DID I KNOW?

Can you guess how I was able to pinpoint many of the common challenges you face without ever having met you in person? I have been organizing clients across the United States for over thirty years. What I have learned is that everyone has pretty much the same amount of stuff. The reality is that getting organized is an achievable goal for absolutely everyone. Give me one year of your life. I'll prove it to you! What do you have to lose except a glut of mental, emotional, and physical clutter that's weighing you down—body, mind, and Soul? The format of a year gives you time to plan carefully and never once be overwhelmed. I have planned downtime throughout the book. This isn't a constant, nonstop, fifty-two-week slog through your physical space. It's a journey to gently create a new life.

A GOOD TIME TO START

Now that I've convinced you it's possible, when do we get started? You know what they say: "There's no time like the present." Every midnight ushers in a new day that we have never lived before. We seem to embrace the message most powerfully as we greet a new year. Perhaps it is the collective impetus of just about every human being on the planet making a wish for a better life. Here's the good news: You don't have to wait for January to roll around. *One Year to an Organized Life* has projects and discoveries that will move you forward in your quest to get organized once and for all. After you're organized, this book can serve as your coach when you need to do those obligatory tune-ups. Imagine the

state of your car if you never changed the oil, checked the fluids, or ran diagnostic tests on its computer. What about your teeth if you decided to save money and never see a dentist? Everything requires maintenance, including your home and work life.

THE PROCESS REVEALED

The projects in this book cover every square inch of your home and every aspect of your life. For example, in a year you will have a bedroom that's a sanctuary, a kitchen that inspires you, and a garage where you actually park your car. Photos will be in albums you share with family and friends rather than tossed into boxes that clog your closets. No hard copies of photos in your living space? Let's tidy up the hard drives where they live and perhaps find an electronic frame for your home or a program for your computer that automatically rotates them. If you never pick up an album, you can still be filled with joy every time you glance over and catch a random smile or memory. Whatever you own and keep needs to serve you; otherwise it's just clutter. It will exhaust and upset you. Zen Organizing™ is after ease, balance, and support.

Do you still have CDs, DVDs, and other forms of entertainment filling up drawers in the family room? Let's cull them, sell them, or get them ready to entertain you. Their life as creative debris has come to an end. Assignments will be turned in as requested whether they are for your children's school or your CEO. You'll be on time for appointments and wearing clothes you love. Any needed piece of paper will be produced in a matter of seconds. You might even find yourself tossing a party for the first time in years. Sounds inviting, doesn't it?

Some months, the work will be time consuming and an emotional challenge. Other months, the projects will be a breeze to complete. Because each of you is different, every reader's journey will be unique. It's not unlike a marathon. The runners line up. They take off after they hear the starting pistol. They all cross the finish line, yet each will have had a unique journey that reflects their training, nutrition, natural ability, and a host of other factors. For our purposes, everyone is a winner. In fact, showing up and making the effort makes you a hero in my book.

Does this sound impossible? Do you fear that getting organized is not a realistic goal for you? One of the reasons why I chose the format of weekly assignments spread out over a year is that it gives you ample time to cover all the bases. The first step, however, isn't something that happens in your physical environment. You don't need to snap this book shut, jump up, and tackle a pile or toss out a stack of anything. You *do* have to make a commitment. After that, you'll want to learn the simple mechanics—what I call the tips and tricks—of getting organized. Everyone loves this part. Tips and tricks are useful, fun, and the nitty-gritty aspect of the process. They do not, however, strike at the heart of the matter. Something deeper

and much more interesting is waiting for your discovery.

The chaos around you is an *effect*. It is the result of a cause that was set in motion most likely, but not always, a long time ago. You probably have never made the connection between a pattern you wish to change and the experience that pushed the first domino in the sequence. Over the course of the next year, we are going to set *new* causes into motion—the kind that yield positive results. Instead of living in an environment that is your adversary, you will live in a space that nurtures and supports you at every step of your journey. You'll have an environment, for example, that's ready to greet guests who drop in without warning. Imagine losing the fear of those unannounced visits your mother-in-law likes to make! I'm going to turn you into a mini Sherlock Holmes. I'm also going to give you tools to control the fear and sense of overwhelm when they inevitably arise. Tools, by the way, you can use for the rest of your life in every situation that stresses you out.

Working with Reality

Roger came into my life in the first years of my business. He is a delight. He was also a slob. Roger had the good grace to realize he needed to change. He was engaged to be married and wanted to get organized before he and his fiancée moved in together. There is a balance in the universe that amuses me. The person who saves everything inevitably hooks up with the one who tosses with abandon. The spender finds his way to the tightwad. And the slob and the neatnik are bound to fall in love. The latter described Roger and his fiancée, Jan, to a T.

We weeded through his belongings. We agreed that only the things he really used, loved, or enjoyed should be brought to the new home. As we sorted through his possessions, I asked Roger what his childhood home had been like. Had he been assigned chores? Did he have to pick up his room? Would he describe one parent as tidy and the other as a slob? Would it be fair to say one parent was organized, while the other functioned as an absent-minded professor? It turned out that not only had he never been asked to be responsible in the home, his childhood environment was chaotic. Human beings often replicate what they see from an early age. It becomes an unconscious part of our emotional DNA.

I spent several days with Roger and made some notes. The bottom line was a simple fact of life: Every action has a reaction. If you never complete your actions, it's like having a thousand golden threads scattered about. Something beautiful could be made from these threads if we could only figure out where the ends were. How did this manifest for Roger? He never closed a drawer all the way. He never shut a cabinet door. Food came out of the refrigerator and languished on the counter. Soiled dishes piled up in the sink. Dirty clothes hit the floor. Any item returned from the cleaners kept its plastic cover and stayed on the wire hanger. Every few hours, a drama repeated itself with the regularity of Big Ben in London.

It was called "Where the heck are my keys?!" You get the idea. Why are these things important? If you don't complete the mundane tasks in life, you probably aren't completing the bigger ones either.

Roger instantly understood. It wasn't really about closing a cupboard door. It was about follow-through and completion. The open cupboard, the food on the counter, and the dirty dishes stacked to the ceiling all represented a lack of caring. To help facilitate change in this situation, Roger and I came up with a series of new habits. It's best to make small, incremental changes rather than try to do a total makeover all at once. That type of experience works on TV to create great drama for the audience. It doesn't work well in real life. You have to make realistic changes to succeed over the long haul. Take a minute and ask yourself whether any golden threads are in your life. By the way, the golden threads in Roger's life are no longer scattered about his physical space. His home is tidy and organized. He and his wife are true partners when it comes to maintaining order in the home. And, oh yes, their children have chores! Habits were the key, and we're going to deal with that in detail in just a minute.

From Treasure to Trash in a Flash

Roger's issues began in his childhood, but that's not the only way life can become disorganized. I'd like to share an experience I had a number of years ago. Yes, even a professional organizer can be thrust into chaos. It happened when the Northridge earthquake hit Los Angeles. At the time,

I had been through numerous small shakers, as Angelenos like to call them. But I had never experienced anything like this. As the song says, "I feel the earth move under my feet." The Northridge quake made the earth move, all right. The three-story building I lived in rocked and swayed like a small boat riding an ocean wave as it breaks on the shore.

When the shaking stopped, I leapt out of bed and called for my Golden Retriever. After five calls, I felt her sweet presence next to me. We raced out of the apartment, and, using a flashlight, I found our way to the manager's apartment, which became command central for everyone who lived in the building.

When the sun rose, we came back to our apartment. I can't adequately describe the destruction. Furniture had fallen over. Books were scattered everywhere. Decorative items and lamps were shattered. Little shards of glass were embedded in the carpet. My kitchen looked like a mad chef had flown through and smashed all my spice jars on the floor. It was overwhelming. I wanted to run away. I went into shock, a protective mechanism the mind uses when reality is too much to bear.

Aftershocks continued to move the earth for days. Had we experienced "The Big One," or was it still to come? Although we were all on pins and needles, my neighbors were amazing. We opened our doors and worked as a team. We helped each other, encouraged each other, checked on each other.

I was particularly devastated to have lost most of the china I inherited from my mother. I came up with the idea that I would match the pieces and glue them back together. Hilarious in the light of day, isn't it? In my altered state, it made perfect sense. My neighbor Nina came in and asked what I was doing. I thought it was clear. I politely told her, and I will never forget what she said. "Honey, you can't do that. You have to sweep it up and throw it away."

I responded: "What? Like so much trash!"

"Yes," said Nina, "because that's what it is now."

About two weeks after the earthquake, I was amazed to see piles of papers everywhere around my apartment! When life was normal, I had a routine. Every day I went through my papers as they entered my home. After the quake, although intellectually I knew exactly what I had to do with each item, I was immobilized. I identified the paper, and it sat on my coffee table. I wasn't consciously avoiding the task indicated; I was caught in the snare of depression. Have sorrow, loss, or depression ever prevented you from tending to your home and obligations?

The greatest gift being organized affords you is having a template to follow. In time, I was able to get my world together; I didn't have to start from scratch. I simply had to "work" the system. These systems are the key to your long-term ability to stay organized. You aren't doing anything extra. You are simply shifting your energy to a different set of action steps. For example, Roger no longer tossed his clothes onto the floor when they were dirty. He tossed them into a hamper. As you examine your situation, you will be astonished to see the complex system you have in place that keeps you mired in chaos.

Every section has an affirmation. Take a photo of the affirmation with your smartphone and read it every morning. These affirmations set the tone for your day.

Affirmation of the Month

A new way of living, coping, and being productive beckons to me. I am grateful for everything that has brought me to this moment in time. Judgment, fear, and negative thoughts are left in the past. I surrender.

WEEK ONE

Dive In

This week, you can

- Appreciate the benefits of order
- Understand how a Zen Organizer™ works
- Consider making a vision board
- Choose your journal
- Meet your first self-care practice

Time required: Devote ten minutes to read this week's material and then fifteen minutes to order your supplies. You'll want another fifteen to thirty minutes to work on your vision board.

THE BENEFITS OF ORDER

I believe that an organized life enables one to have more time, less aggravation, better health, and a chance to accomplish more. There can be no doubt that getting organized when you're starting at ground zero takes a lot of careful planning, time, and energy. It's easy to become overwhelmed. It's common to abandon the cause in midstream. This book circumvents all the traps. It serves as your step-by-step guide to a new life and also introduces you to folks just like you who have taken the plunge and succeeded. You'll be able to create templates that you can alter to suit your needs and use every year. I use the design app Canva, as it has templates for every possible need. There is a free version and one that requires a modest monthly fee. You might enjoy the app so much that you wind up creating infographics, handouts, presentations, habit trackers, chore charts, food shopping lists, and the like for your work, your children, your hobbies, and your family. I have no artistic ability, but Canva makes me feel like Picasso.

WHY DO WE GET DISORGANIZED?

I need to stress the importance of your commitment to the process of getting organized. Without it, a team of the world's greatest organizers living with you for an entire year would be of no benefit. No one can impose order on a chaotic mind. The creation of physical chaos always begins with our very thought processes. We are overloaded, distracted, and unable to concentrate. It continues to be difficult to think clearly, to be calm, or even to be healthy when the atmosphere in which we live and work is a swirling mass of constant upheaval. We know we need to get organized, but fear stops us. Often a lack of simple organization skills accompanies this frozen state. We look around our self-created environments and we are immobilized.

As we grow older, the problems multiply. "Well," we think, "now is not the time to get organized. I have reports due at work, diapers to change, mounds of laundry to tend to, and carpool duties!" If you believe, as I do, that we come here with a specific set of talents to develop and express, you can see how this unconscious state of affairs can lead to weariness that affects every aspect of our lives. Living a fulfilled life shouldn't be the province of a few. It is our birthright. The shift begins the minute you make the commitment to get organized.

Given the parameter of one year, anyone can gradually learn the necessary skills and make the time to achieve transformation. As your physical environment transforms, something magical happens.

Your life canvas transforms as well. Think about it. If living in chaos makes you feel tired and depressed and causes you to lose time and money, think how powerful an organized environment must be and how it can empower you. Who would you be if you felt at peace and had more time and more money? We're going to find out.

MY PERSONAL GOALS FOR YOU

In terms of the purely physical, my ultimate goal is to help you create an environment that is at once beautiful to look at, completely functional, and easy to maintain. I also want to help you understand why you haven't had this up until now (remember Roger) or identify what happened that took you off course (the Northridge earthquake for me). Our life experiences affect us on every level of our being. Too often, we compartmentalize our experiences as if they are unrelated. I hope you will embrace a more holistic approach to your life.

Finally, I believe that you are a Spiritual being having an earthly experience. I don't want to see the process of getting organized become your new focus or hobby. Rather, I want being organized to be a tool in your new self-care tool kit, which might include your Spiritual studies, exercise, diet, circle of family and friends, even time with a qualified therapist. I'll be adding my favorites over the course of this year. You'll find a self-care practice in the introduction to all the sections that follow. You'll be able to incorporate it immediately into your organizing journey for that month. You'll find many of these practices work together, and you'll be able to create meaningful rituals. The world is waiting for the unique contribution you were born to make. Are you ready to create the environment that will support and sustain your best efforts? I wrote this book for you.

GETTING STARTED

Read this section through and then sit with the concepts for a few days. There is a ton of how-to instruction in this book; however, unlike any other book in the organizing marketplace, we consider preparation and view each project as a way to practice a skill we can take into the world. After a period of contemplation, you can continue reading the book in sequence or find a section with a project dear to your heart. Because an understanding of time is key to your success, read the next section and do the indicated exercises for weeks one and two. This will make the hard, physical work of organizing easier because you will know when to proceed, exactly how much time to allot, and you will be sure that the project at hand is part of your overall life goals. Sound lofty? It's a matter of relinquishing a freewheeling lifestyle for one that is directed and purposeful.

Feeling a bit unsure? You can start with those infamous time exercises and the creation of a few positive habits (more on those soon). Take a month to perfect them because the rest of your home will be waiting for you. It didn't get chaotic over the weekend. It took time. It will take time to heal. And habits, by the way, are magical especially when they get strung together to form a routine or ritual.

Please don't be intimidated by words like *habit* or *routine*. I would bet cold, hard cash that your life is already run by them. We're just going to shine a light on them and, in all likelihood, replace them. For example, your current morning routine may look something like this: get up late, take fast shower, race out the door, and pick up coffee on way to work. I'd like to see you get up in time to meditate, enjoy a shower, and make a nutrient-dense breakfast to fuel your day. Rome was not built in a day, and neither will your new life appear overnight. Besides, if I could make that happen, I would refuse to do so because you would be denied the process. *One Year* isn't a signed contract with the Mafia forcing you to a cookie-cutter conclusion that fits every reader.

This is your personal journey to living a Zen Organized™ life.

> I often hear the advice: "One day at a time." From my own challenges, I know that can be overwhelming advice. I like to say: "Advance from breath to breath." We can all do that, for sure! And before we move on, let me caution the speed freaks among us. I understand. I am in your camp, eager always to cross the finish line. Take it slow. A year is the perfect amount of time. You don't want to cross some imaginary finish line, pat yourself on the back, and then resume your old ways like a yo-yo dieter.

WHAT IS A ZEN ORGANIZER™?

As mentioned, I've been a professional organizer for more than three decades When I started working with clients, I was surprised to find that the average home was filled with piles of stuff. Newspapers, magazines, mail, books, CDs, and more were stacked to the ceiling just about everywhere I went. After I organized an area, I noticed that it literally felt different. This was a consistent experience. When it came time to start teaching workshops, I wondered how I was going to describe this palpable feeling to others. One day when I was having this conversation with someone, she said, "Oh, you mean it's Zen-like?" I knew I had my phrase. "Yes!" I said that day. "Zen is exactly what it's like." At that moment, I also had the title for my first book, *The Zen of Organizing*, and a way to describe those who used my techniques: Zen Organizers™!

Take heart: You don't have to become a Zen practitioner, twist your body into difficult yoga poses, or learn how to meditate if you want to become organized following my philosophy. The Zen of Organizing philosophy refers to the creation of a calm, peace-filled, and joyous environment. I recognize a Zen Organized environment the minute I enter one. It's the feel of the room, not just its appearance. If you follow the guidelines in this book, you too will experience what it means to be Zen Organized. Alone in an office that invites your best efforts, cooking in a kitchen that seems to hand you the tools you need, falling asleep in a restful bedroom, you will suddenly smile and say to yourself, "Oh, this is what she was talking about."

After your home and work environments support you to do your best, your life will soar. I promise my clients that they will be rewarded for the hard work they are doing. I ask them to call me when the changes occur to let me know what has transpired. They always laugh as if this is a tease or a sales pitch. But the changes inevitably arrive and the calls always come. You're just beginning this journey, so for now you have to trust me. I invite you to write to me in a year and tell me about the great adventure this work made possible for you!

When I work with my clients, I often encourage them to first create a vision board, which is a wonderful way of seeing your goals in a physical, concrete form. It's also a terrific reference when you're tired or overwhelmed and getting distracted from your organizing goals. Never heard of a vision board? Don't panic. They are easy and fun to create—a little art project. You comb through magazines looking for images, words, or phrases that represent the things you want in your life and paste them to a poster board.

Long to have a tranquil bedroom? Your ideal image is waiting in a design magazine. See how this works? And on days when your energy is low and you need a mental boost to start organizing, one look at your vision board will inspire you to carry on to reach your goal!

I worked recently with a young executive who had a wealth of materials for making vision boards in her office. My client had the poster boards, the magazines, and all the tools for her team. I asked why her team members didn't bring their own supplies when she led these sessions. Her reply stunned me. "Most people have no idea what their dreams are," she said. "If I asked them to be responsible for their supplies, they'd have the perfect excuse not to attend." I've always been a big dreamer, so I was surprised to hear this piece of information. Are you in touch with your dreams? *Dreams*, *visions*, and *goals* are all just words. What do you want to manifest in your life? Don't let language trip you up.

The vision board process can help you pinpoint your ideal space, see beyond the chaos in your home, and visualize the end result. For example, when I come into a client's home, I begin to envision the solution the minute I am presented with the problem. The creation of a dream or vision board will help *you* see the kind of order you want for your home.

The supplies are inexpensive and available from your local art supply store or office supply store. You want a large piece of poster board (22 x 28 inches is standard, but feel free to go a little bigger) and a glue stick. You also want a stack of magazines that you can happily rip apart and sharp scissors. Why not invite some friends over for a vision board party? If everyone brings five to ten magazines to share, you should have no trouble finding images that speak to you. Besides, it's fun to brainstorm ideas and share dreams! If you happen to know a group that wants to get organized, you could even meet once a month to discuss your progress and act as a support system. You'll be budding Zen Organizers™ in no time! In fact, if you decide to do this organizing work with a group (more on that shortly), a Vision Board Meeting would be a great way to kick off your year. You can work via Zoom, so if distance or the pandemic prevent you from gathering in person, you can still make progress.

Have you used the Pinterest app yet? Put my name into the Pinterest search engine and you'll find my Zen Organizing™ board that is updated daily with articles and images that I think will enhance your quest for order. Pinterest literally puts millions of images at your fingertips. No need to purchase magazines to create a vision board.

I have a private board called "Family" where I move photos from my phone. I don't want the images clogging my phone, nor am I going to print them out and make albums. I do, however, want to save them, and a Pinterest private board is my ultimate solution. You'll find there are other ways to use the genius of Pinterest scattered throughout this book in the appropriate places. Hint: Pinterest will help you with gift-giving ideas, decorating, and memorabilia.

My other idea is to use the design app Canva, which has vision board templates you can fill and tweak to make uniquely yours.

For the super tactile among us, yes, you can print out your board! Instructions are refined periodically, so to locate the best choice, go to YouTube and type in "How to print out a Pinterest or Canva board" for the latest and the greatest choices. Before you do, however, ask yourself where you're going to keep this board, why you need a hard copy, and how you'll use it to move your project along. Carefully curate every decision that impacts your physical space. You don't want Pinterest to turn into a new source for clutter!

Changing Your Routine: The Organizing Journal

An important part of becoming organized is to start an organizing journal. What does a journal have to do with getting organized? Many people think not in pictures but in words. Sitting down and putting your thoughts on paper can help you determine *why* you've had difficulty getting organized in the past. If the idea of getting organized strikes fear in your heart, you should go back and understand either who planted that fear or what happened that made you feel inadequate in this area. Seeing the words on paper will help you see the shadow reality at play. Our aim is to replace this with the truth.

And what is the truth? First and foremost, I want you to realize that absolutely *everyone can get organized*. You need not turn into a professional organizer or a Martha Stewart clone. All you need to do is learn the basics. The simple steps in this book will enable you to create a chaos-free physical environment. Like all things that

appear complicated, once you get it, you will sit in wonderment at how long it took you to wake up.

The second bit of truth is a tidbit I use to open all my classes. Are you ready? *You are already organized.* Yes, I swear. Not only are you organized, you work the system you have in place with the fervor of a religious zealot. I can hear you say, "But, Regina, I can never find my keys." Or, "My closet is a nightmare and the clothing spills out onto the furniture." Maybe you're saying something like, "Regina, I just don't cook anymore because I can't find anything in my kitchen cupboards and drawers." Your lament reflects one of the rules you live by. Let's take a look.

If you can never find your keys, for example, it clearly means you walk into your home with the express aim of dropping them in the first clear space you see. It could be the kitchen countertop, a dish on the living room end table, or the pocket of your raincoat. This lack of consistency *creates* a drama for you—the constant surprise of where your keys will be found next. Although they get our adrenaline pumping, dramas take us away from our creative and productive pursuits. Perhaps I should tell you about my father.

My father was organized and chaotic at the same time. How can these polar opposites exist together? In my father's case, he tossed every single important receipt into one large dresser drawer he kept for this purpose. While it was great that everything he needed for his taxes was in one place, finding what he needed always caused a drama.

The weeks leading up to April 15 were never fun in our home. Dad would be looking for a particular receipt and come up dry. He was certain that my mom and I had rifled through the drawer. He would bluster about the house, complaining that he had no support from us. In a day or two, the storm would blow over. My dad always found what he needed hidden in the debris. He never really believed we had taken anything; after all, what would we gain? He was acting out the pressure he had placed on himself. Dad did his own taxes until the day he died. I have no doubt that this self-created drama was an unconscious way of saying to my mom and me: "See what I do for you? See how hard I work?" Perhaps it also expressed an unconscious fear: "I hope I'm doing this right!"

This year you may discover in your own journal work some of the self-created dramas in your life. Trust me. Just about everyone has at least one they consistently create. Our goal will be to see them for what they are and replace them with new behavior that empowers rather than drains us.

My mom's chaos was a horse of a completely different color. I never, ever saw my mom search for anything. She was as organized as they come. In fact, her mantra was that old saw: "There is a place for everything, and everything should be in its place." We didn't have piles of anything in our home. My mother had a regimented schedule for cleaning our brownstone. She taught me these organizing skills as I tackled my homework. So, where did she fall down?

Anything visible was perfect. Anything behind a door or hidden in a drawer—watch out! My mother believed you had to organize what others would see, lest they judge you harshly. Her organizing systems were put into place not so much to make her life easier but because she was using being organized to raise her low self-esteem. Do you identify with her in any way? I think it's important that all aspects of your environment work in concert even if no one is going to see the finished result. You matter. Perhaps this is the lesson you need to learn over the next year. *You matter!*

How to Journal

You will find journal prompts in every section keyed to the task at hand, but they are meant merely as initial guides. Over time you will develop your own and perhaps enjoy a bit of free-flowing journal work to help you understand not only the past but also a present challenge. I have clients who journal every morning to help them gain clarity. Purists like me want only a notebook and time to pour out the answers to questions on the printed page. There are others who turn journaling into an art project. Again, if you go to Pinterest and type "journals" or "journaling" into the search box, you will be astonished by the vast array of choices that present themselves. Bullet journaling, for example, is popular and very creative. My caveat here is that if you relate to a journal style that involves lots of different colored pens and use of shapes and symbols, be mindful! You run the risk of getting addicted to the colorful process rather than seeking new inspiration. I feel this way about complicated calendar programs (the Bullet Journal Method is a crossover). More on this next month when we dive into the calendar, which is a must-have tool for organizing success.

If you get stuck, try writing with your nondominant hand. It is amazing what is revealed. I learned this trick when I worked through the exercises in John Bradshaw's book *Homecoming*. As with every tool, try each one with an open mind and see which help you. Our goal is to understand, not indulge, negative emotions. I would suggest a timer; and if trauma in your past reveals itself as the culprit that holds you back, seek the help of a good therapist. Most therapists now offer Zoom sessions, so you won't be limited to your physical area. You may be limited to your state, however, so check the rules governing licensed therapists for your location.

Choose your journal with care. Do you want a fancy, leather-bound version or would a simple school notebook do? There is no one size fits all. If you love how it feels and looks, you will be drawn to do the work. If you love pens as I do, be sure to purchase a new one for this project. You don't want to run out of ink in midsentence. I know this may sound silly, but you would be surprised how attention to detail helps set you up to win.

Advice from My Dad

In many ways my dad was ahead of his time, and it is only now in the years since his passing that I have come to truly appreciate his wisdom. When I was a girl, we did not speak about "journaling"; we kept a diary. No one guided us into the possibility of self-discovery. We were just having fun recording our likes, dislikes, and, of course, our crushes. I kept asking my parents if I could have a diary. Finally, my dad agreed that I could go shopping and buy my first diary, but he had one caveat. He told me that every day I should review my life and be sure that I had done something worthwhile. It didn't have to be big or even known to others. The action simply needed to have value and be recorded. He said this simple action would prevent me from frittering my life away and having a meaningless journey.

My dad's advice to review my day echoes ancient yogic advice. We are asked to review our day just before we drift off to sleep. Kudos to what we handled well and recognition for the times we fell short. You note them so that the next time they come up (and you know they will) you can recognize your opportunity for a better do-over. This simple practice adds a measure of Mindfulness to our days. Try it and see if you like the process. We all fail at things every day, so remember that guilt; self-loathing and recrimination are not part of the practice.

I suggest you keep your journal private. Even the happiest of couples can have privacy. In the early stages of discovery you don't want a lot of opinions to rain down on your head. You will decide in time who you can and should confide in, if anyone. You will determine which advice is pertinent and valuable to your journey. You want to weed out those who give advice based on their own limitations and fears. Seek out those who will rejoice as your life expands. The latter are a rare species, but they do exist. You are reading the words of someone who has done the work, wants to see you fly, and needs nothing in return. The best part of this journey is that you in time become a nurturer of the best in others because you have given it to yourself.

Breathe!

As human beings we stay alive by breathing. Thousands of years ago, ancient yogis discovered the many benefits of controlled breathing exercises. Please don't panic. You aren't doing these practices for any particular religious or Spiritual benefit unless this is part of your path. Today, Navy SEALs practice breath work to increase their ability to focus, enjoy a feeling of calm, control pain, or improve sleep. If Navy SEALs fearlessly dive into this ancient practice, so can you. And the benefits I just mentioned but scratch the surface. I will offer several practices in this book. There is literally no downside to breathing with intention and control. You are going to breathe anyway, right?

Sit quietly in a straight-back chair for support, if you can. (I once did a pranayama in the cockpit of a small seaplane as we took off, so the absence of a straight-back chair is not a deterrent.) Place your feet flat on the floor. Close your eyes if that is comfortable for you, and place your hands in your lap, palms up, fingers not touching. Yes, this will be the same instruction for meditation practices.

You are probably aware that Gandhi and Dr. Martin Luther King Jr. both espoused a nonviolent approach to change. The principle of nonviolence comes from the East and plays a part in Hinduism, Buddhism, yoga, and Jainism. The practice is called ahimsa and means nonviolent living, including nonviolence to the self. Walking around with an inner dialogue that starts something like *Why am I such a jerk?! I cannot believe how stupid I am!* violates ahimsa. Speak to yourself always (but of course especially when tackling big organizing projects) with the same kindness you extend to others. Progress comes from gentleness not violence.

In fact, you can link the two by calming down with a pranayama and then meditating. But I am getting ahead of myself! Let's take it in stages, shall we?

Let's start with a super simple practice called Box Breathing. Exhale deeply through your nose, letting go of your current breath, and then inhale to the count of 4, hold for a count of 4, exhale to a count of 4, and hold again for a count of 4. As you breathe in, feel the air in your lungs and stomach. As you practice you will find a rhythm develops. Your count of 4 will be different timewise than mine but not more or less effective. Let's say you have chosen today as kitchen organizing day. You have read the kitchen organizing material in this book and are motivated and ready to go. That is, until you open a few cupboard doors. Suddenly the idea of spending a few hours on this task is no longer appealing. You are on the verge of bailing out when you remember the Box Breath.

You sit quietly in a chair that supports your back, with your feet flat on the floor, eyes closed, and hands palms up on your thighs in an expression of openness and receptivity. You begin the practice. Suddenly your mind can't leap from one catastrophic thought to the next because it's busy counting. Instead of unconsciously holding your breath or engaging in a panicked shallow breath, you find yourself getting calm. Two or three rounds make all the difference in the world. You return to the kitchen armed with the instructions from this book and are ready to move, item by item, until the new order is created. You can of course have additional Box Breathing breaks! And feel free to indulge just because you enjoy the peace and calm the practice brings to your whole being. Don't wait for an emergency to use any of the self-care practices.

Breath work contributes to every area of your life. Are the kids making you insane? Is Fido barking his sweet head off? Is your boss being an unreasonable douche? Has journaling uncovered a long hidden trauma? Are you tired all the time and depressed? Did you just get news you can't yet accept like a dreaded medical diagnosis? Breathe your way out of panic. Has your sister, mother-in-law, or best friend just unloaded on you? Excuse yourself and go to the bathroom for privacy. Box Breathe your way out of conflict and into resolution. There is no end to the scenarios that Box Breathing can help heal. There are thousands of practices, and many are geared to specific issues. For our purposes, I will share a few simple practices in this book that can be done by anyone. Experience them for yourself. If you like what happens, you can research and grow a detailed breathing practice.

Teach these practices to your children. Share them with family and friends. We can ignite conflict or power peace. It's an ongoing challenge. Some days I am Mother Teresa and others I am a mental Barbarian. No matter where I find myself, however, I am always a human who has powerful tools at her disposal. I think all the tools in this book are the greatest gifts I can share. None surpass breath work in power except perhaps meditation, and the two are linked. Give them all a chance. When you give in to rage, your body is flooded with cortisol, and it will take hours to return to normal. The next time you fly into a rage when the incident ends, take a moment to scan your body. How do you feel? Not so fabulous, right? Your body is your instrument. All bodies wear out, but you can accelerate or delay the process. I don't have to tell you what my choice is.

Going forward there will be more meditation or breathing practices for your journey. I would take a photo and keep the basic instructions on your phone along with the affirmation for the month. Read the current practice each morning before your day starts and give it three to five minutes minimum to start. Combine practices when you can like breath work and meditation. Maybe have some aromatherapy going as well to deepen your investment. This will help you get focused and replace the negative chatter that was planted most likely long ago and unconsciously by the people in your life. We've all got those monologues in our brains, but with work they can be replaced with positive, loving messages.

You aren't going to carry your book with you everywhere you go, and you want to be able to quickly reference the practices if you find yourself in need. Make a folder on your phone and save them all. At the end of the year, you can scroll through and read/do your favorite practice anytime you wish. You'll have several to choose from, and I will share a few trusted sources in the Resources section so you can continue your journey. Every tool I share has volumes written about it, so be gentle with yourself and with me. I am tossing out nuggets to inspire you to learn more. I am not suggesting that you will be a master of meditation, breath work, or any other tool after reading a few paragraphs. The fun is in the quest; progress is the hallmark of the journey.

WEEK TWO

The Organizing Security Blanket

This week, you can

- Learn the Magic Formula
- Understand the time it takes
- Relish the power of rewards

Time required: It should take no more than ten minutes to read this week's material. I would take fifteen minutes to consider how you might use the Magic Formula and start a rewards list that can be added to over time.

THE MAGIC FORMULA FOR ORGANIZING ANYTHING

When I first started my organizing business, I assumed that every client I encountered would be unique. I had trouble sleeping the night before I entered someone's home for the first time. What if they presented me with something I couldn't handle? Over time, I've learned that the majority of people fall into common groups and that everyone pretty much has the same level of chaos. "Have you ever seen anything like this before?" asks the client with a mixture of fear and shame. "Just about every day for over thirty years!" I reply.

I began to notice another pattern. No matter what the project, I was taking the same steps to create order. It was incredible to me that the same simple steps could help someone organize a closet, create a file system, host a party, or clean out a garage. I call these three steps the Magic Formula: eliminate, categorize, and organize. I promise you that you will find the magic if you follow the steps! Are you ready?

Step 1: Eliminate
Keeping in mind that the whole of anything is overwhelming, we systematically work item by item to see what we can eliminate

from the space. An item may be old, out-dated, broken, faded, tired, or simply no longer to your liking. You decide whether to toss it or give it to someone who will give it a new life. That someone could be a charity or your best friend. Keep in mind, however, that no one wants the tattered, torn, or faded.

Eliminate might also mean returning to a friend or family member something you borrowed a while ago. It might also mean that an item has been languishing in the wrong room. Did you leave a coffee cup by your bedside this morning? Do you find plates and cups in your teenager's room? Or maybe Dad took a glass of water out to the garage last week and forgot to return it to the kitchen. Items are orphaned by everyone in the home. Even Fido leaves a house toy in the yard from time to time.

Step 2: Categorize

As you make your decisions about what to eliminate, you are also deciding what to keep. If you start making categories of related items, you are saving time in the long run. Categories give you instant control as you see what you need. Running low on chicken soup in the pantry? If all soups are on one shelf and sorted by type, you'll know to add chicken soup to your shopping list when you grab the last. This works just as well with paper clips, batter-ies, socks, and underwear!

If you're sorting through papers, creating categories is especially helpful. With catego-ries you can see not only how much material you have on a particular subject but how much you have collected on related things.

Let's say that you have a child in school. You'll have a hanging folder with a tab that says the child's name and inside will be individual manila folders for each aspect of his or her life. For example, you might have the following folders: "Activities," "Medical Records," "School." Your list of folders will no doubt expand as your child grows older. This same kind of grouping works with everything from travel ideas to work proj-ects. You can use the same guidelines if you are all digital.

All around us we see categories. Think about your average department store. While shopping, you go to different departments, right? And then within a department, you find all related items. I might, as an exam-ple, head into the men's department before Father's Day and wander around consider-ing whether it's a tie, a shirt, or some slacks I want to purchase. It would certainly be a chore if men's shirts were next to women's blouses and women's jewelry was next to men's sportswear. You'll find that the com-mercial world is always organized by cate-gory because it saves the customer time. You will discover this at home as well.

Step 3: Organize

At the final stage of the game, when the debris has been removed and everything you want is in neat stacks, you are ready to make decisions about the best way to keep this material in order.

Every profession has its tips and tricks, and the field of organizing is no exception. After a year, you will be so experienced, you'll be able to introduce a lot more cre-ativity and fun into your organizing work.

I use products created for one purpose: to help me solve unrelated challenges. For example, the other day I used a lid holder for pots and pans to keep different size shipping boxes separated and upright in an office!

HOW LONG WILL EACH PROJECT TAKE?

Clients frequently ask me how long a specific project will take to complete. Throughout this book, I will indicate rough estimates based on the *average* length of time required. Can you guess what factor will shorten your time or add hours? Are you ready to be surprised? Ask yourself this question: "How quickly can I make a decision?" That's your key!

I wish I had a more glamorous answer, but speedy decision-making is the reality. For example, if you were a client and we were going through pictures or memorabilia, my job would be to keep you moving quickly through the items. If you were to get lost gazing at every image or reading every card, we would be together for hours. I can't tell you how many times I have had to say to a client: "I really want to hear that story. But we need to accomplish as much as possible in the time allotted, so can you tell me the story when we're done?" Remember that question when you feel you're getting bogged down in an area. I'll be your inner organizer!

You might have a few items you call memorabilia but break out in a sweat at the mere thought of going through your closet. Perhaps your office files are worthy of a magazine shoot, but you weep at the thought of organizing the garage. You see what I mean? We're all unique. Our attachments are different and vary in intensity. There's more good news on the time front: As you move through the assignments in this book, you will be amazed to see your speed increase. You will gain confidence in your ability to make the right decision. Your life will get easier and your physical space more nurturing. You won't want to short-circuit the process by dragging out the decision-making process.

Each project we do in life succeeds in direct proportion to the respect we give the process. An old Zen proverb says it all: "How a man does one thing is how he does everything." Your willingness to follow the steps indicated will be in direct proportion to your desire to succeed.

REWARD YOURSELF

Even though the organizing process yields wonderful results and can be creative, a bit of old-fashioned elbow grease must be applied. Sometimes when a sea of chaos surrounds me, I have to think about the reward at the end of the day. That reward might be as simple as a latte at my favorite coffee shop or as elaborate as a weekend getaway if I have been working for days on end on a big project. Unpacking a family in a new home is the most exhausting work I do, and it's always followed by a big reward.

Many of my clients shy away from the reward concept. They tell me they don't deserve a reward for doing something they should have done long ago. Few things in life are as destructive as the "tyranny of the shoulds." I think all things happen when the time is right. Rather than focusing on what you haven't done, choose to celebrate that today you changed your life, faced a fear, and altered your environment in some positive way. We can't change the past. We can, however, learn from it and move on.

Your rewards do not have to be elaborate or cost an arm and a leg. For example, I bet you'd love to spend some time with your dog walking on a country trail or in a park. When was the last time you gave yourself permission to go to a museum? Window-shopping can be fun. Do you have any friends who haven't heard from you in a long time? Give them a call and catch up on old times. Hop into a nice, hot bath and soak your weary bones. Start reading that book you got a few months ago. Go to a music-streaming site and create a playlist that makes you want to dance (wait for it) like no one is watching you. Stream a movie you have wanted to watch or enjoy one that is your tried and true go-to when you want to feel your best. When I feel down and need to be inspired, I watch Russell Crowe in *Gladiator*. I even have the framed movie poster in my kitchen hanging above the stove. What's your go-to movie inspiration when you need courage?

You can't work 24/7 and not expect to burn out. Nurture yourself body and Soul. When you return to work, you will be amazed at the energy and renewed vitality you bring to the process. Record a list of possible rewards in the back of your journal and add to it over time. When you get stuck and can't summon a single idea, check your list. Have simple and elaborate choices. Sometimes a latte in your favorite coffee shop does the trick while other times you need a safari in Africa. Did I make you smile? I'll have more suggestions in a later section.

WEEK THREE

The Power of Community

I can do things you cannot, you can do things I cannot;

together we can do great things.

—MOTHER TERESA

This week, you can

- Decide if a group experience would enhance your organizing journey
- Contact potential members
- Establish guidelines
- Set a date for the first meeting

Time required: Ten minutes to read and thirty minutes to an hour to make notes and do the necessary leg work if you wish to form a group.

The Power of a Group

When *One Year to an Organized Life* was first released in late December 2007, it included the suggestion that working in a group would add power to all the accomplishments. I envisioned friends gathering once a month in person sharing triumphs and getting support when organizing goals were not met. I watched over the next decade as groups formed and fizzled. I wondered why. In 2018, I formed a group online. We met via Zoom once a week for a year. I wanted to see if my idea was faulty. I learned it was as powerful as I imagined; however, I had assumed that detailed instructions for how to run the group were not necessary. They are. Leadership is not intuitive. It's a learned skill. The road to hell is not paved with good intentions. It is paved with assumptions. Those guidelines are in this edition.

All the participants in my initial Zen Organizing™ group were women. They lived in different cities around the United States. Two had recently experienced personal tragedy. I expected little from them. I intended to be proud of them if they showed up. You can probably guess where this is going: They were the stars of the class, doing every single assignment, moving from grief to transformation with tremendous grace.

Guidelines for Regina's Zen Organizing™ Group

If you want to form a group to follow this book and spend a year cheering each other on, there are some things you need to consider. To wit:

- Make a list of potential members. I would keep the group under fifteen so that everyone gets a chance to share when you meet. Send out an email or text message and see who is interested.
- If you are comfortable, assume leadership of the group. If that is outside your comfort zone, ask someone else to assume that role. Without it, the group will fall apart. This person needs to have excellent communication and people skills.
- Decide how often and when you will meet. If you Zoom, you won't be limited to your immediate circle of neighborhood friends. You can reach out to your best friend from college or a former neighbor.
- We found 5 p.m. PST on Sundays to be perfect. The meeting was kept to an hour. I advocate for Zoom because

 I don't think any trauma is more deeply felt than the loss of a child. We expect our children to bury us. It feels as if the very fabric of life has been torn in some cruel and haphazard way when a child dies. Marlene and Roy lost their adult daughter in a freak accident. They wanted to sell their home and move to a new location. Their home was, however, the place where they had raised their daughter, an only child. They were guilt ridden and conflicted. Would they be leaving her behind?

I believe that long-lasting change takes time to settle in. I assumed ideas would be presented and over the year this wonderful couple would make incremental decisions to change their lives. They fooled me. They understood the concepts I teach in a deep and profound way. The truth they took to heart was that their daughter's Spirit lived on. She was not solely to be found within the walls of her childhood home. They were free to stay vested in life, as she would want. Her death was incorporated into their life experience. It did not define it or impede it.

The year passed and found them selling their home in the country and embracing life in a condo in a big city. They found ways to honor their daughter in the new space. Holiday traditions were continued and new friends were added to the long-standing cast of characters. They felt free and empowered. The last I heard Marlene was thinking of becoming a professional organizer. I suggested she specialize in those who are in grief. She will be a magnificent coach and positive influence.

it eliminates travel time and the need to set up a space or provide snacks.
- With Zoom you can record your meeting. Let everyone know it will be available for one week. As the new meeting starts, the old one is erased. Create a

private Facebook page and post the meeting there. If anyone has a question or wants to make a comment, they can use this forum rather than starting a text or email chain. You may have to subscribe to the basic membership so that you can record for more than forty minutes, but the cost is minimal and everyone can contribute at the start to cover the year. Again, cheaper than providing snacks!

- You will do best if everyone is simultaneously working on the same month. If one or two have specific needs, they can of course go to the most pertinent section for them, like moving or travel. As the leader, you will need to be sure everyone understands and is using the basic tenets of Zen Organizing™. This requires reading the first section and the first two weeks of the second. The leader is the one who ties the common elements together should the group be working on multiple chapters.

- The group should begin and stay together for one year, with no new members admitted during that time. The influx of new energy will disrupt the ability to create intimacy and secure a safe space for sharing.

- The group can't be a free-for-all of organizing ideas, with some doing Kon-Mari and others the NEAT method. You are Zen Organizers™ in training. Every group has one person who needs (unconsciously) to pull focus and spend time on their personal problems. This is why a strong leader is key to the group's survival and productivity. You can say something along these lines: "Jane, we hear you. I am so sorry this happened to you. It's a lot to deal with and no wonder you weren't able to do much organizing this week. I'm going to move on so that everyone gets a chance to share what they accomplished this week or where they need encouragement. If we have time at the end of the hour, we can stop the recording and brainstorm ways to assist you."

- Follow an established agenda so the meeting has structure. I asked everyone to share what she had worked on that week and if she needed any help or encouragement. We gave everyone two to five minutes, depending on how many showed up. Photos of the area, the progress, and the finished product should be encouraged. These can be posted on the Facebook page prior to and discussed during the meeting.

- At the end of the session, the leader can give the attendees a heads-up as to what the next week's assignment covers.

As I write this, the first group is still meeting on Sunday evenings. *One Year to an Organized Life* isn't a mental journey; it involves the heart. After a year the bonds are strong and people may want the connections to continue. My next group completed the year and joined me in year three when I formed Regina's Zen Organizing™ Tribe. Come for a month or stay a lifetime. Details in the Resources section.

WEEK FOUR

A Peek at the End of the Journey

Whatever you can do or dream you can,

Begin it.

—GOETHE

This week, you can

- Change your perspective on organizing forever

Time required: Ten minutes to read this week's material; a lifetime to assimilate it.

TYPICALLY, A PERSON WHO COMES TO me for help asks questions like: "How can I control my email?" This is a legitimate question, but what I need to know first is if email is an anomaly in your life or if the lack of control you experience over incoming information is typical for you. Does your mail pile up on the kitchen counter? Do you go to bed late, wake up early, and skip breakfast? Do you exercise, or were such pursuits left behind in high school?

Why are these questions relevant and important? Because we are one being in one body having a physical experience in time and space; we do not operate twenty-five different ways depending on the area in question. Again, I must return to an old Zen proverb: "The way a man does one thing is how he does everything."

I am interested in all aspects of your life. The email problem is a symptom; it is not the issue. This book will advise you on the power of healthy eating habits, suggest great ideas for exercise, and give you an entire tool kit you can use as needed to stay grounded. Some tools might even open the door to advanced study and in some cases a new profession. Let me know if that happens. I've witnessed that shift over the past thirty years. It always humbles me. People start with a closet, move on to the entire home, and end up making major life changes.

When I started organizing, I too thought of it as a series of tasks that I would perform in someone's home. Had TikTok been around, I would not only have watched organizing hack videos, I would have made them. Deeper, richer implications didn't dawn on me until year fourteen of my business when I was diagnosed with stage III uterine cancer. The words of a good friend not only changed how I dealt with cancer but how I saw my organizing work. Organizing was a tool that fit into a bigger mosaic than I had ever imagined. Let me share the story.

Rock My World

Once you've reached the end of a year of organizing projects, you should be feeling proud of yourself. Those endless stacks of papers, magazines, and newspapers are gone. You can find whatever you need in your closet, in your kitchen, or in that longed for clean garage. Your friends are calling you a Martha Stewart wannabe because you're always inviting them over. Your infamous in-box is under control. You have tools to use when you feel overwhelmed. You know what they say: "You've come a long way, baby."

Now I have a little secret to share with you. It's only stuff. That's right. It's only stuff. On the other hand, the skills you have learned when it comes to dealing with possessions are truly pearls of great price. You have developed skills that will

serve you in all the myriad challenges of life. I had been a professional organizer for over thirty years but didn't know this truth until, as I said, a good friend clued me in.

Sometimes in life you're going along just fine, thank you, when suddenly your world falls apart. We've all been there. On July 27, 2002, my OB/GYN called to tell me the results of a biopsy performed the day before during a D&C. I had cancer. I was to have a total abdominal hysterectomy, with staging for cancer, followed by six rounds of two chemotherapy drugs. I heard only the diagnosis. By the time he got to "staging for cancer," I not only didn't know what he was talking about, I didn't care. I needed to hang up and call Susie, my best friend at the time.

Susie was living in Arizona. I called her about 10:30 in the morning. By early evening she was sitting next to me. As I sat blubbering on my couch, a mass of fear and anguish, my wonderful friend gave me the advice that brought me through the experience. She said: "What is it you teach people, Regina? You teach them that the whole of anything is overwhelming and you have to break things down into small, manageable chunks, right?" I nodded yes, wondering why she was talking about organizing when I had cancer. "Well," said my wise friend, "you don't have to face everything all at once. Every day when you get up, you have to take care of only what's on your plate for that day. For the next month, you need to get strong for your operation. After the surgery, you will have two weeks to get ready for the first chemo, and so on. You don't have to do it all at once every single day." Bingo! I had my modus operandi for the next six months. I found "one day at a time" to be overwhelming, so I lived breath to breath. I needed the tools I share in this book, but most had not yet arrived in my life.

I've cautioned you not to let yourself be overwhelmed when you tackle a big project. This was the project of my lifetime. The Magic Formula took on new meaning. I eliminated everything that wasn't related to my healing or my survival. I categorized. And oh did I organize! During my time with cancer, I wrote my second book, ghostwrote a book for another author, and prepped a one-hour cable television special! Neither the producers nor the network knew of my cancer. You should have seen me in production meetings: focused partly on what was being discussed and partly on the mantra I kept repeating in my head: "I will not throw up. I will not throw up." You'd be surprised what you can accomplish with the Magic Formula. I'm living proof.

I was surrounded by a dozen friends who wanted to be of service. I worked out a schedule so no one would ever feel burdened. I remember the day my friend Diane asked if I needed a ride to the doctor for my pre-chemo regular blood work. "No," I said, "I'm covered." Diane asked if she could take me to acupuncture or buy my groceries. Again I was so proud of myself, as these too were covered. She then asked: "Well, could I run your errands for you?" Run my errands?! It had not occurred to me that anyone would do that, and I promptly burst into tears. I mention this because very often when someone is dealing with an emergency, we say: "I wish there was something I could do." Change your language to: "What can I do to be of service?" Let the one in the eye of the storm give direction. It's a great way to assume a bit of power and feel in control when the floor has dropped out from under you.

If your world is turned upside down, remember that you're a Zen Organizer™. You have a Magic Formula. I just celebrated my twentieth anniversary as a survivor in 2022. How will you use the information in this book to serve you and your life? The closet, the garage, and the kitchen will soon be in order. What's next for you? Life is waiting.

FIRST MONTH SUMMARY

WEEK ONE

Create a vision board, start journaling, and learn Box Breathing.

WEEK TWO

Learn the Magic Formula.

Create a list of rewards.

WEEK THREE

Embrace community.

WEEK FOUR

Learn the real benefit of Zen Organizing™.

BONUS TIP

For a week use a timer to see exactly how long common tasks actually take you to complete. Most people have no idea how they use time. How long, for example, do you think it takes to wash the evening dishes? You might say it's ten minutes, only to find it's double that in your home. Or conversely, you might think it takes twenty-five minutes, only to discover as a single person it's actually eight minutes. Live with reality rather than supposition and empower your every task. Developing a true sense for how long things take will enable you to realistically plan all your projects—from organizing your closet to preparing a speech for a critical presentation at work.

SELF-CARE PRACTICE

Box Breathing is the stress-releasing pranayama we use this month. When we are under stress, we breathe quickly and shallowly. Ironically, we create more stress with this fight-or-flight response. We are in the sympathetic nervous system. Controlled breathing known as a pranayama in the world of yoga moves us into the parasympathetic system. Here digestion and rest are controlled. Counting breaths focuses the mind. The word *pranayama* sounds exotic, but there is sound science for why and how it works. Don't take my word for it. Yoga is a system based on experience. Try it out for yourself. (Detailed instructions can be found on pages 17–18.)

UNDERSTANDING TIME MANAGEMENT: WORKING ON THE KITCHEN

Here's to the incredible voyage ahead...and the
fulfillment of a lifelong quest.

—ANONYMOUS

MANY YEARS AGO, MY FIRST ASSIS-tant said something that forever changed the way I taught and wrote about getting organized. I was preparing for a class the following weekend when suddenly she said, "Regina, you think differently. That's what you have to teach people: how you think about getting organized." I had never considered the possibility that I processed information differently than others. In 1988, there were few professional organizers and even fewer books on the subject. I wasn't sure in those days exactly what people needed to be taught. Now I had a handle.

Here are two things the years of teaching have taught me: Time is a commodity like food or money. We can buy more food or make more money. Time is either used to our advantage or squandered. I'm going to help you harness it this month. The kitchen is the heart of the home. I think it's a great place to start your organizing journey. It is also where we need to go to fuel our bodies and our minds for the sometimes emotionally draining and physically demanding work that getting organized entails. Most people see food as a source of pleasure. I'd like you to add to that and see food as a source of fuel. Before we dive in, however, grab your journal. Let's get focused.

Do This Now

Please take five minutes to think about your life in one year. What would you like to achieve? You will have devoted a good chunk of a full year to getting organized.

What will this bring to your life? How will next year on this day be different? Specifics and details are your friends. Indulge in a little daydreaming and allow no criticisms to derail your vision. If you think you'd like to be living in your own home, for example, rather than an apartment, don't allow your inner critic to get activated and say things like: "You? You'll never own a home. You aren't smart enough, rich enough, nor do you have the right prospects." We all have the critic. I'm suggesting you put tape on his mouth and give him a timeout. Do a little Box Breathing if she won't sit still. She or he is a frightened little child. Give them no power and have compassion.

After you identify your one-year goals, spend ten minutes writing them down in detail. If this feels silly, you just have to trust me. You will refer back to this exercise at a later date. Do it, tuck it away, and forget what you wrote. When I teach my in-person classes, this is the most popular exercise. Students are sad they only have ten minutes (yes, set a timer) because they sense that great joy and fulfillment are on the horizon. I remember one woman who was happily married, owned her home in a posh part of Los Angeles, and had a wonderful career. Doing this exercise helped clarify for her that she had two main life goals, and within a year she wanted to launch both. In fact, she was pregnant a year later and had gathered information for the new profession she wanted to pursue. It took several years to manifest that new career, as it involved going back to school for a degree. At one point she and her daughter sat together to do their respective homework. Goals are not achieved because we commit them to paper. They are achieved as we move them from ideas to reality by understanding the things we need to do to prepare the way. I am not into magical thinking. Zen Organizing™ is anchored in the law of cause and effect.

TIME MANAGEMENT: THE KEY TO SUCCESSFUL ORGANIZATION

As we work our way through this book, one of the things I'm going to help you understand is how to manage time. Soon you'll be automatically creating shopping lists in your head, categorizing the day's mail, taking into account how long it will take to drive from point A to point B to point C, and easily calculating the number of hours to allocate to a project. This kind of thinking will give you more control over your life.

This month, you'll begin by looking to the past for clues about the formation of your present situation. Next we're going to break down your use of time so that you can see if your day-to-day life is set up in a way that will bring your goals to fruition. Too many people are mired in fantasy when it comes to the future. A dream is the starting point. It won't take you where you want to go. A plan of action takes you to fulfillment. You'll be adjusting the way you view assignments, appointments, and relationships. You will acquire helpful tools, such as having and using a calendar to track your use of time. The key to your success is learning how to say "no." Practice makes perfect!

In addition to this mental and emotional work, you'll be up on your feet bringing order to your kitchen. We're going to learn how to balance a quick round of elimination in a room crowded with stuff with a well-thought-out reorganization plan for the space. By month's end, you're going to have a new relationship with time. You will be using it to serve you. You'll be able to enjoy your kitchen and use it with ease. How's that for only the second month of a life-changing journey?

HABIT OF THE MONTH

Psychologists have found that repeating an action for twenty-one *consecutive* days turns it into a habit. Choose one or two of the following actions for this month. We'll add more as we move through the year. Our current habits relate to maintaining order in the kitchen because that's the area we tackle this month. Are you thinking these are so subtle you don't want to bother? Tiny shifts like these can cause seismic reactions. They raise your self-esteem while positively influencing those with whom you share your life. Be prepared to be amazed!

> Wash dishes rather than leave them languishing in the sink.
> Put your clean dishes away immediately.
> If you use a dishwasher, unload it when its cycle is complete.
> Wipe off the counters after each use.
> Once a day, check the trash can and take out the garbage if the can is full.

AFFIRMATION OF THE MONTH

As I open myself to discovering who I really am, my physical environment is healed and transformed. I honor the profound connection between the inner and outer expressions of life. They are in fact one. I have a unique path to follow in this life. I embrace that reality with joy and gratitude. Neither pain from the past nor fear about the future can stop me. I live in the eternal now.

Self-Care Practice

This practice is great on its own or paired with breath work. It is meditation. There are thousands of practices but in these pages you will find a few basic ones from different systems. Meditation is simple and easy but the start of the practice if you are new to it may be a bit rocky. Your mind is like a wild horse running free on the prairie. Meditation calms it and brings it under your control. You know how wild horses fight that process.

Some people like me have meditation as a formal part of their Spiritual practice. It is for us a form of prayer, a way to connect with the Divine. This is not what it will be for you. The practice has been found to yield health benefits. I want you to enjoy these benefits and have a mind that serves you rather than one that keeps you roiled in upset and drama. Let's consider some of the top benefits:

- More focus
- Better sleep
- Less pain
- Reduction in stress

- Improved memory
- Lower blood pressure
- Less depression and anxiety
- More compassion

When you did your breath work last month, your mind was able to focus on counting and how the breath felt. In meditation we try to quiet all the noise and chatter and experience stillness. Perhaps you have tried and you fell asleep? That's normal. It passes. Or perhaps you would tell me that you simply can't sit still? You are too creative to meditate. Well, everyone feels this way. This reaction passes as well. Everyone stands to benefit, so why not give it a try?

Sit in a straight-back chair for support with your feet flat on the floor. Rest your hands in your lap, not touching with palms facing up in an attitude of acceptance. Close your eyes. Take a few breaths and then consciously focus on the act of breathing. Feel the air as it moves in and out of your nose. Do not comment or critique. Simply be present and notice. You can begin your session with two or three rounds of Box Breathing. (Do not exceed three minutes.) The benefits here are instantaneous.

Now move to five minutes of meditation until you are comfortable with the practice. Over time expand to at least twenty minutes. It typically takes about twelve minutes for the benefits to kick in, but we want a slow entry that guarantees longevity. Quick fixes are not part of our Zen Organizing™ thinking! There is no limit to your meditation time. It can only benefit you.

This breath work and meditation combination will ground you in the present moment. In this practice there are no thoughts entertained about the past or the future. All that exists is now and the feeling of the moving breath. Guess what? This is the exact laser focus you need when making decisions about organizing! This practice comes from the world of Mindfulness. If you want more, research Sharon Salzberg and Jon Kabat-Zinn. Begin to see how many daily activities invite your present moment focus from organizing to kneading bread.

WEEK ONE

Why Am I Like This? Time Questions

Without freedom from the past, there is no freedom at all.

–KRISHNAMURTI

This week, you can

- Make friends with your new journal and examine your past for clues to the present reality
- Discover where the time goes and how you currently use it
- Understand your real goals for your life
- Craft a plan to use the time in a way that enables you to achieve your goals

Time required: I've broken down your writing assignments into sections. You should allow somewhere between ten and thirty minutes for each, depending on how much you feel you have to express in each area. Set a timer. If you want to explore further, do so later in the day or week. Work in accordance with your timer rather than allowing yourself to get lost on an emotional journey. This approach will enable you to take your first steps in your quest to master time, rather than fritter it away.

ONE OF MY FIRST ORGANIZING CLASSES was with a group of four women. They were all busy working mothers, recently divorced and raising small children without any help from the dads. The number one interest that day was: How can I better manage my time? We did the written exercises I have outlined for you. At one point, we took a bathroom break. Everyone got up except for one mother who looked shell-shocked. I asked if she was okay. I will never forget what she said: "I have more time than I realized. I'm not managing it well at all."

People allow life to happen to them rather than giving it direction. If you say "yes" to most of the following, odds are good that you are in that boat:

- Are you always late for appointments?
- Are you forever running out to the grocery store for items you need? (Or using an app to have the missing items delivered?)
- Do you turn in assignments (volunteer committee reports, work assignments, homework) late?
- Do you find it difficult or impossible to say "no" to anyone? Do you want to be liked and appreciated?

Do you relate to these issues? A person might not manage time well for many reasons. This week, we'll get to the root cause of your current time-squandering ways. By the way, the mom who came to my class that night was inspired to make a dramatic overhaul of her life. It took time, as all real change does. However, she made a plan and accomplished her true goals. Today she is happily living in Europe practicing her dream profession. Her children are grown and out of the house and see their mother as an incredible role model. You can accomplish your goals if you set your mind to managing the business of time. Remember, however, that organizing isn't a magic bullet. If you are in need of talk therapy, for example, to heal deep-seated issues, that can be done concurrent with your organizing pursuits. I was in therapy

for over a decade and much of what I learned refined and enhanced my work.

LOOKING BACK

Take out your organizing journal and answer the following questions. I recommend you allow ten to thirty minutes, depending on how much you have to say and how quickly you write or type answers. If you want to go back later and write more, please feel free to do so, provided you believe it would be helpful. We need to set parameters for this first pass so that we don't...well, you know, waste time! Are you ready?

1. Think back to your childhood home. Were your parents on time, or do you remember both of them being chronically late? What specific memories do you have regarding time? If you have blocked out specifics from your childhood, I invite you to chat with a sibling or friend who might be able to refresh your memory. Sometimes looking at old photographs has the same effect.

     For example, I remember my mom as someone for whom arriving on time was critical. She fell apart, however, when she had to attend a social event with my father. She put on just about every outfit in her closet during a fashion frenzy that she created before they left the house. My dad never said a word. He just calmly read the paper. He'd ask for a fifteen-minute warning, and can you guess what happened? He'd still walk out the door first! From this one-act play I witnessed throughout my childhood, I learned to plan my outfits well in advance.

2. How were you affected by parental dramas regarding time? Did you have one on-time parent and one habitually late parent? How did you feel about each of them? Often we identify with a parent and emulate their behavior. Perhaps you're always late because you wanted to be just like your tardy dad. We choose political, Spiritual, moral, and ethical values to win our parents' love. Did you ever think that your tardiness was an unconscious paean to one or both of your parents? On the other hand, we also choose behavior as a way to rebel. I'm a baby boomer and I'd have to say that my generation had rebellion down to a science. Is it possible that you're late because you wanted to rebel against your mom, who forced you out of bed each morning so you would be on time for school?

   See if you can be the Sherlock Holmes of time. Investigate the emotional links with time and your past. Did you develop your current use of time to identify with or rebel against a parent?

3. Moving forward, were you a person who was always on time until something happened that derailed your usual modus operandi? For example, the arrival of a new baby often puts a young couple through unanticipated changes. It's never like it is in the movies, is it? Or perhaps you changed after a sudden death in the family or a move you didn't want to make?

   We all hear people say, "I used to...and then one day I changed." It's powerful to understand the impetus for any change. Sometimes circumstances move us in positive directions. When they don't, we want to take back the reins. We want to be the architect of our life, not a victim of circumstance.

4. Let me ask you a question about your reaction to being late. Does it bother you? Often being late is how we draw attention to ourselves. It can become the tool we use to feel special. "Everyone is waiting for you!" cries the unconscious. "How special you are!" It's pretty heady stuff. Is it possible that you are manipulating time to become the center of attention?

   If arriving late makes you feel terrible about yourself, do you think you have low self-esteem? Perhaps the glares and nasty comments of family and friends are how you unconsciously reinforce your poor self-image. Can you pinpoint the origin of those feelings?

You might be thinking that you don't have any big emotional bogeymen in your closet. You just don't have a clue how to get from point A to point B without being late. Well, I have good news for you. Using time well is a skill just like getting organized. This week and next, we'll look at the strategies you can use to improve your time management. And you have a year to master this one!

SETTING GOALS

Be specific about the changes in your life that you hope to see after you learn how to manage your time. Always write in the present tense rather than the future. Saying "I no longer lose important papers" is powerful. Saying, "As soon as I get organized, I will no longer lose important papers" puts your good result in the future, just out of reach. In a way, it takes you off the hook. Part of successful time management is being accountable.

Your list of positive life changes may look something like this:

- I show up on time for all appointments. I release the need to be the focus of attention because of tardiness.
- I protect myself by planning my life at least a month at a time. This way, work time, play time, and downtime have their place. My life is balanced.
- The word *no* is now part of my vocabulary. I no longer seek to be loved and accepted by sacrificing myself to others. My physical, mental, and emotional needs are important to me.

Next, be sure your stated goals are realistic and truly hooked into the concept of time management. For example, let's look again at the student I just told you about. She had a job as a receptionist in a law office. She barely made ends meet. In Europe, she had been an attorney! She had not gotten her US certification when she moved here because, like many women, she assumed she would be a stay-at-home mom. When her dream was shattered by divorce, she had become immobilized by depression. Her current situation reflected her low self-esteem.

After my class, she vowed to better her situation. She hired me to organize her physical space. Then she made a plan. Her initial goal was to study and take the certification exams here in the US. After a few months, however, she realized that she could provide her children with immediate health care and make a good living just by moving back home to Europe.

Never feel you are stuck with the first decisions or plans you make. As time passes, your decisions about your life and your goals may change, as they did for my client. The bottom line is that once you understand what you want to accomplish, you will automatically use time to help you succeed. You will be moving inexorably forward. And you will end up exactly where you are most needed, wanted, and appreciated.

WHERE YOUR TIME GOES

Let's look at your life. What takes up your time now? Make a list in your journal. As an example, here is what would be in my journal, in no particular order:

Work: clients and writing
Time with my animal companions
Time with family and friends
Exercise
Spiritual pursuits (attendance at a house of worship, meditation, yoga, etc.)

Travel

Volunteer work

Errands, grocery shopping, and so on

Your list reflects who you really are. For example, if you say you are looking for a relationship and your list reveals that you have no time to find a partner, much less date, your expressed wish is just a fantasy. If you are in a relationship and realize it's suffering, ask yourself how much time you devote to it. Perhaps you need to eliminate something so you and your partner can have more quality time together.

What else is on your list that isn't on mine? Would you like to add some things to your life? Would you like to eliminate some things? Give yourself at least fifteen minutes for this list. It's a key ingredient in creating the life you want—you know, the one being organized is going to support.

After you have your list, if you think it may not be complete, run it past your best friend or partner. See if he or she wants to add something. Often others see us more clearly than we view ourselves because we are caught up in emotion and judgment. After you're happy with your list, please mark next to each item the percentage of your life and energy it gets during an average week. In other words, how much time are you spending on each pursuit?

If you are like most people (me included), you will find that your life is out of balance. Work is usually the culprit, whether that's work outside the home or you are a mom raising a family. Moms frequently discount their work because it doesn't come with a paycheck. Please remember that raising healthy, happy children, running a home, and maintaining a good relationship is the most exhausting job on the planet. It counts. It counts big time. Money is a highly overrated measure of success.

Now let's do some work to consciously shift your current reality to one that is balanced and leaves you feeling fulfilled. Write your current list with the percentages indicated on the left side of an 8½ x 11 sheet of paper, and draw a line down the center of the page. On the right side, write the elements that you want to have in your new life. Perhaps it will be the same list with different percentages. More than likely it will be a slightly altered list with new percentages.

As you record your answers, they may lead you to other areas that add more detail to your issues with time. Feel free to create additional questions for yourself.

I have a client who, at seventeen, had been eager to marry her high school sweetheart and start a family. When I met her years later, she was at a crossroads. She was turning thirty, had three children, and wanted to have a career when they left home. She needed a college degree. It was amazing to watch her use the exercises (the journal, the vision board, and so on) and completely redesign her schedule. She investigated the degree she would need for her chosen profession. Which schools offered a program? What were the costs? How many hours of class time would there be? Here are some of the ways she redirected her time to achieve her goals.

Chores were no longer an option. Everyone had to step up and assume more responsibility in the home. She needed to shave time off every area of her life so she could use that time for her studies.

She asked her children for their support. She joined them at the dining room table after dinner. They did their homework as a group. Have you ever considered the possibility of doing homework with your children rather than just checking theirs? If you aren't in school, do you have work projects? PTA assignments? Homework in school prepares us for all the life assignments we will face. You can demonstrate this to your children without saying a word.

All of the children were in school, so she took part-time classes at the local community college. This way, she could still take them to school and pick them up.

Her husband was totally on board. When the youngest child entered high school, his wife would be entering the work force. Guess what he decided? That's when he would go back to school and get his degree!

Instead of weekly trips to the grocery store, they stocked up on the basics at a big home store like Costco. Her husband picked up the fresh produce and dairy needs once a week on his way home from work. Once the pandemic started, every large chain store set up a delivery service. If the delivery fee is modest consider how you will use the time you save. There are also services that will supply someone to run your errands whenever you need the help. There are apps for that and the app will supply almost any service from putting together your IKEA furniture to, yes, getting organized. You have the help without making a regular commitment to someone as a new employee. TaskRabbit is the one most of my clients use.

My client loves crafts. This is not only her favorite way to relax, it is something she shares with her kids. However, she had to pack up and store her supplies. Now she works with her kids on projects only in the summer, when school is out. This was a big personal sacrifice for her, but she needed those hours for homework.

It's probably most difficult to alter your schedule when you are in a family situation. My clients have shown me that anything is possible if you learn how to manipulate time to your advantage and if you have the support of everyone in the family. Think of the unspoken lessons this couple taught their children about possibility and partnership along with time management and basic organizing skills!

To summarize:

- Decide what you really want from life.
- Do the research necessary to make your dreams come true.
- In your calendar, schedule the steps you need to take to achieve your goals.
- Communicate with those with whom you share your life. A positive change for you has a positive effect on everyone else.

STRENGTH IN NUMBERS

Although I think journal work is best performed in private, feel free to do this with your chapter of Regina's Zen Organizing™ Tribe. But I have to stress one important caveat: Do not invite anyone into the group who is not a loving communicator with your best interests at heart. It sounds absurd to say, doesn't it? Sadly we all know the person who means well but finds fault with everything. Or maybe your life has a person in it with an inferiority complex that is fed by belittling others. This group isn't a friendship circle or for fun. Nor is it a place that tolerates cruelty of any kind. Gather like-minded Souls and you will soar. If you want a group and can't find anyone interested in making a commitment, come and join my Zen Tribe. Details in the Resources section.

After your journal work is finished, you can take out your vision boards and work on them, crafting a little more each month. At the end of the year, see how close the new life you have created comes to the one you put together on your vision board. My first group created some keepsake vision boards. Again, if you don't want to do this, you can share your Pinterest- or Canva-created version. You can all use the screen share feature on Zoom. You won't notice you aren't literally in the same room.

The Zen Tribe members can monitor each other's progress. You can also help each other with bigger projects. Why not document some of the projects with before and after shots? You'll always have a reminder of how far you've come. Just like a professional organizer, you can coach a tribe member who is stuck in the details of a type of project that comes second nature to you.

If you decide to work alone because that's what suits your personality, you will make the same progress. I'm an only child and I thrive when I work alone. We're all different. Learning to respect who you are and working in the way that makes you most comfortable are two of the goals of the steps we've taken so far.

WEEK TWO

Creating Schedules and Routines

This week, you can

- Learn the beauty of working with a calendar. Whether it's the one on your computer, a system like the Bullet journal/calendar, or one you create, there is no better way to keep your life on track.
- Start practicing the fine art of knowing when and how to say "no." Remember: It adds power to every "yes" you utter.
- Begin to think like an organizer. Is there a jumble of thoughts in your head? Let's bring order to your mind while we're clearing out the physical space.
- Start creating routines that will save you time and in the long run money and emotional energy.

Time required: Approximately two hours.

INVEST IN A CALENDAR

One indispensable tool that everyone needs is a good calendar. (After all, how are you going to schedule organizing time for yourself this year if you don't have a calendar?) As you've probably experienced by now, it doesn't work to keep doctor appointments and school trip dates on scraps of paper or Post-It notes. My favorite calendar system is the Executive edition of AT-A-GLANCE. However, nothing is wrong with the Franklin Planner, the Bullet system, or any other brand on the market. You can buy one already assembled or you can purchase only the shell and create a customized version. You can get a month-at-a-glance (my favorite), weekly, or daily view setup.

I sent one of my clients, a visual artist, out to shop for a calendar. She needed to see her choices in person and touch them. The online experience was out. She wasn't pleased with anything she saw in the marketplace, so she decided to buy only the inserts she needed. She got a plain binder and decorated it so that it would be as unique as she is. A simple task became an artistic project.

Let me caution you to be aware of the fine line between making something you love to use versus spending time making something so that you can postpone the hard work to change that will be done inside the pages of your journal. Only you can tell the difference.

A Cricut machine will give you a wonderful opportunity to make fancy labels for items like food containers in the kitchen after you decant from the store-bought packaging. You can also make decorative labels for the bins you use in your closet. If you love to craft, label making offers a new outlet for your creativity. It will give any area the appearance of professional level organizing. A simple Brother P-Touch will also do the trick.

If you are a total computer person, feel free to use the calendar installed on your computer or phone, or download a calendar app. Don't forget to sync the two! The bottom line is to follow your personal comfort and style. I will say this more than once because it bears repeating: There is no system that is inferior or superior. If you love it and use it and it serves you, it's perfect. I wouldn't care if you did a combo. Let's say you plan your life in your written journal, but you keep appointments on your electronic calendar. If someone asks if you are available on such and such a date, you will know instantly. No guilt.

WHERE IS EVERYONE?

If you have a large, active family, it is confusing to remember where everyone is on any given day. The more children in the home, the more after-school activities and the more invitations to parties there will be. One of my favorite clients kept a very large calendar behind a door in the kitchen. With one glance, everyone knew where every member of the family was at that moment. What I so admired about her was her sensitivity to the children who would come to visit or play. That's why the calendar was hidden from view. She didn't want anyone to see a party that they had not been invited to and have their feelings hurt. Today the more popular choice would be a family-centric app that every family member has access to. I have a friend who works outside the home, as does her husband. Each family member has access to the family schedule and they can update it instantly. They also use a tracking app and can pinpoint the location of every member of the tribe. As your children get older they may balk at this level of family security. Keep the lines of communication open and tell your children that freedom is earned by being responsible.

You have no doubt noted that I do not mention any particular app. This is because the choices change over time. Ask fellow parents and even teachers what they recommend. My clients currently use Google calendar, Evernote, Cozi, or Trello. Go to the app store and download the free version of any recommended app. See if the interface of the app is in sync with the way your brain works.

No shame. I proudly use a paper calendar, but I only write professionally using a computer. The organizing police have yet to toss me into jail with a big fine.

THINK LIKE AN ORGANIZER

Everything you do needs to be scheduled. If you get in the habit of seeing your life a month at a time, you will be in a better position to balance your schedule. Let's say that after a long week at work, the weekend's plans include a dinner dance sponsored by your school's PTA. Let's take another step and up the ante. You are not only going, you are on the committee responsible for decorations. You arrange for a sitter. You provide food for everyone at home. You take a change of clothes. You and your spouse race to the school to help decorate the gymnasium. By the time Sunday comes around, you are pooped. I would be careful to block off the next weekend to share some much needed quiet time with my family. Get the idea?

When you start planning your life with an overview, you safeguard two things: your energy and your goals. Using a calendar enables you to see in black and white whether you are keeping to the percentages you think are best for your life activities. Inevitably when we plan, we also save money. Do you drive everywhere like we do in Los Angeles? You'll save gas if you have a shopping list and make related stops in one area. I know so many people who stop for groceries every night after work so they can get whatever they discovered

they were running out of that morning or whatever they need for dinner. How much gas are they wasting? How much time is frittered away that could be spent with the family? Time, money, energy, and reaching your goals are intertwined like stitches on a beautiful needlepoint canvas.

If you get into the habit of scheduling your activities, you won't run off like the proverbial chicken with its head cut off in response to every request that's made of you. So many of us were raised to be people pleasers and get our self-esteem boosted by taking care of the needs of others. Have you ever noticed that happily married people never immediately say "yes" to an invitation? They always say that they have to check with their spouse first. Guess what? You and your calendar are now an official team. You can't go anywhere without it, and you can't say "yes" until you consult it.

Do you have trouble saying "no"? Your calendar is your out. Ignore the knee-jerk "yes" response and say that you need to check your schedule and will contact the person later. (They don't have to know that the schedule is with you. And if they see it, say you haven't checked with your family so your schedule isn't up to date.) This ploy will give you a chance to formulate a response that's comfortable for you. And stick to your guns! If your "no" really means no, your "yes" will be appreciated and respected. Learning to say "no" is a skill you will develop over time. I think the biggest surprise for many is that it's not the end of the world when we say "no." It all works out even when you aren't the point person for every job, every committee, every friend, and every project at work. If you're feeling overwhelmed, let someone else have a turn.

Or do you volunteer for everything because you are a control freak? One of the reasons no one else can chair that committee is that you will not give them a chance! How about assuming the role of mentor or teacher? I'm not suggesting you announce at the next meeting that you realize you should have said "no" years ago and you now resign! I'm suggesting you find a way to let someone else have a turn. The amazing part of this experience is that it frees you to learn and do something different yourself.

One of the most common reasons we hold on to positions is that we are afraid of coming up short in a new arena. There is a false sense of security in the same old routine. *False* is the operative word. Perhaps it isn't fear but a lack of personal identity. "Who would I be and what would I be doing if I relinquished this position?" The most common underlying fear is that no one will love or care about you if you say "no." You may indeed lose those people from your life, but I assure you that they were never friends to begin with!

Finally, change might also be a way of pretending that time is not passing. "It's spring so I have to chair the annual charity ball for my church." Whatever the cause, it's time to put on your Sherlock Holmes hat and do a little journaling. You will find that change comes more easily when you understand why you are frightened of it. By the way, we're all afraid of change

in some way. You move to the head of the class because you aren't afraid to identify and conquer your fears.

THE POWER OF ROUTINES

One of the best ways to save time is to establish routines. Take a few minutes to identify where in your average day you lose time. Most families, for example, have a struggle in the morning. Discovering that you are out of your child's favorite cereal at 6 a.m. puts a damper on your whole day, doesn't it? After you organize your kitchen, one of the most common elements of a typical drama is eliminated: Your pantry setup will alert you when an item is running low.

Do you eat breakfast as a family? Try setting the table the night before. Break your morning routine into steps and, if you are part of a family, assign them to your children as chores. One child sets the table the night before, another clears it and loads the dishwasher the next morning. Perhaps the chores shift each month so that everyone experiences all the aspects of the breakfast setup. If you are a working mother, you might want to investigate the most nutritious quick cereals and save time by making pancakes, eggs, or homemade oatmeal on weekends.

Decide what you are going to wear the next day and lay it out the night before. If you don't have a pull-out bar in your closet, use a deep hook on your closet door and hang your selections there. You can install one or get a sturdy plastic one that hooks over the door frame.

Do you drive to work? Keep an eye on your gas tank. You don't want a family member to discover at 6:45 a.m. that you parked the car last night with a near-empty tank of gas! You don't want to do that to yourself either.

Got an electric vehicle? Make a habit of charging it when you come home at the end of the day.

Make a list of the most common time traps in your home. Then create an easy-to-follow routine that will eliminate this source of stress and wasted time for good!

After you've streamlined your home situation, don't forget to look at your work life. How do you squander time on the job? Here are some common traps to help you make your own list.

When you have a report due, do you find yourself responding to unimportant emails or answering voice mail messages that could wait? Do you have a knee-jerk reaction to respond to text messages instantly? Give that up. Unless someone is bleeding in the ER, they don't need an immediate response. They may feel entitled to one, but that is not your responsibility. Do you wander into the kitchen area and decide to make a fresh pot of coffee or clean out the refrigerator because you don't want to face your workload?

Do you skip breakfast or lunch in an attempt to save money or time? Do you notice how this makes you feel? Are you exhausted, grumpy, or finding it hard to focus? It may be time to feed your stomach and your brain!

What are the ways you squander time? Put the antidote in place! If you see a pattern of avoidance, begin doing the reverse. For example, if checking your email and voice messages first thing in the morning throws you off course, begin your day with thirty minutes of work on the project report that's due.

Very often gaining time is a matter of being in the moment. What do I mean by that? The next time you find yourself wandering into the kitchen on your way back to your desk from a bathroom break, ask yourself why you feel impelled to stop and tidy up or make coffee. If you're busy, go back to your desk. If it's a slow day, knock yourself out being helpful in the kitchen. Rather than being rigid, be conscious.

Let me give you a personal example. Recently I painted my office. I decided to move the furniture into different positions to shake things up a bit. The new formation doesn't please me as much as the old. As I write these words, I am on a deadline to complete the requested editorial changes for this manuscript. My mind tells me I should take the time to move the furniture! I have to stop myself because this would be a big project. I am amused how artful the subconscious mind is at sabotage. You must put your nose to the grindstone at times and complete assignments. And remember to schedule a reward. How is your list coming?

Create a new morning routine that is a productivity power boost:

- Drink 8 ounces of room temperature water before you have your coffee, tea, or food.

- Start with a few rounds of a breath practice (there are several in this book) followed by at least five minutes devoted to meditation.
- Move your body! Take a quick walk, do a yoga routine, or take a Zoom Pilates class.

You can tick all of these off your new morning routine list in about fifteen minutes and set your day to run with all cylinders firing instead of feeling behind the eight ball. Over time extend your meditation to twenty or thirty minutes and try your yoga postures before you do your pranayama and meditation.

GETTING THE KIDS ON BOARD

To get the entire family on board with your goals, start by making changes that make life easier for them too. No fanfare. No announcements. As the Nike ads say, "Just do it." A well-organized kitchen is an ideal place to start. Invite everyone to join you with your example rather than command them with your words.

One rule, however, must be enforced: Whatever is used must be returned to the spot from which it was taken. This rule will maintain the environment. It also establishes that everyone must have respect for the work you do.

Make organizing something fun and rewarding. Is it going to be an easy switch?

No! This is especially true if all everyone has ever experienced is chaos. Even the most positive change in the world is difficult. However, after three consecutive weeks of strict enforcement, the odds are in your favor that order will replace chaos as the new normal.

Plan surprise rewards such as serving your family's favorite cake on Sunday evening to celebrate a week of chores completed. Enforce the rules by having consequences when the rules aren't adhered to. Lost entertainment, computer, or phone privileges head the list of consequences guaranteed to get the attention of young children and teens.

A word to all you busy moms: Have you ever noticed how children and animals pick up on your emotions? The success of Operation Organization starts with you. If you believe this is going to succeed and you are enjoying the fruits of your labors, so will everyone else. It's uncanny the way this works.

If you are still feeling overwhelmed by time management, do the work indicated for this week and know that there is a bonus practice at the end of the month if you need additional help tying it all together. Expect the change, the control and the comfort to grow over time. It takes nine months to gestate a human baby and two years to gestate an elephant. Things take the time they take. Giving up or carrying on with the same old, same old are no longer options.

WEEK THREE

Kitchen Questions

Man did not weave the web of life, he is merely a strand in it.
Whatever he does to the web, he does to himself.

–CHIEF SEATTLE

This week, you can

- Learn how to analyze a space to see what it reveals about you
- Understand how you currently use your kitchen and how you would like to use it; these are often at odds
- Perform a speed elimination of all extraneous items
- Learn how to set up your kitchen zones
- Organize your pantry so it supports your kitchen activities, whether your pantry is a few shelves in a cupboard or a separate area
- Create a shopping list and an emergency contact list

Time required: Two to three hours for organizing and shopping; one hour for journal work.

EVERYONE GATHERS IN THE KITCHEN. I think it's tribal instinct—our way of gathering around the campfire. This week I have a series of questions to ask. You don't have to write down the answers unless you are particularly stumped about the direction you want to take. After you read the questions, I have some down-and-dirty preliminary work for you to do. It's time to get on our feet and start organizing!

Want to play a little game? Turn on the TV right now and find a program you have never seen before—a one-hour drama or a situation comedy. When you see the home of a character, don't you instantly know a lot about him or her? A professional set decorator works with the director to mirror in the physical space some of the characteristics of the main protagonists. Your home is your canvas. You are the set decorator and the director. You are also the star! What do you want to reveal about yourself? And what are you revealing now? We're going to go through the home one room at a time, so don't panic. Let's look at the questions for the kitchen.

What do you like about your kitchen? Be specific.

What do you dislike? Again, be specific. If the things you don't like can only be fixed by a remodel, are you planning to do that soon? If you rent or can't afford a remodel right now, are there any cosmetic changes or tools you could introduce that would make the space work better in the meantime?

Do you have things from past generations that don't serve you other than giving you a sense of familial devotion?

If you are sharing your home with another person, do you have a lot of duplicate items?

Are you eating off chipped plates and drinking glasses? Stores such as IKEA can set you up with a new set of dishes for four for about $20! The prices for glasses are equally inexpensive.

Do you like the color of your walls? If not, are you handy with a paintbrush and paint roller?

Is the lighting adequate?

Do you have space for furniture in your kitchen? If you have furniture here, do you like it and use it?

How much time every day is spent looking for things? If a lot, is it due to a total lack of organization or are you sharing space with someone who never returns items to their designated spot?

Do you have counter space to prep meals, or has that space been usurped by children's papers, the daily mail, and stuff from work?

Do you cook every day or just on special occasions?

If you aren't cooking every day, are you a microwave king or queen?

Do you ever bake?

Are the items in your kitchen the right size for your family? For example, if the children have gone off to college, you probably don't need that six-slice toaster eating up counter space. Is the garbage overflowing because your garbage can is too small?

Rate everything you see that is meant to be useful.

As you look around your kitchen, do you see some things that you wish I had asked about? Please create your own questions and make some personal notes to understand exactly what you like and don't like about your kitchen. My questions are a jumping off point, meant to spark your inner Zen Organizer™!

HOW DID THIS HAPPEN?

At this point, you may be wondering how your kitchen ended up this way! Although much clutter can accumulate over time, a kitchen can fall into disarray from the start. Most people get to a new residence and toss things into cupboards and drawers in an effort to unpack their boxes and get settled as quickly as possible. In some cases, a close friend or relative is the one hurling things into the dark recesses of cabinets. No need to fret; it's understandable and fixable.

SPEED ELIMINATION

Now let's look at the actions you can take. I want you to set a timer and give yourself a minimum of fifteen minutes to literally tear through your kitchen. What exactly do I want you to look for? Easy things that you can eliminate quickly. For example, do you really want those stained pot holders or the frayed dish towels? Those twenty coffee mugs? Do all of your plastic storage containers have lids?

Don't forget to see what's lurking in your drawers. Consider tossing grandma's ancient potato peeler. Do you have little gizmos and gadgets you can't identify? Toss them.

Very often I find multiple sets of dishes sitting on upper shelves. Someone's grandmother or maiden aunt passed away and my clients are sure that "one day" they're going to use that set. "One day" has been waiting in the wings now for a decade, but hope springs eternal. Can you relate? Do you have your own version of Aunt Tilly's china? Perhaps it's time to pass these items on to another family member or sell them on eBay or through Replacements .com. If you do need to hold on to them or own china of your own choosing, be sure they're safe. You'll find a wide variety of holders available for safe china storage—I use the traditional padded containers.

Of course, you will have to consider some items carefully. We'll deal with them next week. Don't let indecision slow down the process. This week is about speed. If you need to negotiate with your partner, please make a list of those items.

Tools of the Trade

Next, allow twenty minutes to take another walk-through of your kitchen interior. Look for areas of your kitchen—cluttered countertops, cabinets, drawers—that you find frustrating. For example, the lids to pots and pans haphazardly strewn in a bottom cabinet are usually an issue. Make a note of your frustration and create a shopping list of organizing products that might help, as well as a list of items you need to discuss with your spouse or partner.

Be sure you count the items that need organizing before you go shopping. Organizing five lids is a different challenge than organizing twenty. In addition, read through the material for week four. I suggest product usage as I go along. If you think you need something, add it to your list.

USEFUL ORGANIZING PRODUCTS: KITCHEN AREA

In this section you'll find a list of my tried-and-true favorite kitchen organizing products.

Shelf creators: These make labels on cans more visible by creating three levels in one area. They come in various depths so you can use one for big food cans and a narrow one for spices. The middle size is great for canned soups and vegetables. Most units are expandable.

Shelf dividers: Use on pantry shelves to keep food categories separate. They are sold in the closet section of your favorite organizing department.

Drawer organizers: Is it a fight to find anything in a drawer? You can get several different sizes of drawer organizers and create the perfect pattern for the specific items you need to keep in the drawer. Or you can pop expandable dividers into the drawer and divide the space without using containers.

Decorative pitcher: Something like this can be used on the stove to hold your most frequently used tools. If you are short on drawer space, this will relieve the congestion and keep your favorites handy. Be sure you use a container made for this purpose or one you have on hand that's not too delicate. You want a sturdy vessel that can take a beating.

Drawer liner: The best-organized drawers can dissolve into chaos if there isn't some kind of liner to hold items in place. My favorite is a thick weave that reminds me of a paper towel and is washable. It comes in colors so you can find a roll that goes with your décor. In fact, I'd get several rolls and do just about every drawer in the house. There's another version called Zip It that is also easy to use and keep clean. You tear it into the size you need. No cutting required! I am not a fan of contact paper.

Two-step stepstool: Many people shy away from using the top shelves in cupboards, thinking that no one can reach them easily. This is remedied with a two-step stepstool. They have ones that fold flat for easy storage. In fact, these stepstools are so inexpensive you might want to hide several around the house so that all of your high shelves are in use. Let me add one caveat: If you are older or a bit unsteady on your feet, get a stepstool that has a back. You'll be able to hold on if you feel you are losing your balance. These don't fold as flat, but safety is always our first concern.

And while we're focused on safety, be sure your stepstool has nonslip pads on the steps and on each leg. Be sure the screws are tight if it's wood and that no one would describe it as unstable or rickety. I once broke my arm in a fall from an unsafe stepstool when it got launched out from under me. It had no slip guards on the steps and the feet had felt tips so it wouldn't scratch the floor. I did a move I shouldn't have and went flying into a wall like a piece of shrapnel! Learn from my costly organizing mistake.

Lid storage unit: If you have a small area to keep all of your pots and pans and you can't keep individual lids on the pot or pan they belong with, a lid storage unit is your solution.

Baskets and totes: These are great for sorting categories of cleansers under the sink or for use on the pantry or laundry room shelf. Containers come in an assortment of materials (think acrylic, bamboo, rubber, and wicker for starters) and are usually either small squares or rectangles. Most have handles for easy transport. Look for sustainable materials whenever possible, but also note how the tote will be used and in what area.

Under the sink in the kitchen, use rubber or acrylic containers because they are easy to wipe out. Wicker or bamboo baskets might make a large pantry organized and beautiful. Note: If you have lots of fresh produce like potatoes and onions, you can save money by using cotton canvas storage bags instead of baskets. Of course they are on Amazon, so start your quest there. When you do purchase petroleum-based products, be sure the quality is superior, and you will have the items for decades of service.

Spice racks: The variety is almost infinite! You can use one that's like a miniature lazy Susan and keep your spices in a cupboard. You might want to use the narrow shelf creator referenced earlier. If you have a free drawer, you can put in a spice holder. It lies flat, as will your spices, so you can look down and see your selection at a glance. If you have counter space, however, go for a spice rack that's functional and beautiful.

I like to keep my spices in alphabetical order. I have clients who balk at the very idea. They think this is too much and

just keep their favorites handy on a shelf near the stove. What will you do? Remember that while spices are placed logically near the stove, you don't want them too close to the heat. Over time, it will compromise their potency. In addition, you don't want to keep them more than a year because their freshness fades. If you like to experiment with spices, buy the small size in case the experiment fails!

Roll-out drawers: Are you blessed with deep cabinets but find the contents in the back get forgotten? All big box stores have an organizing department now, and you should be able to find a sliding unit you can install that will give you instant access to everything. You can also order it from Amazon.

Pet food containers: These have snap locks to ensure freshness. The one on wheels is my favorite. If you use canned food, you can pick up some generic covers to keep the contents of the can fresh in your fridge.

Under-the-sink caddy: This keeps your products sorted and portable. When you purchase a unit be sure you have noted the configuration of the pipes.

Canisters: Use these for storing dry goods, such as flour and sugar. These can be an on-the-counter decorative ceramic set or acrylic ones made specifically for the pantry. To save money, the planet, and preserve uniformity, try good old-fashioned mason jars. They come in an array of sizes and are cost effective. Slap on a fancy label and your mason jars will look magazine-shoot worthy.

Let me say one word here about decanting most of your pantry supplies. It will be beautiful but you have to keep it up. If maintenance is difficult for you, forget this step. Be realistic.

Finally, there are clear holders for flour and sugar that allow you to plop the package inside and lift the container with an attached handle. No decanting necessary and you always know which flour/sugar you have on hand just by looking.

Mindfulness is more than a meditation practice or a way to handle difficult challenges like organizing. It's literally a way of life. It's an exercise in staying present to the total reality of every situation we find ourselves in. How we eat is central to our survival and yet the vast majority of us eat unconsciously. Here are a few ways to bring Mindfulness into our entire experience of food.

On any day that you have special demands on your time, like a big organizing project, try to eat without consuming processed food, dairy, white sugar, or more than 3 ounces of meat. You will experience more energy. If more energy isn't of interest, consider this: factory farming is a contributor to climate change. Help reduce the impact on the planet by giving up meat one day a week. If meat is a permanent part of your food consumption, try to find a local farmer who does regenerative farming and raises and slaughters creatures in as humane a way as possible. This choice enables you to power the local economy and support those with whom you share a community. Regenerative farming will rebuild and preserve healthy, living soil for generations to come. These measures benefit the planet, but in the end you go the extra mile to benefit your own body and its state of health. Conscious consumption of food is Mindfulness in action.

WEEK FOUR

Whip Your Kitchen into Shape

This week, you can

- Sort your cooking tools and gadgets into related categories (prep/ cook, bake, and store)
- Divide your kitchen space into activity zones in keeping with the preceding categories
- Complete the elimination process
- Decide how to make the best use of your counter space
- Bring the pantry to order
- Conquer the scary areas of the kitchen, including under the sink, the refrigerator, and the junk drawer

Time required: Five to seven hours.

THE LAST WEEK OF THE MONTH, YOU'LL be on your feet working hard. I want you to be at your best when you do this work. The following tips will help guarantee a successful day. Being prepared will make you feel energized and in control, so be sure to have all the tools you need on hand. You wouldn't want to go into surgery and hear your doctor exclaim, "Darn! I was sure I had that scalpel. Where do you suppose it is?" You'd shout, "Didn't you check that before you got here?"

HOW TO PREPARE FOR AN ORGANIZING PROJECT

Be sure to reference the following checklist each month before the start of all major organizing projects:

- Choose the time of day you are at your physical peak. Is that 7 a.m., 11 a.m., or 4 p.m.? Plan accordingly.
- Eat a nutrient-dense meal before you start and have lots of fresh, healthy snacks on hand. If you need sugar, think carrots rather than candy bars.

Think (vegan) cheese and crackers instead of cake.

- Drink lots of water throughout your workday.
- It's best if you have a table nearby to serve as a workstation. For most of us, that's the kitchen table or the dining room table. The latter might need a protective cover. Spread a sheet over it, if necessary.
- Don't answer the phone, check your email, or look at text messages while you are working unless small children are involved in activities outside the home.
- Have your tools ready. Your standbys for most projects will include heavy-duty garbage bags meant for outdoor use, a label maker with extra cartridges (black script on a white background), and the organizing products you purchased for the task at hand.
- Be sure you will not be interrupted during the time you set aside.
- Create an atmosphere that encourages your best work for the project at hand. Some people like music and others work best in silence.
- Plan a reward. The physical work won't exhaust you, but the decision-making process will wear you out. It's best to have something to look forward to at the end of the day.

SPEED ELIMINATION, ROUND TWO

Last week you eliminated the easy items from your kitchen. Today, having had some additional time to think and consult with your family, you are ready to do the final pass. After this, everything that stays will be something you know you must organize. Work in a systematic fashion. Begin at one end of the kitchen and do all the drawers. Then return and do all the upper cabinets. Your last task will be to peer into the lower cabinets.

When this is finished, you will have successfully worked the first step of the Magic Formula. Now we need to create categories for what belongs in the kitchen and decide where these things go. By the way, if you no longer cook except on special occasions, you can donate, pack away, or store more than the average reader. For example, if you have hosted Thanksgiving dinner for many years and would like to pass the baton, do so. And pass the turkey roaster with it!

THE KITCHEN TRIANGLE

The average person can divide the contents of the kitchen into the following traditional areas: prep/cook, bake, clean up/store. These three areas form the traditional triangle for kitchen design. We also all follow a basic template for kitchen organization. Walk into a strange kitchen and you'll be able to find a drinking glass and a dish. The glasses will be in a cupboard on one side of the sink and the dishes on the other. In a top drawer close by, you'll find the silverware. Pots and pans will be near the stove as will pot holders. After that, it gets dicey. That's where the kind of planning you've been doing comes to the rescue. Please remember that the basic difference between tidying up a space and organizing it is that the latter includes a system of maintenance. Basically, if you return everything to the place you designate for it, you'll be home free.

You'll want to assign a specific area for each category. For example, keep the large food prep items in one cabinet and use the drawer above it for smaller, related tools. Dedicate one shelf to your small prep tools and gadgets. Put items such as your mixing bowls on another shelf.

As you organize, be sure to wipe out your cabinets and drawers. We don't take everything out that often, so it's nice to freshen up before you put in your drawer liner and introduce the contents. If you purchased any slide-out drawers, now is the time to install them. Another useful tool I suggest for every home is a label maker. In a home with a large family, especially one with teenagers, labels make it easy to honor your hard work as an organizer. You don't have to remember where things go. You just have to read. Labels are a true blessing when your in-laws come to visit or you give a party and the kitchen is suddenly filled with those who want to be helpful. They can only be helpful if everything goes back to the designated spot. And labels are your guarantee they will.

Let's work one area at a time.

I had a client who cared for her collection of cast iron skillets like they were her children. One day she came home to her husband happily using steel wool on her favorite cast iron frying pan and almost had cardiac arrest. Here is her foolproof tip to clean your cast iron but preserve the finish. After use, fill your pot half full of water and add a few tablespoons of salt. Bring to a boil. Gently scrape the pan with a wood spatula. Voilà! Cast iron has a long life, no chemical coating, and adds iron to your food. It's worth the investment.

Cooking Tools

Your pots and pans should be kept as close to the stove as possible. I like to keep lids on the pot or pan they go to, but I realize this isn't always possible. Did you get your lid storage unit last week? Do you have other items tucked in with your pots and pans? Pull them out and place them on your work area. One trick is to turn a lid on a large pan upside down with the handle facing into the pot; now put a smaller pot and lid on top.

Food prep items include the following:

Air fryer
Blender
Colander
Food processor and attachments
Hand mixer
Instant Pot
Measuring cups
Mixer
Mixing bowls
Salad spinner

Prep tools you might find in a drawer include:

Assortment of knives
Knife sharpener

Spatulas
Wooden spoons

Do you have a corner cupboard with a unit that turns? It enables you to use all the corner space. Put heavier items on the bottom. You want to balance the weight on the shelves so they neither spin too fast nor get bogged down.

Most folks have multiple can openers, wine bottle openers, nutcrackers, cheese spreaders, and bottle openers. I frequently find several garlic presses and potato peelers as well. The watchword is "less is more." Now is a great time to take a second look at these types of tools because the surplus only creates debris. If you didn't eliminate the overflow last week during the first pass, now is your opportunity.

Take-Out Stuff
Do you frequently get take-out orders? I'm going to bet you have extra chopsticks, not to mention tiny packets of sugar, mustard, ketchup, salt, and pepper tossed into several drawers. I would also wager that you have a collection of take-out napkins stashed in these drawers. Unless you are that incredibly rare individual who actually uses these items, I suggest that you ditch them, donate them to a shelter, or take them to work. They take up space like nothing else. We think, "Well, I paid for this, so I have to keep it." Trust me, you don't. You paid for the food you ate. These items are included as a courtesy in case you are moving or eating on the go. If you fall into neither category, reclaim the space in your drawer.

In the average kitchen you will find paper and plastic straws in this category. Why not use metal straws at home and try bamboo for when you are out and about?

Large Equipment
If you have big equipment items such as a bread maker or an ice cream maker, be honest about how frequently you use them. You may want to give them away or park them elsewhere in the home. For example, if you rarely eat ice cream in the colder months, you could pack away your ice cream maker in the garage with other seasonal items for summer. Are you without a garage? The area above the refrigerator is traditionally a cavernous spot. It's a good place for rarely used equipment. (Be sure you are truly using this area for infrequently used or seasonal items and not turning it into an appliance graveyard. If it doesn't work, get rid of it!)

Countertop Items
When I was into cooking, I kept my food processor on my counter. It was constantly in use and I saw no reason to haul it out every day. If you have lots of counter space, use it wisely. Remember, we're creating categories, right? Cluster related items on your countertop. For example, if you use a coffee maker, put it on the counter just underneath the cabinet where you have your cups and sweetener. If you grind beans for every batch of coffee you brew, let the grinder sit out by the coffee maker. Keep the toaster here as well. Now you have a breakfast area on the counter.

In much the same way, if you have an assortment of knives in a wooden holder, it should sit near the stove. If you like your kitchen tools in a pitcher, keep it on or near the stove. Remember that surgeon I mentioned who was missing a scalpel? Well, when you're in need of a kitchen item, you want it close by the area where you intend to use it. By the same token, less is more. Keep it out if it makes you work more efficiently. What is too much? It all depends on the size of your kitchen and how much counter space you have.

Baking Gear

If you are not a baker, you'll have more cabinet and drawer space to devote to the other categories. If you are, remember that the rule of thumb is the same. You want all tools in one area and all smaller items in the drawer above if possible. This can be an area far from the sink and the stove.

Here are some typical baking items:

Baking molds
Cookie cutters
Cookie sheets
Hand beater
Muffin pan
Rolling pin
Sifter
Spatulas
Wooden spoons
Whisks

If you bake only during the holiday season, you might want to put holiday-specific items such as Christmas cookie cutouts into your baking molds and store them up high. If you love to bake with your kids year-round, you'll want all of these tools nearby.

Food Storage Containers

I hope you have whittled your food storage containers down to a precious few that have their lids intact. Most people have a true Tupperware graveyard with orphan lids and bottoms. The common belief is that one day the other half will show up and—voilà!—you'll have yet another container to add to the ones already in service. Ask yourself how often you actually use what you have. If you are part of a large family, the answer may indeed be frequently. For most of us, however, the space these items hog is not commensurate with the service they provide. Start tossing if you haven't already. Or give these containers to a small child for paints and other craft supplies.

Try to replace your exiting petroleum-based storage containers over time with glass ones that have snap-on lids. You can get a set with varying sizes to start your new, conscious kitchen journey. Giving a friend a gift of leftovers from your dinner party? Let the old Tupperware go home with him or her and not return.

Paper and Plastics

When it comes to the wrap and plastic bags we use to store food, it's best to have them all in one drawer close to the sink. With that said, if you buy in multiples, you might have to store the backup elsewhere. The pantry is the logical place if you have one. A makeshift pantry for overflow items can be created by placing an inexpensive baker's rack in the garage. Set it next to the door you use to enter the house. Use this spot for storing all your excess paper products, such as tissues, toilet paper, and paper towels. Remember that big area on top of the refrigerator? If you haven't filled it with rarely used equipment, consider placing a portable, deep shelf here, and then use the divided space to house paper products. Now that you have a stepstool handy, this will become accessible real estate when you need it.

If you are willing to experiment, you can use beeswax wrap that lasts several months with proper care. If you are crafty, you can make your own! Find instructions on Pinterest. I use parchment paper. It rinses off and I get multiple uses from each sheet. Glass storage containers can replace some plastic bags. Or you can do a combo and simply reduce your reliance on those handy-dandy tools we have come to rely on. By the way, those convenient bags take at least twenty years to break down. Shocked? It takes plastic bottles 450 years! I know. We humans have put ourselves in a pickle through the magic of invention, chemistry, and in the name of convenience. We got ourselves into the mess; we can consciously get ourselves out. I try to find companies making products out of plastic bottles. The shoe company Rothy's is a case in point: stylish, instantly comfortable, and good for the planet. It's the ultimate trifecta.

Dish Towels, Pot Holders, and Aprons

Dish towels and pot holders should also be found in a deep drawer near the sink. Some cooks also store their aprons and placemats here. But if you have huge stacks of each stuffed here, everything will be wrinkled. Put a few in the kitchen to keep them handy and store the rest in the linen closet (provided it's not too far away), in the laundry room (if you have some shelving for storage), or in the dining room. Are all of the drawers in your hutch full?

Wrinkled, tattered, faded, or torn items make us feel depressed when we look at them, much less have to use them. When they get to that state, tuck a few away for use as cleaning rags and toss the rest. As you purchase new items try to buy "Made in the USA" sustainable cotton. It degrades faster and is compostable. Remember that when you are shopping for clothing, linens, or any other item that has an all-cotton alternative. Polyester and nylon take a long time to decompose, and they release micro-plastics into the waterways.

> A little trick for gaining more space in your dish towel drawer is to roll the towels. You can repeat this trick with great success in other areas. For example, do you need space in your T-shirt drawer or in your suitcase? Is your linen closet a tight fit? Give it a roll!

The Pantry

Food is what the kitchen is all about. Nothing is as wonderful as a separate pantry. If you are like me, however, you have to use some cupboards as your pantry. Once again, no matter what your setup, remember to divide your food and shelf space into categories so that you always know when you are running low on an item.

The most common food categories are:

Baking supplies: flour (e.g., cassava, soy, white, whole wheat, whole wheat pastry), sugar (e.g., brown, confectioners', white)
Canned vegetables
Condiments
Flavor enhancers (packages of instant soup, salad dressing, and the like)
Grains (e.g., oats, quinoa, rice) and potatoes
Pasta and sauces
Snacks (e.g., candy, cookies, crackers)
Sodas and water
Soups

You can use some basic tools to bring order to your food categories no matter where they are stored. For more information, see "Useful Organizing Products: Kitchen Area" on page 51.

Shelf dividers were invented for use in closets, and they work wonders when it comes to keeping your sweater stacks from collapsing into each other. They also keep your categories in the pantry separate, marking off where one territory begins and another ends. Never again will your bags of pretzels and potato chips slide over into the soup can area. This may not sound important, but if you preserve visual calm in your home no matter where you look, you will feel at peace.

Pet Food

Do you have pets? If you feed them kibble, be sure to use an airtight container to ensure freshness and protection from ants, roaches, and other critters who will think you have set out a feast for them. I've seen two sizes of containers for this purpose; the larger of the two is on wheels. Is that convenient or what? You can up the health benefits of your kibble by adding a bit of fresh raw food. There are numerous versions frozen in your local pet store freezer. There are now wonderful frozen raw pet food delivery services like The Farmer's Dog, Nom Nom, and JustFoodForDogs.

I have small dogs and they are fed Small Batch (beef) sliders exclusively, but if I had a giant breed the cost would be prohibitive. A holistic vet can partner with you to get the perfect kibble/raw equation for your pet's breed, age, and weight. Rodney Habib is an animal nutritionist with a huge following and a new book with holistic vet Dr. Karen Shaw Becker called *The Forever Dog*. You can do your own research, starting with them. As you clean up your diet, you will want your furry children to eat in a healthy fashion as well. I would rather spend money on food than on medical conditions brought on by kibble. "Nutrient dense" is the mantra for all living beings in our Zen Organized household.

If your pets eat canned food, be sure their food has its own area on a pantry shelf or in a kitchen cupboard. You'll want to be able to see which variety you're choosing for the evening. Why not make use of a shelf creator here? Treats can be kept here as well. I store mine in a cupboard and keep a selection on the counter in glass jars. They look pretty and my dogs appreciate how quickly they can be rewarded. My counter space is limited, so I have these out rather than cooking equipment or a canister set for flour, sugar, and coffee.

The Refrigerator

While you're bringing order to your kitchen, don't neglect your refrigerator. Give it a good cleaning today and eliminate any lingering mystery containers. Don't forget those unmarked packages in the freezer that could be anything! Amazon has "Use By" labels and freezer labels you can use that cost very little. When you think of the tossed food and mystery freezer frustration they save, they are worth their weight in gold. You can, of course, simply use colored duct tape and a Sharpie!

While you're tossing, check all jars, like that jelly you bought a long time ago. Most food packaging has an expiration date to make this process easier. You'll be surprised that you still have things to toss after last week's purge. No doubt you'll also notice that it's getting easier. I call this developing the trash muscle. As the ability to toss the unwanted or no longer needed gets stronger, you'll see that fewer piles develop in your home. Why? Because piles are simply unmade decisions made visible. And now you're ready to take control.

Divide the food in the refrigerator into categories and designate specific areas for each. When you're shopping for organizational supplies, see if they have a storage solution for an item you buy in large quantities. For example, if your family loves cold soda on demand, pop a soda can dispenser in the refrigerator. When you take a can out, the next one rolls into place. Sodas will all be contained in one area and you'll see at a glance when it's time to refill. Anyone in the home looking for a chore? It's your job to refill the dispenser!

The Front of the Fridge

Refrigerator people come in two basic types: those who cover theirs with magnets, notices, and photos, and those who like an unadorned refrigerator. I would urge you to either join the latter group or at least pare your items down to a minimum. Over time, we're all so busy, things just collect. It's the rare person who puts up a notice from Johnny's swim club and thinks to take down the old one at the same time. You can find photos of the children from birth to college and beyond on the refrigerator door or spiraling down the side. It looks messy and feels chaotic.

Put the photos in an album. Have a binder in the kitchen that holds all current schedules and school notices. If you have a large family, use tabs to create sections for each family member. Use individual sheet protectors to keep the information clean. Designate one place to keep your binder so everyone knows where to find it.

Display your child's artwork on a bulletin board. I had a client who had a huge corkboard in the mudroom. As you entered, you put your keys in a dish. There was a place for coats and a bench for you to sit while you removed your shoes. This utilitarian space was turned into a make-shift art gallery with the addition of the corkboard!

Do you have an unused area in your home that's ripe for a corkboard? Change the artwork regularly. When drawings collect on any surface, they become clutter and we no longer see them. Keep an artist's portfolio for the best of the best. At the end of the school year, you and your child can sort through and see what will remain as part of his or her memorabilia. Portfolios are sold at art supply stores and are quite inexpensive. You don't have to feel bad as you toss artwork because its digital image can live on Pinterest!

With that said, perhaps a refrigerator can have two things on the door: doctor contact information and a list of emergency contact numbers, especially if young children, pets, or elderly family members live there. This list should include mobile and work phone numbers for everyone in the home. It might be prudent to list the local police department, fire department, and, if you have one, your alarm company. Create your list on a computer. It will look neat and be a breeze to update.

Yes, I know you probably have this on the cell phones of your immediate family because you are all using the same app. In an emergency the teenage babysitter or famous Aunt Tilly may need a quick reference. Did you remember to share that info with them before you walked out the door? If you don't need these lists printed out, you'll save some trees and space on the refrigerator. I'm about options because humans are never one size fits all.

Shopping Lists

Now that your food and storage categories let you know by sight when you need to restock, you'll want a place to make a shopping list. Here are several ideas to help you stay on top of your fresh food needs and pantry supplies. I literally have something here for everyone.

- Keep a pad of paper on the refrigerator. Divide each sheet into sections: one for each store where you shop. This way it's all organized when you tear it off and head out on grocery shopping day. If you enjoy computer work, you can create a standard shopping list. Check off the items you need. Keep the master in your computer where you can update and print out as needed.

- You can use a family app with a shopping list built in that all family members can access. Cozi, for example, allows you to create one master shopping list or separate lists for all the stores you frequent. You might be a Google Calendar and Google Docs devotee. At the moment there is a bevy of choices, including Evernote, Maple, and Trello.

- Most of the time you can use a free version first to see how you relate to the interface before you purchase the app. Noodle around and find the one that works with the way your brain functions. Finding the right app is like dating. You don't want the first person that appears. You want to make an informed choice, right? Same with organizing tools. I'll have the Resources section in the back of this book on my website so I can update it with the latest trends.

- Do you have Alexa or Echo? One of my clients barks instructions while he prepares dinner. Alexa times his food and keeps his grocery list current.

You guessed it. Pick one solution, get everyone on board, and stick with it. This is one of those actions that isn't performed every day but does get ingrained over time. There is no right or wrong. For example, picking up your phone may be second nature for every need if you are under thirty. When I am in the kitchen busy cooking, if I need to add to a shopping list, I prefer to use pen and paper. Here's what matters: keeping the fridge and pantry stocked. The tool you use to achieve that goal isn't significant.

The Pantry: A Cautionary Tale

I have clients (a married couple) who are both practicing attorneys, albeit in different aspects of the law. They have five children, with housekeepers and nannies. They both come from large families and are neighborhood favorites, hosting frequent sit-down dinner parties. Every day is a festival of food prep to feed this large gang. The husband is a phenomenal cook and loves to unwind after work by wandering around the aisles of the local high-end supermarket. He is a fresh food freak. Clearly, my kind of human;

however, there is a downside. As he wanders, he buys items on sale. He buys in large quantities just because something is on sale. He not only buys more than the family needs, he tends to buy items they never eat, like (wait for it) Spam.

The upshot is that an astonishing amount of food is tossed each week from the fresh food bins and periodically from the pantry. Do you relate? Cooking fresh food is the best way to achieve my goal of nutrient-dense meals. But if your meals are not planned and you buy on impulse, you will clog the available space, wasting food and money.

Remember too that spending money produces a high because it releases endorphins. We think of clothing as the shopping demon, but it can be anything you don't truly need—from food to clothing or craft supplies to a new car. I had a client who drove a high-end vehicle she loved. She didn't want her dog's slobber in that car, so she bought him his own vehicle. You know my advice by now, right? Be Mindful. Be present. There is no downside.

KITCHEN BLACK HOLES

We all have black holes in our kitchen, don't we? Those areas where clutter collects. And isn't that where your mother-in-law goes first? Let's bring them to order for good.

Under the Sink

Every kitchen holds a terrifying area. It's under the sink. Household cleaners, ant and roach spray, trash bags, plant supplies…it's a volatile jumble of chaos and poison. The most important thing you must do if you have children or inquisitive puppies or kittens is install a childproof lock. Poisonous items are best stored up high in these situations.

Take a good look at the construction under the sink. Depending on the configuration of your pipes, you might be able to put at least one container here. Several styles are designed to work under the sink. Some have two levels with drawers that pull out; others have one container on a track that allows it to slide out. See how many categories of items you have under the sink and divide them accordingly. I might keep cleaners in one tote, polish in another, plant care items in a third, and so on. By the way, a key item for under the sink is a small fire extinguisher. Be sure you know how to use it. You won't have time to read the instruction manual if a grease fire erupts!

The Junk Drawer

Let's face it: What kitchen is without a junk drawer? The problem arises when there are several! Whittle down what you really need in this drawer. Many times, for example, I find multiple tools here. Granted, a small hammer, a flat head screwdriver, and a Phillips head screwdriver are handy, but the rest of your tools should live in a toolbox. You can park this in the pantry if you have a large one, under the sink if that is spacious, in the garage, or in the laundry room. If all else fails, try the back of the hall closet.

It's nice to have handy some paper (not enough to write the great American novel) and pens or pencils (again, not enough to supply the local grade school). Mechanical pencils are good because you do away with the need to have a sharpener. Remember that pens dry up if they aren't used. A large cluster of pens will just take up space while they lose their effectiveness. If you have a lot of items in this drawer, use some drawer organizers to fashion the perfect design for what you want here or buy a junk drawer organizer and tailor it to your needs.

The COVID-19 Conundrum

During the COVID-19 pandemic many families merged to live in one household. With housing prices on the rise, this trend may continue for the foreseeable future. If you had adult children, relatives, or friends move into your space, chances are good they came with kitchen equipment. We humans get very territorial about our favorite cast iron skillet or the way we make coffee. Living in a community means sacrifices. The owner of the home has, I think, first dibs on what stays and what is not needed. But why have an argument when you could have a fun experiment? Spend one weekend using different coffee makers and see which one aces the taste test. Do some research and see which pots and pans have the best reputation for safety. Who has some fun cooking tools like a waffle maker or a potato ricer that will make meal prep easier? You get the idea. This way compromise is reached via experience and research not edict.

Take a realistic look at your situation. Is this a temporary move or a permanent one? If it is permanent, why not find a local charity that helps immigrant families find housing? The items you can't currently use could help feather the nest of someone who has come to your country from an ordeal even more difficult and emotional than the one you experienced that caused you to return home or live with friends. Let your items have a new life and be a blessing.

CREATING NEW HABITS

Remember at the start of this month I told you that psychologists say it takes twenty-one consecutive days to turn an action into a habit. If you miss a day, you need to start over. It sounds so simple. It can be quite a challenge! Here's the good news: You already have lots of positive habits ingrained. You wouldn't run out of the house and suddenly realize you hadn't combed your hair, brushed your teeth, or changed your underwear, right? These are just some of the actions we take for granted.

The kitchen habits I suggested at the start of this section also make wonderful chores for your children. In addition, after you organize an area and have it labeled, you can assign a child to check it once a week to be sure the system is being maintained. Your children can be responsible for setting and clearing the table for meals, filling salt and pepper shakers, or keeping the sugar bowl full. If they are old enough, let them decant flour, sugar, and grains so your pantry is always ready to serve whoever is on deck to make a family meal. Be sure you assign chores with an eye to what is age appropriate. You don't want to set up a child for failure.

In a large family, rotate chores. This way, as your children mature, they will know how to manage an environment. Sadly, this is all too commonly an unknown skill set for many college-bound teens. If you say: "It's just easier if I do it," not only will your children never learn how to take care of themselves, your martyr's robe will get heavier with each passing year.

In my book *The 8-Minute Organizer*, I had the idea to add exit rituals to key rooms. These were a series of actions designed to keep the room tidy and ready to serve the next family member to enter, whether that's you or you live in a multigenerational household. You can take a snapshot, print it out, and use a magnet to keep it on the refrigerator until everyone gets the steps into their DNA, or just share it via the family app you use to communicate. Some chapters don't have an exit ritual, so if the area we tackled (basement, attic, guest room, etc.) is in frequent use, feel free to create your own.

THE KITCHEN EXIT RITUAL

- Put away all food.
- Put clean dishes back in the cupboard.
- Place dirty dishes in the dishwasher or quickly wash by hand.
- Wash any pots and pans. The exception is a pot or pan that needs to be soaked for a while.

- Return kitchen tools to their designated spot.
- Give the table and counter a quick wipe.
- Check the trash. Empty if needed.
- If it's after dark, turn off the overhead light and turn on a table lamp.

Consider a compost pail. If dealing with worms or fear of nasty aromas strikes fear in your heart, there are now kitchen counter-size electric composters that never smell or use worms. You would be amazed how much waste it eliminates and you end up with fantastic soil for your plants. Not a gardener? Someone in your life or your neighborhood will be beyond grateful. Within the next decade, look for citywide compost ordinances and programs. Get on the bandwagon now and be an example to the reluctant in your community.

Healthy Dining

Once your kitchen is ready to serve you, it might be the perfect time to consider planning healthier meals. It's certainly going to be easier now that you know where everything is and how much you have of every item. Here are five simple tips to help you on this next phase of your journey. Try one or two to start. Ease into change.

- Use small plates. I stopped using traditional dinner plates unless I was hosting a dinner party. I eat exclusively off salad plates and out of bowls. It provides automatic portion control.
- Consider the visual. I pay attention to the colors of the meal itself. I might use china I inherited or pieces I've purchased from a local potter. Nurture yourself from the visual to your taste buds. It all matters.
- I use salt when I cook but I never put it on the table. Be mindful of the salt you use, from type to portion. There is a world of salts waiting to intrigue your taste buds.
- If you are serving a family or hosting dinner parties, eat in the dining room and serve food from the kitchen. People will reconsider seconds and thirds if they have to get up to get it.
- Swap in healthier ingredients and if you are cooking for a family (or hosting a party) do not clue anyone in. They will object before they taste the food! Tofu by the way is high in protein and can be whipped into a desert or a salad dressing as easily as it can be the main course. My favorite tofu cookbook is in the Resources section. Buy organic.

To close out this section on food, I'm sure you are using your own reusable cotton shopping bags to bring home groceries, right? Guess what? They need to be laundered after use. Why? The conveyer belt that your food travels on as your checker charges you for each item has had many bags on its surface. You get my drift? By the same token if your bags come home with you via your car or public transportation, they may pick up more germs. More reason to toss them in with a regular load of laundry! Finally, if you place your bags on your kitchen table when you get home, give it a wipe with a disinfectant when all the food is put away. What can I say? I did this before the pandemic.

SUMMARY

WEEK ONE

Please be sure you have your journal, your calendar, and your vision board supplies.

Answer all questions in your journal.

WEEK TWO

Begin to schedule your activities and establish routines.

WEEK THREE

Acknowledge your kitchen's weaknesses and strengths; decide how you want this room to function and look.

Eliminate the easy items.

Create a shopping list and, if you need one, a discussion list.

WEEK FOUR

Make the first checklist, "How to Prepare for an Organizing Project," your guideline before you organize the kitchen from top to bottom.

Establish your habit of the month.

Decide on your maintenance routine for the kitchen.

BONUS TIP

We often enter the kitchen in the evening for something quick such as a glass of milk and a cookie. Instead of turning on the overhead light, have a small lamp lit on the counter if you have the counter space. It creates an inviting ambience, saves electricity, and can also serve as a night-light. I have a small lamp on my counter. You'd be surprised how much light a 15-watt chandelier bulb gives off!

BONUS TIME EXERCISE (IF NEEDED)

1. Please draw two lines down an 8½ x 11 sheet of paper and then draw two across. Yes, it looks like you are going to play tic-tac-toe! At the top of the squares, put the days of the week. Divide the last square to create your weekend.

2. Take another 8½ x 11 sheet of paper and create three columns. The first is your "Do or Die," the second is "Important but Flexible," and the last is "Miscellaneous."

   a. Please list all the activities in your week that must take place in the first column, such as work, taking kids to school, or picking them up.

   b. In the "Important but Flexible" column, list items such as food shopping, laundry, or exercise that are key but can be moved if necessary.

   c. Finally list all the items you want to include in your week like learning a new language. Your lists will be unique to you.

3. In black ink put all the items from the first column onto your mock-up calendar page. In pencil write in the flexible items.

4. Take some time to study your typical week. Do you have more time than you thought or less? Do you overload some days? Can some items be removed? Could some items be grouped and done on the same day?

5. What can you delegate to another family member or outsource, such as ordering groceries for delivery?

6. Look at your "Miscellaneous" list. Do you realistically have space for any of those items in your current situation? If not, keep them as a list in the back of your journal. Every six months you can do a review.

Remember that exercise you did as the month began and I asked you to put it away? Read it now. Are you doing concrete things to move to your stated new life or is it a fantasy? Time to either pat yourself on the back or do a little journal work to discover how you need to start manipulating time to serve you. We state goals and forget to break them into the steps that carry us to achievement. We get lost in the day to day and because we are so busy, it feels like we are living a purposeful life. It may just be a busy one. You are in the driver's seat. As the great poet Mary Oliver asks: "Tell me, what is it you plan to do with your one wild and precious life?"

CREATING A BEDROOM SANCTUARY

Our contribution to the progress of the world must, therefore, consist in setting our own house in order.

—GANDHI

HOW WOULD YOU DESCRIBE YOUR bedroom? Would words like *sexy, comforting, nurturing, inspiring, cozy, elegant, sophisticated, homey, fun,* or *joyful* be on your list? If not, I hope they will be by the time this month draws to a close. Our main focus will be on creating a bedroom that is a sanctuary for you, no matter your romantic status. After all, if you don't love yourself, how will you have anything to give to others?

HABIT OF THE MONTH

Return your clothing to where it belongs every single day. When you take off your clothing at night, put it in one of three places: back on its hanger, in the hamper to be washed, or in a bag intended for the cleaners. This habit will also keep your clothing off the floor or your bedroom chair.

AFFIRMATION OF THE MONTH

My bedroom is a place of peace. Within its walls, I am comforted and healed. I appreciate and wear the clothing I have. As I give away what I no longer need or use, I am blessed. There is only abundance in my life.

Self-Care Practice

This pranayama is another one that involves counting but it has a twist I think you will enjoy. Its benefits include:

- Stress reduction
- Ability to fall asleep faster
- Control cravings
- Reduce the anger response

The great holistic practitioner Dr. Andrew Weil favors it for sleep. In fact if you want to have a demo, he has one on YouTube. It can be helpful to watch someone do a pranayama with a twist. For some reason, I love it for stress reduction especially when I am angry. You try it and see if you enjoy it and how it affects you.

Sit in a comfortable straight-back chair with your feet flat on the ground. The instructions for pranayama practice or meditation are evergreen. Empty the lungs of your current breath through your mouth and breathe in through the nose for a count of 4, hold for a count of 7, and slowly breathe out of your mouth for a count of 8. This pranayama is known as 4-7-8. A humble name for such a powerful tool, is it not?

You breathe in through your nose and breathe out through your mouth. Easy, right? Here is the twist: place the tip of your tongue lightly behind your front teeth. Keep it there for the entire series. You will feel a ridge. As you exhale make a hissing sound and allow the breath to escape on either side of your tongue. I know. It sounds little odd but what you are doing is directing energy. You can run a mile in flats but with running shoes the whole experience is elevated, right? I imagine you are alone, so just seek the experience and embrace the results.

Do this two or three times until you get comfortable. If you have difficulty with this one, entertain no worries! You can shorten the count to 2-3-4 and build up over time. As with all yoga-based practices, never strain.

WEEK ONE

Bedroom Questions

This week, you can

- Diagnose your bedroom's shortcomings (design and structural).
- Devise a plan to transform your bedroom (including what you should donate, what you need to purchase, and what, if anything, you should move).
- Take a clinical look at your wardrobe. Do you have to get uniform hangers or a new dresser? Do you need to purge those two or three sizes of clothing from your past or is a shopping trip in order?

Time required: One and a half to two hours.

DO YOU HAVE AN EMOTIONAL DISCONnect with your current bedroom? If your home is your sanctuary from the world, your bedroom is your place of ultimate rest from all the challenges that dog your every waking minute. You can answer the following questions in your journal.

1. What kinds of sleeping arrangements did you have as a child? Did you have your own room or did you share with a sibling? Did you like the room and the arrangement?
2. Did you have a lot of control over the décor in your room growing up? Is your

current room an outgrowth of that early style or has it changed completely?
3. Do you like your current bedroom? If you do, be specific as to what pleases you.
4. Are there things about your bedroom you don't like? Be specific.
5. Can the things you don't like be remedied easily (for example, will a fresh coat of paint help or could you move the furniture around)? I have a long, high window in my bedroom. I would love to lower it so that I could read in bed and look out at the mountains, but this is impossible because I rent. I

could, however, dress the windows in a way that's pleasing to the eye. What are your solutions?

6. Ask someone close to you if they feel you are truly reflected in this space. Their comments can be eye-opening.

7. Are you sharing this room with someone? How do they feel about your treasures? Walk into this room as if you have never been here before. Is one person the dominant force? Do you now realize you have been a space hog? How do you think that makes your partner feel? If the shoe is on the other foot, can you negotiate with your partner for a more equitable setup?

8. Is the room filled with things from your past? Why is that? Perhaps you are a twentysomething and your room is crammed with items from your college dorm room. Perhaps you are an empty nester and you cling to the now-tattered rocking chair you sat in when you were a nursing mom. If everything from the past has belonged to you, do you realistically still need it? It's okay if you feel you do. I just want to make you aware that the past may be a big part of your present.

9. Do you notice that the past is heavily represented in your space, but it's all possessions that mean nothing to you? Are you the guardian of the past in terms of antiques, furniture, and memorabilia for your family? If you don't love having these things, perhaps it's time to ask other family members to take them.

10. Many years ago, I met a lovely lady who told me that she was the good girl in her family. Her four brothers and sisters had no interest in the furniture from their childhood home. Neither did her parents, who gave it all to her when they moved to another state and redecorated from scratch! Can you imagine? My client had a house full of furniture in her basement. We good girls and boys get saddled with the family stuff. Inevitably, it's one child in the family who assumes this role. If you don't enjoy this role, it's time to quit your job.

11. I had another client who adored the old furniture and decorative items that had been passed down to her from various family members. As we walked from room to room, she took me on a tour of her family history through her furniture. Her voice was full of the pleasure and pride she took in these objects. If that's you, please continue to enjoy what you have.

12. If you share your bedroom with your spouse, did you move into a space that he or she had lived in before? This is traditionally a difficult transition. Do you feel you have been able to express yourself adequately? Or is it time to renegotiate?

These exercises are meant to awaken you to the possibility that your bedroom, perhaps the most sacred room in the home, may not reflect who you are. It's equally legitimate to discover that you have done a masterful job and who you are at your core or Soul level is on display. If you're in that situation, you may simply pat yourself on the back and enjoy the organizing process.

MAKE A PLAN

At this point, I'd like you to make a list of all the improvements and changes you'd like to make in your bedroom. If you know you won't be able to do everything this month, draw a line down the center of a page in your journal. On the left side, list what you can do this month; in the opposite column, list all the things you will do over time. For example, you may be ready to off-load some family antiques. If they have significant value, you may first have to do a little research and see if you want to use an antique dealer or an eBay assistant.

Perhaps you will purchase all new bedding this month, but you need to wait a few months before you paint. There are no rules as long as you have a plan. Making changes over time is tantamount to having projects in the hopper. However, you must take the next step and schedule them in your calendar for the appropriate month. Lots of items that will transform a bedroom don't cost an arm and a leg, such as lighting, throw rugs, and decorative items. By the way, if you are a big reader, instead of using floor space by the bed or burying your nightstand in stacks of books and magazines, put a nice bookcase in your room. And if you don't want to paint your walls because you rent rather than own, consider painting a piece of furniture.

Take a good look at the entertainment or office equipment in your bedroom. Can you relocate those activities? If you live in a tiny one bedroom in a large city, you probably cannot. If you live in a house,

it might be time to transform your guest room into a home office and watch TV in your family room or den. Ideally, your bedroom is a place for rest and pleasure. When we turn it into a satellite office or the place where we watch the news, the energy in the space is affected. I am only suggesting what I think will help you get the most pleasure from this room. Please adjust to suit your personal taste.

If you need to work in your bedroom, can you set the area off with a rug or hide it behind a screen? Small rugs are amazingly powerful because they create separate zones in a room. I had a client whose office had to be in the living room. He hated the fact that when friends came over to visit and watch a game, his work was in the same room. We created an office area by placing the desk, chair, and filing cabinets on the wood floor. We put the couch on the large rug facing the TV with its back to the work area. It worked like a charm. If you and your partner work from home, you may use this trick to set up a work zone here and make the dining room or the kitchen work for the other person in the unit. We'll look at these choices more in the Office section. Working in the bedroom is never my first choice for anyone but I honor that it may be necessary in some circumstances. Let's make it a separate energetic zone so it doesn't invade the quality of your rest.

If you fall asleep with the TV on, please give some attention to the unit it sits on. I remember organizing a large, elegantly appointed bedroom with an armoire directly across from the bed. This couple made their living in the movie industry, and as you might imagine they had a large-screen TV and lots of entertainment choices in terms of DVDs and VHS tapes. When I looked over at the unit from the vantage point of the bed, I had to smile. Prominently displayed was a set of VHS tapes they had purchased from the History Channel. It was wonderful educational material, but unfortunately in front of them each night were several tape spines with one large word across them: *Hitler.* I suggested we take Adolf to the den. His name isn't the last thing you want to see as you snap off your lights. I realize that streaming and cloud storage have made VHS tapes pretty much obsolete. Is there anything facing you that would cause an unconscious disruption in your psyche?

HAVE CLOTHES TAKEN OVER YOUR BEDROOM?

Now let's turn to the need to organize your room, including your closet. Please answer the following questions. Most of these require a simple "yes" or "no" rather than a journal entry.

- Can you sit on your chair or is it forever draped with clothing?
- Are dirty clothes tossed onto the floor? Hint: You need a hamper!
- What about your dresser drawers?

Are they organized or chaotic? Do you need more drawer space?
- What else besides clothing is stored in your closet?
- Is there space in your closet or is everything smashed together?
- Do you use uniform hangers or the wire ones your dry cleaner sends home?
- Is there a huge space between the shelf and the ceiling in your closet?
- Do you have multiple wardrobes in your closet because your weight fluctuates?
- Is the closet floor a shoe graveyard?

Working through these questions is more than enough for the first week of this new month. By the end of the week, you should have a handle on what is working and what level of self-expression you have achieved in your bedroom. If you have a partner, please be sure to have a conference with him or her before you go out and start painting or moving furniture. And don't forget to comb through Pinterest, online design magazines like *Domino* or *Architectural Digest*, and the websites of your favorite interior designers looking for ideas to help transform your bedroom on a shoestring. I have a few designers listed in the Resources section to get you started. If you are a do-it-yourself type of person, you might be measuring for new curtains this week!

WEEK TWO

Get to the Bottom of Your Closet

This week, you can

- Understand how your attachment to clothes may be emotional
- Clean out your closet of all unwanted and unrelated items
- Make donations to charity or to friends and family

Time required: Three to five hours in your closet, depending on the size of the closet and the number of clothes you have to go through. Add two hours for distribution of donated items, unless you arrange for them to be picked up. In that case, allow thirty minutes for the required phone calls.

WHEN WE FEEL VULNERABLE AND powerless in our lives, we frequently do one of two things: we gain weight or we weight ourselves down with too much stuff. Fat and stuff are both buffers against a world we perceive as threatening our well-being. This year is all about owning your own power. Let's exercise it in the bedroom. Let's shed the excess.

My clients frequently ask me what are the rules for eliminating clothing items. Some organizers suggest that if you haven't worn something in six to twelve months, out it should go. Others suggest that every time you bring home an item, you have to get rid of something you've had for a while. If these rules work for you, by all means follow them.

I prefer to understand the emotional attachment. When I work one-on-one with someone, I ask about each item. "Do you like this? Do you want to keep it?" If the answer is an immediate "yes," I move on to the next item. If the client is unsure, we talk about it. Your closet reveals the story of your life. I want to reveal the story through our investigation, not bind you to arbitrary rules about when clothing items need to leave your possession. Here are some examples of things I've learned.

Some people save items they purchased during a happy time in their lives. They reason, albeit unconsciously, that if they hold on to the item, they will be capturing forever a piece of that time in their lives. In my first book, I told the story about a client who wanted to save all the cashmere sweaters she had worn in high school. Now in her early sixties, they would never fit. They were in boxes in the back of a closet. Their presence helped her feel connected to the girl she had been. Just because you are blessed with lots of closets doesn't mean you have to keep them full to the rafters. They won't ever bring the past to life. It lives inside you in your heart and memories.

Others hold on to things that were given to them by someone who is now out of their lives. Perhaps a relationship ended or the person moved away? Do you have gifts and letters from old lovers? Saving some things from a meaningful relationship is certainly appropriate. Saving everything is interesting from an energy standpoint if nothing else. Feng Shui practitioners would caution you that a new relationship may be delayed if there is no space for that person in your life. You may also be expressing the fear that another relationship will never be yours. You need to keep these items because they are proof that at least once someone loved you. Is that your reality? I've had lots of single women clients who, for this very reason, secretly kept stashes of relationship memorabilia from men who treated them poorly. Be ever mindful what reality your stuff reveals.

When it's the death of someone dear, after an appropriate period of mourning, remember to pare down what you are keeping to a precious few items. The next stop on our eternal journey doesn't require stuff. No one ever comes back and asks what you did with their possessions, do they?

Can you relate to any of these? As you go through your closet, ask yourself questions about each item. Get to the bottom of the story that has made you hold on to this item of clothing. If you are still unsure, take a clinical look. Is it out of date, inexpensive, tattered, faded, worn, or stained? Let it go. If you have a friend who can help you make a decision, that's great. Remember, the key is that your friend has to ask the questions and help *you* decide. She can't make the decision for you, as in, "That's trash and it's going out today!" You are trying to build *your* decision-making muscle. And you don't want to regret anything that happens today.

Remember to check the list of preparatory actions I shared in the last section. This is incredibly emotional work and you want to be feeling your best. Feed your body and brain with nutrient-dense food; drink lots of fresh water; have healthy snacks on hand; give Fido a spin around the block or take an abbreviated Zoom Pilates or yoga class; and of course get a good night's sleep. When the demons get released, calmly beat them back with the winning combo of breath work and meditation. You got this! Remember too that these steps are not exclusively for organizing projects. You should make them knee-jerk steps for everything you do. What project would be better served by a hungry, sleep-deprived, dehydrated human who hadn't exercised in months? We're doing life here. It just looks like organizing.

STAYING ON TOP

So how do you take on your closet without getting overwhelmed? I have read directions for closet organizing sessions that say everything should be taken out and placed in a pile on the bed or the floor. I disagree. My goal is to streamline your life not make it more complicated.

If you get interrupted, you'll have clothing everywhere. And where will you sleep if the closet contents are now on your bed and you have to finish tomorrow? If something you want is at the bottom of a stack, it's going to be wrinkled by the time you get to it. Now you must add ironing to your closet organizing to-do list. If you made your piles on the floor, will you trip in the night if you need to go to the bathroom? Will your dog or cat nest in your clothing pile? Please. It's a nightmare directive. I am not a fan. Finally it feels disrespectful to the clothing to dump it all into a pile. Let's take a Mindful approach.

Set yourself up to win. I happen to have a portable, lightweight rack that I sometimes take to clients' homes. These are inexpensive and store flat. You might try a portable rack; another great use of these racks is to help plan your wardrobe in advance of going on a trip. But be careful with all the tools you purchase to help you get organized. If you don't really need the item, you are in fact adding to the clutter.

Be sure to have trash bags on hand for clothing that will be donated or thrown away. Sturdy garbage bags designed for grass clippings are perfect to hold clothes. You don't want to be hauling a bag of clothes down the stairs to the car or the bus stop only to have it rip. And be sure not to overfill the bags; otherwise they might be too heavy or unwieldy for you to carry. Attention to little details like this will ensure not only your success but the ease in accomplishing the task at hand.

Work one section of the closet at a time, as if nothing else existed. If you're weeding out the clothes on the right side of the top rack, don't get distracted by your belt collection or the shoes on the floor. You'll get to those later.

Go through hanging items first. I would advise you to remove all the plastic and wire hangers. If you have empty hangers taking up space, remove them. I store a few extra hangers in the closet and then I distribute the rest around the home. You will be astounded by how much space this simple action frees up.

If you have garments such as evening gowns or summer whites that need to be protected, you can find canvas covers in any organizing department. They make them for individual garments or wide enough to accommodate an entire category of clothing. Be sure you get canvas; vinyl does not allow your clothes to breathe.

By the end, everything you want will be left hanging and everything you're going to donate will be in bags ready to go to their new owners. After you work through the hanging items, turn your attention to the shelves. Again, do one at a time, working item by item or decision by decision.

After the shelves, check the floor. Your closet is designed to hold clothing. What else do you have here? Unless you live in a tiny space with no appreciable storage, please move nonclothing items out. My students are always shocked when I share the story of the strangest item I ever found in a closet: the ashes of the previous wife. Yes, I couldn't make this up. You probably don't have ashes in your closet but you may have family photos, gift-wrap supplies, memorabilia, or holiday gifts. Believe it or not, the most common items are portable fans and free weights. Take a minute to put all these items where they really belong. You'll find storage and organizing solutions for most of the preceding items in this book.

When it comes to the free weights, they usually find their way into the closet as a way to jog your memory. Does this work for you? Or have they become part of the décor? If the latter is the case, find a home for the weights where you will actually use them or add them to the donation pile. If it's summer and the fan comes out every night, why not give it a space in your room instead of hauling it out each night? If it's the off season, store it with other seasonal items. By the way, room circulators store more easily than the taller fans. The latter are going to be bumping into your hanging wardrobe if this is indeed the only spot you have to store fans. Your closet is the designated spot for your wardrobe. It isn't meant to be a dump site, gym, or off-season storage facility. Remember: We're creating a sanctuary here!

At the end of this session, you may peer into the now relatively empty space of your closet and experience a profound sense of loss. This is probably because you are accustomed to filling up the space around you with stuff. Enjoy the freedom of empty space. Vietnamese Buddhist monk Thich Nhat Hahn says that when he consumes all the tea in his cup, it is then full of space. Think about that for a minute. Space isn't empty; it's full of energy. Consider also that all the good that is meant to come to you now has a place to reside. What is that law of physics? Ah, yes. Two objects cannot occupy the same place at the same time. Indeed, they cannot.

You'll have some cleanup work today. Before next week, you'll want to have all your items donated or returned to the friends or family members who loaned them to you. Don't forget to clean out the clothing you have stashed in drawers. Here is where the old, tattered, outdated, and stained usually reside. You know what I'm referring to: the holey underwear that you feel safe no one will see, the stained T-shirt from college, and that Hawaiian shirt that looks good only on the beach in Waikiki. Do you have a picture of yourself in the T or special travel shirt? Could you cut a swatch and use it in a scrapbook? Fearlessly clean it all out. Next week will be the fun part!

If you have a car, you're in the catbird's seat in terms of donating your bags of goodies. If you don't have a car, call a charity that makes pickups and have your appointment scheduled for the day after this work session. Items that stay in bags for days tend to magically migrate back to the closet. Trust your judgment. Let it go.

I bet one of your fellow Zen Organizers™ has a car, and, if you give a few dollars for gas, you'll be on your way to less clutter in no time. Maybe you can do your donations together. After the drop-off you can share a reward, such as a special outing to your favorite coffee shop.

Minimalism versus Maximalism

As we deal with our collection of clothing, I think it's a good time for me to say a few words about minimalism and it's polar opposite, maximalism. You probably think I have a favorite, don't you? I don't. I would not want to see either sweep the world creating cookie-cutter environments.

In the minimalist mindset I see great value. Use what you have. Don't devote your life to needless acquisition. Enjoy the ease of maintenance when a home or a life has only the bare necessities. There are Facebook groups in which the members trade items so that the need for new purchases is kept to a minimum. I think the way a minimalist expresses themselves will change over time as life's demands change.

Maximalists seem to be less popular but certainly loud and proud about the mix of patterns in their environment and the vastness of their collections. I think if you love what you have, organize it, know where every item is, and if you have the space, go for it. I've seen a video of the incomparable Iris Apfel's home and it's got for me what would be a suffocating amount of jewelry. But would I urge Iris to divest herself and go to the minimalist side of the equation? Never! Are you a hoarder who calls yourself a maximalist? You realize that's a horse of a different color. This isn't an elegant phrase but it conveys the intent: You can't put lipstick on a pig.

As I say frequently to my clients: You do you. Your home should reflect you, your life story, and what you hold dear. My home looks like a real human being lives in it. I have zero clutter. There is also no resemblance to a Zen monastery that is ironically what everyone expects. If you feel austerity makes your Soul come alive, that is absolutely what you should create. I'll do me while you do you. Aren't we lucky?

WEEK THREE

Take Time for Your Space

Misplaced gold is easily found, misspent time is lost forever.

–LOY CHING-YUEN

This week, you can

- Create a shopping list for any organizing tools you need
- Return to your examination of time and uncover your true goals
- Consider how you can maximize your closet space

Time required: Thirty to sixty minutes for journal work; thirty to sixty minutes to examine items and create a shopping list; thirty minutes to measure your closet and, if necessary, arrange for a closet company appointment; two hours to shop for supplies.

I F YOU ARE DOING AN ORGANIZING SYS-tem installation yourself, you will have to allow for a trip to the store to create the design and the time to do the installation work itself. The time will be governed by the size of the closet and the complexity of the system. Your skill at this type of job will also affect the time you need to devote to the process. Try to purchase your system at the same time you pick up your supplies. This will save time.

We're going back this week to add to our understanding of time. We're also going to develop our shopping list for the bedroom in terms of the organizing supplies that will make our lives easier. Transforming this space from ho-hum to sanctuary takes time and thought. Rushing the process will leave you feeling incomplete or, worse, that you made a mistake to even try. I want you to have time for your projects, especially those of you who are going to be making bold strokes such as painting, moving furniture, or shopping for additional pieces.

WHAT'S IT ALL ABOUT?

Let me ask you some questions about the direction you want to take for your life. You are working an entire year to get your personal and work environments to support you. What are they supporting you for? It's important to know. When we live our days buffeted by the needs of others, our lives fall into the "same old, same old" rut. In the average home, fall means back to school and nights of fighting with the kids about homework. Summer means taking a trip or trying to enjoy our backyards or the city we live in. The holidays go by in an exhausting blaze of activities that we repeat every year. One day we ask, "How did I get here in my life?" The key to getting, being, and staying organized is to make decisions. Stacks and piles are unmade decisions made manifest. If these decisions aren't consciously made, you will arrive not at your goals but at a destination created by chance or, worse, by others.

You have dedicated yourself to the process of getting organized over the course of an entire year. What made you do that? What are you seeking? How will this work change your life for the better? Be as specific as possible.

Has there ever been a time when you knew exactly what you wanted to do with your life? Did you stick to those goals or did something like falling in love, having a baby, or a death force you to take an unexpected new direction? How do you feel about this change?

Are you in the middle of life changes now that come at expected times, such as the children leaving for college or your retirement from work? Even though you knew they were coming, have they knocked you for a loop? Has that manifested in your inability to keep up with your environment? Can you open your heart and imagination and think about what you would like to accomplish in the next phase of your life?

What do you do well? Are you great at sports? Do you create scrapbooks that people admire? Do you have a natural aptitude with languages? When a party is planned, does everyone beg you to cook or bake? It's important to be in touch with the things you do well. Acknowledge them now with a conscious, detailed list. Is there a way to make money using these gifts?

If you could do anything you wanted in life, what would that be? Dream big and be honest as you write it down. Let's say you wrote, "I'd be a movie star." Well, if you're fifty that might be out of your reach, especially if you've never studied acting. However, it would be possible to take a class in acting at a community college or join the local theater company. If you've carried this dream around for a lifetime, do something about it just to make your Soul happy.

These journal entries are likely to be emotional. We're going to continue this work as we move through the year. Learning to control your time means more than learning new techniques. It's about living your life differently. The habits of a lifetime die slowly. Be patient.

ORGANIZING TOOLS

Let's balance out the week with a nice left-brain task. You'll need to figure out which organizing tools you might need during our blitz through your bedroom and closets before the month ends. You begin and end your day in this room. You change your outfits here. We need to be sure it's a functioning room that supports your daily activities, even if changes such as painting and new furniture remain on the vision board for a few more months. If it's important to you, you'll make it happen even if it takes a bit of time!

The most common organizing tools that might be needed in your bedroom are described in this section. Please jot down the items you know you need and some you may want to research at the store.

Hangers

Uniform hangers are a must. I love wooden hangers. They used to be prohibitively expensive but are now available for a song in the closet department of most home stores and places such as Bed Bath & Beyond. If you have a large closet and the finances, go with wood. If your closet is small, thin coated hangers will take up less space. The coating doesn't come off and it prevents slippage of delicate garments like silk or those garments with spaghetti straps. If you use wood, find a version with notches at the ends. Your spaghetti straps will be so happy you provided for them!

Unless your closet is very large, padded hangers will take up too much room. If an item is that delicate, fold it and place it in a dresser drawer or put it on a shelf in a container.

Shelf Dividers and Stackable Drawers

Use shelf dividers to mark off which space on a shelf is dedicated to a specific part of your wardrobe. Usually I use them to separate sweater stacks to prevent implosion.

In some climates, the need for a large wardrobe of sweaters is clear. You can house them in many ways. I like to sort them by color and stack them using shelf dividers. You might want to keep them in individual zippered pouches. You will also find plastic stackable drawers that can nicely hold sweaters. If you put them on a shelf, be sure you have a two-step stepstool handy. If you have floor space, stack them under some short items such as tops. The drawers slide in and out easily.

Throughout this book I recommend a few products made in acrylic. I am not into expendable plastic that will wind up in a landfill after a few months. Quality products can be with you for decades and the way you use them can change over time. Let's say you move from NYC to Los Angeles as I did. Suddenly you might not be filling up those acrylic drawer organizers because the need for warm sweaters has been reduced to a precious few. Do you craft? Do you have children with toys? Could you store linens in them? What about categorizing holiday decorations? You might even use them in the back of an office closet for archival papers. You are only limited by your creativity.

Acrylic Hatboxes

Some organizing stores have see-through acrylic hatboxes. I use them for items such as scarves, evening purses, and metal belts that can't be hung. Of course, if you have hats, you'll never wonder which one is in which box again.

Shoe Racks

It's a must to get shoes off the floor. Expandable shoe racks are great for women's shoes. The shoe must have at least a small heel to keep them securely on the bar. Wood shoe racks designed for men's shoes will also handle women's flats or athletic shoes. If you get one in cedar, you'll simultaneously be combating moths. I also like the canvas over-the-door shoe bag for exercise shoes and flip-flops. Get one that attaches so all those shoes don't go *thwap-thwap* every time you open and close your closet door.

Jewelry Organizers

Where is your jewelry now? Do you need a jewelry box? Could you empty out the traditionally narrow top drawer of a dresser and put your things there? You can use the same drawer organizers we used in the kitchen or you can use padded ones made for (high end) jewelry No matter how much jewelry a woman has, she almost always wears the same key pieces each day. I have a small decorative wooden box on my bathroom counter. Each morning I take out my favorite pieces. The jewelry in boxes in my dresser is for special occasions or when I need a change. This saves me steps in the morning, which means I save time. I'm organized but I move slowly in the morning. It's best if everything is laid

out for me. Those boxes by the way have their lids underneath the box itself. I can open a drawer and see the entire collection. Opening and closing boxes would make me weep.

Drawer Organizers

Do you have a large collection of exercise socks that threaten to spill out over the floor every time you reach for a pair? I like to fold dress socks neatly and tuck them into sock organizers. I keep that group in a dresser drawer. There are inexpensive drawer organizers for items from bras to socks. You can also go crazy and get them in wood or lined with beautiful material. I toss athletic socks into an open container that stays on the floor of the closet near the exercise shoes. I wouldn't roll them and use the top of one sock to hold them in place by pulling it over the two. Yes, it keeps them together, but it also stretches out the fabric. Roll them or fold them. This fold-over technique is all the rage. I'm just not a fan of stretching fabric.

Belt and Tie Organizers

A belt and tie organizer mounted on the wall is ideal if you have the wall space. If not, use hangers made for this purpose. When it comes to belts, if you don't have a large number or you're a woman with a lot of metal belts that can't be hung, consider placing them in a nice lined basket (or that hat box I mentioned above). Of course, you need shelf space for this solution, so plan accordingly.

THE CLOSET SPACE ITSELF

Let's turn our attention to your actual closet space. I used to work with a closet designer who had a saying: "Now the space is the space." No matter how organized you are, if you have too much stuff, it's not going to fit in a tiny closet. Be realistic about the demands you're making on the closet space you have. Maximize it. Don't overload it.

Be sure you take the following steps *after* you have cleaned out your closet. It would be silly, for example, to set aside space for fifteen business suits if in fact you are only going to keep four. If you own a home, I would suggest you have a closet designer come out and give you a professional design. There is no charge for the design itself. If you take your measurements to The Container Store, they will design a custom closet for you. The Elfa system is less expensive than one installed by a closet company, and you can take it with you when you move. The Container Store has added a line of high-end closets as well, so you can talk to your rep while you are in the store about the differences. If your budget is limited, you rent, or the design is for a child, teen, or guest room, use Elfa or the Pax system from IKEA. If you want to add resale value in the primary suite, go high end with The Container Store or a company like Closet Factory. If you are in the middle of a remodel or know a good contractor, he or she may be able to design and build a system for you. However, that's a very expensive way to go!

A carpenter will probably not use pressboard or melamine but real wood. And that's where you rack up the high fees.

A word of caution: I have been hired many times to organize a newly installed closet only to discover the designer never asked about or saw the existing wardrobe. You can have *the* most beautiful design, but if it doesn't accommodate what you have, it's just an art installation. Do your eliminating before you design and give your designer a list of your clothing categories and the number of pieces in each.

If there is a very tall person in the home, be sure to measure their shirts and suit jackets. You want them to neatly hang above the lower bar, not drape over it. You may need to add additional long hang space for their needs. Finally, some closets use high-end wood and extra holes are not provided. Yes, you need a few! Being able to adjust the configuration of a custom closet is worth its weight in gold.

If you need it and have the space, put up a second bar in at least one area so you have double hanging capacity. These bars should be adjustable and removable so the configuration of your closet can change with your needs.

If you lack space for a dresser in your bedroom proper and have a walk-in, see if a small dresser will fit there. You might be able to score one second hand. With a coat of paint (check out Annie Sloan's chalk paint) and new drawer handles (I love the creative selection at Anthropologie), you can transform almost any furniture. This is a form of recycling, right? If a dresser won't fit, do you have hanging space to use a multi-compartment canvas sweater organizer? They attach to a rod and hang down, giving you mini open drawer storage space. They make narrow ones for shoes. You can, of course, get creative with the items you store in either size!

If you rent and don't want to invest in a closet system, here are some easy things you can do to make a space work better. Just about every closet has one shelf, above which is a cavernous space. Place a bracket on either side and add a shelf. You can paint or stain the wood if you like. I like to leave it plain. Any handyman can do this for you at a minimal charge.

If you have sliding doors, you know what a pain they are. If you don't want to put in doors that open, remove the sliding doors and hang a curtain that you can either roll up when you need to access something or pull aside. If you want to keep the sliders or have no place to store them because you're in a rental, be sure you place your clothes in the closet in the order in which you take them out. For example, let's say you work in an office. Just about every day you wear a nice blouse and a skirt or pair of slacks; on rare occasions, you wear a suit. I'd have the blouses in the front so that when you slide the first door, that's what you see. When you slide the second door, there you'd find your slacks and skirts. At the end of the row, behind door number three, I'd tuck your rarely worn suits. Organizing a closet like this is critical. Otherwise; you'll be sliding those doors back and forth wasting time and energy. But you probably already knew that, didn't you?

Does your closet go deep inside a wall on one side? It's the dead zone there, isn't it? You can use that space for off-season storage, either hanging or on shelves (such as sweaters, scarves, gloves, and hats). Items on shelves can be in containers if you like. In the absence of shelves, do a stack of acrylic drawers or some decorative storage containers. It's still going to be difficult to access, but access isn't as much of a priority for off-season items.

Every closet needs good lighting but some don't even have an outlet! You can find lights that attach to the wall and go on when tapped. They are usually battery powered. If you have the option, I would call an electrician and add an outlet. By the way, I once had an infestation of clothes moths. It seems they like to eat in the dark, so I now have a light on 24/7 in my closet. I also use cedar-scented wood chips and lavender sachets. Replenish both every six months. The door is only closed at night when I go to sleep and yes, the light stays on! It's low wattage and not a fire hazard.

By the end of this week, you'll really understand the space you are dealing with and how you can best maximize it. My only word of caution is to avoid the cheap version of a good solution. If you are going to install a system, you need to brace it securely so it can support the weight of your clothes. I was shocked to find a cheap closet system installed in an expensive high-rise in Manhattan. Can you guess what happened? I was folding clothes when I heard a loud crash. All of my client's beautiful hanging clothes were on the floor. That was not the only time that happened to me, so remember: You get what you pay for!

This week requires a commitment of time and energy, but the result will be more than worth it. Next week you will have a lot of fun putting your products in place and seeing your sanctuary come to life. It's play time for sure! Take a deep breath this week. By the way, do you have a reward planned yet? There's no time like the present!

WEEK FOUR

Create a Bedroom You Love

This week, you can

- At last—organize all the clothes in your bedroom, from closet to shelves to dressers
- Organize your handbag
- Learn what to avoid; there's no sense wasting your time or money on worthless products

Time required: Three to five hours, depending on the number of items and the size of the space (closet, dresser, shelves, and so on).

THE MOMENT OF TRUTH HAS ARRIVED. The time for fun begins. Putting a closet together is one of the most creative tasks I do for my clients. I hope you will relax and enjoy this project. The hard work is behind you. By the way, after your closet is organized, don't be surprised if you see a few more items you don't need. It happens all the time.

THE GROUND RULES

Have you ever tried to organize your closet and not known what to do? In this section, you'll find keys to creating a visually beautiful and fully functioning closet! Just be sure the eliminating phase is not only complete but all those items are out of the bedroom before you begin organizing. With fewer items your closet should already feel less intimidating and be easier to use.

Please clear the bedroom of any items that are destined to leave the house, whether it's to the trash/recycle bin, a charity, or a friend. Consider one section in your closet at a time. Go item by item in that section. As the closet empties, you will see what you actually want to keep and can decide if you need to make new sectional assignments. Have you utilized the space well up to now?

Move items around if you need to and if it's a big walk-in closet remove one section at a time if you wish so you can do a thorough cleaning. Place clothing sections/types on that nice clear bed. I told you it was a great place to stage! As you return the items to the closet, you know where they are going and you can now put each section in color order. You can purchase an inexpensive clothing rack for this project and store it under your bed. All your friends are going to borrow it when they see how efficient you are in those videos and photos I know you plan to share on social media!

The Dark Side of Fashion

I lived the first part of my life in New York City. Every time there was a change of season, people dressed differently, so I had a large wardrobe. Life in Southern California is different. Contrary to the myth, it is not always summer. I would say we have three seasons. Even in the coldest of winters, after a few days the sun returns and it's in the eighties for a day or two. We don't have warm parkas, snow boots, fisherman's knit sweaters, or gloves. Our wardrobe is pretty much a constant. Your age, socioeconomic status, and career will largely dictate how you dress. It's a much more casual atmosphere, and I confess I have adapted the blue jean uniform. It really is an amazing garment that can be dressed up or dressed down. One day I discovered that, like all clothing, jeans have a dark side, and I don't mean the shade of blue.

The fashion industry is a major polluter. We shop for fun. We discard our clothing with ease. We purchase cheap clothing because it is expendable. Have you ever considered the possibility that child labor in a foreign land made that garment and gifted you an affordable item because they worked in deplorable conditions for a pittance? We pawn off our discards on a local charity, never giving a thought to what will happen to items they don't want because they can't resell them. The fashion industry produces 10 percent of all humanity's carbon emissions. Stop and let that sink in. Fashion is the second-largest consumer of the world's water supply, and pollutes the oceans with micro-plastics. I could go on, but you get the picture. It isn't always a pretty bargain.

We don't have to freeze the wardrobe we have and never purchase another article of clothing to make a contribution. In fact, that would lead to you making your home a private landfill. We can, however, become conscious consumers. You can reduce your consumption by making fewer purchases of higher quality items that will last several years. Skip synthetic fabrics when possible and purchase natural fibers. Mend your clothes rather than replace. Shop sustainable companies whose garments are made in countries with strict production controls. Eschew fur and leather and become a fan of their faux brothers and sisters. A word of caution: Just because something is faux doesn't mean it was made without polluting the environment. A rule of thumb is to check the country of origin. Again, do a little research and become a devotee of certain brands. In the case of faux leather and faux fur, at least you have taken animal death for human adornment off the table. That's always a win.

Finally, recycle by finding someone who will appreciate the garment you no longer need. I do not mean personally seeking out the new owner of every single item you wish to discard. This would be a full-time job. I trust the Universe will direct the perfect person to the charity of my choice when I donate. There are, however, items we can go the extra mile for and find a charity dedicated to that garment. Dress for Success will take business clothing for women and help someone look the part when they go in for a job interview. In the Resources section you will find other charities doing creative and helpful things!

There are charities that will take your bridal gown for the military bride who can't afford one (Brides Across America). Many brides will enjoy your dress and have a special day. You can donate your gown to a charity that will make a burial dress for an infant who has died (The Angel Gowns Project). Your bridesmaid dress could be donated to a charity that helps teenage girls find prom dresses (Operation Prom). If you have high-end clothing and feel the local Goodwill or Salvation Army storefront is not the right fit, call them and see if they have a storefront that will take high-end clothing. Yes, they exist.

And let me say also that just because you dropped off items at Goodwill doesn't mean they are duty bound to sell them. Some people donate items that are not usable but giving them to a charity brings up warm feelings of having done a good deed. If an item is destined for a landfill because no one is going to use it, be honest and do the dumping yourself. My favorite misguided donations are those weddings dresses that are sent to a region that has suffered a disaster. No one who has lost a home wants your wedding dress. Yes, people do that!

You can take your clothing to a local consignment store or sell it online via programs like thredUP and Poshmark. I like the Farfetch program because it's multifaceted. You can sell on eBay or on Facebook Marketplace. The choices are exploding as I write this. Investigate these programs and see which is a fit for your personality (i.e., how much time do you have to invest) and your clothing. If you are off-loading designer duds try The Real Real. Green America has a clothing brands scorecard so you can see how conscious your favorite brands really are.

The easiest way to go is just to mindlessly stuff discards in a bag, drop it off at a Goodwill collection center, and be done. I'm offering a few suggestions to help you make money or turn your special discard into a bonanza for someone who can't afford to buy it new. You will most likely receive a tax deduction but sometimes the fact you helped a fellow human being trumps the financial reward. Mix it up. You don't have to devote the rest of the year to this project or become Mother Teresa. We're going for conscious not sainthood.

Clothing

Various types of clothing will stay together. When you want a pair of slacks or a blouse or a pair of shoes, you want to know exactly where in your closet those items are kept.

Place every category in the same color order. I use the following:

White/Off-white
Beige/Brown
Blue/Purple
Pink/Red
Green/Yellow
Gray/Black

When I organize a closet for a client, I put sleeveless blouses first in each color category, then short sleeve, and then long sleeve. I place patterns at the end. I tell my clients that if this is too much to deal with, just keep the colors together. Decide what works best for you. You'll find that the use of color to organize all the sections will make the closet feel very Zen. It will calm you every time you have to get dressed.

Sometimes a client will have a large wardrobe dedicated to a particular sport, such as golf, horseback riding, or tennis. In this case, let those pieces have their own section. It will be that much easier to choose your outfit for the day.

Learn to fold your sweaters just like they do in department stores. Neat stacks of sweaters, in color order, look great on a shelf. When you want a sweater, it will be easier to lift up the ones on top if they're folded. Yes, it takes an extra ten seconds to replace sweaters in a stack, but the visual peace it brings is well worth the effort. I use a smooth acrylic square to slip under the sweater just above the one I need. Lift one sweater or a stack and gently pull out the one you need. Use this tool when you go to add or replace a sweater to the stack.

It works like a charm. You can find them on Amazon. You'll find acrylic squares, but they are designed for other purposes. You know my directive: think outside the box. You'll probably have to purchase a few but place them in all your closets or share with your friends. Even closet designers don't know this trick!

Have you ever pulled out a favorite wool sweater only to realize it's pilled? Special, inexpensive shavers take care of this. You can find them online or at the corner drugstore, but in a pinch, run to your bathroom and grab a pumice stone!

You will be surprised how easy it is to find things in drawers if they are neatly folded and in color order. I like underwear containers for bras, panties, boxers, briefs, and dress socks.

Shoes

Whether you put your shoes in clear shoe drawers and stack them or line them up on a shoe rack or stand, keep them in the same color order as your hanging clothes. As I said earlier, you may want to stash your play and workout shoes in an over-the-door canvas holder.

If you find that you don't have room for all your shoes and you're using built-in shoe shelves, try this trick: turn one shoe in each pair in the opposite direction. It will give you more space instantly! Also, if you have very deep shelves and want your shoes out, put one in front of the other. You'll have a row of different shoes facing you and you'll know exactly where the mate is.

If you can't afford to purchase acrylic storage drawers for your entire collection, get a few for your evening shoes. I like to toss the boxes that shoes come in because the sizes and colors vary so much. If you want to keep yours, sort your shoes by color but put a photo of the shoe on the outside of the box.

Purses

Keep your purses on a shelf and in color order. To keep the purses from falling into each other, use shelf dividers to keep colors separate or purchase a unit made for this purpose. It sits on the shelf and gives each purse its own space. One nice touch is to keep them stuffed with tissue paper to help retain their shape. It's also easier to prop them on a shelf and not have them fall into flat heaps of leather or material! You can tuck the tissue paper into a small cloth bag; that way it all comes out and returns as one unit. If you purchase high-end shoes and purses, your life may be overrun with these cloth bags. If not, you could also repurpose organic cloth produce bags made for the pantry or purchase cotton shoe and handbag storage bags made for this purpose online.

The best way to organize your handbag, ladies, is to dump out the contents on your bed or on a table. Examine each item and ask yourself if you realistically need to haul it around with you each day. It's wonderful to save the day and pull out some esoteric item once a year, but it's not really important, is it? Let someone else be the Girl Scout.

THE CLOSET CHECKLIST

- Have everything facing in the same direction.
- Use one type of hanger. No wire hangers, ever!
- Throw away plastic covers from the cleaners.
- Keep specific types of clothing together.
- Arrange everything in color order.
- Keep shoes off the floor on a shoe rack; use acrylic shoe drawers for special pairs like evening shoes and employ an over-the-door canvas holder for sport shoes and flip-flops, if needed.

Periodically replace or refresh whatever type of moth protection you use. Please do not use mothballs. The chemical that kills the moths has been outlawed in the EU and other areas. It is thought to be carcinogenic and can cause many health issues.

Just for fun, take a look at your closet before you start organizing. Is everything facing a different direction? That makes it difficult to see items when you're looking for something. Your upper torso is bobbing back and forth as you move through the row. Are the clothes facing the same direction? I like everything facing the door if you have a walk-in closet. When everything faces the back wall, I get the feeling you don't really want to leave your house!

There is a popular organizing trick that recommends you turn all your clothes hangers backward on the bar. As you wear each item, hang it correctly. At the end of six months, you will see what you don't wear. I find this a silly use of your time and it creates an unattractive visual you have to deal with for six months. If you truly don't know what you wear, you have too much and need a purge.

After you whittle down the contents, look at your categories. Keep related items in separate containers. Makeup is a great example of a category most ladies have. Makeup in your purse is about having the tools for touch-ups, not every item in your arsenal to help you glam up for a prom!

Do you carry more keys than you need? Do you have an oversized decorative item on the ring?

I had a wallet for credit cards, the majority of my cash, and my automobile information; a change purse for coins; and my checkbook. To make it easy to find everything, I had my wallet and checkbook in a separate zippered container like the one for my makeup.

Today I frequently leave home without a purse! I just use my phone as my wallet and carry no change or cash. I do have my debit card at all times and one credit card to pay for meals where I can earn American Airlines miles. Now that's good multitasking! I will carry a purse if I am going to a social engagement so I have makeup with me to refresh after I eat.

As you look at the financial information and money you have with you, what's the best way for you to keep it all in order? The size of your category and the size of your purse will dictate your solution.

If you have separate items that you like to have handy that are unique to you, transfer them to a small tote. This will help equalize the weight on your shoulders. For example, perhaps you like to have a book and some water with you. These are heavy items. Save your body. Balance the load by carrying both a purse and a tote. Let me remind you that if you download the Kindle or e-reader app of your choice, you can have hundreds of books at your fingertips.

Each evening, I look in my purse to pull out the items I have added that day. I put tax-deductible receipts into my "To File" folder (more on that in the Office section), toss extraneous material, and refresh anything that got depleted. For example, I might need a fresh travel pack of tissues. If you find a nightly ritual overwhelming, go through your purse every Sunday evening. You'll be streamlined for the week to come.

QUICK FIXES

If you find as you organize that you're running out of space, try to keep jackets in the hall closet. Very often jackets and coats eat up a lot of room in a clothes closet. Another space eater is ski clothing. If you love to ski, try to keep these things in the guest closet if you're lucky enough to have one, or in a container if you need the hanging space. Space bags are wonderful ways to store bulky items from clothing to linens. They really work, so if you haven't tried them yet, treat yourself. They're like large Ziploc bags except you suck out all the air with a vacuum cleaner. Don't worry: they don't ruin or wrinkle your items. They work best with items that are flat by nature. If you have super fluffy pillows they might break the seal. Know the limits of your products and you will never be disappointed. I guess I could say that about people, couldn't I?

You can place hooks that extend out a few inches over the door. You could hang your bathrobe and pajamas or nightgown here. Don't forget you could use this hook on the back of the bathroom door. That's where I keep my PJs and robe. If the closet is tiny and you happen to have a lot of drawer space, fold your sleepwear, T-shirts, and sweats and keep them in drawers. Conversely, if the closet is large and drawer space is at a premium, hang those items instead. Those narrow coated hangers will assist you in maximizing the space.

TO HANG OR NOT TO HANG?

One question I am always asked is how to hang pants. You can do long hang if you have the space. You can fold them over special pant hangers. If we're talking about casual slacks and especially blue jeans, you can fold them on a shelf or toss them over a wood hanger. Here's the sticking point: If you have a lot of pants you rarely wear and you use hangers with clips, you will have marks on the pants from the hangers no matter how padded the clip is. It's another reason to purge. If you want, have a small portable or travel steamer to help smooth out those wrinkles. Before you go crazy, however, ask yourself if the mark is going to be covered by a belt, blouse, or jacket.

A TOOL I AVOID

Do you have one of those long metal hangers that hold multiple pairs of pants or skirts? I find that it simply grows wide, eating up space. Good luck taking one item off without several others falling. Ditch it.

I never use skirt or pant hangers with clips that have no or inadequate padding. Your clothes will be notched with those dreaded marks in the fabric.

IN PRAISE OF UNIFORMITY

Finally, let me say that, as much as possible, you want to use uniform containers on your closet shelves. For example, if you are using acrylic shoe drawers, you might want to also use the various size acrylic storage drawers. If you have wood hangers, you might like to incorporate leather, wood, or natural fiber containers such as cloth covered or bamboo. Check out these products online. You design the visual that will be equal parts functional and beautiful.

Your closet needs to be utilitarian, but that doesn't mean it can't have a touch of class. If you peer into a closet and see all kinds of containers in various colors and textures, it instantly jangles your nerves. Remember, we're Zen Organizers™!

PUTTING THE ROOM TOGETHER

As you complete the obvious projects in your bedroom, such as your closet and dresser, don't forget to consider what other elements you can add to make this room your sanctuary. Here are a few ideas:

Add a large comfortable chair or a rocker if you like to read or do needlecrafts.

Perhaps next to your chair, replace the basket for yarn with a small computer stand on wheels to hold your laptop. I'm not suggesting you work here! I am suggesting you take some private time to stay in touch with friends and family or just play solitaire for an hour to let your brain unwind.

If you love to read, add a small bookcase. Be sure you have adequate lighting.

Don't forget to look at the décor in the room. Beautiful curtains or drapes and magical touches such as a dream catcher will also help create the sanctuary feel. A luxurious bedspread or duvet cover will also have a strong effect on the ambience of the room.

I've seen bedroom suites as big as studio apartments in New York City! If you are so blessed, you may want to add a small refrigerator for snacks. Try to keep it behind a cupboard door so your sanctuary doesn't start looking like a kitchen.

In a large bedroom, I've also seen an area where a coffee pot can be set up. This works for the kind of pot that turns on automatically. If you love coffee, your sanctuary can be filled with the aroma of a fresh brew every morning!

What elements will you add to turn this utilitarian room into a private sanctuary? If you are in a committed relationship, don't forget to consult with your partner.

THE BEDROOM EXIT RITUAL

- Make the bed.
- Put clothing in your closet, hamper, or dry-cleaner bag—these are the only three options! Never toss garments on the floor, drape them over a chair, or leave them on your bed.
- Place shoes on the shoe rack, in the shoe drawer, or in the hanging shoe bag.
- Return miscellaneous paraphernalia (from children's toys to pet toys to your books) to their designated spots.
- Return dirty dishes, glasses, and all food items to the kitchen.
- Turn off the lights.

Both order and chaos are created by dedication to the steps that create them. Change your focus from confusion to calm, and your actions will follow. The result will be a place of peace waiting to nurture you whenever the stresses and strains of daily life threaten to overwhelm you.

As you complete the projects in this section, your environment will become calmer and more peaceful. The energy of a space exerts an unspoken influence on everyone who enters. If the kids seem less stressed and your spouse is more loving, I wouldn't be surprised. Something about saving time and emotional energy makes a body happy.

SUMMARY

WEEK ONE

Do your journal work this month with an eye to understanding exactly what you want to create in your bedroom so that it reflects who you are at a Soul level.

WEEK TWO

Clear your closet and your dresser of all excess so we can make a plan to organize what you want to keep.

WEEK THREE

Complete more exercises to help you understand the concept of time better.

Create your shopping list for next week's organizing work.

WEEK FOUR

Create order in your closet and dresser!

BONUS TIP

Aromatherapy candles and oil diffusers are wonderful in the bedroom to help you set a mood. Don't forget that essential oils have a long and rich history as natural healers. You can also make your own personal body products such as lotions and cleansers.

If you would like an introduction to the power and use of oils, I invite you to visit the website of one of my favorite yoga posture practitioners, Elena Brower. She has a free thirty-day course you can sign up for that will introduce you to oils and the exquisite doTERRA line. They are one of the gold standard companies in the marketplace along with Aura-Soma and Young Living Essential Oils.

I tell my students they can experiment to see how serious they are about the world of aromatherapy. You can purchase an inexpensive diffuser and inexpensive oils from Amazon. If you find you don't like the process, you haven't invested much and can pass it on to a friend. This is how I eased into the world of oils. Now I use doTERRA. I give the inexpensive duo as a gift to introduce my friends to this powerful, fragrant tool.

I have an exquisite glass diffuser from doTERRA and tuck my inexpensive plastic one into my suitcase when I travel. It's lightweight and I can diffuse tea tree oil or eucalyptus to clean any hotel or guest room. Finally, there are many books on the subject, but I personally love *The Complete Book of Essential Oils and Aromatherapy* by Valerie Ann Worwood. Consider using aromatherapy all over your home and make it another powerful tool in your healing kit that is growing every month.

ORGANIZING THE BUSINESS OF LIFE

Rest a little, but as soon as you can, get up and carry on. Because ever since your goal found out that you were traveling toward it, it has been running to meet you.

–PAULO COELHO

WHETHER YOU ARE RETIRED AND HAVE just a few files, are single and have a home office with piles everywhere, or are a stay-at-home parent with a kitchen nook work area, this month we bring order to the business of life.

THE PAPER BOGEYMAN

For some reason, paper seems to strike fear into the heart of most adults. Paper is the average adult's bogeyman. If getting organized is about making decisions and piles are merely stacks of unmade decisions made visible, why is paper so scary? I think it's because we fear we'll make a mistake. If I throw out a blouse and later regret it, it's a personal matter. If I toss out something I need for my taxes or lose a legal document, I can be in quite a pickle. Rather than make an error, most people tend to hold on to everything.

Here's a rule of thumb to live by: Anytime you wonder about the fate of a legal document, ask yourself, "What broad category is this document related to?" After you identify your category, find an expert in that field. For example, say you aren't sure how long you need to save your tax returns. Call the person who prepares your return, your tax attorney, your CPA, or a professional tax filing firm such as H&R Block.

If you have documents from prior real estate transactions and wonder which you need to keep, call your real estate agent or your real estate attorney. If you have no professional help, research the current guidelines on the internet. In other words, let yourself off the hook by asking someone who makes his or her living in the field. Are you starting to relax?

Although I would prefer that you check with *your* accountant, real estate agent, or attorney, CPA, or insurance broker for the last word, here is an outline of record retention requirements to give you some direction. This is how the experts in my life have advised me. You can also use a search engine such as Google and type "record retention guidelines." For income tax questions, go to www.irs.gov.

Record Retention General Guidelines

- Credit card receipts: Keep until verified on your statement if they represent general purchases; keep with tax material if the expenses are deductible.
- Warranties: Hold on to the receipt for the life of the warranty or as long as you have the item, whichever comes first.
- Insurance policies: Keep for the life of the policy.
- Mortgages, deeds, leases: Keep six years beyond the agreement.
- Real estate records and improvement receipts: Keep six years beyond the sale of the property.
- Pay stubs: Keep until reconciled with your W-2.

Hold Forever (Digital Format Is Preferable)

- Income tax returns
- Retirement and pension documents
- Legal records
- Investment trade confirmations

Tax Receipt Retention

- Federal return backup materials: Three years
- Federal return backup materials if you are incorporated: Seven years
- State return backup materials: Check with your tax preparer because requirements vary by state; California, for example, is four years.

It pays to keep documents like these in a fireproof safe or box. You can also scan key information onto a disc for storage in your safety deposit box and store a copy in the cloud. Needless to say, you wouldn't scan all of your tax backup materials (aka supporting documents)—just the actual returns.

In today's world most insurance companies will send you your home, medical, and automotive policies via email. I receive legal contracts and royalty statements this way. If you resist digital retention of documents, consider these ideas:

- Having documents digitized means you will never have to search for important documents or precious photos in case of a fire.
- You will never have to frantically call home asking your spouse or partner to search for a document you need because you have access to it on your phone.
- If you are totally old school, keep hard copies in your office and digital versions of this file system on your computer and phone.

Now, wasn't that easy?

Remember you can always find the latest and greatest news on any subject on the internet. Google has changed our lives forever—and it's only one search engine available. The internet allows us to be discriminating about the number of hard copies we feel we need to save on any given topic. However, let me sneak in one caveat: If you have lots of online articles saved in a cyber file or you have burned countless CDs of information just in case you need it, or you have a knee-jerk reaction to save *everything* in the cloud or on an app like Evernote, you are creating a new kind of debris. Don't weigh yourself down with the unnecessary. Our goal is to fly free, taking with us only what we truly need. Think lean and mean. Well, okay, lean and organized!

Max's Story

Before we organize our papers, I'd like to tell you the story of a dog I met a few years ago. One night I agreed to help a friend's daughter babysit. When we got to the house, the mom and dad were engaged in last-minute preparations to leave for dinner. We were introduced to the toddler, a beautiful little girl of three, and the newborn, a handsome young man if ever I saw one. I, however, was drawn immediately to the sound of incessant barking coming from the backyard. "Oh! That's Max," said the mom with a notable edge in her voice. "He's always barking." As a result, she didn't like the dog to be in the house. "He gets so excited!" she said. "He drives me crazy."

As I opened the door to the backyard, my heart broke. The dog was tied up on a short leash by a small doghouse, even though he had a huge yard to call home. "No wonder he barks," I thought. Max was frustrated. Dogs are pack animals, and Max wanted to be inside with his pack

members. He also wanted to be in a position to protect his mom and the children, which he couldn't do effectively from the backyard. I instantly felt the barking was the equivalent of a human cry: "Hey, let me inside, okay? I've got a job to do."

When the parents got in their car and drove off, I untied Max and let him in the house. He ran around once to check on everybody and every room, then spent the entire evening sitting quietly at my feet. Hours later when his parents returned home, they were surprised to find Max in the house and so well behaved.

That night, Max brought home to me the importance of work in our lives.

* * *

In the final analysis, everybody needs a job. Our self-esteem rises when we are acknowledged for a job well done. Our work helps define us. What's that popular cocktail party question? "So tell me, what do you do for a living?" It seems to me that our work begins the minute we are born and ends when we draw our last breath. Think how difficult it must be for a baby to learn how a human body works and master the language being spoken around him or her. The job of a child is play. Our life's work changes from age to age and decade to decade. We foolishly think it's only the work that comes with monetary compensation that counts. But I know mothers who work harder than corporate executives. I know children who play with more passion than most adults ever experience at their jobs. Because work is so key, let's set ourselves up to actually enjoy the space we use to do our work no matter how lofty or mundane. Let us set up these work areas to empower and support us.

For example, having your paperwork organized is critical, so the big event this month is learning how to set up a file system. Are you an "out of sight, out of mind" kind of person who eschews the creation of a file system? I have creative solutions for you to try. The bottom line is that paper piles must be tamed; otherwise you'll feel out of control every time you have to do something as simple as pay a bill.

Imagine trying to get to your great file system in an office that was set up to flummox you at every turn! We're going to make the outer office as streamlined as the inner workings of your file cabinet. After you're sitting down to get at the business of life, you may uncover numerous clever ways you short-circuit your productivity. Don't worry; this is oh so human. We continue our study of time management to iron out the kinks. We're adding the word "no" to your vocabulary and delegating tasks to others. We're becoming a little less available via phone, text, and email. This is a busy month, so grab your journal and let's dive in!

HABIT OF THE MONTH

This month we take bold steps to tame the paper monster once and for all. Each day as you open your mail, fearlessly toss all extraneous matter. You don't need any junk mail cluttering your desk. Nor will you need the ads your credit card companies tuck in with your bill. (You can eliminate all ads by receiving and paying your bill online.) Want that catalogue? Toss the ten just like it that you've been saving. If you fall behind, dedicate some time on Sunday to catch up.

AFFIRMATION OF THE MONTH

I am grateful for the work I have to do today and the people with whom I interact. I protect and manage my time. The future I see in my dreams comes into reality as I handle the details of today with respect, care, and attention.

Self-Care Practice

I have been a devotee of acupuncture for over thirty years and have it performed regularly. If there is one common denominator to all the systems I have studied and share with you (breath work, meditation, yoga, Feng Shui [more on this in a later section], and acupuncture), it is that all work with energy. If you see the world as energy, you realize that it gets encapsulated into form. The human body is one type, and a building is another. Acupuncture needles release blockages of energy in the body (called stagnation in Western medicine), and Feng Shui deals with blockages in the literal space of our homes and offices. You can spend a lifetime exploring any of these avenues.

Paper tends to wear my clients out, so I thought this month I would give you a breathing technique that can be done lying down. In fact, my acupuncturist asks me to do it as she exits the room so I can be calm while the needles do their work. Close your eyes. Breathe normally but imagine that the air is entering your third eye, traveling down, and exiting your navel. This practice is from Qigong, a Chinese art that originated like yoga over five thousand years ago. It is based on the principles used in acupuncture. Are you with me?

The third eye is that area between your brows about a half inch up that is referenced a lot in meditation. It is a chakra or energy center. The navel is basically your belly button area, and it too is an energy center or chakra. Don't worry about these terms. Just do the simple practice and enjoy the relaxing benefits. This practice can be done for fifteen or more minutes. Build up if you need to and remember to focus literally on the movement of the breath and to release thoughts of judgments or fear. I'm not offering you a single technique in this book that will harm you in any way.

WEEK ONE

Home Office Questions

This week, you can

- Uncover the reasons why you find the world of paper so daunting
- Read several case histories of others who found a way out of paper chaos and into order

Time required: Sixty minutes to write in your journal.

ARE YOU UNSURE ABOUT YOUR LEVEL of chaos in this area? Let's look at a few things that will be clues. If you nod your head "yes" to most of these, this part is for you!

I have the money in my account, but I forget to pay my bills on time.

The minute I see a legal paper of any kind, I become immobilized. I just don't deal with it.

I could be more productive at work if I didn't have a million voice mail messages, emails, and text messages to respond to.

If you want something done right, you have to do it yourself. Good help is hard to find.

I'm too busy with other things to file my papers.

These represent the most common complaints I hear. We're going to go inside first and allow some journal work to give us the key to the origin of the choices you are making and the fears you harbor. Yes, it's true. Just about every one of the previous statements is based on fear.

Some people fear they will toss something they need, so they save everything. Others want to be liked by everyone, so they respond to every request for their time no matter what it does to them. There's balance hidden in those piles of papers and we're going to rout it out this month, turn fear into freedom, and enjoy the process.

This week, grab your journal and carve out some private time to investigate your past and your relationship with work. You'll find that your past always holds the key to your present circumstances and expectations. This is why each month begins with the same kind of investigation. Discovering the link between the past (causes) and today's reality (effects) puts us in the driver's seat. If we don't like the causes set in motion in the past, we can consciously replace them with new ones today.

Following are some journal questions designed to help you understand how the world of paper turned you upside down.

1. What do you remember about your childhood in terms of the work lives of your parents? Did they enjoy what they did or did you get the feeling that work was a burden?

2. How did your parents relate to paper? Was yours the "House of Piles" or the "Home of the Neatnik Family"?

3. Did you pick up after yourself as a child or did someone do that for you?

4. Were you a good student with effective study habits? Or was school something you couldn't wait to put behind you?

5. If you are being treated for ADD or ADHD, have you learned to work with the way your brain functions rather than let a diagnosis rule your life?

6. If you have siblings and you remember something dramatic about your childhood and the way the business of life was handled, give your sibling a call and see if his or her perception is the same.

7. Are you married? Are you the one who handles the day-to-day business? Do you feel that you are appreciated? Would you be happy if you could turn the reins over to someone else, whether that's your spouse, an assistant, a CPA, or a bookkeeper?

8. Everyone has paper in his or her life. We have bills to pay, reports or homework due, trips to plan, moves to organize, and hobbies to learn. And these are just a few areas that generate paper. Are you on top of this aspect of your life? If not, has it always been an issue? Or did something derail you? Identify what that was and why and how today is different.

Here are three stories to help you understand more clearly how the past affects your current life. See if you find your situation in these stories.

Rebecca: Loyal to a Fault

Rebecca grew up in a large family in the middle of the country. Everybody had chores. Her mom took care of the home and her father worked in the city for a large and powerful union. Every day around 3 p.m., her dad would call to inquire about available work the following day. Rebecca remembers long stretches of steady employment, including overtime, and dry spells when her parents fretted about their ability to pay their bills.

Rebecca assumed they were the typical American family living from paycheck to paycheck. She grew up, moved to the East Coast, and started a successful consulting business. When I met Rebecca, she wanted to organize her home office to help her be more productive. As we went through her papers, I noticed that Rebecca made a very nice living. And yet she seemed on edge about her finances. It was at this point that I asked her to talk to me about her childhood. I was struck by the fact that she seemed to have internalized the day-to-day money drama of her parents. It was as if she were more comfortable waiting for the other shoe to drop financially than to embrace the success she had achieved in business.

It's quite an achievement to create and run a successful business. It's hard to enjoy the fruits of your labors, however, when your office is awash in paper. It's important to balance your work and home life, but difficult to do so when you carry your schedule in your head. If you can't see how you spend your time, you will no doubt be overworking yourself. The human body needs sleep, good food, fresh air, and exercise to function at an optimum level. Rebecca was just like her dad. All she did was work. And if the environment was difficult to deal with, that was a twisted bonus for her: It took more time to do everything so it was clear how dedicated she was to the business. Human beings are so clever at slapping a positive label on a negative action!

Rebecca told me something that floored me. Her father lived by a financial rule he never shared with his children: When money was deposited into the bank, it was never to be touched. Rather than living from paycheck to paycheck, Rebecca's father had salted away a fairly generous inheritance for his children. They had in fact never been in danger of losing their home. The lean times were inflicted by her father and his personal financial code. Rebecca's story reveals how we internalize a system we see without ever questioning its validity. The tension she created matched that in her childhood home whenever money was the topic of discussion. She was unconsciously copying a financial system without knowing all the details of the operation. Have you done something like this?

Mike and Jenny: The Honeymoon Is Over!

As newlyweds, Mike and Jenny decided that Mike would control the finances in their marriage. Jenny was delighted to turn over bill paying and investing to her husband. She quit her job and settled into her new life as a homemaker. In short order, a dream was fulfilled with the birth of twin boys. The years passed, and one day Mike lost his job. When bill collectors started calling the house, Jenny sat Mike down for a talk. She wanted to know what was going on with their finances. It turned out that Mike had taken over a task he was ill equipped to handle. He had paid multiple credit card bills late. He had taken cash from these cards to pay bills. Not only had they incurred huge and unnecessary finance charges, but the cards now carried the highest interest allowed by law. It was a disaster.

At this point, Jenny assumed the financial reins of their life. I was called in to help her set up a file system that would make keeping track of bills and investments relatively easy. Jenny returned to the work force, and Mike took a job outside his field of expertise to pay the mortgage and keep a roof over their heads. It seemed like a solid plan was in place.

Yet after they got back on their feet, Jenny did something mysterious. She turned their financial life back over to Mike! Once again, they got into a pickle. I was reminded of my father's words: "It doesn't matter what sex a person is; the most qualified person for the job is the one who should have it." Managing simple financial tasks such as bill paying eluded Mike. And yet, as the "man of the house," he felt it was his job. It would have served this couple well if they had shared this work rather than delegating their financial affairs to one member of the team exclusively. Does the arrangement in your relationship benefit both of you?

Bob and Gwen: Another Day, Another Dozen Diapers

Finally, we have the story of Bob and Gwen. When I entered their home, I wondered why I had been called in to work with Gwen. Their large home was tastefully decorated and spotless, and there wasn't a pile in sight. And then I peered into a kitchen cupboard. Like many moms, Gwen felt the kitchen was her power center, and she wanted to do her paperwork here. The house had been built before the kitchen work nook concept became

popular. Gwen had no place to put her papers before or after she dealt with them. The result was that several cupboards had been turned into stuff-it zones.

From my perspective, the fix was an easy one. Gwen needed a portable file box. I suggested she get one in wicker or bamboo with a lid. It would blend in with the décor of the family room that opened out directly from the kitchen. We got some basic office supplies and set up a file system based on the categories I discovered as we sorted through several years' worth of piles. We established a place for incoming mail to be deposited each day. And her husband agreed that their three toddlers needed to have some daddy time each weekend outside the home so that Gwen could do her paperwork.

What saddened me greatly about Gwen was the tremendous guilt she felt about what she had created. "Why did I let this happen?" she lamented. It was clear to me; I couldn't believe she had to ask. Gwen had a large and beautiful home, but she had no help keeping it clean. She had three children under the age of seven. I don't think she had stopped changing diapers until recently. In addition, she breastfed each child for at least six months. Something has to give when you have this much responsibility and aren't sleeping through the night. And so the mountains of paperwork piled up. As you examine your situation, can you identify how a birth, a death, a change in circumstance, or something else I haven't mentioned derailed you? That's all you need to do.

Acknowledge it. Guilt has no place in Zen Organizing™. Neither does shame or fear.

The goal of this first week is to uncover your personal relationship with the "business of life." If you are working with a group, share your perception of how each of you handles paper. You'll find that one person may have mastered this aspect of his or her life, but the kitchen is a mess. I remember a minister saying that we all have areas that need to be healed. You may also be surprised to find that what you think is an organizational disaster is a reflection of a shaming mechanism that was internalized by a parent or partner. Your group may hold the key to opening your eyes to a new reality. No group involvement for you? Grab the phone and call your best friend.

After this week you will have shed light on the dark corners of your paper plight. Next week we bring out the big guns: the tools that enable you to put into practice your desire to manage time better and conquer those paper stacks.

You can also convert some of your bonus rooms into more useful spaces:

- If you need a space to create a home school, you might look at the finished basement for inspiration. Carve out a corner if you already have it dedicated to another purpose.
- Do you and your spouse both work at home now? There was a funny piece in the *New York Times* during the pandemic citing the things spouses learned about each other when forced to work in the same room. For example, your partner might just be louder than you thought possible on the phone during business calls. If you can, schedule different parts of the workday to be in the office space while your better half uses the dining room table. Remember to share and schedule childcare and home maintenance assignments. I saw a great sign in a real estate office kitchen once that applies: "Wash your dishes. Your mother doesn't work here."
- My favorite COVID development is the addition of an outside structure for those with a big property, including he-sheds or she-sheds, a mother-in-law apartment, or an Airbnb to make extra cash. Along came COVID, and they are now tricked out with all the conveniences of a formal office.

I can't see into your home or your bank account, so it's impossible to list THE correct solution for you. If two adults are working from home and children are present, it's a prescription for insanity.

Here are a few more guidelines:

- Dedicate areas as work zones. Be sure the area has a strong Wi-Fi connection.
- Keep your supplies on-hand and restock as needed.
- Schedule times when each family member needs to use the space. Do this even if you are alone. No free floating of time, energy, or supplies. Schedules and predictability are great for productivity and sanity.

- Note levels of noise (TV, computer, chatter, or music) in adjacent areas. Be respectful of the needs of the person working, whether it's a project for work or a school assignment.

- Get dressed. No Zoom meetings in pajama pants! Wash your face, brush your teeth, and so on. You will be more productive if you prepare as much as possible like you're going to the office.

WEEK TWO

Save Time

This week, you can

- Learn how to be an effective multitasker
- Delegate tasks and chores to others
- Say "no" with ease and add power to your "yes" response
- Learn to visualize your goals
- Tame your electronic pests

Time required: Sixty to ninety minutes.

REMEMBER THE WORK WE DID IN JANuary concerning time? We designated not only the various aspects of our lives but also the percentage of time we dedicate to each. I am going to bet that your life is a little out of balance and the culprit is work. As I admitted before, I am in the guilty zone with you. So let's take a look at some ways we can save time. Saved time can then be allocated elsewhere. These tidbits will also make you more productive.

PLEASE, SIR, CAN I HAVE SOME MORE?

Whenever I teach my class or work in a corporate setting, the inevitable question arises: "How can I do more multitasking?" In our modern world, we feel that we need to be using the phone and the computer, shuffling paper, and reading today's new text messages simultaneously. And that isn't enough. We want to do more. Corporations downsize. Now you're doing the work of many and the only solution seems to be to do more at the same time.

I have to tell you that my response comes directly from yoga. When you splinter your focus like this, you fry your nervous system. You may get a promotion, but when you retire, you're going to need a solid medical plan to heal that exhausted vehicle you live in. In fact, every breath work exercise and meditation practice in this book is designed to help you focus like a laser beam on one task at a time. The quality of what yogis call one-pointedness is second to none. The results from multitasking are poor. Do I denounce multitasking? No. But I think it's an art, and this week I'd like you to cultivate the healthy way to multitask.

The first step is to jot down in your journal at least five ways you currently multitask. We all know the classic example of the young mother with the baby on her hip, a phone nestled in the crook of her neck while she stirs a pot on the stove. It's often used to show how amazing women are but I see nothing but accidents waiting to happen: phone falls into pot, baby gets burned, pot contents hit the floor, and Mom's legs are scalded in the process. Women are indeed extraordinary, but we can also be safe and focused. Why laud a dangerous scenario?

List your examples in a column, leaving a few lines in between. After you have your examples, please take a minute to recall the last time you did each one. Write down how you felt when you finished multitasking. Think physically and emotionally. Were you tired? Elated? How did your body feel? If you aren't used to checking in with your body, try to become more conscious of what it's saying to you. It's always talking to you, but you may not be in tune yet with the message.

One day a few years ago I was giving a lecture on organizing techniques to the managers of one of the big hospital complexes in the Los Angeles area. When I opened up the session to questions, I was amazed to learn that the staff was shorthanded and multitasking like maniacs. And what did they want to learn? How to do even more multitasking! I asked one manager to give me an example of how she multitasked. She said that when she was on the phone, she answered email, read reports, and wrote notes to her assistant. I asked how she felt at the end of the day. "Exhausted!" she said. "Well," I responded, "I'm here to help you balance your life, not fry your system at a faster pace!" I gave them the tools I'm presenting to you this week.

Now that you have your crazy-making multitasking list, I'd like you to think of five positive, non-draining ways you could multitask. I'm going to give you a few examples to get you started. Here are my personal favorites:

Always have something on hand to read or a notebook to write in if you know you're going to be in a waiting room (such as a doctor's visit), traveling on public transportation (airport terminals, flights, trains, buses, and so on), or waiting in a restaurant. Nothing is accomplished by staring at the walls. Personally, I don't like to make phone calls in public places. I don't want to inflict the sound of my voice on others who may want some private time. You can of course use a notetaking app and have electronic books on your phone or iPad.

When watching TV, have something to do during commercials. When I did needlepoint or hooked rugs, it was perfect! Now I use those breaks to skim the NYT app on my phone. God bless the mute button on my remote! Did you know that the television has a hypnotic effect on your brain? Ever find yourself wanting to go to bed but falling victim to the "just one more segment" demon? You can break the spell by getting up. The same rule applies when you go down the Instagram, YouTube, or TikTok rabbit hole. Yep, just get up and walk around the room. I wish all spells were this easy to break, don't you?

Are you a stay-at-home parent with a busy after-school schedule? If you find yourself sitting in the stands at soccer practice, for example, find a spot away from the other parents and return some phone calls. If you are at a distance, your voice shouldn't disrupt others, and you can still keep your eye on the field.

I see lots of people walking their dogs while deeply engrossed in a phone conversation. I think Fido deserves your full attention. These same good folks frequently walk right into me or trip and fall. It's tempting fate to be unconscious while awake! Needlepoint that on a pillow. If you are walking and looking down at a device or absorbed in a telephone conversation, you might miss something beautiful like the sky at sunset or something dangerous like a pothole. Mindfulness isn't just a practice for the Zafu (or meditation pillow).

Let's say you are making dinner. All the prep work is completed. Something has to simmer for twenty minutes, after which

you're going to add more ingredients. If you have a kitchen nook office area, this is the perfect time to peruse today's mail. You're cooking and paying bills without making yourself crazy.

The common denominator in all these examples is that the first action is suspended and the time can be filled with a second activity. The goal is to be productive, not exhausted. You'll find multitasking examples scattered throughout this book. Be on the lookout!

HOW TO DELEGATE

Are you filling your life with mundane tasks that someone could easily do for you? Sometimes we do this unconsciously because we don't want to face something that scares us a little. Let's say you have to prepare a report for work. You dread it but you know it has to be done. You set aside Saturday morning to put it behind you. Miraculously, by noon you find that you have left your desk a hundred times. You didn't write the report, but the plants are watered, the pencils are sharpened, the dog has been taken out so many times he's confused, and oh yes, you've raided the refrigerator to the bone. If you are part of a family, all of those actions save the last would make great chores for your kids. Your version of this kind of avoidance will be unique to you, but be comforted in knowing that we all have a version!

Other times our need to control is revealed with a desire to go it alone. The old saw "If you want something done right, do it yourself" will keep your universe very small. Imagine someone like Oprah firing her staff because she believed that she needed to give her personal attention to every aspect of her company. It would be the death knell for her empire, wouldn't it?

To delegate successfully, you have to understand how to do it properly. First, you need to find the right person for the job. Second, you want to put into place a deadline that gives you a little wiggle room in case there's a problem. (If I'm running late for a deadline, one of my favorite questions is, "What's the drop-dead date?" One is always waiting in the wings, and it's never the first one you received.) Finally, you need to understand all the aspects of your project so you know what you can give away to others and what you have to do yourself. Delegating frees your time and makes you more powerful. You can have several people reporting to you and doing work it would take you hours to accomplish. Learn to be the Big Boss, not one of the minions.

If you have children at the appropriate age, do they vacuum and dust their bedrooms, keep them picked up daily, clean their bathrooms, do laundry, prepare simple meals, or take out the garbage? No time like the present to start. Unless, of course, you have visions of them staying at home forever!

Could someone at work help with the mundane tasks you have to perform each day? Do you find yourself saying to others: "It would take me longer to explain how to do this than to just do it myself"? Let's shift your thinking a bit. You can take this task off your plate and help another person advance. Don't think of the time it will take to explain it once. Think of the hours you will save never having to do it again!

This week, as you think about delegating, see if you can experiment and give something away to another person. If a little teaching is involved, think of yourself as a mentor. Whether it's your child or a coworker, let someone else learn something this week.

JUST SAY NO

"Just say no" isn't only a slogan to fight drugs; saying "no" will empower you in terms of your time. I hear pretty much the same song from everyone who has an issue with saying "no" to requests. It's always along the lines of wanting to be helpful. They see themselves as good people who are always there for others, always willing to help. In fact, they are taking on too much, they may be exhausted, and their home and work life suffer. But they reason that it's all worth it because they are perceived in their circle as the good guy.

I understand how this works very well. I was raised to be a people pleaser. It's not really about being a good person. It's called codependency. If you have this issue, I have some useful tips for you. First, I want to assure you that no one will drop dead because you said "no." (If they do drop dead, they had issues beyond your control.) If they end their relationship with you, it wasn't a valuable relationship to begin with. Thank them for the favor they did. The elimination process is key to being organized. Sometimes human beings are the clutter in our lives.

The book that opened my eyes to healing this aspect of my life was John Bradshaw's *The Homecoming.* I recommend it highly. Recently I read *What Happened to You?* by Bruce D. Perry, MD, PhD, and found it to be a profound way to understand trauma and its impact on life, including codependency. We think of trauma as catastrophic events like rape or war, but we can be traumatized in a thousand small ways that add up to a compromised life. We have the choice to forever be run by what happened to us or allow it to inform our healing and better understand those with whom we interact. The next time you want to ask someone "What is wrong with you?" consider instead: "What happened to you?" Ask it of yourself as well.

Finally, I promise you that it's great when you learn to say "no" because you find that you now relish when you get to say "yes" to what interests you. You will be amazed how people respect you more. When you say "yes," it has meaning. Let me also say that just as there are those who have trouble saying "no," there are those who have no trouble taking advantage. You help them when you say "no" because they need to learn how to do things for themselves. Empower them and free yourself.

SAYING NO TO ELECTRONIC PESTS

Don't forget to apply your new skill to your computer and your phone. How? You do not have to reply to every voice mail message, text, or email that's sent to you. You also don't have to answer the phone just because it's ringing. Voice mail is a great invention. Ask yourself, "Do I need to take this call or am I looking to avoid the work before me?" Face the task at hand and put it behind you. Do you have a phone call to answer and you know the person is a Chatty Cathy? Send a text or email and say you are on a tight deadline. Ask her or him (yes, there are chatty guys) to send their requests through email and you will respond at your first opportunity. If you have an assistant, see if he or she can return the call.

Understand that I am not advocating that you be rude, thoughtless, or insensitive. I want you to be polite with all of your communications. One technique that will serve you well with those who can't accept "no" is to acknowledge what they have said, and then simply repeat your "no." It goes something like this: "Jenny, I am so honored that you thought to ask me to serve on your committee. Unfortunately, I simply can't in all good conscience say yes because there are so many demands on my time right now." If Jenny persists, you say, "Jenny, I hear what you are saying and again I acknowledge how much it means to me to have been asked. Unfortunately, I must repeat that at this time I cannot help you. Please ask me again in the future."

With good manners in mind, you don't have to be polite with some people. You know who I mean: the strangers who call and solicit donations. They never take "no" for an answer, do they? I say "no" once. When the request is repeated, I simply say, "I am so sorry. My answer is 'Not at this time.'" If I like the organization, I may add, "Please feel free to contact me in the future." If I am not interested, I ask to be removed from their list. In either case, if the stranger persists, thereby not respecting my word, my time, or my boundaries, I hang up. I don't need a new best friend. That position is filled. My concern can't be about hurting the feelings of a person I don't know. It has to be about conserving my time. Better yet, register your phone numbers with the National Do Not Call Registry at www.donotcall.gov. Most cell phones and smartphones have a "Block This Caller" option.

THOUGHTS ARE THINGS

A basic belief in metaphysics is that thoughts are things. You probably have heard of it in a different way. You know the word *visualization*, right? Well, taking a few minutes to be quiet and to see in your mind what you want to create in your life is what visualization is all about. Your vision board is a visualization in physical form. You already use visualization techniques. All of us do. Instead of planning for the good things in life, we imagine all the terrible things that might befall us. "What if I lose my job and we can't pay the rent? We could be homeless." "What if I never get pregnant and have a child of my own?" "What if I never become successful in my chosen career?" "What if I never find a spouse?" "What if I never get to travel?"

"I can't fly because the plane might crash." "I can't visit California because of earthquakes." Do you see what I mean? Dark fears rumble around in all our psyches. When they get playtime in our minds, that's a negative visualization. We attract what we think about, so it's wise to learn to be in control of what you're entertaining in your mind.

WHAT REALLY MATTERS?

We've done quite a bit of work meant to help you realize what is important to you. Please take a few minutes to write down two goals. One is short term: Name something you want to accomplish this year. The other goal must be long term: What would you like to accomplish in the next five years? After you have those in place, pay attention this next week to everything you do or agree to do in the not too distant future. Every activity will fall into two broad categories: those that move you closer to your goals and those that aren't relevant.

Don't be surprised if you discover that little you do has any relationship to your stated goals. It takes practice, focus, and a lot of dedication to bring our everyday life into alignment with our goals. In much the same way, it takes practice to learn how to run a marathon, play the piano, or become proficient at anything. You have to do something to achieve your goals. This conscious way of plotting your course in life allows your dreams to come true.

WEEK THREE

Make a Plan

This week, you can

- Clear out the obvious paper clutter
- Stock up on appropriate office supplies
- Be sure you have a file box, holder, or cabinet and all filing supplies for next week

Time required: Thirty minutes for a quick purge and cleanup; thirty minutes to assess the situation and create a shopping list; sixty to ninety minutes to shop.

WE'VE BEEN SO CEREBRAL THIS month, now it's time to have a little fun. I have two tasks for you this week. First, we're going to do a quick raid on your collected papers to help save time next week. Then, we'll talk about the products you may need to help create order.

SPEED ELIMINATION

I want you to set a timer for twenty minutes. Tear through the piles and pull out the obvious things you know you don't need—the garbage. Please don't give this a lot of thought; you *don't* have to sort. Go

fast and trust your instincts. And remember one of the golden rules of Zen Organizing™: After it hits the trash, it's there to stay! What am I thinking about for this exercise? Here's a list of things that clog a space and need to be tossed:

- Ditch old magazines and newspapers. Cut or tear out newspaper and magazine articles if you absolutely have to keep them. If you do research on the internet, organize links into a "To Read" folder (clean it out periodically) or in folders by topic. I did that while I prepared to update this book. The file was called "Revisions" fittingly enough.

- Are there flyers and catalogues for sales that have expired? Toss them. If you receive physical catalogues, remove your name from their mailing list or, if they still interest you, sign up for an online subscription.
- Do you have old bank statements and bills? Save what you need and toss the envelope it came in and all the junk that arrived with it. In general, if your expense is written off on your tax return (i.e., you itemize), hold on to the statement for the time designated by your tax preparer and keep the statements with your tax receipts. This is especially important if you are self-employed as a consultant. In the event of an audit, the IRS will want to peruse your bank statements for all deposits. On the other hand, if you work at an office and your household expenses are not deductible, I would save the statement until the following month. Be sure you have been properly credited and then toss or shred. Your best friend in the war against identify theft is a shredder. They are not expensive and there are compact ones perfect for the home. Your rule of thumb should be to shred any document you are tossing that has an account number or your social security number.
- Toss invitations for events that have passed.
- Toss expired coupons.
- Do you have warranties and instruction sheets for things you no longer own? Toss them.
- Junk mail goes into the trash without opening it! Did a charity send you return address stickers or note cards? Save them only if you intend to use them. Otherwise, out they go. Don't feel guilty about using them if you can't make a donation. Note cards usually have the name of the charity on the back. You're giving them a little free PR.
- Photo holiday cards get tossed. Your friends wanted you to see how much Johnny has grown. They don't expect you to make a scrapbook for him! People say to me, "I can't throw children in the trash!" Indeed, you cannot; but you can toss their holiday portrait.
- If you have old cell phones and smartphones, consider donating them to a women's shelter. Be sure you wipe the phones clean of all personal information like stored credit card numbers, etc.
- Old monitors, computers, and laptops also clutter our offices. Again, wipe them clean of personal information and then donate, trade-in, or sell. If any of these items are true antiques or unsalvageable, check with your local government for the correct e-waste disposal location.

What can you add to this list? Set your timer and work in those twenty-minute spurts. You can return to a room more than once this week if you have the time. Make this an archeological dig into your past. It's a game, not a homework assignment, and it's developing your trash muscle. That muscle is every bit as important as great glutes! By the way, if your building or neighborhood recycles, be sure to get rid of your trash in accordance with those guidelines.

IDENTITY THEFT

Identity theft is part of our lives now. You have to be vigilant in a way that past generations never had to consider. Don't be overwhelmed, alarmed, or depressed by the possibility. Be super vigilant! Here are some tips to help sharpen your level of smarts in this dangerous arena:

- Protect your accounts with passwords that would be difficult to guess. Never use obvious information in a password (mother's maiden name, pet name, or birth date). And change your passwords every six months.
- Never carry your social security card with you, give the number to strangers over the phone, or have the number printed on your checks. If a legitimate company asks for your social security card for ID purposes, ask to use another form of identification.
- You are entitled to one free credit report each year from each of the three credit reporting companies: Equifax, Experian, and TransUnion. Spread your requests out over the year. Go to www.annualcreditreport.com or call toll free: (877) 322-8228.
- If you are a victim of identity theft, write via email to each credit bureau and freeze your accounts. Include a copy of your police report. (Contact information for all three is in the Resources section at the end of the book.) You'll also want to alert all of your credit card companies as well as your bank and any other financial institutions.
- Do not sign the back of your credit card. Instead, write: *photo ID required*.
- Check the activity on your credit card accounts every week. You don't want to find out at the end of the billing cycle that someone was using your card for a month-long shopping spree!
- Don't save electricity: Make liberal use of a shredder! Licensed and bonded companies will shred for you at their premises or yours.

PAPER ORGANIZING TOOLS

As you work through your piles, you will be jogging your brain about what's important to keep. Next week we'll be doing the big project of the month. We'll be knee-deep in the paper aspects of your life, setting up a system that will support you and last for years. Now is a good time to tell you that file systems need to be cleaned out periodically; I'd say every one to three years, depending on how extensive and volatile yours is. Files are storehouses of the active information we need. They are not meant to be paper cemeteries.

Let's talk about some products you may find invaluable in your quest to become organized.

First we have the office basics everyone should have in the home:

Calculator (there's one on your smartphone)

Computers were supposed to save paper. Instead, we're all madly printing everything from work projects to the annual holiday letter. How can you save on paper? Turn a useless copy over and print on the opposite side! Does your project have multiple drafts? Print each phase in a different color. You'll have instant recognition!

Large and small paper clips

Letter opener

Paper shredder

Pens and pencils

Post-It notes

Rubber bands

Scissors (these come in inexpensive packages of three or more, so have one stashed in every room)

Stapler, box of staples, staple remover

Tape

If you have a good size desk and you like symmetry and design, by all means purchase a decorative matching desk set. Now let me say a few words about the preceding items. If you are a retired person, for example, you want one small box of paper clips. You would not benefit from making your office supply purchase at a store like Costco because you'll be clogging up your space with supplies you will most likely never need. Sometimes a bargain is a burden.

Most people have a computer and either an inkjet or a laser printer. You're going to want a stash of printer paper and ink cartridges or toner. Check with your local supply store and see whether they have a policy of accepting your old printer cartridges. They will recycle them for you and sometimes give you a credit toward your next printer cartridge or toner purchase. Some manufacturers also accept their empty cartridges back and cover all expenses for the return.

While you're stocking up on paper, may I suggest that you get a paper tray to hold the open package of paper? Even the most organized and tidy of my clients will open a package of paper just wide enough to grab a handful for the printer and then leave the package in that semi-opened condition. It looks so sloppy. In fact, it looks like a little mouse came along and had a snack.

Speaking of trays, let's talk about your in- and out-boxes. These are usually stacked one on top of the other. They are not meant to be substitute files! I like to refer to them as physical conversations. Your assistant comes in and takes everything from your out-box. He or she can then place all the items that need your attention in your in-box. Use Post-It notes for clarification. Work has been accomplished. A conversation happened, and not a word was spoken. How efficient! If you have no help, you are your own assistant. Keep your completed and incoming or to-be-processed materials separated.

A tall stack of trays takes up too much room on a desk unless you use them artfully and truly need them. For example, these are ideal if you work in graphic design and need an array of paper in front of you at all times. Most people, however, use them as a giant, overflowing, unorganized to-do holder. You know what they say: "Stop the madness!" In week four we're going to organize your to-do materials in a far more efficient manner and, in the process, win back all that valuable space.

Speaking of rescued desk space, I've been in home offices that had so much equipment they looked like the bridge of the starship *Enterprise*. Electronic gadgets come down in price or go on sale. Be a prudent shopper. If you don't need it, you are losing valuable desk real estate.

FROM PILES TO FILES

It takes some concentration and elbow grease to transform your scattered piles into files you can actually reference, but it's worth the effort.

Storage Space
Everyone needs to store their important papers someplace, whether it's a file cabinet, file drawer, or file box. Examine which one makes the most sense for your household's needs. In 2007, I had two two-drawer file cabinets as well as one file drawer in my desk, which was more than enough filing space for me. I also had a dedicated office with a storage closet for office supplies and archival material like tax receipts.

I downsized eight years ago and now I have one active file box that I access so rarely it sits in a hall closet. The other file box is purely archival, and the active box

sits on top. This evolution was also caused by material being stored on my computer. Who, for example, has tax returns now in hard copy? I don't even visit my tax preparer's office. We do everything electronically. With the app DocuSign I can add my signature to legal documents with ease.

Without a dedicated office, I have to work on the dining room table in the main room of my apartment. A laptop would be easier to manage but an iMac screen makes writing easier. I live alone and so others are not inconvenienced. When I want to entertain, it's like moving a dinosaur into my bedroom. My work life, however, trumps my social life. Like me, you have to use the tips and tools that are available in a way that works and may be unique to you.

If you want to store your archival files as cheaply as possible, use cardboard file boxes. I have one word of caution if you take that route. If you intend to store these boxes in the garage, the attic, the basement, or an off-site storage facility, remember that critters such as roaches and rats feast on cardboard. I would use heavy-duty plastic or rubber containers instead. Nothing is foolproof where rats are concerned, but any noncardboard choice gives you an extra line of defense.

Your Filing System
When it comes to creating a filing system, you will want to be sure your file cabinet is set up with rails to support hanging file folders. Don't panic if you don't have them, because you can purchase the rails and pop them into the drawer. Just be sure

you measure the length of the drawer and know whether you have letter-size (8½ x 11) or legal-size (8½ x 14) capacity.

If you have a legal setup that isn't adjustable and you rarely get legal-size documents, don't be shy about using letter-size folders. Just because a file drawer is set up for legal hanging folders doesn't mean you have to put legal files inside.

For those of you who have never had a file system, here is the basic setup: file folders and hanging folders. You put your papers into a file folder. You use the tab at the top of the folder to identify the file. The file folder lives inside the hanging folder. The latter gets identified with a detachable tab that you can read on sight when the drawer is opened. Not all tabs are created equal! You want long tabs so you can be more creative with your titles. Okay? Are you building your shopping list as we go along?

If your setup is basic, you can use manila folders. They are inexpensive and adequate. I use them for mundane information such as automotive receipts, banking records, business expenses, and medical expenses. If you have a business, you may want to use another color to identify these folders. For example, I use blue for my business files and red for my writing material.

Perhaps you have a job with a company outside the home, and you work on different projects. You might consider color-coding your individual projects. If you have sensitive material that should never leave your office area, a color folder will automatically alert you if someone is taking a file from your office. Office managers, for example, love this idea for their personnel files.

I use my handy label maker machine all over the house. In the office, it is a must. No matter how neat your handwriting, the uniformity of the print on a label from a machine is visually calming and saves time. After all, you may be able to read your handwriting, but can everyone else? Many of my clients prefer to generate labels on the computer. The choice is yours. For next week, be sure you have extra cassettes for your machine or an extra package of labels for your computer. Black ink on white background tape is the easiest to read.

Remember the liner we used in the kitchen and those wonderful drawer organizers? I use them in the office as well. Do you need to add these to your list?

YOUR OFFICE

This is a good week to assess the condition of your home office if you have one. Is your desk big enough? Perhaps it's too big? Is your chair comfortable? Is it ergonomically designed to save your body over time? Is the lighting adequate? Would you like to have a plastic liner under your chair so you could be more mobile in the office? It would save time and steps if you could just roll from your desk to your file cabinet, wouldn't it? Take a look at all of these details. If you can, make some big changes while we're creating the internal system for information. It's all part of the whole.

If you lack a dedicated home office and use a desk and chair in another room such as your den or guest room, do they have their own area? Perhaps a small rug would mark this territory as a work zone. Or perhaps you could hide the area behind a screen. If you have the kitchen nook setup, be fearless in organizing your files and designating this area as your work zone. This area is prone to becoming a catchall for everyone's junk. It's okay to park something there temporarily, but at least once a day you need to return orphan items to their rightful homes. Make this a habit!

If the pandemic era has moved you and your partner into a permanent or semi-permanent work-at-home situation and you don't have separate desks much less separate offices, try to make the work area benefit both of you. Now when I say "work area," I mean without a designated home office, it's the space where you can work, be it the family room, the finished basement, the kitchen office nook, or any area with a table, chair, electronic support, and preferably abundant natural light.

Each person can come in with his or her laptop and perhaps a file box when their designated work time is indicated. Yes, set up a use schedule and honor it. Base your schedule on the need for quiet, time to make phone calls, and who has childcare duties. At many offices now, there are no designated desks. You come in with what you need and get assigned a desk for the day. Being flexible will bring success at home and at work.

By now you probably have your shopping list in order. Please take a minute to read through the material for next week. If you find an organizing solution you'd like to implement, add the tools you'll need to your shopping list.

The Flex Future

Personally I have never liked the bullpen, the no-privacy open-workspace layout. Imagine how delighted I was to read these words in *The New Yorker*: *Companies must move away from surveillance and visible busyness, and toward defined outcomes and trust.*

I am eager to see how many permanent changes the pandemic brings to our lives. As an only child who works well on her own in silence and who is an introvert by nature, I thrive being my own manager. My best friend from college on the other hand is a total extrovert who needs humans and noise to flourish. With flex-time, we could both shine in the same company albeit in different settings on different days. Individual contributions are the parts that make up the whole of the company. I see great benefit.

Workers who can spend more time at home will not have to commute. That's probably ninety minutes saved each day. This time can be devoted to self-care (this book is lousy with ideas on that front) and to quality time with one's family, friends, or community, depending on your age and work status. I just watched a documentary series on PBS examining the changing face of work. I was aghast to discover that most people use their saved commute time to work. Your body is a machine, and it needs downtime. Zen Organizing™ is a quest for balance, not burnout.

WEEK FOUR

Say Goodbye to Piles!

This week, you can

- Create a working file system
- Learn how to organize paper in other creative ways
- Discover what goes on your desk and in your office space

Time required: Five hours.

I PARTICULARLY LOVE THIS QUOTE BY philosopher Jiddu Krishnamurti because it's the goal of our work this week: "To have inward solitude and space is very important because it implies freedom to be, to go, to function, to fly."

We want the business of your life set up and organized in a way that unleashes your creativity. I want you to fly. First, let's read the instructions. Like the pilot of a jumbo jet, you want to be familiar with the controls before takeoff!

This week, you'll need to set aside that five-hour block of time. And don't forget to follow the tips for success that we established in week one of the section on organizing the kitchen. No matter how many piles you have, remember that you are going to work with only one at a time. When you have your pile chosen and in

front of you, remember it's just one piece of paper at a time. Here are your guidelines for the process:

1. Ask yourself if you need this piece of paper. If the answer is "no," it gets tossed or shredded. If you think you are going to have a large amount of papers to shred, put everything in a separate trash bag. Most large cities have professional companies that shred documents at your home or office. You can usually take your papers to them and have them shredded at their site for an even lower fee. Even the local office supply store now shreds on-site for a small fee.

2. If the answer to your question as to whether you need the piece of paper is "yes," place the item on a cleared workspace. As you collect related material,

your stack will grow. Examples of common paper categories are articles on hobbies, recipes, travel articles, bills, and children's school activity sheets. Place a Post-It note in front of the pile to identify the category. This way, you won't forget or become confused. You'll be able to move along quickly.

3. When this phase is complete, you will have worked the first two steps of the Magic Formula: What you no longer need is eliminated and what you do need is in logical groupings by category. Now it's time to organize each category. If you need a break, now is a good time to take it.

Just when I assume that everyone has gone digital and these instructions are obsolete, except to help you learn to think in an organized fashion, I get called to an office that still has paper files. Lots and lots of paper files in banks of file cabinets. This issue is a little like the one we faced earlier in the year when some assumed that a calendar app was superior; and my response is the same. The system you will use is superior. The system that makes you feel comfortable is superior. And the system dictated by your profession. You can have paper *and* electronic. You can do one exclusively. Who cares? Here's the bottom line: Can you find what you need the second the need arises? Bingo!

CALL TO ORDER

Everyone has everyday business papers, such as mortgage or rent payments, automobile insurance, mobile phone bills, and medical insurance information. These are best kept in manila folders in your file cabinet or portable file container. Take a look and see if some of your categories are related. For example, one way to organize is to use a hanging file folder and create a label for the tab that reads "Household Expenses." Put that tab on the left side. Tabs on the left side indicate major categories. Tabs on the right side indicate subdivisions within that category, such as "Automobiles" and "Insurance Policies." This way, the folders for the household's cars are together in the "Automobiles" folder rather than scattered throughout the file cabinet. It might look something like this:

Household Expenses (left side tab for hanging folder)

Automobiles (right side tab for hanging folder)
BMW (tab for manila folder)
Camry (tab for manila folder)

Insurance Policies (right side tab for hanging folder)
Automobile (tab for manila folder)
Disability (tab for manila folder)
Homeowners (tab for manila folder)
Medical (tab for manila folder)

Legal Documents (right side tab for hanging folder)
Birth certificates (tab for manila folder)
Credit cards (tab for manila folder)
Passports (tab for manila folder)

You can have photocopies in a safety deposit box, or uploaded to the cloud.

Why the latter? If your passport is lost on a trip abroad, you can quickly show a copy of it at your local home country embassy. If someone needs to see your birth certificate, you can produce it in seconds. If you're a parent of a school-age child, you have been asked to produce such docs in a matter of hours and can relate.

> Mortgage Payments (right side tab for hanging folder)
>
> Phones (right side tab for hanging folder)
> Landline (tab for manila folder)
> Smartphone (tab for manila folder)
>
> Utilities (right side tab for hanging folder)
> Electric (tab for manila folder)
> Gas (tab for manila folder)

I keep my attached file tabs in a straight line, in alphabetical order. When you stagger the tabs, it gives you what I call "brain dance." Your mind gets tired as your eyes dart back and forth. Use file folders with the tab in one location as well. If you eliminate an attached tab or file, your staggered pattern is off. Try the straight-line approach for the tabs on your hanging files as well as the folders you insert in them. You'll like it!

If you have projects to work on, you can divide them in the same way. When it comes to projects, have a little fun. For example, you can find wild, colorful, fun file folders; lovely pastels; or traditional primary colors. Designate a color for each project. If you are a mom with a large family, assign a color for each child. It might look something like this:

Family/Children (left side tab for hanging folder)

> Edith (*pink* files/right side tab for hanging folder)
> Activities (tab for manila folder)
> School records (tab for manila folder)
> Medical information/records (tab for manila folder)
> John (*red* files/right side tab for hanging folder)
> Activities (tab for manila folder)
> School records (tab for manila folder)
> Medical information/records (tab for manila folder)
> Tom (*blue* files/right side tab for hanging folder)
> Activities (tab for manila folder)
> School records (tab for manila folder)
> Medical information/records (tab for manila folder)

Moms, if your children come home with a lot of paper for you to read from their school, set up a portable desktop file holder with a file for each child. Make it their responsibility to deposit the information they collected at school that day in their personal file. It then becomes your responsibility to peruse it after dinner while they are doing homework or at whatever time seems most logical.

In today's world, it may be more expedient to have these files on your computer because most schools and teachers will email you directly. This cuts down on lost paper and it gives you a golden opportunity to demonstrate to your children just how an organized adult handles the paper that fills our lives. Remember to delete the messages that need not be referenced.

My teacher friends tell me they send paper home and write emails, so you'll have to create a system that works with how each teacher communicates. One issue they all shared about parents is that most children's backpacks were never cleaned out. Not only did paper for parents not get delivered, but lunch containers were not washed. I see an opportunity for habits and chores if this describes your situation.

Finally, a huge category of material found in most families is warranties and product manuals. I usually find them dumped into an empty drawer or stashed away in an old box in the back of a closet. It would take hours to find whatever you need. Let's transform that situation. Go through your material and toss the papers or manuals for items you no longer own. Toss warranties that have expired. If you own your home, it's nice to have all the material for the big appliances like refrigerators, washers, and stoves to pass along when you sell. If this material has come to you via email, designate files for them. Going forward, you can ask at the time of purchase if this material lives online. No need to save paper when the electronic version is not only evergreen but most likely regularly updated.

For large amounts of information, you need box-bottom hanging file folders, which are designed with a wide bottom to accommodate large amounts of related material. To keep the bottom of the hanging folder flat, you use a cardboard insert. I wouldn't go wider than two inches because the added weight in three inches or more will cause the folder to rip. Divide everything into categories, and put these individual categories in folders in alphabetical order. The overall category tab can simply read "Warranties/Product Manuals."

Here's what a typical setup looks like:

Warranties/Product Manuals (left side tab for hanging folder)

Appliances (right side tab for hanging folder)
Cameras (right side tab for hanging folder)
Entertainment (right side tab for hanging folder)
Garage (right side tab for hanging folder)
Home Office (right side tab for hanging folder)
    Computer (tab for manila folder)
    Equipment (tab for manila folder)
    Small office purchases (tab for manila folder)
Household (right side tab for hanging folder)
    Art (tab for manila folder)
    Furniture (tab for manila folder)
    Jewelry (tab for manila folder)
    Small household goods (tab for manila folder)
    Toys (tab for manila folder)

I keep TV and other electronic manuals and related items in the "Entertainment" folder. I keep the kitchen blender info in "Small Household Goods" rather than with "Appliances." I have the refrigerator, the stove, and the washer and dryer in mind for that file. The "Small Office Purchases" file would include a new label maker. Scanner or fax machine information would go into "Home Office, Equipment." (I use apps for those activities now.) You might want to make a category for phones. Some households have more phones these days than the Pentagon even though all family members have a personal mobile phone.

Before we leave this section, let me say a final word about paper versus electronic records. Some people function better if they can hold a manual, receipts, or school records in their hands. If they are going to attempt a repair, for example, their brains don't work as well reading on a screen. Honor what works for you. I hate electronic calendars and I love my paper calendar with a passion. On the other hand, I write my books using a computer because the days of yellow legal pads feel like the Dark Ages.

Here is a list of simple apps to help you launch your electronic adventure:

- DocuSign: Sign legal documents
- Dropbox: Store documents and images in digital folders
- eFax: Virtually send and receive faxes
- Evernote: Popular digital note taker
- FreshBooks: Digitally invoice clients

Make the Toughest Call

Once you have assets, it's important to have a will or a trust. It's equally important for the key players in your estate plan to know where everything is and who your representatives are in terms of attorneys and insurance agents. This is something an adult needs to take care of; it isn't meant to hasten your demise or that of a loved one. Keeping your environment organized is another end-of-life gift you give your heirs. Consider periodically downsizing

the maintenance you need to do so no one person has to purge a lifetime of acquisitions, as I had to do for my parents.

As the elders in your family advance in age, have these conversations with them. Should they need to move to assisted living, you want all the information that runs their lives to be organized and easy to reference for all appropriate family members. You can use literal paper files, binders, or your computer. Make categories along these lines:

- Agents (lawyers, doctors, investment advisors)
- Banking
- Household expenses
- Insurance
- Investments
- Medical information
- Property (deeds, etc.)
- Will or trust details

Each of these master categories will have subheadings. Let's look at "Household Expenses":

- Gardener
- Housekeeper
- Rent or mortgage
- Utilities

Let your elders know that you downsize possessions periodically and would be delighted to help them. If they can't part with items, remind them that you will be doing this work one day when they are gone and you don't want to have to guess what their wishes are. Empower them to be in charge of their lives. Ask the difficult questions. Would you want to live at all costs? Do you want to be buried or cremated? If you wish to be buried, has a plot been purchased? (They are cheaper if purchased before your passing.) Where would you like your ashes scattered? Is a funeral or a memorial service more in keeping with your style? If they are at least in their late teens, be sure your children have an idea how you are helping their grandparents. One day they will be doing this for you. Organizing is the gift that keeps on giving.

OUT OF SIGHT, OUT OF MIND

Many of my clients tell me that if they can't see it, they forget it exists. Is that you? I have a solution for you. It comes in two parts. First, you do have to create a file system for the mundane aspects of life. Take the time to create a master file list on your computer. Simply make a list of all the files you have created! Print that and keep a hard copy inside a sheet protector. Keep "gotta have it at my fingertips" information such as this in a narrow binder. (I like a red binder for this purpose because it's easy to find.) Put a label on the spine that says "Reference," and voilà! You are at once more powerful and in control of your world. You can let your fingers do the walking when you can't remember where a file is located or if one exists. You will have to keep the list current, but you'll discover it's a small price to pay for the convenience it affords. Not into binders? Keep a reference folder on your computer and smartphone.

WHAT'S COOKIN'?

After you sort recipes into categories, you may decide that you'd like to have some or all of them closer to you in the kitchen. This will be especially convenient if you are an avid cook rather than an occasional one. Put your recipes into individual sheet protectors and keep them in a large binder. You can separate your categories with tabs. If you have a vast collection, use both files and a binder. Keep your ideas in the folders and your proven recipes in a binder. Feel a little old school? I've got you covered.

Scan your favorite recipes using a scanner app on your phone and keep them in a file on your computer. You can prop your iPad on a book stand (with a splash guard) and follow step by step in the kitchen. This method saves your original image. But wait! There's more!

Use an app that will allow you to scan and organize all of the recipes in minutes. It translates the handwritten note into type. Not only will the family's culinary secrets be safe, you can email the entire collection to everyone on your family tree! They can cook without having to make space on a shelf in the kitchen for one more cookbook. Use one of the handwritten recipes as a cover image for the collection. You know someone is going to want grandma's handwriting. It's one and done.

If you have a home assistant like Alexa, she can read the recipe and respond to your questions. "Alexa, was that one-quarter or one-half teaspoon basil?"

Don't allow yourself to be overwhelmed by choices and do nothing. Craft a solution that works specifically and uniquely for you. Be grateful that you have choices. Very little is one size fits all.

For projects, however, you can keep material at your fingertips in two ways. The first is to use binders. Your binder is the equivalent of a box-bottom hanging folder. Inside you divide the various aspects of your project with index tabs. This is the equivalent of individual file folders. You can keep your binders on a shelf behind you or on your desk, depending on the size of your desk, the number of projects, and the configuration of your office.

In addition to binders, you can purchase small boxes called, aptly enough, project boxes. You can put the various components of a project in here. Use the slot in the front for a label. You can choose one of these solutions or use a combination. See how creative organizing files can be? You can find many ways to put your unique stamp on your material. By the way, when it comes to binders, you can buy an inexpensive one and decorate it to suit your personality. When people tell me that artists can't be organized, I tell them this is hogwash. Everyone can get organized, and artists can put their unique stamp on this process.

Many of my clients like to have current project or reference files on their desk in one of those graduated stands that elevates the files so you can better see all the tabs. If this works for you, far be it from me to deny you. What I don't like about this solution is that the stand is open on the sides and therefore precarious. I envision reaching quickly and having a cascade of materials flying all over my desk and the floor. Consider either the flat version of the file holder with all files on one level or

using a small desktop file holder. It's a container really. It not only prevents accidents but is portable.

Let me close this section by saying that there is one other solution for the "I gotta see it" crowd. It doesn't work for me, but I have lots of clients who swear by it. What is it? The old-fashioned expanding or accordion file. I find them awkward, and that brown color is so unfashionable, isn't it? Guess what? The creative folks at www .seejanework.com now carry attractive versions of the expanding file. You can use this solution and be stylin' at the same time!

DEALING WITH THE DEADLY DAILY MAIL

Has a week's worth of mail—or worse, a month's—piled up on your kitchen countertop? The best thing is to flip through your mail the minute you pick it up and do the following: Trash what you know you don't need (junk mail, anyone?); put your bills in a "Bill" file (coming up next, don't panic!) and toss the envelopes they came in along with all those wonderful ads that get stuffed inside to tempt you; and put magazines in a magazine holder and catalogues in a different holder.

Decide how many months you're going to save your magazines. My rule of thumb used to be a generous one year. Now it's down to one month. If I haven't set aside the time to read an issue by then, clearly it's not going to happen. If you find that you never have time for a particular magazine, don't renew the subscription when it runs out. Whenever you see an issue you want to enjoy, pick it up at the newsstand.

It takes time to be able to process mail quickly, but eventually these decisions become second nature. If you are too busy to do this kind of sorting when you first pick it up, please toss the obvious junk and then place the day's mail in a basket. This could be on a table by the front door if you live in an apartment or on a kitchen counter if you drive in and enter through a door in the garage. Later in the day, you can execute the previous directions.

ACTION!

We all have things we need to take care of, don't we? We have bills to pay, phone calls to make, letters to write, and things to keep track of. You want all this information in files. But you don't want it buried in alphabetical order in your new system. That will mean hunting for it when perhaps all you have are a few precious minutes. At the front of your file system should sit a special section called "Action Files." The following are the most common:

Action Files (left side tab for hanging folder)

Bills (right side tab for hanging folder)
Log (right side tab for hanging folder
Pending (right side tab for hanging folder)
To call (right side tab for hanging folder)
To do (right side tab for hanging folder)
To file (right side tab for hanging folder)
To read (right side tab for hanging folder)

If you were to show me your computer screen, would I be able to see your screen saver or is it covered in files? Sadly, many have the latter scenario. You think you are placing these files in front of you to prompt you to take care of whatever tasks they demand. What you are really doing is creating an ersatz display that is material for an "Action" folder. Corral those individual files into category folders and enjoy your screen saver.

"Bills" Folder

One of the most important considerations is how to remember to pay your bills. Here are several choices that I have used or seen over the years:

- Pay bills on the first and the fifteenth. Be sure you have a stash of return address labels and stamps.
- Set up e-billing. This step saves postage and has the added benefit of being good for the environment.
- Mark in your calendar when each bill needs to be paid.
- Set reminders with your computer.
- Turn over the process to a bookkeeper or a CPA and check the statements once a month.
- Have bills that are always the same (think car payment) automatically deducted from your checking account. Check the amounts each month on your bank statement. One word of caution: Choose one system and stick with it to see whether it works for you. Don't bounce from one to the other.

Note: If you pay your bills exclusively online and/or via automatic payments, you won't need this section. It's wise to review your statements to be sure no computer glitch occurred, say, at the water company, for example, and you were charged four times as much as usual and it was paid automatically.

"To Call" and "To Do" Folders

For some of my clients, the calls they have to make get placed in their "To do" file. This is a matter of choice. I separate them because I might like to take a break from writing or investigating online. In my "To call" file, I place invitations so I remember to RSVP. First, of course, I check my calendar to be sure I can go!

Not everything in "To do" is of the same importance, is it? You can therefore create two folders: "To do/ASAP" and "To do/Personal." My "To do/Personal" folder gets checked once a week. My "To do/ASAP" gets checked each morning.

"Pending" Folder

"Pending" is an invaluable file, but not everyone uses it correctly. If you take an item from your "To do" folder and take action, you may still not have completion. Perhaps someone has to call you back. Or perhaps you must wait for a follow-up letter in the mail. While you are waiting for more information or time to pass, the related papers go into "Pending." I check my "Pending" file every Monday morning to see whether I need to pull something out and put it back in my "To do" folder for the next phase.

"To File" Folder

In your "To file" folder, nothing should be placed without being cut down to the smallest size possible. If you have someone helping you, put on each item to be filed a Post-It indicating the destination. If this is a new file, before you create it, ask yourself if more information will be added. You don't want a series of file folders, each with one piece of paper! This is where one "Miscellaneous" file folder is indispensable.

TAX MATERIALS

People always ask me how long they need to keep their tax supporting documents, backup materials, and their returns. The latter is easy: forever. Don't ask me why, but Uncle Sam wants you to have your returns with you from the first time you file until the day you die. The current rule of thumb on supporting documentation and backup material is this: Save it for three years for federal purposes or seven if you have a corporation. Each state asks you to save this material for different periods. In California, for example, it's four years. With that said, when you visit your tax preparer this year, ask for his or her preference. After all, if you get audited, your preparer will be going with you, not me!

Create an archival section for yourself. It might be in the bottom drawer of a four-drawer file cabinet. It might be in a cardboard or plastic file box in the back of your office closet or in the garage. The location is not important. What matters is that as projects move out of your day-to-day life, they need to have a location all their own. You want to be sure your file system reflects the present, not the past. If you have a file cabinet in the garage, be sure you keep it locked and everyone knows where the key is.

PERSONAL DESK ITEMS

Whether you work at home or in corporate America, keep your decorative items and photos to a minimum, especially on your desk. I can't tell you how often I find clients who have barely enough room on their desk to sign a letter because the available space has been given over to memorabilia, photos, or decorations.

Do you have children? How old are they in the photos on display? Here again I will frequently find multiple photos on someone's desk of small children, only to find that they are now in their late teens. Take these old photos home for the family album. Here you need the space!

Another form of desktop clutter is having too many tools. I often find three staplers and multiple containers of pens and pencils. If you want all those containers, at least separate your stash with pens in one, pencils in another, Sharpies and highlighters in a third. Test them at least twice a year because ink dries up over time.

If you are now in a flex situation at your office and no longer have a permanent workstation, it is imperative that decorative and all personal items be cut to the bone if not completely. If for no other reason than the fact you have to haul it all with you to work several days a week. Here's a cheat sheet to help you feel you

are in control because floating can unmoor us emotionally.

The Person with No Desk Who Floats

This human has *the* most difficult assignment because they have no agency over their workspace.

- The minute you arrive put any obvious trash in the wastebasket and then put any papers or tools that you won't use in a drawer. You deserve a clear workspace.
- If you have had this job for any length of time, it should be easy to make a list at home in a few minutes of all the items you need. Need is the operative verb here. You want to learn the difference between need and emotional support items. Print out this list and have it in your briefcase/backpack so you can always do a quick check the night before or keep it on your phone.
- Pack your briefcase/backpack the day before so you know if you are short on any supplies. The devil is in the details. This can become a calming routine if you think of it not as a task but as a way to smooth your workday once you arrive.
- If many of your supplies are at work (logo stationery, for example), be sure you take a sample of whatever you might need so you have it on hand for the ultimate challenge (company runs out). Don't bring home a huge stash, just enough for a typical day at work.

- If you are someone who likes to be surrounded by personal items, be sure you bring work-related items from home. For example, a designated sleeve for your laptop to travel in or a mug or thermos for your coffee. You get the idea.
- If there is a communal kitchen your own mug and a travel set of bamboo cutlery and a dish will help save the planet. These kits are inexpensive, timeless, and available on Amazon.

The Person with a Designated Desk

You are in the catbird's seat if this is your situation.

- The list of what you need can be checked as you leave work to see if you have to order anything or bring something additional from home on the next work day in your flex schedule.
- I would limit the personal photos and plants. I love both but some people crowd their literal workspace with these items and make what they need to accomplish more difficult. If you feel comforted by photos, put a program on your computer that will show random images when in use.
- Check the number of tools you have. Are any unnecessary items clogging the space, like three staplers or four tape dispensers? Something needs to go. Check for small supplies you no longer use like large binder clips.
- Unless your income allows for lunches out, at will, I would pack an insulated

bag with lunch and my bamboo cutlery and bowl or dish.
- I would also invest in a thermos rather than drink bottled water. There is no point adding to pollution when it's easy to do our part! I presume your office has a water cooler or filtered water.

Heading Home

- I would take all personal items like the bamboo cutlery and dish that need to be washed and reused. (It's ideal if you can wash them at work.)
- In today's world most people will take work home to complete so you can email the docs you need or put them in Google Docs or any other program designated approved by your management. Your company will probably have an online setup for work sharing; if not, suggest it!

Remember, if you repeat an action for twenty-one days, it becomes a part of you, an ingrained habit. At first you might balk at more things to do or steps to take, but please consider our lives are lousy with habits...negative ones that keep us mired in chaos. I'm just suggesting ones that bring peace, calm, and control. Adjust my tips to suit your situation.

PLACEMENT OF FURNITURE

If at all possible, sit so that you are facing the door but not directly in line with it. This is an old Feng Shui tip. Sometimes clients fight me about moving their desk. And then we try it and they immediately feel more powerful. Feng Shui isn't a religion. You aren't betraying your personal Spiritual beliefs if you follow a tenet or two from this five-thousand-year-old philosophy.

Be sure you are set up so that you save steps. You don't want equipment that you access regularly to be so far away that you have to get up to use it. For example, when you print something, you want to be able to grab it and continue working. Haven't used that scanner on your desk in a year? eBay is waiting, or just stash it in your office closet until you do need it. You might also consider donating old equipment to your local charity or school system. Your space taker is their treasure! Their treasure is your tax deduction. It's truly win-win.

At the end of the day or work period, put away your completed work and all the files you pulled out to reference. If you have an ongoing project, you can leave the material out provided you take the time to tidy up. Think about coming in tomorrow morning ready to work and faced with a mess. The act of simple office maintenance is a great way to express how much you appreciate yourself. Soon you will naturally and automatically return everything to its designated home no matter what room of the home you're in!

This is one of the toughest weeks in your year of assignments. Working with paper is time consuming and often emotional. Take heart. After you have this system in place, you will save time, money, and energy. You'll be much more productive. And your self-esteem is going to go through the roof! Do you have a suitable reward planned?

SUMMARY

WEEK ONE

Journal alone or with your group to investigate your personal relationship with paper.

WEEK TWO

Learn some simple techniques to safeguard your time.

WEEK THREE

Do a quick sweep of your office proper or work area, and create your shopping list of needed supplies.

WEEK FOUR

Set up your new file system.

BONUS TIP

Never underestimate the uses you can make of an old dresser or armoire. In the office it can hold your office supplies if you lack a closet in the room. Refinish the wood or paint it a bright color; just don't let it go at the next garage sale before you look around and see whether it might not be able to help you get organized. A coat of paint and some new drawer pulls and your old friend will look refreshed and ready to serve you in new ways.

BATHROOMS: CHASING YOUR CARES AWAY!

Don't grieve. Anything you lose comes round in another form.

—RUMI

After several months of hard physical and deep emotional work (if you are following the sections consecutively), during month five we take a much-deserved break. It's the perfect month for a quick and cathartic makeover—one that will contribute immensely to creating a soothing, Zen environment in your home. I'm talking, of course, about clearing all the small bits of junk from your bathroom!

By month five I feel comfortable using a bit of organizing shorthand with you when it comes to the instructions. I hope by now that certain things are becoming a natural part of how you plan. For example, don't forget to check your calendar for the perfect days to shop and organize. Be sure your organizing activities are scheduled with as much care as a day at the office.

Before you start a project day, be sure to review the "How to Prepare for an Organizing Project" checklist introduced in the second section (pages 54–55). For example,

have you chosen the ideal time for your body to start, eaten a nutrient-dense meal, blocked off your five hours, stocked up on healthy snacks, and slept well the night before? I hope your family is going to give you some private time to get the bathroom in order. Your shopping should be complete. And, like a surgeon preparing to operate, you have all of your tools ready to go.

The goal of Zen Organizing™ is always to create an environment that nurtures and supports you. To accomplish this goal, the steps taken must be treated with respect. You will find a direct correlation between the respect you pay a goal and the results you achieve. This month, through your organizing efforts, you'll be creating a room that treats your body with respect. Too often, the bathroom is a sloppy, carelessly put-together room. We're going to get as close to the feeling of a spa as we can.

You will be amazed how wonderful this room feels the minute you declutter it! It's ripe for so many decorative touches that will draw you in at day's end for a relaxing bath. We're going to check every detail from the condition of the towels and the shower curtain to the number of hooks and shelves. We want a room that is a pleasure to relax in even if you're a shower person. Are you ready to get started?

HABIT OF THE MONTH

Every single time you use your bathroom, wipe off the counter. You can purchase those special sheets that pop up from a dispenser or simply keep a pretty sponge handy. The bathroom counter attracts and holds hair, product residue, and general grime more than most surfaces. Wiping the counter helps the room stay inviting. Be sure you put everything away when you have completed a task. No toothbrushes, hairbrushes, or makeup left carelessly tossed across the bathroom counter. Debris flies in the bathroom and the floor gets dirty quickly. If you have a large bathroom, keep a dust buster handy and clean up hair and occasional product spills off the floor quickly before they become a hot mess. No space? No need to fret! I have my trusty dust buster plugged into a kitchen outlet and out of sight. I grab it as I need it. Those few extra steps help me reach my daily step count.

AFFIRMATION OF THE MONTH

I honor the body I have been given for my earthly adventure. I keep it clean. I release tension. I relax. I am at peace and all is well.

Self-Care Practice

This one will surprise you. It's a common activity, but I'm tweaking it to give it an upgrade.

You know I advocate that you do some exercise to get your energy moving. I never suggest you train for a marathon (unless that's your thing); just take Fido for an extra spin around the block. Sitting is the new smoking in terms of being destructive to our health. It can be watching TV or a computer screen or sitting in your car for long regular commutes. I am careful where I gather information to share with you. When it comes to medical research findings, I can't do better than the Mayo Clinic. Here is what they have to say:

> Research has documented that sitting for long periods of time is associated with a higher risk of heart disease, cancer, diabetes, depression and anxiety. Studies have found decreased hip mobility is one of the main reasons that older people tend to fall. Chronic sitters have tight hip flexor muscles and weakening of the legs.
>
> In addition, researchers from UCLA discovered that adults without dementia who spent more time sitting in the day had greater thinning of an area of the brain that is important for making memories (medial temporal lobe).

Okay, I am convinced, but are you? There's no point having this fabulously organized environment if you are too weak or sick to enjoy it. Here are some Mayo Clinic tips to counter the evils of sitting:

- Spend five minutes doing standing activities (walking the dog, folding laundry, taking out the trash) for every hour of sitting (this is sufficient to combat sedentary behavior).
- Set alarms on your phone to remind you to stand up and move every hour.
- Walk around while talking on your phone.
- Stand up during television ads and walk around the room.
- Take a short walk (ten minutes) after each meal (this can reduce the risk of type 2 diabetes).
- Take the stairs when that is an option.

One simple lifestyle change: reducing the time you spend sitting is the key to a dramatic difference to your physical and mental health. You have the key!

For those of you who can't walk due to physical disability or injury, consider chair yoga. I know it sounds a bit Mickey Mouse, but trust me: You can work up a sweat. If you are able to walk but find it a bore, consider yoga, Pilates, swimming, or a sport you love. Create a program using exercises from physical therapy. Move your body to avoid the inevitable consequences from stagnation of energy. This is not a new concept, as Traditional Chinese Medicine has espoused it for thousands of years, and now it is a huge focus in Western medicine. Movement is the healing practice we honor this month.

Walking Meditation

Yes, walking can be a Mindful meditation practice. It's not done for cardio benefits or to counter sitting. It is like all meditation a way to help your brain focus and for your body to calm the cortisol storm most of us create with great abandon.

Here are some guidelines:

- Find as distraction-free a location as possible. The ground should be flat and free of hazards like ficus tree roots that threaten to trip the most sturdy on their feet.
- Begin with a few calming breaths before you start walking. No counting involved; just be aware of the feel of your breath as it enters and exits your nostrils.
- Now walk slowly and move your awareness from your breath to your body. How does it feel? Are you stiff or sore from other activities? Feel your legs as they move you through space. Put your attention on your body. As thoughts, feelings, or judgments arise simply note them. Do not engage with them. Keep moving your body. Have an open heart and extend goodwill into the world. The pace is slow and the area covered is small.

If you have a seated meditation practice, you can do a short walking practice at the end to help you center back in your body. You will find as you practice that you can turn almost any action into a Mindful one. I find organizing to be ripe for a Mindfulness practice. We can make the best and the fastest decisions if we are anchored in the present moment and not entertaining regrets from the past or hope for the future.

WEEK ONE

Sing a New Song

This week, you can

- Devote yourself to uncovering the unconscious story of your life that you most like to tell
- Learn how to write positive affirmations

Time required: Thirty to sixty minutes of journal work.

T HE FIRST WEEK OF THIS MONTH, I want you to think about just one question. Ponder it at odd moments throughout your day rather than sitting down to record your immediate response. What's the question? What is the same old song you've been singing to yourself and anyone else who would listen? This "song" is not a popular, published one. It's a refrain unique to you. Let me tell you a story and explain.

My friend Constance is the personification of elegance. You can tell the minute she enters a room that she has something to do with the fashion industry. What impresses me most about Constance is that her beauty is not just skin-deep. She is compassionate, generous, and kind to a fault. And one day, she taught me an important life lesson.

Constance had been happily married to a man who is a famous actor. They traveled; they had the big house; and they were luxuriating in the fruits of a life of fame and wealth—when he announced he wanted a divorce. At the time, Constance was devastated. But as she told me this story, now happily in the past, she paused. She smiled wistfully and said, "I haven't talked about this in a long time. One day I realized that this saga was becoming 'my story.' And I stopped telling it. I didn't want one event, no matter how painful, to be what identified me. The minute I made that decision, I went on with my life."

Your assignment this week is to think about the story you habitually tell about your lack of organization. After four months of work with this book, are you still singing the same old song about a lack of order, an inability to manage time, or how stuck you are in your situation? "I can't have people over because of the way my home looks." "My friend Janice has as many kids as I do but somehow she finds the time to do things like scrapbook. And her home is spotless! I don't know how she does it." "I am so stupid. I don't know why I can't get organized."

Here's a secret that Constance discovered: After a while, even your best friend is sick of the same old song. If you change your tune, you not only encourage yourself to better your life, you uplift and encourage others. If you think you need the added boost, journal about your childhood or recent past. How did this song start? Sometimes it frees you to know where or how you got hooked into a negative pattern. Constance saw herself getting stuck in her broken heart. Be conscious about the new tune you want to sing.

Every month I've created a special affirmation for you to repeat out loud. This week you are going to write some for yourself. You have uncovered the sad or negative story you like to tell. Please write down some of the personal descriptions that accompany this story. The most common go something like this:

"I can't believe how stupid I was to (trust, believe . . .) him/her."

"I can't do that. I'm not (pretty, smart, good) enough."

"I'll never accomplish anything with my life. I don't have enough (time, money, luck) to make a difference."

You get the idea. Your personal negative beliefs probably come out in the same way all the time. Listen to that story you're telling. Are you a victim in it? Write down as many negative descriptions as you can. The more you uncover, the better off you are! After you have them, you are going to create affirmations that are the positive antidote. Always speak in the present tense. We want to alter our belief system now, not at some future time.

Here is how I would counter the preceding examples:

I am a strong and intelligent individualized expression of Spirit in the world. I trust my judgment, instincts, and decisions regarding all matters in my life.

In this moment in time, I declare that I am enough. I am pretty, smart, good, and accomplished enough to achieve my goals. These include the complete organization of my home and work environments. I am unfazed by the negative comments of others.

The resources of the universe are at my disposal. I align my thoughts with the Divine and manifest whatever I need to succeed. The right teacher/business partner/finances/dating opportunities are now free to enter my life and assist me. I accomplish with ease the work I came here to do.

Your affirmations are meant to guide you and move you forward in a positive manner. There is no right or wrong. There is no test, grade, or judgment coming your way. If you feel empowered as you say the words you write, your affirmation is perfect! Be on the lookout for those negative statements. When you hear them coming out of your mouth or bouncing around in your head, immediately utter the truth.

You will be amazed how this simple exercise can transform your life. Now we need to turn our attention back to the bathroom so the attractive, successful, and talented version of you can get cleaned up in style!

WEEK TWO

Goo and Gunk Be Gone!

This week, you can

- Grab a garbage bag and start pitching the junk
- Consider hosting a product swap party
- Put the products you want to keep in categories
- Design a morning routine to save you time
- Start your bathroom product shopping list

Time required: Two to three hours to eliminate, categorize, and plan future steps.

THIS WEEK, IT'S A GREAT IDEA TO clean out your bathroom. It's amazing how much we pack away in this little room. Even if you're working this program alone, you may want to call friends and suggest that you have a product swap party later this month. This is a clever way to find new homes for those perfectly good products that you no longer use but that are taking up valuable real estate under the bathroom sink, on a shelf, or in the shower.

There are two big space takers in the average bathroom. The first category is the glut of products we've purchased over time that simply didn't work out as we expected. Let's consider a typical example.

We decide we don't like a particular shampoo after using it just once. However, we feel wasteful tossing it, so it becomes a space hog. It may even be part of that second type of space taker: products that come in multiples. Was the shampoo you didn't like part of a double package you got at a big warehouse store like Costco? Our desire to be thrifty now demands that we have not one but two large bottles of shampoo we're not going to use.

To compound the matter, there may have been enough plastic wrap and cardboard in the original packaging to clog that area under the sink all by itself. When we were organizing the office, I suggested that you get a paper tray to hold the paper you need for your printer and fax machines. It looks so much tidier to have paper neatly stacked in a tray than to have it peering out from a partially torn package. (It really does look like a woodland creature nibbled it!) Well, that same visual might be assaulting you all over your house! Two bottles of shampoo is one thing. One bottle stuck in a half-opened package with a second bottle roaming around elsewhere is a waste of space. What about that monster twenty-four pack of toilet paper? Is it still in its plastic packaging? Does it take up the entire area under the sink? Something we fail to understand is that often our attempt to be economical means we have squandered our space. We don't stop to consider how this affects us. Every time you struggle to find a needed object through a minefield of debris, you waste time and energy and cause upset. Every time you come home with a product you need and realize you have no place to keep it because the space you have is filled with a jumble of stuff, you are not treating yourself with respect. Let's dive in and change all that, shall we?

FIFTEEN-MINUTE SPEED ELIMINATION

This week, try a few more rounds of speed elimination. As with the bedroom, work one area of the bathroom at a time. As you clean under the sink, the drawers, the cupboards, the shelves, and the shower area, decide what you want to toss and what you

could swap (or give away). Remember to work quickly.

CATEGORIZING YOUR PERSONAL CARE ITEMS

Now let's figure out what you use in this room. How much makeup do you have, how many prescription bottles are in the medicine cabinet (check their expiration dates), how big is your first aid collection? Do you really need three hair dryers, six hairbrushes, and three combs? Has your collection of hair grooming aids grown over time? Can you whittle down this category? When you go shopping for your organizing tools, the size of your category and the available space will dictate what you purchase.

If you find items from one category in several cupboards, house them all in one area. Just like in your pantry, you'll have automatic control over your product needs. When something such as shampoo, soap, or toothpaste runs low, you'll know to add it to your shopping list.

After you have a category, don't be afraid to refine it in an attempt to reap space rewards. For example, I like to keep general first aid in one container and cold remedies in another. If space is limited, I would keep first aid in the bathroom and cold remedies on a shelf in the linen closet or wherever you create satellite bathroom storage. You don't need to think about stuffy noses when all you need is a Band-Aid.

If you have makeup that is strictly for special occasions, keep it in a separate container. You don't need to wade through the glitter and the gloss to get to your every-day lipstick. It will be more of a treat to take these items out for a special occasion. Check with your favorite makeup rep or the website for your favorite brand about the shelf life of your cosmetics. Nothing is forever. Especially your mascara!

As always, lined drawers will hold treasures in place. Small bamboo containers work well in these drawers because they wipe clean. Divide the small products in your life: nail care, makeup, eye care, bobby pins, safety pins, and teeth-cleaning products are good examples. If you have extra countertop space, check out the wonderful containers designed for makeup, cotton balls, and Q-tips.

Here are a few key "what to pitch" guidelines:

- Is it expired, outdated, or broken? Out it goes. To inspire you, think old prescriptions, fad makeup, and cracked mirrors.
- If your lotions and potions smell funky or have separated, pitch 'em. If we're talking about a high-end product, such as La Mer versus the generic body cream from a store like Rite Aid, call the company for guidance.
- Assemble all your hair care tools and ask yourself how many you really use. Think combs, brushes, hair dryers, curling irons. Keep the everyday handy. Store the special event products. Toss the rest!
- Separate cold and flu remedies from general first aid. Check expiration dates.

Here are some makeup guidelines direct from my client Christina Zilber, the founder and creative director of Jouer Cosmetics.

Determining the age of your makeup: It is FDA law that all manufactured makeup have a batch code or lot code on or under the label; for tubes this is crimped into the end of the tube. The code is usually three to five digits or letters or both and is a record of when the makeup was produced. Each brand and lab has a different system, but you can call customer service, give them the code, and find the age of the makeup. For example, F61 in Jouer language stands for "June-2006-1st batch that month."

Anything SPF, including powders, gloss, lipstick, and foundation: Toss after two years! Most SPF chemicals are good for only two to three years in cosmetics, and you don't want to use anything that has expired. Most SPF products in bottles or tubes have expiration dates; tubes usually have this date crimped into the end of the tube.

Powders such as eye shadow and blush: These last much longer then you'd think. Most are good up to five years, but pigments can change over time or oils used in the powder can dry out, making them chalky and dry. They are not harmful if old. I say, test it on your skin. If it applies nicely, keep it; if not, toss it.

Wax-based products such as lipstick and cream blushes: These tend to have a nice long shelf life, I'd say often three to five years. Same advice. Test it. Some formulas dry out and get clumpy.

Wet lip gloss and liquid foundations: These should be tossed after one to two years. The ingredients often start to separate. You don't want to allow your skin to absorb old ingredients.

Mascara: If it's used and older than six months, toss it. If still sealed, it can last a few years on the shelf.

- If you have pocket change and pens in your bathroom drawers, take them out. If either of these items has been loose and touched an item you use in your body, such as a toothbrush or a Q-tip, trash it. Get a drawer organizer and a piggy bank!

If you're planning a product swap party, remember the following:

- No one wants your trash! Items that are ripe for swapping include shampoos, conditioners, hair gels, mousse, body creams, and face creams that have been used *once or twice* only!
- I swap makeup that came as a free sample with purchase rather than any products I have tried and used, even one time.
- You can swap products that you have used such as brushes or combs, provided you clean them first. Be sure they are in good condition!
- Lots of people love sample sizes of products. Check all the items for quality and expiration dates. Sewing kits, travel-size toothbrush and toothpaste, and wrapped cotton balls or Q-tips can be given out like party favors if you have enough!

What items will you trash or swap that I did not mention here?

ORGANIZE FOR YOUR MORNING ROUTINE

When you're rushing in the morning, you can use a combination of storage solutions to help you move quickly. You might have some items on the counter (such as lipstick in one of those acrylic makeup holders so you can refresh all day long), some items in your drawer (such as your toothbrush and toothpaste in those clear containers), and other things in containers you pull out as needed. Most women use multiple brushes and combs to get ready. A small container or basket can hold these and your hair dryer. Take out your container when you need these products and then put it back under the sink, in a deep drawer, or on the shelf outside the bathroom you set aside for this purpose.

I play a little game with myself in the morning. I take out the products I need to get ready to leave the house. The makeup, the deodorant, the fragrance, and so on all go onto the counter. When I get out of the shower, I can gauge how well I am doing for time by how quickly those items go back to the places they have been assigned. See whether something like this works for you.

After you have sorted through all the cupboards and drawers in the bathroom, it might be a good time to give this room a special cleaning. As much as I love aromatherapy, sometimes the sweet, clean smell of a freshly scrubbed bathroom makes me just as happy. Check out the end of this summary for some ideas on making your own natural cleaners! You can save money and the environment at the same time.

WEEK THREE

Reinvent the Space

This week, you can

- Examine your large bathroom products such as towels and the shower curtain to see what needs to be replaced
- See whether you need to do any redecorating or plan to make any structural changes
- Decide whether the current room setup is adequate for you and your family (for example, are there enough hooks, cabinets, and shelves)
- Take a look at your linen closet as it works with the bathroom
- Add to your shopping list, if necessary

Time required: Sixty to ninety minutes to examine and strategize; sixty to ninety minutes to shop.

THIS WEEK YOU'LL BE OUT SHOPPING for the organizing tools you need as well as for specialty items such as candles and bath oil. You might even put together a special playlist for those relaxing bubble baths that are now on the horizon. Most of the bathrooms I have been in over the years feel utilitarian. I think the bathroom can be another area where you express your creativity. Let's take a look now before you go shopping and see if you can purchase something to make your bathroom more inviting.

Is there a window? What kind of window treatment do you have? If it's just smoky glass or a pull-down shade, what about adding a pretty curtain? If you have a window, do you have the counter space for a real plant? Could you hang one?

Do you have an eclectic collection of decorative items on the counter? Can you either banish a few to the area under the sink or pick up a matching set?

We've mentioned towels. Don't forget your scatter rugs. Do they need to be updated?

What about your shower curtain? Is it playing host to mildew? Does it represent an old style of decorating that once attracted you? If you still love your shower curtain, could you jazz up the look with new shower curtain hooks?

Speaking of hooks, do you have enough in the bathroom? What about towel bars?

Do you have space for a hamper in this room?

What about your trash can? Is it an adequate size for the number of people using the room?

If you read in this room, do you have a discreet holder for your magazines? Or do you have a holder for your smartphone? You know, so it doesn't fall into the toilet when you stop reading and get ready to exit.

WALLS

Let's not forget the bathroom walls. Do you have anything hanging on the walls now? Are you ready for a change? Bare walls look as if you just moved in and have yet to assume ownership of the space. Most people have a stash of pictures hidden in the back of a closet. Do you have an old framed poster you love? Perhaps a needlepoint canvas you completed years ago is languishing in a drawer. Why not frame it?

THE TUB

If you have a tub and can't remember the last time you used it, why not treat yourself to some special bath products? A relaxing soak is one of the most restorative and economical treats you can give yourself. Add an aromatherapy candle and some music and you will wonder what you had been waiting for. Every so often, add a small box of baking soda to your bath or one cup of apple cider vinegar. They have wonderful healing properties—and, no, you won't smell like a salad! You can also invest in a tub pillow and tray. This way, you can relax and read some of those magazines you swear you never have time to flip through. Just promise me you won't bring work-related papers or periodicals into this situation. The operative word here is *relax*, not multitask!

THE LINEN CLOSET

After cleaning out the interior areas of the room, let's turn our attention to the space itself. Start with the towels (and the nearby linen closet if that's where you store your entire collection). Is it time to replace the sets you are using? Are they old, faded, tattered, or threadbare? Add at least one new set to your shopping list, if necessary. Your local animal shelter or animal hospital would love to have your old towels and sheets. It may not be a tax deduction, but you'll be giving a wonderful second life to things you have outgrown. Why do they want towels and sheets? They can use them to line cages and clean up after the sick animals.

Does your family constantly destroy the order you create in the linen closet as they rummage for matching sheets and towels? Try this trick: Put each sheet set inside a pillowcase. Keep all the linens and towels for a particular room on one shelf. You can also keep them organized by size: twin sets in one area, full on another shelf, and so on.

Often the shelves in a linen closet are unevenly spaced. You can purchase an inexpensive portable shelf. These shelves come in many lengths and depths; some are even expandable. Place one on your shelf and now every inch of that cavernous space is utilized! This is the kind of tool you can easily order online without viewing in person. Amazon has a nice selection of organizing tools. One way to save the environment is to select a weekly Prime delivery day rather than have multiple items arrive on random days. We all love the idea of instant delivery, but that keeps delivery trucks on the road and planes in the air. There are no free lunches.

I would label the shelves so that all family members know where to return sets when they do the laundry. The latter is a great chore for children. After all, you want them to know how to wash clothes when they move out. You'd be surprised how many college-bound kids don't have a clue.

STORAGE SPACE

Make a list of any of the basic bathroom items you may need: toilet paper, shampoo, soap, and so on. Do you have a place to store backup items? Some bathrooms are blessed with lots of storage. If yours doesn't fall into that category, could you put up a shelf or two on a wall or get an over-the-toilet unit to add storage? If your bathroom is the size of a postage stamp, you will probably need to use some area outside the room itself. If your linen closet is nearby, you might be able to use part of a shelf in that area.

Take a peek under the sink. Does the pipe configuration give you any space to store necessities? One reason why I like to use a container is that in the event of a leak, you have to take out only a few containers rather than an eclectic collection of bottles and jars. If, however, this is a tiny space, see if you could use one of those shelf creators we talked about in the kitchen section. The extra-wide ones made for large cans will help you see the collection of hair care products and body lotions at a glance.

If you remove the paper from your soap and let it dry out just a bit, it will last longer. If the soap is scented, tuck it in with your lingerie. Be sure to use a soap holder that drains water otherwise every day your soap will be melting away after each use. If you prefer liquid soap, purchase the largest size container available and then refill smaller ones you place in the bathroom (or kitchen). Do the same with shampoo, conditioner, and body wash.

WEEK FOUR

Watch Your Personal Spa Appear

This week, you can

- Have your fellow Zen Organizers™ or best gal or guy pals over to swap products
- Put your newly purchased organizing tools to work
- Create a home spa for yourself

Time required: Ninety minutes to plan the party; ninety minutes to shop for snacks and drinks; sixty minutes to set up. Two to five hours (depending on the size of your bathroom) to introduce the new products.

Note: A major project like a full-room paint job should be scheduled for a separate day. Don't forget to note the time you feel you'll need to complete this task.

THIS IS THE WEEK TO HAVE YOUR product swap party with your fellow Zen Organizers™ or pay a visit to a local shelter and donate your items. Do you travel often? You can also donate those samples the airlines give first-class passengers, as well as the samples from hotels. If you work for a large corporation, why not put out a call for all the execs to donate these items? These are appreciated and useful at shelters. These samples are being phased out, so this is one source of clutter that won't reappear.

Wouldn't creating a home spa be a lovely goal? Instead of going into the bathroom and finding a room devoid of color, humor, or design, you can create your very own relaxing spa. Stress relief is a huge component of good health. Think of your bathroom spa as a step to a healthier you!

Remember to put your new bathroom together one area at a time. Have a workspace set aside, even if that's the floor. I would start with the small interior areas first (cupboards, drawers, and under the sink) and make the splashy changes last.

Every big project should end with a planned reward. I hope tonight yours is a luxurious bubble bath!

Remember at the start of this book I told you that I knew you? Well, right about now, some of you are thinking that you just can't get organized. You have some special issue. If you find yourself in the middle of a trauma or a transition, be gentle and patient with yourself and the progress you can realistically make.

However, if your sadness is rooted in the distant past, I invite you to let go of your identity as a person with this problem and embrace today. I want to tell you about a client of mine who inspires me every time I think about her. Vita is, as they say, "a woman of a certain age." I've never asked. I presume her to be around seventy. Did you just picture a little old lady? Think again. Vita is beautiful, always impeccably groomed, and has more energy than any teenager I know. She and her husband of forty years lived in a beautiful home near the ocean in Los Angeles. They raised five wonderful children. The one and only sadness in their lives was his cancer. Vita's husband fought a valiant battle for more than ten years.

Many women in Vita's situation would have shut down their lives. They would squirrel away all their funds for the children. I've never asked, but I feel certain she was advised to downsize to a condo and live out her days quietly, simply, frugally. Vita, however, is fully invested in life, not just hanging around waiting for death. In addition to traveling the world and having lots of beaux, Vita loves to entertain.

As you work your way through this book, see your home as a vehicle that enables you to nurture and care for yourself, your family members, and all those who enter. This view adds the sacred to what might otherwise be something else you *should* do: get organized. The "tyranny of the shoulds" will kill you.

Vita is also an example of a woman who had every right to sing a sad song. She lost her best friend, the father of her children, and the companion with whom she shared her life and her youth. Instead, Vita chooses to find joy in every breath she takes. I hope Vita's story has inspired you.

SIMPLE STEPS TO SUCCESS

Remember when you were a child how amazed you were that your mom always knew when you had to go to the bathroom? I was sure my mom was clairvoyant. It didn't occur to me that the jumping around I was doing gave me away. Years later as an adult I was in an exercise class with a particularly wonderful teacher (we used to call her Gumby!). One day she looked at me and said, "Regina, when you are struggling, you hold your breath. Breathe!" When I checked my body, I was astonished to realize that I was indeed holding my breath. How in the world did she know?

Now it's my turn to be like your all-knowing mom or that wonderful instructor. When you think about getting organized, do you become engulfed with fear or guilt? When you start to organize, do you become immobilized? I bet you stop breathing. Here's my directive for the month: Breathe! I have two magic bullets to counteract fear: Breathe and drink water. Try them. You will be amazed. You have two breathing practices under your belt now and you have started a simple meditation practice. Use these tools daily.

BATHROOM EXIT RITUAL

- Seat up or down will depend on your family members. Choose one.
- Wipe off the counter as you leave.
- Hang used towels for reuse or toss into a hamper.
- Return all products used to their designated locations.
- Check the trash can and empty if necessary.
- Check the toilet paper and replace if necessary.
- Refill shampoo and conditioner shower products if necessary after your shower or bath.
- Check soap and—you guessed it!—replace if necessary.

SUMMARY

WEEK ONE

Uncover the habitual life story you tell others.

WEEK TWO

Clean out the bathroom of debris and consider how to better use the space. Create your shopping list.

WEEK THREE

Shop for the organizing tools and bathroom products you need.

WEEK FOUR

Create order in the bathroom—your own personal spa.

BONUS TIP

Why not replace your professional chemical cleaners with homemade, nontoxic versions? You can use these all over the home, but the bathroom is a nice place to start. Your best friends in the war on dirt are in your kitchen and include: baking soda, lemon juice, and vinegar. Here's a hack I love. I put a half cup of hydrogen peroxide in the toilet weekly and let it sit for twenty minutes to naturally kill any bacteria that may be lurking. Guess what? I also make a paste of baking soda and hydrogen peroxide to brush my teeth. I got that tip from my dentist. Use a soft bristle brush and don't bear down like you are scrubbing a pot. Be gentle. This paste is a natural tooth whitener. I just saved you a fortune in over-the-counter teeth whiteners.

You'll find a wonderful guide on homemade cleansers in the Resources section on my website. You can also use Google for some quick, easy tips to get your adventure with natural cleansers started. If you prefer to learn by watching, don't forget the treasury of cleaning-with-natural-products videos on YouTube, Instagram, TikTok, and eHow.com.

TACKLING THE HIDDEN AREAS: ATTIC, BASEMENT, GARAGE, LAUNDRY ROOM, AND GUEST ROOM

It is easy to shield our bodies against poisoned arrows from without but difficult to shield our minds against poisoned darts from within.

—SHAKYAMUNI

How would you like to waste some money? You know, just go crazy with a tidy sum and toss it to the winds. You could gamble in Vegas, go to the Empire State Building and let hundred dollar bills flutter to the street below, or race to the dollar store and purchase dozens of meaningless trinkets. What? Are you saying you would never do that? Well, guess what? If your attic is jammed to the literal rafters with stuff, if the basement has become a storehouse instead of a space the family might enjoy, if your garage hasn't seen a car in years, or your guest room is a junk room, you are wasting space with the same abandon that gamblers squander their money. Let's devote this month to reclaiming the bonus areas in the home.

Bonus areas all share one common denominator: They are places in the home that traditionally get used for some type of storage. Mind you, these areas don't store things we really need, but rather hold items that, for the most part, we are reluctant to make decisions about. Hiding physical items in these spaces has an emotional counterpart. I am reminded of a wonderful client I had a few years ago.

When Ben's wife, Betsy, was diagnosed with a terminal illness, he was shattered. For several years, Ben had nursed her at home. I didn't know him then, nor did I ever meet Betsy. Their son Charles hired me to help Ben get organized several years after Betsy had passed away. It was time to move forward.

When I entered his house, I was struck by the old-world charm of the home. I could easily imagine the wonderful parties Ben and Betsy had been famous for. Ben gave me a tour. The first floor was unremarkable. I had no clue why I had been called; I presumed the chaos waited for me in the private living areas. What greeted me, however, was a surprise. Sometimes having space, time, and money work against you. They give you the luxury of putting your life on hold. The downside to this is that the time we lose can never be recaptured.

Ben slept in one of the guest rooms. The primary bedroom was clogged with the energy of the past. It was full of Betsy's clothes, as if she were expected to reenter at any moment to dress for dinner. The fact that she had been gone for several years was not apparent. I have, of course, seen the clothing of the deceased left untouched; I've also seen rooms turned into de facto museums. But it was in their primary bathroom that my heart broke.

Betsy, like many terminally ill patients who spend their last months at home, had many medications to take and lots of special equipment to assist her. Ben had left all these items in their primary bathroom. His reasoning, as you might imagine, was that it was all expensive. He hadn't been ready to part with it nor had he wanted to be wasteful. Although I am certainly not in favor of coming home from a funeral and summarily tossing every single item the deceased has ever used, there comes a time when we have to realize that our loved one has moved on. We're never going to hear the words: "Hey, thanks for saving that for me!"

Ben was ready to begin the process. We started in the primary bathroom. Over the next several months, we worked together once a week. As the items of the past exited the house, the energy of the present grew stronger. I knew my work was finished when Ben announced he was moving back into the primary bedroom. I have enormous respect for the emotional, physical, and psychological work he had been willing to do. I found Betsy's personal things hidden all over the house.

I believe that just as we free our spaces and ourselves when we let go of stuff, we also exert an influence over the Souls of our loved ones. Now they too can move forward. We have set them free.

HABIT OF THE MONTH

This month I want you to be hypervigilant and listen for this phrase: "I don't know where this goes. I'll just put it here for now." Stop yourself immediately when you hear this sentence come out of your mouth. Replace this phrase with the following bit of wisdom: "There is a place for everything. I will now find the perfect place for this item. My search begins by identifying the broad category it is part of."

This is not the traditional "habit of the month," but it will change your life. I have chosen it because this month you are organizing the areas that most frequently absorb the orphan objects that enter the home.

AFFIRMATION OF THE MONTH

I am a good steward of the blessings that are given to me. This stewardship extends to all areas of my life including the physical. I make use of all the areas in my home. In this way I express my thanks.

Self-Care Practice

There are thousands of pranayamas and meditation techniques. I have but opened the door to practices that can enhance and expand your life experience. Instead of adding another practice this month, I'm going to introduce you to a related practice you can do while you are consciously breathing or in meditation. I hope you like this twist.

Statues of Buddha have been all the rage in decorating for several years now. Have you ever noticed that his hands are in different positions? These are not random choices by the artist. Each gesture conveys a special meaning. If you are more drawn to Christian images, you may have noticed Christ is frequently depicted with one hand on his heart and the other raised facing out with his ring and pinky fingers bent toward his palm while the index, middle finger and thumb are straight. This position sends out a blessing to all and strengthens the immune system of the person holding the position.

These hand positions are called mudras and each has a meaning. They also serve to positively strengthen and direct the energy in the body. In most images of a person meditating we see their hands on their knees, palms up with the index and thumb touching and the other fingers out straight. This mudra is your healing practice for the month. As you do one of the pranayamas or sit in meditation, you can do what is called the gyan mudra. The intention is to improve concentration and sharpen the memory. Who doesn't want this in their life? Do the practice and experience the results for yourself. The benefits can only make the work of getting and staying organized easier. And that is our quest.

WEEK ONE

What's Hiding in Your Space?

When we practice mindfulness in our daily lives, we open to the
wonders of life and allow the world to heal and nourish us.

–THICH NHAT HANH

This week, you can

- Find out what a true pack rat is. Are you one? Do you live with one?
- Take a clinical look at the bonus areas in your home (attic, basement, garage, laundry room, and guest room). What works in these spaces and what doesn't?
- Decide what concrete steps you can take to make these areas work better
- Begin your shopping list for the month's projects

Time required: Varies.

WHEN WE HOLD ON TO TOO MANY physical objects from our past, we are in fact just like Ben. We're clutching a shadow world that has ended. What's up in your attic or in a box high on a shelf in the guest room closet or lurking in the recesses of the garage? If we were to work together, would I find the sweaters you wore in high school? Or perhaps the trophies you won in Little League or your cheerleader's outfit? Would some of our discoveries be broken or falling apart? Nothing brings back the past. Waiting for its return by hanging on to the artifacts from bygone eras only robs us of the joy, the opportunities, and the beautiful reality of now.

HELP, I'M A PACK RAT!

I don't have any probing, emotional questions about your past this month. These areas of the home don't usually figure heavily into the relationships we develop with "stuff." If you feel that your situation is unique, please do engage in an exploration of these rooms from your childhood or any other era in which they play a role. One of the most common possibilities would be if you were raised by a pack rat parent or live with a pack rat now. This is probably an opportune time to say a few words about this often misunderstood condition.

Many clients tell me they have too much stuff because they're pack rats. The reality is that they have never been taught how to organize. If you have piles in your home from time to time, you are not a pack rat. If you haven't created a file system because you have no idea how to go about setting one up, you are not a pack rat. If you have several sizes in your closet because your weight goes up and down, you are not a pack rat. Hoarding is a medical condition that affects the brain. It is not about being sloppy, willful, or obstinate.

Many books deal with the pack rat syndrome, or compulsive hoarding. The most important thing to understand is that the hoarder has no choice. He or she is as much a slave to his or her destructive behavior as the alcoholic or drug addict. They aren't creating piles everywhere to get back at you or make you angry. They are in essence looking for security. If you find yourself involved with a pack rat, ask yourself why, out of all the people on the planet, you chose someone with this issue. If you are a blood relative, ask yourself what you think you might learn from being in this situation. We can't control other people. Thankfully, we can control our responses and ourselves.

You need to have tremendous love for the pack rat, especially if you happen to be one. We are all too eager to grant forgiveness and extend love to others while we berate ourselves with abusive thoughts and actions. Perhaps this situation is your opportunity to learn how to love and forgive yourself.

The way out is to engage with a therapist who specializes in this condition and who can administer appropriate drug therapy when indicated. There are also professional organizers who work exclusively with those who have this condition. You can find one by contacting the National Association of Productivity & Organizing Professionals (NAPO) or your local chamber of commerce. A great place to start, especially if you can't afford these avenues of assistance, is by joining a Messies Anonymous or Clutterers Anonymous group. These organizations are based on the twelve-step program used by Alcoholics Anonymous. If you can't find a chapter, contact your local AA, and they will direct you.

PLAN OF ATTACK

We need to do some planning before we get going this month. It's time to grab your journal and begin! We're going to consider each area or room in turn. Please read all the sections even if you don't have the area in question. You never know where an invaluable tip may be hiding! Next week I will present diagnostic tools and cures that apply to all the areas. You'll be able to mix and match as you see fit. How about that for a touch of personal creativity?

Create two lists for each room (attic, basement, garage, laundry room, and guest room).

1. First, write down all the things you like about the current state of the room.
2. After you have finished, directly across the page in a separate column, note all the things you don't like. Being human, the second list is probably going to be longer!
3. And don't forget to create your shopping list.

These lists will help bring clarity to the work you need to do in these areas. Feel free to make additional notes as you read along.

WHAT'S IN YOUR ATTIC?

The attic is a bonus space that more often than not looks like the landscape from the moon. There seem to be two kinds of attics: those that are in fact like an extra room and those that are barely a crawl space. My first word of caution is to consider the temperature in this space. You don't want to put boxes of photographs up here if the area is subject to temperature extremes. Nor do you want this space, if it's large, to be a dumping ground for furniture. It's like having a cemetery of the past over your head. Not a pleasant image, is it? Take a few minutes to rummage around in your attic, even if you are absolutely convinced you know what's up there, and make a list of your erstwhile treasures.

After you have your list, what do you think about these items? Do you have things you have been saving for your children or grandchildren? Ask them if they want them. If they do, are they in a position to take them now? Your home isn't a storage facility. As you look at these things, do you think they might be worth some money? You can sell items you have outgrown in numerous ways. We'll look at these issues next week when you make your plan.

THE BASEMENT: NOT JUST FOR HORROR MOVIES!

When I first moved to Los Angeles, I was amazed at the price of the homes and the fact that you rarely saw basements, which are common back East. If you are lucky enough to have one, let's make good use of it.

The Kid Zone

Is your basement a crash pad for teenagers? Parents frequently use furniture here that has stood the test of time. A wayward spilled soda or some melted chocolate won't be the end of the world. No matter the age of your children, this is an important gift to them. It's impossible to expect children to always be careful. Sometimes their lack of coordination or level of social skill will handicap them. Let them have a space like this if you can. This room usually has a couch that opens out to accommodate guests from out of town. Does this sound like your setup? If it does, let me ask you a few questions.

Does the room look thrown together? Just because it's casual doesn't mean it can't be inviting. If it is a kid zone, ask them to be part of the new decorating theme project. Along with this privilege comes responsibility: The upkeep of the room is ripe for chore assignments. We all have to learn to put things away when we are finished. Today it's the clothes you wore or the papers that need to be filed. Yesterday it was the toys you played with. It's the same skill with a different application. No time like the present to learn how it works and feels.

This project doesn't have to cost a fortune. New curtains, a new afghan for the couch, a few scatter pillows, and maybe some containers for toys are all you need. If the kids are older and will be entertaining friends here, you might want to check out a store such as IKEA that specializes in inexpensive dishes and glasses. If you pay $20 for a set and something breaks, you won't have a meltdown. You might even want to use unbreakable materials designed for outdoor use.

How about hanging a few framed posters on the wall? Does the room need a bookcase? Is there a TV here?

Lots of stands and holders are available to help you organize your entertainment choices. The best thing is to pack away the items you no longer listen to or view and take a count of what's active. Whether you shop at high-quality stores or the organizing section of your local home store, you can match your needs to what's available.

One of my favorite choices is the use of a binder with special sleeves that hold DVDs and CDs. You can either toss the jewel cases or pack them away. I would separate by category or genre and not bother with alphabetizing. Otherwise every time you add something, you might have to rejigger an entire category. One word of caution: These binders can get heavy, so be mindful of who is going to handle them. We divided a massive collection in the home of two professional actors into organized leather binders that were works of art. When we were done, the wife informed us that due to rheumatoid arthritis she could not lift any of them. Oops! We had to shrink their size.

By the way, if you have your old vinyl records but no player, pack them away in special boxes made for this purpose. Whatever you do, don't stack the boxes! The weight can cause the records to warp. You may not be listening to them right now but there are frames made for the album covers. The visual will remind you of the good old days until you get a new record player! Records are in a class by themselves. Many music aficionados believe the sound is superior. My suggestion is to make your collections accessible rather than making them space hog memorabilia boxes.

What else would you add to this do-over shopping list?

The Empty Nest Basement

If this was the playroom and now the children are grown and gone, would you like to make it a more adult-themed guest room? Perhaps it would also be the perfect spot for a craft corner. Are you always wrapping gifts for parties? Why not take advantage of this space and have your supplies set up and ready to go? Setting aside an area in your basement means you can work whenever the mood strikes.

In this post-pandemic era with many people continuing to work from home, the basement may be the ideal space for a combo of guest room and second office. You can define areas using rugs, screens, or furniture placement as we have discussed in other sections. You may have to call your cable company or get a signal booster so you can work online. You don't have to invest in a high-end desk or file cabinet, but I would spare no expense when it comes to your chair. Get an ergonomically correct model and save your body. Not in your budget? Secure a supportive pillow.

Moving around the house to work in different zones is not unlike moving around your company's office now that there is no assigned seating and you leave personal effects in a locker. Some days working in the company office will give you time away from family life and not commuting; the other days will give you time with the family. I know. Nothing is fabulous 100 percent of the time. Embrace the advantages of the day.

Would you like to be able to exercise on a regular basis? You might want to put in a Murphy bed (one that pulls down from the wall) so that you can divide this room into separate zones: workout, scrapbook or craft area, gift wrapping, and so on. Very often we hold on to the past by not changing a room long after the original function has ceased to be performed there. If this room became a mausoleum after the last child left home, get busy and reclaim the space. When we stay vested in life, we demonstrate to our children how each decade is full of blessings. You aren't just doing a little weeding out and redecorating, you're teaching a life lesson.

The Dungeon

At the opposite end of the spectrum is the basement that has space for some storage but no possibility of being used for any kind of social interaction. Very often this area has the guts of the home, such as the furnace. In many new homes, this is the area housing a computer that automatically runs many of the home's functions. If you need to store some things here, be sure they are in airtight containers. I love the ones that can be stacked and have wheels. You can stack an entire category, such as holiday decorations, and just roll them out when you need them. Don't forget to label your containers, preferably on all sides so in the event they get moved you can still immediately ID the contents.

To capitalize on your wall space and keep storage containers off the floor, you can add an inexpensive shelving unit. A home store will have the heavy-duty, inexpensive rubber shelves made for this purpose. A higher end store will carry metal ones on wheels. Your choice will be dictated by what you have to store, how you have chosen to pack it, your budget, and the amount of floor and wall space available.

As you look at the basement, no matter what kind you have, be sure you are using the space in a way that serves you. With so many design resources available to accommodate any budget (check the Resources section on my website, www.ReginaLeeds.com, for some of my favorites), make the space a fun place to be. Regardless of size, make it an organized and completely functional space. Your best guide is to be sure you really need and use what you are storing. Don't let the past or your desire to hold on to things for others turn your real estate into a cemetery.

THE GARAGE: WHATEVER HAPPENED TO THE CAR?

I live in a lovely neighborhood filled with beautiful homes. Inevitably, the owner of a home I have fallen in love with will leave his or her garage door open. I jump back in horror. It's dirty, confusing, filled to the rafters, and a car hasn't been inside in eons. In a temperate climate like Los Angeles, you can park outside all year long. But do you want to waste valuable real estate like this? How does a space fall into such disarray? Every time you don't want to make a decision about an item and you exclaim, "I know! Let's put it in the garage!" you contribute to the creation of the Chaos

Monster. Let the Sword of Order slay this monster once and for all!

If ever a space called for the dumpster approach, the garage is it. This is likely to be the most difficult bonus space you tackle. Let's assess what we have here:

- Have you always wanted to call a garage company and have built-ins installed? Will your budget allow you to do that this month? If not, why not purchase some utilitarian shelving units at your local home store?
- Is the garage large enough for you to install a pulley system and fly some of your stored items? Or could you add a loft?
- Do you have wall space that isn't being utilized well? For example, you can store your bikes on special hooks and free up floor space. You can also attach holders for brooms, mops, and other tools.

If you have two cars and live in a temperate climate, one can live outside and one can be in the garage. You could convert the other side of the garage into a workout or hobby area. I have friends who converted their entire garage into a rehearsal space. The wife is an actress and the husband has a band. How creative is that?

The bottom line is to think outside the box. The garage is designed to house a car. If you have inadvertently turned it into a storage facility, take back the space. How you reclaim it and for what purpose is where your creativity can flower. Speaking of creativity, remember that most large closet companies also outfit garages. You can ask one of their designers to come out and give you some ideas. Usually they will give you a simple space plan at no charge. This design may be just the thing to help you come up with the perfect solution.

Take advantage of all available resources when you are in the planning stage. Some design companies do only garages, and they too will happily give you a free estimate and either a plan or some ideas. The Container Store will also space plan a garage for you and help guide you in outfitting it to solve your personal needs. Why not look at a few plans and decide which works best for you?

Many large families revel in going all out to decorate for the holidays. As you repack your decorations in sturdy containers, don't forget to be willing to downsize. As we get older, too many decorations will seem like a big burden at the holidays. Why not give some treasures to family members or close friends? Just letting go of holiday decoration boxes may free up valuable real estate in the garage!

THE GUEST ROOM: WHO WANTS TO SLEEP IN THIS BED?

In my travels, I see two types of guest rooms: The room that is set aside exclusively for guests, and the room that serves many purposes. The most common multiple purpose is the guest room and home office combination, which is the most difficult to pull off.

The combo room is tough. The greatest challenge I see is the everyday office that doubles as the occasional guest room. If you have this setup and your guests get a futon couch, a pull-out bed, or a Murphy bed, it can work. (If you work at home, however, you must have ground rules so your guests don't prevent you from performing your duties. If you have to call the opposite coast at 6 a.m. and Aunt Gertie sleeps till noon, there will be trouble in paradise.) But I can't tell you how often I walk into a room and discover a queen-size bed taking up most of the space. I am told that this is because Mom and Dad visit once a year. Stop and consider the reality at play: The comfort of one or two people who rarely visit is more important than the work you need to accomplish each day. It doesn't make sense, does it? If you have this setup, how will you go about making it work for everyone involved?

Finally, if this room is where you keep items you use periodically, such as your festive ribbon and gift wrapping paper, be sure it's organized rather than falling all over the closet floor. I used to tell my clients to store wrapping paper in a tall garbage can (you don't use the lid). Now they make tall containers for the wrap with lids that hold supplies such as tape and a scissors. One of those in the corner of the closet wouldn't bother your guest at all!

The dedicated guest room is a luxury, and bravo if you can offer such convenience for your guests. I would take a survey of the room and see whether you need to update anything or change some things. You might notice that the bedspread, the towels, or the sheets are a bit tired and need to be refreshed. How fluffy are those pillows? Have they turned into rocks when you weren't looking?

When it comes to making guests feel welcome, comfort is in the details. Take a stroll over to the closet. Do you have a nice selection of uniform hangers or does it look like you tossed in some leftover wire hangers from the cleaners? Is there floor space for shoes? Sometimes the guest closet gets used for storing off-season clothing. Is yours bulging at the seams? When guests walk into a room and there is no space for their personal belongings, it's as if you've hung out a sign that says, "Hi! Thanks for coming. You're not staying too long, right?" How does your guest room stack up?

You may find that you need to organize this closet. If you're following the parts in order, organizing a closet is a snap for you. If you haven't done your closet yet, you may want to read the directions in "Creating a Bedroom Sanctuary" first. Don't forget to put in an extra shelf if there's space. You can store your off-season items on the top shelf and leave the bottom one for guests. Off-season clothing is ideally stored in space bags or storage bags from my friends at organizemeusa.com. By the way, don't forget to look under the bed. In America, this is a popular place for storage. I follow the suggestions of Feng Shui, which teaches that you will sleep better if this area is left open. The choice is yours.

And importantly, don't forget to leave the Wi-Fi password!

THE LAUNDRY AREA: A LEAN, MEAN CLEANING MACHINE!

If you are lucky enough to have a laundry area or room in your home, it can be demoralizing if it's in perpetual chaos. Let's consider the main problems and their antidotes and see if we can't make this room as inviting as the rest of the house.

Most laundry areas have cupboards above the machines. Let's take a look at what you have stored here. For example, do you have a mixture of open and unopened laundry detergent containers? Be sure the detergents and other products you purchased and used once are eliminated. We all experiment with detergents, don't we? Keep the tried and true. This is an area of product waste like the bathroom. Put the detergent and fabric softener you're using on the dryer. Keep the backup on a shelf in the cupboard.

What other items do I find here? The usual suspects include stain spot removers, light bulbs, household cleaners, and rags for cleaning. If they get used, this is a fine location for them. As you look at what you have, would anything be stored more logically in the kitchen, a bathroom, or the pantry? Are there any products you want to toss? By the way, if rarely used silver and brass polish or jewelry cleaner is taking up space under the kitchen sink, put them on a high shelf in one of these cabinets.

Keep related items together and, if possible, in containers. For example, remember the totes I suggested for use in the kitchen and bath? They would be great here. Put your light bulbs in one and your cleaners and spot removers in another.

Did you get a label maker yet? Labels on the shelves and the containers will help family members maintain the order you create.

If this is where you need to store mops and brooms, can you put up a simple holder for their handles? This will keep them off the floor, tidy, and easy to find. These holders are at home stores, cost little, and are easy to install. All you need is a little wall space!

If the laundry is a separate room, can you hang something festive such as a favorite poster? Is there a window? How about some pretty curtains? These may sound silly, but if you want to be on top of the laundry or assign it as a chore, you don't want the room to look like a prison! What about a fresh coat of paint? You could use magnetic paint on one wall and put your child's artwork here. Or maybe this is the place for a corkboard. What will you do to spruce up this room?

When we tackled organizing our paper piles and streamlining our schedules, we talked about how to successfully multitask. Remember? Tossing in a load of laundry is a great example of something you can do with almost any other task. On the phone with a friend? Fixing a snack? Watching TV? I invite you to toss in a load of laundry.

Doing laundry is a great example of a chore that can be assigned on a rotating basis if you are part of a family. Is there anyone who doesn't need to know how to do laundry? Whether you live alone or are creating a chore chart, be sure you schedule when the laundry is to be done. If you make it the same day and time each week, it will become a rote task.

In many cases, the problem isn't the laundry itself; the problems are folding the items and putting them away. Again, if you are part of a family situation, these can be additional chores. If you live alone, be sure you're doing the laundry when you can complete the task. Leaving the house with the dryer going is not only a fire hazard but will also hopelessly wrinkle your dry clothes. Household items that heat up and need to cool down are all sources of home fires. Think automatic coffee pots, dryers, dishwasher, and irons. One of my clients lost half of her home to a fire when her dishwasher exploded at 3 a.m. Fortunately she had fabulous insurance coverage. Still, moving out of your home for six months is never a picnic. We think putting a load of laundry in the dryer or turning on the dishwasher as we leave home is superior multitasking when it's a scenario for a fire. Which reminds me: Unless you love to iron, look for fabrics that require little or no care when they exit the dryer. Folding, by the way, can easily be done while you're watching TV or listening to music. Another example of positive multitasking!

FEELING PRESSURED?

At this point you may be feeling a bit overwhelmed. Don't worry, that's normal! On the off chance that you have every area or room mentioned here, you've done quite a bit of work this week. You may be wondering what it will take to get these rooms under control. Well, just in time, next week we're going to look at a host of tools you can use to make your projects easier. You didn't think I would leave you in the lurch, did you?

And don't be surprised if you are also feeling a new sense of ownership concerning your home. The bonus areas are often treated casually, sometimes without respect. They can easily turn into a dumping ground. After this week, however, you should begin to see new possibilities on the horizon. Think how great it's going to be to drive into your garage, spontaneously invite someone to spend the night in your guest room, or know that your attic is no longer a fire hazard!

LAUNDRY ROOM BONUS TIPS

Every bedroom and bathroom in the home should have a hamper. If you use a decorative one with a lid, be sure it has a heavy-duty canvas drawstring bag that you can pull out so you can easily transport your laundry to the washer!

If you have a lot of dry cleaning and your vendor doesn't supply you with a bag, you can use another canvas drawstring bag for transporting items to the dry cleaner. Hang the bag on a hook in your closet.

Lightweight hampers are great for the kids' room. They have handles and your children can be responsible for bringing them to the laundry room.

No room for cabinets? Put up a shelf or two. (Be sure these are braced to support heavy items such as laundry detergent.)

Don't have room for shelves or cabinets? Try using a laundry storage cart on wheels. You'll have three deep drawers for product storage and a usable flat top.

Are you hiding your ironing board behind a door? Does it fall all the time and make you crazy? If you have some wall space, use an ironing organizer, which keeps your board and iron together, off the floor, and no longer in danger of falling!

If you are blessed with a large laundry room, be sure you have a pole with extra hangers. It's also great to have a large, multi-compartment hamper so you can have the family sort their laundry as they bring it to the laundry room. (Chore, anyone?) Some of these units are on wheels and have a bar across the top where you can put your hangers.

If you need to wash a lot of delicates and don't have time to do them by hand, invest in a fine washables bag that you can toss into the wash.

For delicates that you don't want to trust to a dryer, purchase a drying rack or, for sweaters, a sweater dryer. I used to have one that was large and a pain to store. Now they make ones that pop open and are a breeze to put away.

Special note to all apartment dwellers! I too have to take my laundry to another location in my building to do the wash, so I understand the issues. It was a literal drag for years until I made one glorious, life-saving purchase: I got a cart with wheels. It's sturdy and yet folds up for easy storage in the back of my closet. This is an especially critical purchase if you have to do your laundry outside your building. I did that for many years in Brooklyn, so I also know how difficult that can be. Invest in a cart. You'll never regret it. You can also use it for transporting groceries!

WEEK TWO

Help Is at Hand: Resources!

This week, you can

- Consider the tools at your disposal, such as the dumpster, consignment shops, charity organizations, eBay, and Facebook Marketplace
- Learn about yard sales: the pros, the cons, and how to organize one
- Make arrangements for the tools you're going to use (rent your dumpster, put an ad on Craigslist, and so on)

Time required: Varies.

LET'S BANISH ANY FEELINGS OF BEING overwhelmed by developing that strategy I promised. Remember what we learned early on? The whole of anything is overwhelming. We always need to break things down into manageable chunks. Every person will be in a unique situation. Whether it's one area or all, the first order of business is to eliminate what is no longer needed.

Create a worksheet for each room. Don't let the word *worksheet* scare you. For this context, worksheet is just a detailed to-do list. Look at the notes you took last week for that area. As you read the information for this week, decide the fate of the stuff in these rooms. Do you need to rent a

dumpster? Will you be asking a charity to come out to make a pickup? Are you going to be interviewing experts to see what goes to auction, on eBay, and to a dealer? Know what you want to accomplish and who you need to contact to achieve success. If you get stuck, use the sample worksheets at the start of each of the next two weeks. These are abbreviated worksheets that will point you in the right direction.

GET EVERYONE INVOLVED

If you are part of a large family and everyone has items stored in these areas, you may want to call a family meeting. It can be disconcerting to come home and discover that your possessions have been tossed or donated without having had a chance to express your feelings. If your children have left home, ask them to pick up their stuff. If they have to pay for storage, they may see those soccer trophies in a new light! After all, after their stuff exits, you might have an area for a mini home gym or enough room for a hobby such as woodworking.

If your children are young, help them make decisions about what they really need. If you are just learning how to get organized, share with them that as a family you are all learning how to let go. Talk them through the process just as I have done with you through our journal exercises. For example, suppose that little Johnny has three bicycles. You bring to his attention that the garage can hold only one of his bikes. He has the luxury of choosing which one stays. He can also accompany you to the local charity resale shop so a less fortunate child can enjoy the two bikes he doesn't need or has outgrown. As the parent, you set the guidelines, the parameters, and the consequences. Children are fast learners, so don't be shocked when little Johnny points out the five boxes of your old college memorabilia that have to be whittled down to one!

DUMPSTERS

Often people have the "what was I thinking!" moment when they get into a deep excavation of the hidden areas of the home. Should you have all the bonus areas we're looking at this month, you might want to research renting a dumpster. From the tiny to the mighty, the one you need will be delivered and, once full, it will be carted away. Your neighbors might think you are moving. When you tell them what you are doing, don't be surprised if you are the first organizing domino on the block. Downsizing and organizing are as contagious as the flu! Zen Organizers™ will be sprouting up like weeds before you know it, and it will all be thanks to you and your good influence.

CONSIGNMENT SHOPS AND DONATIONS

When I work with families, we often take lots of furniture to the local consignment store. Local storefronts as well as online venues such as eBay and Facebook Marketplace are but three ways to lighten your possession load. They also put money in your pocket that you can in turn use for organizing tools, new decorative items, and furniture.

If you live in a large city, there may be agencies helping refugees get settled in America. You won't make money or get cash but you will help our newest Americans get settled. All four of my grandparents were illiterate immigrants who settled in America, who worked hard, and whose progeny have contributed to society.

Habitat for Humanity has a robust website that helps you decide when to donate, reuse, or recycle. In larger cities they have storefronts and can accept donations. If you have time and building skills, you can also volunteer with them.

For high-end goods, you can always contact an antiques dealer or auction house. If you'd rather have the tax deduction than the cash, many charities will come and pick up those former treasures from the past. Very often women's shelters can use furniture to help their graduates set up new homes for themselves and their children. Isn't it beautiful to consider that the furniture you have stashed away in your attic could help a young family get back on its feet?

YARD SALES

My clients frequently ask if I do yard sales. Let me be candid. It's just not my thing. I don't enjoy going to them or organizing them. Why? Because I went to hundreds of antique stores and yard sales with my mom when I was a little girl growing up in Brooklyn! If you want to have one, I bet you can find one or two friends in your circle who are experienced at this kind of activity. You want to be with folks who love yard sales. You'll stand a much better chance of having a fun day and a profitable event. A successful yard sale takes planning and patience with the public to be successful. Here are some of the most important considerations:

- Choose a date at least two weeks in the future. And of course check the five-day weather forecast! I would have a rain date in your ads or flyers. I would also be specific about the start and end times.

- Decide how you are going to advertise. Will you design and post flyers? (Canva to the rescue!) Will you put an ad in the local paper? Will you post a notice online at a community site like Facebook? A combination of strategies should attract a nice crowd.

- Travel around town and check out garage sales before you host yours. Talk to people at the end of the sale day. Don't be shy. Ask them what they know now that they wish they had known at the start. Listen carefully and profit from their mistakes.

- You will probably want folding tables and chairs and perhaps even a few clothing racks. Be generous and warn your neighbors about your plans. In addition to having the supplies you need, they might even add to your goods. In fact, why not invite them to schedule their own yard sale for the same day? The more the merrier for the planners and the shoppers.

- Shoppers will be more attracted to items that are artfully displayed. If it's all tossed on the lawn like trash, it may sell but for a song. Launder, scrub, and polish everything you want to off-load. Fold it, drape it, hang it. Make it look like gold.

- Keep items in categories. If you can, have family members or friends staff the different stations. Tell your children that they can keep whatever money they make from what they sell. You will of course have the final say over the choice of their sale items. "No, Johnny, you cannot sell your PlayStation 5!"

- You'll want to tag everything and price it to sell. Be prepared at the end of the day to deliver the "remains of the day" to a charity. Promise me that you won't drag it all back into the house or the garage.
- Be sure you have at least fifty dollars in singles so you can make change easily. Keep the money on your person. Don't leave it unattended. Offer to take money via Zelle, PayPal, Square, or Venmo. People may not carry cash, but they will have a debit or credit card for sure. And they will have a smartphone with them.
- If it's a hot day, perhaps an enterprising child can set up a lemonade stand.
- Direct your customers to the nearest public restroom. Strangers should not be allowed to enter your home, nor should you answer a lot of personal questions about the reason for the sale, the size of the family living at the house, and so on.
- Even if you have the sweetest dog in the world, let him stay inside and bark if anyone slips past you and gets to the front door. My late Golden Retriever Miss Katie wouldn't hurt a fly, but her bark would lead you to believe otherwise.
- Start collecting bags and boxes about two weeks before the sale so you can pack up your buyers' treasures.
- When the sale ends, be a good neighbor and remove all the flyers you posted.
- In this instance, many hands do make light work. Don't have a sale all by

yourself. You'll be so exhausted that no amount of money will be worth the effort.

HOW TO IMPLEMENT YOUR PLAN

Decide which areas are right for you to tackle now. You should also consider how much time and energy the transformation will take. What's going on in your life right now? A retired person, a working parent, a stay-at-home parent, and a busy executive all have different schedules and available time. I don't want you to feel that you have to drive yourself to complete all these areas over the next two weeks. If you aren't traveling or moving, you'll have all the time in the world to get these projects finished.

This week, research the resources available in your city to implement your plan. Start your quest with Google. If the companies, vendors, or charities you choose aren't well known, don't hesitate to check out their record with the Better Business Bureau. And as always, the experience of friends may hold the key to the best in your area.

Take out your calendar and start making appointments! If you're meeting with a group of friends, you can compare your research before you make calls. Perhaps someone has experience with dumpster rentals or knows of a great charity in need of furniture. In fact, with one call you can set up appointments for everyone in the group! Social media sites like Facebook also offer a gold mine of information in the form of those who excel at yard sales. One reminder: Look ahead and pencil in any remaining projects for this month on your calendar. You don't want to forget them.

The work you do this week is time consuming, but it will put you firmly in the driver's seat. After you have a plan, a sense of control is free to enter the picture. You have a lot of hard work coming up in the next two weeks, especially if you have many or all of the bonus areas! Just remember: You'll be reaping the rewards for years to come.

WEEK THREE

The Projects Begin

This week, you can

- Begin your first project!

Time required: Varies.

FOR THE PERSON WITH ONE PROJECT, this month is a cakewalk. For the person blessed with all these bonus areas, it's a different story. I'm going to do a garage worksheet as a sample. This is for a two-car garage that would take a full two weeks to get organized. If you find the idea of creating a project worksheet difficult, the sample worksheet should help.

Next week I'll show you worksheets for two small projects. One project might take one day (the guest room) and the other might take two (the laundry room). The amount of time depends on the size of the space, how much stuff you have, and how many changes you want to make (paint a wall, put up some racks, and so on). Is that panic you feel in your gut? Let me stress again that you don't have to do everything this month. You might have a crawl space attic and get it cleared out and organized in a matter of minutes. You might want to focus on your finished basement because relatives are coming to visit and will be using this room. Perhaps you're having a cold snap and working on the garage would be impossible. Develop your goals, set a strategy, and make appointments with yourself and outside vendors to complete those goals. Next month we're dealing with travel and you may have no plans to go anywhere. You can get caught up then. And if you aren't moving this August, you have even more time at your disposal. Can you feel the panic subside?

WHAT'S THE TIME COMMITMENT?

You may have noticed that this month I did not indicate the time needed at the start of each week. These areas have so many variables it's hard to pinpoint even a ballpark time. I would allow at least two days for cleaning out large areas like the garage and basement. When it comes to the laundry room or your guest room, you might get lucky and find a half day will suffice. It all depends on the current condition of each area to be organized. As a rule of thumb, be generous with your time. If you work faster than you anticipated, you can give yourself that extra time to play. Or move on to the next step on your worksheet, and your project will get finished in record time.

You may find that in addition to cleaning out items, you need to move some of those you intend to keep. For example, let's say you have the majority of your photo collection stored in the basement closet. You discover that photos are in the attic and the garage as well. Move them to one central location and ultimately digitize them. We think of electronic frames being for our current photo dumps but you could have one for your memorabilia. Why not? Then every time you are in your office or family room, you can be surprised by a memento from the past. We stash these items away and never see them. We feel strangely comforted that they belong to us. This is one way to literally enjoy them while no longer being burdened by literal physical objects.

Before creating a garage worksheet, you would have written your two lists: the things you like about the space and those you don't like and want to change. These lists are the starting point for the worksheet. Here's my sample. Does yours look anything like this?

THINGS I LIKE ABOUT MY GARAGE

- My garage has one large window. I appreciate the light that constantly fills the space.
- The garage door opens onto an alley that is mostly free of traffic. I can work on my garage without the whole neighborhood knowing that I am decluttering and organizing!
- If it were organized, the garage would be a large space capable of holding two cars.
- The garage has lots of wall space and a high ceiling.

THINGS I DISLIKE ABOUT MY GARAGE

- I have stored items that stopped working with the hope of one day restoring them. These include the old washer and dryer that came with the house. In truth, they are just taking up space.
- Holiday boxes have been used and reused for years. They are falling apart.
- Sports items like basketballs roam around the floor while the bikes fall over.
- The garage needs some type of shelving.

From this evaluation, I would create my worksheet. Please note my sample includes some clarification notes to help you understand my thought process.

WORKSHEET FOR THE GARAGE
WEEK ONE

1. Dumpster delivered on Monday (The dumpster is scheduled to be picked up Friday morning.)
2. Set aside two to three hours a day to
   a. Toss items into the dumpster
   b. Choose items suitable for eBay, a yard sale, or online resale
   c. Find items that need to be repaired
   d. Return items that belong to family and friends
   e. Make additional phone calls
3. Call neighbors to see if anyone is interested in a yard sale. If someone wants to organize a yard sale, we need to set a date for the sale as well as schedule our first planning meeting. (I want all items out of the garage as quickly as possible, so the sale date can't be set too far in the future.) If no one is interested in a yard sale, I will add the yard sale items to the charity pickup.
4. A charity is scheduled to pick up the washer and dryer and other miscellaneous items on Friday, late afternoon. Secure receipt for taxes. This happens at the end of the week because until the debris is tossed into the dumpster, no one can reach the washer and dryer! Many charities, such as Goodwill, repair donated items. Be sure to let them know

the condition of the items when you call to make your appointment.

5. On Saturday morning, put all items designated to remain in the garage into categories. I can make use of the open floor space to keep everything neat and tidy. I need to assess these so that I know what kinds of storage containers to purchase and how many.
6. On Sunday, shop for containers. Check out simple shelving at the local home store: I need to know what's available in terms of design and cost.
7. This weekend, photograph items and post for sale on Facebook Marketplace or eBay. (Alternatively, I could take them to a professional who will do it for me. These are private individuals or storefront operations that work on commission. Be sure to check the references of the vendor you decide to use. Your best friend, your personal organizer or decorator, or a local antiques dealer may have a referral for you.)

WEEK TWO

1. Monday morning, a space planner from Closets by Design will be here to give me an idea how the garage could be professionally outfitted. This meeting will help me decide whether I need a professional system now or whether I should use simple shelving until a later date.
2. Tuesday (assuming I decide to wait on the professional system), return to the store and pick up the necessary shelving units.
3. In addition, pick up any special equipment that I might need to complete

the organization of the space, such as bicycle racks or bike hooks for the wall, a tool holder for the wall to grip the handles of mops and brooms to keep them off the floor (as suggested for the laundry room), a pegboard with hooks to hang tools and keep them accessible, and a sports center to hold all sporting equipment.

4. Assemble the racks when I return home.

5. Wednesday, transfer all items to their new containers. These will be labeled and placed on the shelves.

6. All special storage supplies, such as the bike rack or hook, will be installed today as well.

7. At the end of the work session, sweep the garage and, if necessary, hose down the floor.

8. Thursday, return all borrowed items.

This will give you an idea about how to accomplish a big project such as the garage, the attic, or the basement. You could probably compress your activities and do everything over the course of three days, especially if you have help. This slower pace allows you time to research, shop, clean out, set up, and organize without exhausting yourself. Who knows? You might even enjoy the process!

By the way, if a job is really big and requires heavy lifting, why not consider asking for help? Is there a teenager in your home or on your block who needs to make a little cash? Would you like to ask a neighbor and then offer to help with his or her garage? What about those wonderful grown kids of yours who are going to rent a truck and pick up their stuff? Maybe they'd like to help you. Never be afraid to ask. We all need help from time to time.

As you organize your garage, be aware of the importance of placement. What do I mean by placement? For example, you need your holiday decorations once a year, right? If you're putting in a loft, that's the perfect spot for those containers. If you're using shelving, put those containers on the top. You want the items you need during the year to be more accessible. Similarly, don't bury the new sports center in the back of the garage. Keep it near the front so the kids can grab items easily.

It's good to have some emergency supplies. Place them so they will be accessible! And check expiration dates every six months to a year. You can make a date on your calendar or set an automatic computer reminder. When water expires, use it for your plants or lawn. By the way, the Red Cross can provide you with a list of emergency supplies at www.redcross.org. You can sign up for their free monthly newsletter with information geared toward your community.

You want to factor in the size of your family (don't forget Fido and Fluffy!) and how elaborate you want to get. Obvious items include flashlights, batteries, a battery-powered radio (or one that uses solar energy or is wound like a clock), a large first aid kit, water, canned and dried food, and some camping equipment. If you live in a city dominated by personal transportation, don't forget to have some supplies in your car! Next month we'll be organizing the family car and I'll have some additional pointers for you.

Remember how we established zones in the kitchen? Well, you can do the same here. You may have the following: sports equipment, hobby area, emergency supplies, holiday decorations, gardening supplies, and automobile care. No matter what room or area, you want to save steps, which in turn saves time. And knowing what you have saves money. How's that for motivation? The ultimate trifecta: physical energy, time, and money saved just by creating specific spots for your categories!

Try to start with a project whose completion will reap obvious rewards. Wouldn't it be cool to have your neighbors envious that you can actually park two cars in your garage? Wouldn't it be nice to enjoy doing laundry instead of having your heart sink at the thought? How about the fun of your first movie night as a family in the newly organized basement? Bonus rooms are a gift. After this week, one or two of them will be ready to serve you. Are you ready for another week of reclaiming space in your home?

Has it been years since you've driven into your garage? Here are four tips to make your reentry a smooth one:

- Hang a small ball from the ceiling so you know exactly where to stop the car when you pull in.
- When you're establishing your zones, be sure you leave enough room on either side of the car so you can open the car doors with ease.

- If you enter your home from the garage, put down a small, heavy-duty mat by the door. You don't want to track dirt into the house with you.
- Do you live in a four-season climate? When the rain and snow start, put a simple shoe rack by the door leading from the garage into the house. Put out a pair of comfortable shoes or slippers for each member of the family. This will cut down on the dirt everyone tracks inside.

WEEK FOUR

Call More Areas to Order

This week, you can

- Complete a big organizing project from last week or move on to a new project
- Consider my off-site storage guidelines
- Let's consider your memorabilia stash

Time required: Varies.

ARE YOU NOTICING HOW THE MAGIC Formula (eliminate, categorize, organize) repeats itself in every challenge you face? Here's a word of caution concerning the last step (organize) and the use of containers. They come in all sizes and shapes and are a blessing to anyone interested in creating order. However, they do not excuse you from the elimination process! You want to pack up and label only the things you need. Getting a huge tub that will hold every stuffed animal your child ever touched is not the way to go, especially if your child is now forty with kids of his or her own.

RECLAIM THE LAUNDRY ROOM

Readers of my books tell me they are amazed how much personal information I share. I think we're on a great adventure together, so you might as well know who I am. In keeping with this philosophy, I must confess now that I love to do laundry. When people tell me that their laundry piles up, I have a hard time understanding why! Clean clothes are such a joy, what can I say? Make your laundry room a pleasure to be in because it's pretty, organized, and functional. It won't take long for you to share my passion for doing laundry!

Here's my mockup of the two lists I would create for this room and a worksheet to help you see how you could transform a laundry room into a place you enjoy. I've made it a two-day project. If you don't paint or change the floor, you'll be finished in one day.

THINGS I LIKE ABOUT MY LAUNDRY ROOM

- There are two nice cabinets with three shelves each for storage.
- The small window lets in light that brightens the room.
- It's off the kitchen so I can multitask while cooking.

THINGS I DISLIKE ABOUT MY LAUNDRY ROOM

- The walls need to be painted.
- The linoleum is old and ugly.
- The machines are small, so I have to do more loads.
- The light fixture needs to be replaced. There's a bare bulb in the room, and it looks dreary.

WORKSHEET FOR THE LAUNDRY ROOM

DAY ONE

1. Clean out old, expired, or no longer used products from the cupboards. Take things to other areas to see whether they would more logically be stored there. Sort what will remain here into categories. Make a list of containers needed.

2. Go to the store and purchase paint (enough to freshen the room plus magnetic paint for one wall), two rollers, two brushes, and a few disposable drop cloths. Find suitable organizing containers. Go to the flooring section and choose some do-it-yourself tile squares. (Be sure to have exact measurements.) Select a new fixture for the light. Price new washers and dryers. Take brochures. Pick up a hanging crystal for the window and some magnets.

3. That evening, put all items in their new containers. Wipe off the shelves. Label both the shelves and the containers. Put containers on the shelves.

DAY TWO

1. Paint the walls. (Magnetic paint will require several coats.)
2. Put in new flooring.
3. Hang the crystal in the window so that on sunny days the room will be filled with rainbows.
4. Spend some time surfing the internet to comparison shop other washers and dryers. Find the best price. Check finances to decide if now is the time to purchase new machines.
5. When the paint dries (follow instructions carefully), surprise the kids with a display of their latest artwork!
6. Create a house rule: No more than four pieces of art (or whatever number you decide is in keeping with the size of the wall) can be up at any one time. New artwork needs to replace the old, not join

it if the number exceeds four! As art pieces are tossed, if they are special in some way, snap a digital pic and have a board on Pinterest ready to display them. Should you have a large family of budding artists, you might have a photo frame that rotates photos in the kitchen. Load nothing but artwork photos. Your kids will have their own electronic art gallery.

GET THE GUEST ROOM READY

Whether you use it for a family reunion, a spontaneous sleepover, or a part-time office, a guest room is a treasure. Let's work to make it as inviting as possible.

THINGS I LIKE ABOUT MY GUEST ROOM

- It has a bathroom so guests can have their privacy.
- It's a nice size with a sitting area as well as a queen-size bed.
- The room is in the back of the house away from street noises.

THINGS I DISLIKE ABOUT MY GUEST ROOM

- The bedding looks tired and worn, as do the towels in the bathroom.
- The window treatments do nothing for the room.
- The closet is full of clothes I no longer wear.

WORKSHEET FOR THE GUEST ROOM

DAY ONE

1. Measure the windows. Go to the store and pick up new bedding and matching drapes for the windows. Also pick up fresh blinds for the windows. Get a set of new towels for guests and some aromatherapy candles. In the organizing section of the same store (probably Bed Bath & Beyond because I have discount coupons), pick up a few sets of hangers for the closet, as well as a shoe rack and a hook for the back of the bathroom door. Pick up an inexpensive bathrobe so guests don't have to bring their own.
2. Spend the afternoon weeding out the clothes I won't be wearing again. Put the bag of clothes in the trunk of my car to drop off at a charity in the morning, ask a friend to drive me, or call the charity for a pickup.
3. Take a few minutes to organize the closet. My clothes should take up no more than half the closet and should be arranged by type of clothing and color order, just like in the primary closet. In the other half, place hangers and a shoe rack for guests.
4. Check the bathroom to be sure my guests have ample amenities such as shampoo, conditioner, toothpaste, toothbrush, and toilet paper. Put out the fresh towels and empty the trash.
5. If the COVID-19 era has found you and your partner both working from

home and you need this room as a second office, you might need to secure a smaller bed and add office basics like a desk, ergonomic chair, and a good lamp. I realize that mattresses are expensive. Think outside the box. Get a gently used mattress from a friend or family member. Mattresses generally are ready for replacement after ten years. You can now buy environmentally friendly ones like those made by Avocado and avoid that chemical smell as normal mattresses off-gas for days. One of my clients assured me he could not get a new mattress because a king-size mattress would not make the turn at the top of his stairs. He was correct. It would not, but he was delighted to know Avocado arrives rolled in a box, as do many other brands.

APARTMENT DWELLERS AND OFF-SITE STORAGE

Some of you are saying, "Regina, not everyone owns a home!" I understand. I don't have a house any longer. I've lived in some tiny studios in New York City in my day. Believe me, I understand the problems. I guarantee that you have found a way to stash your stuff outside your apartment. Do you have a storage locker in the building? That's your garage! Did you leave things at your parents' house? Ah, that's your off-site storage. Do you store your off-season clothing at the local cleaners? Do you have a friend with a house in the country who lets you store a few boxes

in his garage? You get the idea. We all find a way.

Sometimes off-site storage is an invaluable tool. I love those pods that get delivered and picked up after you fill them. But be sure that you really need what you are storing. You don't want to waste money in lieu of making decisions. I couldn't begin to calculate how much money is squandered each year in this manner. If you do have storage, and you legitimately need it, be sure you have it organized. If you face a sea of boxes when you open the door to your storage unit, you are making life difficult for yourself. Here are some guidelines to help you:

- Be absolutely certain you need what you are storing. I may be beating a dead horse here, but it's a key issue.
- If an item can be packed, put it in a plastic container. Label the container clearly. Group categories together.
- Make use of wall space with containers on wheels or with shelving units. You want to be able to walk into the center of the area and start grabbing what you need.
- Keep the key to your lock in one place. Make a spare just in case and store it in a different location.
- Check to see if your renter's insurance covers this location before you buy additional on-site insurance from the owner of the building.
- Be sure to choose a building that is well maintained, is well lit, and has reasonable access hours.

- Rent a unit that is secure. I have seen storage units whose walls don't go all the way up. If you're thin and agile, you can visit all the units in that row!
- Know exactly why and for how long you need off-site storage. Your monthly rent is money that you could be saving to make a down payment on a home.

⠿

After these bonus rooms are decluttered and spruced up, you are going to feel as if a weight has been taken off your shoulders. "Why didn't I do this before?" will cross your mind every time you enter one of these now organized, useful, fun-to-be-in rooms!

Next month we turn our attention to travel. Please don't feel left out if you're staying home this summer. Completing the work from this month will be a worthwhile way to spend the next month.

Do read the material for travel because you never know when you might have an unexpected opportunity to leave home. This time you will be prepared in a way you've perhaps not experienced before.

If you're staying home, why not go out and buy a beautiful magazine about travel? Or perhaps a travel guide to a place you've always wanted to visit? Or just download them onto your iPad? You can take some breaks from the hard work your bonus rooms are demanding and start dreaming about where in this world you'd like to go.

STROLL DOWN MEMORY LANE

Get out the tissues—it's time to tackle your memorabilia. The areas we tackle this month are very often the repositories for the past. Because I love to toss things out, people assume I am not sentimental. On the contrary, I am very much so. I simply want the cream of the memorabilia crop in my home, not the entire field!

One day I tossed all the paraphernalia from my acting career. Pictures, résumés, demo tapes: it was all part of a past life. Friends ask if I save my notes when I'm writing a book or if I keep the galleys. "Why would I?" is my response. I have the finished product. I believe that every experience builds on itself and nothing is wasted. And the best is always yet to come.

WHAT'S IN YOUR PAST?

I have some questions for you about your memorabilia before you gather it and start going through it. This is a difficult and often extensive area, so we need to have a plan. Grab your journal. What types of memorabilia do you have? Please be specific.

Here are some typical examples to help you get started:

- Do you save letters and cards?
- Do you hold on to all of your children's artwork?

- Are you attached to the textbooks you used in college, medical school, or law school?
- Do you keep every receipt you acquire when you take a trip, especially if it's colorful or in another language?
- Do you have boxes of old photographs?
- Is your computer hard drive awash in digital photos?
- Do you see budding collectors in your children? Is every Beanie Baby ever produced living in your home next to every sports trading card ever printed? Take time to create a personal inventory of all the various categories that you are currently attached to. For our purposes, any collections you may have will fall under the general category of "Memorabilia." You can create three lists if you like:

  o Stored collections (Are hundreds of sports trading cards hidden away?)
  o Displayed collections (How many pieces are on display?)
  o General memorabilia, such as cards and love letters

After you know what you have, the big question is: Why? Jot something down next to each category on your list. "Just because" isn't a reason. Dig deep if that's all that comes to you.

Here are some questions to ask yourself if you don't know the reason why you're saving a particular category. (I hope you find yourself saying: "There is no reason! Out this stuff goes!")

Is this a large collection? Does it eat up space in closets and cupboards that you need for everyday life? Did it grow to this size without you realizing how extensive it was? Is it wise to go on sacrificing this space?

Was life more exciting or interesting when you started your collection? Do you think you hold on to it in an attempt to recapture days gone by?

Do you hope this collection will one day be worth money?

Do you believe that your children will be grateful when they are presented as adults with their childhood artwork, papers, and books?

Are you perhaps more vested in the past than the present? This is common. Do you walk through your days while your mind relives the past? Do you pine for the good old days? Is it possible your collection represents that time?

I read an article once that said most people feel they peaked in college. And then there's my friend Hank.

One night I had dinner with Hank, a funny, intelligent guy who usually tells great stories. This night he told stories nonstop for well over two hours. We laughed that he must have had too much coffee because he couldn't stop talking. This night, however, was odd because all his tales were about his high school years. How could anyone in his fifth decade of life possibly remember in such vivid detail what happened when he was thirteen or fourteen? I was beyond mystified and, quite frankly, bored.

I remembered an article that mentioned the notion of people peaking in college. I asked him if he thought that was true. "Oh no!" said Hank. "I think the average person peaks in high school." I almost fell off my chair! Are you like Hank? Do you look back fondly at high school or college and feel it was indeed the best of times? Honoring the past is a beautiful gesture of gratitude. But getting stuck in the past robs us of being fully invested in the miracle of today.

AT THE WEIGH STATION

In light of Hank's story, when you look at your list of memorabilia, do you now feel the energetic "sticky glue" that's binding you? I know women who, in middle age, still sport the haircut they had in high school. I know people who have lost a loved one and turned the deceased's room into a shrine. I bet you could give examples from your life experience. Stop now and write a few sentences describing at least three ways you have personally experienced people having a death grip on the past. I have two stories for you. One will touch your heart, and the other, I hope, will make you laugh.

Catherine's Story

I had a client who was as full of life as any human being you will ever meet. She supported everyone in her circle of friends. I lost track of how many clients she sent me over the years. I'd get a call and be told that "Catherine says I need you!" When we organized her home, I was fascinated to see how she would fearlessly part with most things, while others were bound to her with emotional superglue.

The latter included love letters and photos of guys who had broken her heart. I wanted a ceremony in which we burned all this and scattered the ashes in the ocean. Catherine saw them as treasures. During her yearly tune-up, I'd ask if the time to part with them had arrived. It never did.

Catherine was audited once and it put the fear of God, or should I say Uncle Sam, in her. She was completely unwilling to let go of anything that was remotely related to taxes. It was early this decade and yet her receipts went back to the 1970s! I begged her to toss these boxes, but again I hit the brick wall of resistance.

My beloved client and friend passed away about a decade ago. I was given the privilege of helping clean out her apartment. Things I had begged her to part with were now tossed out like the trash they were. I thought of her and all the conversations we had had. Now her friends and relatives were throwing away her fears. Out of fear that she would never be loved, she saved everything her emotionally abusive boyfriends had ever sent her. A smart woman afraid that she couldn't make the right decision about paper. Fear that she would toss something she needed. The men who had hurt her were perceived as being "better than nothing," and their communications, no matter how cruel or dismissive, were held as proof that yes, she had been loved.

On this day, it could be said that Catherine was at last free of her fears. In the end, I was reminded that it's only stuff. If you don't toss it, someone else will. Think about Catherine when you're on the fence about some item or collection. Give your trash a loving send-off! I assure you nobody else will. It's time to roll up your sleeves and get to work! Do have a nice stash of heavy-duty garbage bags at the ready. I'd like you to bring one category of memorabilia at a time to your designated work area. If your memorabilia is vast, be careful! If it threatens the serenity of any room in your home, bring it to the area in sections. Build up what I call your trash muscle. Some of my clients swear to me they can't part with anything. By the end of the first day, they are surrounded by bags of stuff. They are exhausted but are ready to do more. Develop your trash muscle with as much devotion as you would your abs or biceps.

Let's be brave and save the best of the best and let the rest go. What constitutes the best of the best? Well, that's a personal judgment call. Here are some ideas to help you make your decisions.

Parents, you do not have to save every single thing your child ever touched, drew, or played with. I can assure you from personal experience that this gesture will not be appreciated. But a single notebook or one or two treasured pieces of art your child created will be.

If you worked for years in corporate America and are now a stay-at-home parent, you don't need all those items of business attire, no matter how expensive they were. Donate them to a program such as Dress for Success, which gives suits to underprivileged women.

If you have extremely expensive designer clothes, take them to a resale shop. Save one or two, if you must. If the day comes when you need suits again, I think you'll want something fresh and new, don't you?

Do you have baseball caps and T-shirts coming out your ears? If you can't part with this collection, be creative with it. Here are some ideas to consider:

Take out two or three caps and T-shirts you actually wear and store the rest in containers. Be sure you know why you're making this effort! Are the T-shirts and caps potentially valuable because they commemorate a special event? Box those. If it's a generic T-shirt that's sold on the beach in Waikiki every day of the year, reconsider this choice.

Do you have pictures of yourself in some of the T-shirts and caps, preferably at the place where you purchased them? Have a special photo album to show off your collection rather than having them take up space in your closet. It's okay if you're the only one who ever looks at these photos! By the way, they make memo photo albums. Next to the photo you can say a word about the experience.

You get the idea. Be creative! Find a way to *enjoy* a big collection.

The trick is to rotate your items if the collection is large. Let me make a point by playing a little game with you. Let's pretend we've been trick-or-treating on Halloween. I'm holding a deep bag full of candy. You want a small bag of M&M's. I tell you to reach in and take whatever you want. You can't find the M&M's because there's so much candy! We wind up spilling it all out on a counter. Suddenly it's easy to spot.

Even if you were to crowd all your memorabilia into the casket with you, it's not making that final journey with you. Save one or two things that represent the gratitude you feel for having had the privilege of that experience. Let the rest have a new life via a charity. Or if it's time, toss it. Look at it all with fresh eyes and see if in fact it has become trash when you weren't looking.

Following are some of the creative ways we've considered to store memorabilia:

- If you find yourself with items that you want to pack away, like those famous love letters, keep them in a container and store them respectfully, preferably out of sight!
- If you have a large collection, use a container on wheels. If you have a small collection, and you'd like to look at it periodically, use one of the pretty project boxes we considered in the office section from organizemeusa.com.

- Choose key items and keep them in a shadow box or have them professionally framed. If you are crafty, consider the magic of scrapbooking, which combines photos and memorabilia. Could you save a few ticket stubs from your trip to Paris to make your album more interesting and decorative, and then toss the rest?
- Put some items from a collection on display and pack the rest. Once or twice a year, rotate items from the stored part of the collection.
- Donate as much as you can so others can enjoy the things you no longer use.
- Whittle a sentimental collection down to a few key items.
- If you think a collection is valuable, have it appraised and decide if it's time to sell. Depending on the size of your collection, an appraisal may take more than a week.

Guess what? If your curio cabinet or display shelves are crammed with goodies, no one will be able to appreciate any of it—not even you. Rotate items with the seasons. I promise you that people will ask whether you made some new purchases or redecorated. It's also easier to keep a few items clean. Let's see, what is that phrase I love so much? Oh, yes: "Less is more!"

Exit Rituals

Every bonus area is not only different in size but in when and how often we use it. The one rule of thumb as you leave any area for the last time each day is to check to be sure every item has a designated spot to be and you returned it after using it. Did you bring in something new? Find it a home. One careless placement will lead to more. You are working too hard to let that happen. Consider the feelings of the next person to enter this room. Yes, even if you live alone and that person is you.

SUMMARY

WEEK ONE

Examine each bonus area of the home to identify your likes and dislikes.

Find out if you are a pack rat.

Begin to create a shopping list.

WEEK TWO

Examine the tools at your disposal for organizing special challenge areas (such as renting a dumpster).

Devise a battle plan for each room.

Make phone calls to outside vendors if necessary to book appointments (call a garage design company, contact a charity to arrange a pickup, and so on).

WEEK THREE

Organize at least one bonus room.

WEEK FOUR

Tackle your next bonus room.

Consider the special needs of small city apartments and when and how to use off-site storage.

Develop a plan for your memorabilia.

BONUS TIP

I love the study of color. I am amazed how different cultures and pursuits give it meaning. For example, yogis see yellow as a color of protection while Feng Shui practitioners see it as the color representing health. I once organized a color expert in the fashion world who had literally thousands of swatches for every color. If you told her your favorite color was red, she'd point to her one thousand plus swatches of red and ask, "Which one?" Learn more about color to deepen the conscious way you use it in your home, your fashion expression, and your healing work. A modality that marries aromatherapy oils, energy, and color is Aura-Soma. It's a unique self-care system that harnesses the power of nature's color, plant, and crystal energies in products created using the highest quality organic and biodynamic ingredients. Apply them to your body, energy field, or environment and you'll experience improved ease, well-being, happiness, and vitality. You may find Aura-Soma a powerful ally in that tool kit you are building over time. I added a consultant for you in the Resources section.

TRAVELING LIGHT

To straighten the crooked, you must first do a
harder thing—straighten yourself.

—BUDDHA

IN THE FALL OF 2006, MY FRIEND SHAY and I traveled to China. It was a long-held dream of mine to walk around the Forbidden City, see the Great Wall, and visit the Terra Cotta Warriors at the excavation site in Xian. Shay is quite possibly the most wonderfully even-tempered person I know. Like just about every human being on the planet, Shay takes way too much with her when she travels. I have always marveled at the number of large suitcases people drag around with them.

We traveled from Beijing to Shanghai by plane, had a bus take us around the famous coastal cities near Shanghai, and then flew to Xian. When it came time to pack up and return to Beijing for the flight to Los Angeles, Shay was in a pickle. She'd purchased lots of souvenirs and her suitcase had been bulging from day one. You can't really help a friend in this situation. Too many hands in a suitcase are the enactment of that proverb: "Too many cooks spoil the broth." So I did what any good friend

would do—I sat on my bed and teased her mercilessly. I even took a photograph of that exploding suitcase before she tamed it. To her credit, Shay laughed the entire time. Of course, there was a time when I was just like Shay. My mother taught me that there was a place for everything in the home; she also warned me to travel light. I wish I had taken these words to heart the summer I turned seventeen.

As an incredible gift from my parents, I was sent to live with my favorite cousin in Brazil for three months. My dad wanted me to travel in style, so he bought me a large, high-quality suitcase. "Large" is the operative word. The seasons in Brazil are opposite those in New York. I was heading from the start of summer to the beginning of winter. We all believed I needed warm clothing. Although my mom was a minimalist and a champion packer in her own right, she felt we had to bend the rules because of the length of my stay. This trip was when I learned the meaning of the phrase "less is more." My battleship suit-case and I left New York in June right after school ended.

Dragging that monstrosity around Bra-zil was the bane of my existence. I found there were creative ways to stretch a ward-robe without having a huge stash of new outfits. I vowed to travel light for the rest of my life. The rubber hit the road the next year when I spent a summer traveling around Europe. I had a small suitcase that could fit in the overhead compartment. To this day, this is the only size suitcase I own. No airline can lose my bag because it's always with me. I can dash off the air-craft at my destination and set about the business at hand. I'm going to teach you too how to travel light.

HABIT OF THE MONTH

This month we're going to be concerned with completion. Do you walk into rooms all day long and think, "Oh yeah. I forgot I was in the middle of…" Get into the habit of finishing whatever you start. If you do this with simple physical tasks, you will do it with every aspect of your life. Living with the intent to complete whatever you start will keep you centered, focused, and oh yes, more organized.

AFFIRMATION OF THE MONTH

I consciously relax into the present moment realizing it is the only reality. The past is over, I cannot change it. The future is unknown. Today is the gift I embrace as I feel, hear, see, and experience life to its fullest.

Self-Care Practice

Chances are there are two kinds of peo-ple in your life: those who do breath work themselves and are excited you joined the fold and those who think it's crazy. We aren't going to worry about the latter group. We'll just respect them and carry on. Those who do pranayamas will ask if I taught you alternate nostril breathing, and I don't want you to disappoint them. If it feels uncomfortable or weird to you, try it once and go back to one of the basic prac-tices I shared. We have to honor your body and how it feels. I have a deviated septum, so alternate nostril breathing is a practice I can't do for any extended period of time. I still do a few rounds because it's so great for balancing the nervous system.

Sit in your favorite straight-back chair, feet flat on the floor, hands on your thighs with palms facing up or in the mudra I shared earlier. Do a few clearing breaths, and when you are ready place the thumb of your right hand on your right nostril to close it while you slowly inhale through your left nostril. No count is taken. Then pause and gently close your left nostril with your right ring finger and exhale through the right nostril. Repeat, alter-nating inhaling on the left and exhaling on the right, for a few moments. This is a great practice to lead the way to a medi-tation. Start with three rounds but do no more than five. Five rounds are all anyone needs to achieve results.

WEEK ONE

Travel Questions

This week, you can

- Learn how to use your organizing skills to plan a trip
- Glean tips from past travel mistakes for future adventures

Time required: Thirty minutes to two hours, depending on your travel experience, where you are going, and how soon you are leaving!

THIS WEEK I'D LIKE YOU TO JOURnal about past trips. I want you to note what you have learned about travel. Do you ever find yourself saying something like this: "I can't believe I did it again! You'd think I would learn." Well, after this week, all those travel blunders will be a thing of the past. Let me give you two personal examples of things I've learned through trial and error.

When we went to China, I knew that we'd be on a tour bus every day. I needed good walking shoes. I didn't need any dressy clothes. I made the mistake of taking only one pair of shoes. Although they were broken in and consistently comfortable, I longed to give my feet a break. You can be sure I'll never again travel without a spare pair of comfortable shoes!

Over the years I've learned that when I stay with friends, I can count on finding certain items in their home, such as shampoo and toothpaste. I can probably borrow a bathrobe. Add up the weight and the bulk those items represent and my suitcase stays light and roomy. (By the way, I call ahead of time to get the okay from my hostess!) You don't need to write about your experiences. I'm looking for a simple list of lessons learned.

Do you need some questions to help jog your memory? Here are the ones I would ask you if we were working together:

1. Do you travel a lot for business or are you pretty much a once-a-year vacation traveler?
2. If you are primarily a business traveler, do you like this aspect of your work or do you endure it? Whatever you answered, explain why.

3. If you mostly travel only on vacation, would you like to travel more? If so, what has stopped you?

4. Do you like to stay in your relative geographical area or do you like to venture far from home?

5. Please make a list of two or three successful trips you've taken. Think for a few minutes about what made these travels so special. What were the reasons behind the ones you selected? In lieu of a lot of writing, you can simply jot down key phrases.

6. Looking at each of those phrases, do they translate into things you can repeat? They don't have to, of course; I'm just looking for clues.

Let's switch our focus to trips that you didn't like. Please list four travel adventures and write a few key phrases to understand why you didn't enjoy them. I would bet cold, hard cash that the nightmare trips yield solid evidence of things you want to avoid at all costs.

Let me give you a personal example of the "won't ever do that again" trip. My mother died not long after I graduated from college. I nursed her at home for the last eight months of her life. I was exhausted body, mind, and Soul. A friend suggested we take a trip to Europe. I had the worst time ever, even though I adore traveling abroad. My loss was too recent and the pain too raw. In retrospect, I might have profited from basking in the warm sun on a beach somewhere. But we live and learn, don't we?

In summary, here are some things my travels have taught me:

- Take at least two pairs of shoes (previously worn and well broken in).
- Call ahead to friends (and hotels) and see what amenities are available. I like to know what can be left out of my suitcase.
- Travel with a lightweight diffuser and bring oils that purify the environment. Whether hotel or guest room, I am ready to stay healthy.
- Always travel with an herbal first aid kit. I can stop diarrhea, vomiting, and motion sickness in their tracks! Have you ever become sick while you were traveling? It only has to happen once and you learn to be prepared.
- Don't travel too soon after a personal loss.

Learn from the past. Let it be your teacher and your guide. This attitude will help you let go and continue to move forward. And guess what? The freer you are mentally and emotionally, the less stuff you find yourself accumulating. Now you should be ready to make your list.

A second and equally important list I'd like you to make is a list of the items you have either forgotten once or consistently leave at home. "I can't believe I did it again!" We're going to use this list next week so that these dramas are never again repeated. I remember the old days when forgetting a hair dryer was a huge mistake. Now, thank goodness, most hotels provide them in the room. What did you forget to put in your suitcase?

I have one final list for you. This one will be painful. You have to promise you'll be honest with yourself. Please list at least four things you always take with you but never use. Remember the first line of this book? "I know you." Okay. Tell me four things you take and never use! I want you to leave them home in the future. And remember, unless you are going camping or to a developing country, I bet you could replace them in a pinch, whatever these items are.

Before you start writing, let me tell a quick anecdote about me. My assistant was taking me to the airport for a long business trip home to New York. I was nervous about leaving my old golden retriever, Miss Katie. I was so wrapped up in the fear, I didn't acknowledge it. Instead I let it run me. And how did it manifest? I pitched a fit in the car because I had left a package of gum on my kitchen counter. Can you imagine? My wonderful assistant looked at me and said ever so calmly, "I just bet they sell gum in New York City, Regina." We burst out laughing.

I learned two things that day. First, you don't have to take every item you use if it's easily found at your destination. The most important lesson, however, is to be conscious of your emotions. When you start to feel yourself acting in an irrational way, ask yourself, "What is driving this upset?" Dealing with your emotions guarantees that you won't be alienating anyone around you with an out-of-character emotional outburst.

Okay. Your turn. Start writing!

ORGANIZING A TRIP

When I was eighteen, I returned home from my second trip abroad. My parents gave me an extraordinary gift in the form of a challenge. I could leave home for the entire summer the following year *if* I did the research for and planned the trip myself. They wanted to know where I'd be every day for the entire ten weeks I'd be abroad. I had to make all hotel and flight reservations. I needed to research train and bus transportation within the countries we'd be going to (I was traveling with a college friend). The letters to all hotels had to be written in Spanish or French. (This era was pre-internet.) And, oh yes, I had a budget! Is there any doubt as to how I became the Zen Organizer™?

One of my favorite pastimes that year was wandering up and down Fifth Avenue in New York City. I collected more travel brochures than you can imagine. I wanted to be sure I saw everything in all the cities we were to visit. I went to consulates to get visa requirements. I went to the airline office and researched flight information. I got the names and addresses of hotels and, yes, I wrote in French or Spanish! (We traveled to the Iberian Peninsula and Morocco.) What took me months to research you can now do in a few hours. Today, the internet puts the world at your fingertips. Whether you're collecting cyber data or hard copy brochures, however, you need a way to keep track of the information.

My file system has an area called "Travel." Within "Travel" are hanging folders. Within each hanging folder are manila folders for each of the countries or states in which I have an expressed interest. If a category is particularly robust, I switch to a box-bottom hanging file folder to hold all the material comfortably. If you are confused by these terms, please refer to the creation of a file system section in "Organizing the Business of Life." That is where we conquer paper and banish piles! Here is what my "Travel" files used to look like. Feel free to adapt this format to suit your needs and style. And remember that the file system you have on your computer can follow this format.

Travel (left side tab for hanging folder)

Europe (right side tab for hanging folder)
England (tab for manila folder)
France (tab for manila folder)
Italy (tab for manila folder)

United States (right side tab for hanging folder)
California (tab for manila folder)
New York (tab for manila folder)
North Carolina (tab for manila folder)
Washington, D.C. (tab for manila folder)

If you are going to an area rich with history, you may want to read about it in detail beforehand by purchasing an extensive guidebook. Download it on your e-reader. You can take a library of reference material on your phone! If you are a lover of books and only purchase hard copies, I would suggest that you copy key pages rather than drag the entire book on your trip! You can use a scanner app and have those pages on your phone for quick and immediate reference. If you have a simple list of what you feel you need to see, you can supplement the list with local publications. We covered memorabilia in the last section, so it's a good time to suggest that you don't have to bring the local guidebook back home with you. I know that's heretical to some of you. I'm just planting the seed! In the same way, you needn't save every ticket stub from every museum, amusement park, or flight you take. Unless, of course, you are a mad scrapbooker and you will actually make use of those receipts in the scrapbook you intend to make of your trip! I would take a photo and instantly add it to a special Pinterest board (automatically adding copies to other sources like the cloud or Dropbox). Your family and closest friends should know the password to unlock this board. You can make it public after you return home. You don't want to advertise your location as you go so that thieves know your home may be unattended. This goes for Instagram and all other social media sites.

If you are traveling to a foreign country, go to their consulate online to check their visa requirements for entry. They will also advise you if you need any special shots. Before I went to China, I called my internist for advice. He suggested that I speak with a doctor who specializes in travel medicine. Ask your regular physician if such a specialist is located in your area. If you are working with a travel agent, he or she can advise you on these matters as well.

Do you belong to an organization that provides roadside assistance like the Automobile Club? They are also a first-class travel agency. Speaking of inoculations and visas, don't forget to apply well in advance if you need a passport. The wait can be up to six months. If you intend to do any driving, be sure your license is current. Are there other legal documents you need to tend to for the trip to your chosen part of the world? Today of course the list includes proof of COVID vaccination. I have my paper proof, and I have a record on my phone.

After you choose your trip, be sure you pull the existing material out of the general files and create a new setup for the current trip. For example, I pulled my "China" folder out of my "Travel" section. I transferred it to my "Action Files" section. As time passed, I put all pertinent information here. When it came time to pack, I knew just where to look for all the legal docs and research I wanted to take with me. It isn't possible for me to direct you to all the sites and agencies that will make your trip a reality. My job, as your professional organizer, is to teach you how to keep track of all the information you are gathering. You want it to serve you rather than become a new source of chaos and frustration. Be sure you enjoy every step of the journey rather than rely on the actual days away from home as the sole reward. Today you can find blogs documenting the experiences of travelers to all your desired locations. Firsthand accounts are gold, aren't they?

I always have my boarding pass on my phone, and I get a copy at the airport from a kiosk. If the computer systems suffer an outage or your phone runs out of juice, a paper copy of vital travel materials will save your organized behind.

When your itinerary is finalized, be sure you take a copy with you. You want to have all hotel names, addresses, contact phone numbers, and confirmation numbers with you. You should also leave a copy at home and email it to a family member or friend. In the event of an emergency, you want to make it easy for your loved ones to reach you. You can also install a tracking app on your phone so that your family literally knows where you are every second, if you feel comfortable with that.

Be sure to check with the TSA for the latest instructions regarding what is allowed onboard.

Fast food and snacks at the airport not only cost a fortune, they are filled with empty calories. Pack some healthy snacks, such as high-quality trail mix (pre-made comes with salt and sugar; make your own raw version), healthy food bars (consider making your own), dried fruit, and dried meat, or grab some fresh fruit. For the latter, think of something like a banana that comes in its own protective wrapper rather than a fresh peach that might leak its beautiful juice all over the inside of your purse. Not such a beautiful outcome.

Your vacation fun begins with the dream. The more organized your preparatory phase, the fewer hassles you will encounter. And as an organized person, if hassles do occur, you will dispatch them with ease!

WEEK TWO

The Travel Checklist

This week, you can

- Create travel lists so you understand what's really needed
- Learn how to pack a light suitcase

Time required: Thirty minutes to two hours, depending on how close you are to your next trip.

Now I want you to create a personal travel checklist. You may find it easiest to enter your list in Excel so that you always have the master. This is just like the master file list you created for your office files in "Organizing the Business of Life." Over time, you can tweak this master travel checklist as well. For example, if you are the mother of a new baby, your checklist is different from the mom who is traveling with a six-year-old and a nine-year-old. It's also different from the business traveler or someone on a pleasure trip.

How to begin? Make categories and start listing. When you're finished, save it as your "Master Travel Checklist" file. When it comes time to take a trip, you can make a copy on your computer just for that trip, using the "Master" file as your

guide. After you create your individual trip checklist, you can print it and keep a hard copy in your suitcase. When it comes time to leave home, you can check your list as you pack. You might even want to laminate it. Take it with you and check off items as you get ready to return home. Shay left her toiletries bag hanging on the back of the bathroom door in Xian. If she had had a list like this, she would never have left those expensive toiletries at the hotel.

You may find that you have lists like these provided in one of your computer programs or available for tweaking on an app you use. This is your assignment, but it isn't meant to be homework. Have fun and be creative! By the way, if you are a frequent traveler, you will find that this list becomes a part of you. One day you'll discover yourself checking items off in your head.

Here's a list to get you started. Of course, not everything on this list may apply to every trip. You just check off what you need at the time. As we get older and busier, established lists save us time. We don't have to create a new one for every trip we take. We can just check off what we need. I used to think my mother forgot things because she wasn't vested in life. If you live long enough, you discover your mental computer goes down periodically. I think less now about mundane things such as shopping and packing. I just grab my trusty list and start checking!

BASIC GROOMING

Contact lens solution and a few extra pairs of contacts

Deodorant

Disposable razor

Fragrances

Glasses (as a backup if you wear contacts regularly; a pair for reading if you need them; and if you wear glasses exclusively, an extra pair in case something happens to your favorite) and, of course, sunglasses

Lotion (body, suntan, and face)

Nail file or emery boards

Nail polish (for repairs)

Nail polish remover wipes

Shaving gear

Small packets of tissues for your purse or pocket

Soap (liquid or a bar, and soap leaves for your purse)

Toothbrush, toothpaste, floss, and mouthwash

Note: a Swiss Army knife will combine several of the above into one tool. Purchase a lightweight knockoff and you can have it with you daily, not just when traveling. You will want this tool in your checked bag.

MAKEUP AND HAIR NEEDS

Blush

Dry shampoo

Eyebrow pencil

Eye shadow

Foundation

Hair brush, comb, pick

Hair gel or mousse

Hair spray and gel

Lipstick

Mascara

Powder

Shampoo and conditioner

Sunscreen

Tweezers

Note: If you use wigs or hairpieces, you will need special products to keep them looking fresh.

FIRST AID

Antiseptic wipe packets

Band-Aids

Face masks (be sure you cut off the side loops when you toss the disposable version)

First aid cream in a tube

Hand sanitizer

Oral thermometer (non-mercury, non-glass)

Scissors (leave out if traveling by plane unless you plan to check a bag)

OVER-THE-COUNTER MEDICATIONS

Allergy, if needed

Antacids

Birth control pills

Headache medication

Insect repellent and after-bite cream

Lip balm

Moleskin for blisters

Motion sickness tablets (dimenhydrinate) or patch (scopolamine)

Sleep aids and ear plugs

Vitamin supplements

PRESCRIPTION MEDICATIONS

Extra written prescriptions in case of emergency (for life-saving medications)

CLOTHING

Bathing suit, sandals, aqua shoes

Blouses

Coat

Crushable sun hat

Dresses: day and evening

Dress pants

Exercise clothing

Jacket

Jeans

Leggings or tights

Shirts

Shoes: sport, casual, dress

Shorts

Skirts

Slacks

Socks: dress, sport, casual

Suits

Sweaters

T-shirts (unless you plan to pick up some souvenirs)

UNDERGARMENTS AND SLEEPWEAR

Bathrobe and slippers

Bras

Pajamas or nightgown

Underwear

DOCUMENTS

Directions and maps

Driver's license (REAL ID if your state issues them)

Emergency ID list and personal contact info

Friends' and family addresses for postcards (be sure the contacts on your smartphone are updated or post on social media to reach everyone)

Global Entry (includes TSA pre-check) expedites check-in for domestic and international travel. If you have a travel credit card, your yearly membership may cover the fee.

Immunization record, if applicable

Insurance documents: medical, travel, etc.

Itineraries, hotel, and contact information

Memberships that provide discounts, such as Auto Club

Passport, if applicable, and copy of passport (bring extra passport photos in case yours is lost or stolen)

Photo ID if you don't have a passport or driver's license

Tickets (airline, bus, and train, as well as any theater or show tickets you purchased)

(If most of these documents have been electronic issue only, be sure you have them in one folder on your phone, in a travel app, and backed up on the cloud.)

MONEY

Cash

Credit card (notify your credit card provider that you will be traveling abroad so you don't get flagged for potential fraud)

Debit card (be sure there are no foreign transaction fees)

Foreign currencies, if applicable

Traveler's checks, if applicable

MISCELLANEOUS ITEMS

Binoculars

Calculator for foreign currency (check your smartphone)

Camera (don't forget batteries or battery charger!)

Emergency sewing kit (the size you get in a first-class airline gift bag)

Feminine hygiene products

Flashlight (small for backup because your smartphone can function as a flashlight)

Jewelry

Laptop computer or iPad

Puzzles, games, deck of cards

Reading material (load the Kindle or e-reader app on your phone)

Small, flat carryall for souvenirs

Small travel umbrella and a raincoat or a disposable rain poncho

Smartphone and charger (use smartphone as your alarm clock and your camera to save items)

Sporting equipment, if applicable

Suitcase locks (TSA-approved for air travel; if they need to examine the contents of your suitcase, they will be able to open it without breaking an expensive lock)

Travel notebook and pen (or use a note-taking app on your phone)

Wet wipes (for your purse or pocket)

Wet wipes for stain removal

Work documents, if applicable

Ziploc bags (various sizes)

TRAVELING WITH CHILDREN

Books have been written about the subject of traveling with children, and tons of information exists on the internet. Probably the best advice will come from the more experienced parents in your circle. Go to all sources to compile a list that works best for you! Remember to create subheads for specific types of trips. For example, theme park vacations, beach vacations, travel by air, and travel by car will all have special needs.

I flew recently from Los Angeles to Detroit. When I got on the shuttle bus to go from the parking lot to the terminal, I saw something I could not believe. A woman was traveling with a young boy and a baby. She had a large suitcase, a smaller suitcase, a carry-on, her purse, and a stroller. I had to ask, "Is all of this yours?" I told her I was a professional organizer and I was in awe of her. I could tell she had travel and packing down to a science. I asked if her husband appreciated what a remarkable woman she was. She laughed and said: "Oh! He thinks this is easy." We all know a mother like this. She's your best guide.

While I prefer to see children use activities that engage them like reading or playing a card game with a sibling, there is no question that electronic screens have a hypnotic effect. If you need peace at the airport or on the flight, I say distribute those devices with abandon. But confiscate them upon arrival and time their use throughout the day.

Finally, let me say that as a frequent traveler, I do not want your child to kick my seat all the way across the country should I be sitting in front of him or her. Too many parents say nothing and leave it to a stranger to school their child in good manners. If "you do you" condones rude behavior, I am not a fan.

KNOW WHERE YOU'RE HEADED!

When I was a teenager in Europe, traveling with a group of other college kids, I set off

on my own one morning. Suddenly I realized that I didn't have the name of the hotel with me. I had no idea where I was staying! Because I was meandering for pleasure, I also had no idea how to retrace my steps. What saved me? A letter from my mother! It had been waiting for me at the hotel and I had grabbed it as I left. In that moment I realized how important contact information can be. Be sure you always have your itinerary and contact numbers with you. It's only one piece of paper, after all, so fold it up and tuck it away someplace safe. And again, a phone battery can run down, and a phone can be lost or stolen. Yes, have a battery pack, but you don't want to be stuck when a single piece of paper can save the day.

WHAT'S A PERSON TO WEAR?

Clothing should be chosen based on length of stay, activities, and climate. The cardinal rule is: less is more. Literally. You want to pack garments that can be mixed and matched to create new outfits. You want solid colors and easy care, wrinkle-free fabrics. Wash-and-wear is the ideal fabric-care tag you're seeking when you look through your wardrobe. Grab shoes that are broken in and guaranteed to be comfortable. Leave your jewels at home and bring out the costume pieces. Of course, if you're going to a special event like a wedding, you have to add additional items. Usually those trips don't involve sightseeing, so there will be room in your suitcase as other items like your shorts and crushable sun hat get left behind.

Before we went to China, I checked with a Chinese friend who had lived in Beijing and with the weather service. October in China is similar to the weather in New York City. I took a warm blazer and wore it on the plane. On the long flight over, it was my blanket. During the trip if it was a bit nippy, I was prepared. Shay, on the other hand, came overprepared. She had a warm jacket that was perfect. She also had a heavy winter coat. She never wore it. It didn't fit in her suitcase so she carried it all over China! I can't say enough about checking the weather service.

I'll tell you about something neither of us had. It was one of those travel lessons. Now I'll never leave home without one. What is my new find? An inexpensive rain poncho! We had a light sprinkling of rain one day in Xian. In two weeks that was the only precipitation we experienced. A couple from Texas had rain ponchos they had purchased at the dollar store before they left. Those ponchos weren't meant to last a lifetime, but they kept them dry in Xian. For a dollar they could be trashed at the end of the trip. And they were a lot easier to carry than an umbrella, even a travel-size one. If it's not the rainy season where you are headed, go to the dollar store today!

Let's take a pretend trip together and plan the clothing. You'll have the basic outline and can alter it again and again to suit your needs. We'll plan a five-day trip to Paris in late September. We're on our own. No tour bus or group to contend with. The purpose of the trip is to explore the City of Lights and have fun. We do have one business meeting on the fourth day. It comes late in the day, and afterward we will be taken to a lovely Parisian restaurant. Are you ready?

The first and fifth days are long travel days. I'd want to be comfortable and wear loose-fitting clothing on the plane. For me, that would be a comfortable pair of jeans and a nice sweater. We're going to be doing a lot of walking, so I'll be sure to wear those broken-in shoes on the plane. My warm blazer will serve as my only coat on the trip. I'll tuck a small travel umbrella in my bag. I don't want to bring a cheap poncho to Paris!

The second and third days we'll be up early and sightseeing. Europeans recognize Americans on the street because we're always in blue jeans. I would pack a nice pair of woolen slacks. I'll bring another sweater and a blouse. If there's a fall nip in the air, I have the sweater and, if it's warmer, I'll go for the blouse. Paris is a big city, so I'll have access to neighborhood cleaners if the need arises. Hotel services are my last resort because of the high fees they charge.

On the fourth day we have that meeting and dinner. I'll wear a skirt, a simple silk shell, and the one pair of heels I brought along for this event. My blazer will be a classic that seamlessly goes from business to fun. Each day what will change will be my scarves and jewelry. I once went away on a business trip for a weekend. No one noticed I wore the same pant suit but kept changing my blouse and my jewelry. (And I was one of the speakers, so believe me, they were looking!) If clothes make the man, then accessories make the outfit. For this trip I'd have a scarf for the plane and two for Paris. The company White and Warren is famous for its cashmere travel wraps. On travel days, it's your blanket. On location it's your shawl or wrap. It's an investment for a lifetime.

TOTAL

One pair jeans
One pair woolen pants
One skirt
One blazer
Two light sweaters
Two blouses
Three scarves
Two pair shoes
One umbrella
Jewelry

If you live in a city with a change of seasons and storage space is at a premium, remember to use your empty suitcase as the perfect off-season storage container. And always pack your shoes in shoe bags so that the dirt of the street isn't sitting in your suitcase waiting to grace your off-season wardrobe.

My wardrobe is simple by design. Now, you don't have to be quite this austere. You might want to return to the hotel each afternoon and change for dinner, which might require an extra outfit. The most important thing is to have a specific plan for every single thing that hits the suitcase. You don't want to be an emotional packer: "Oh! This is lovely, I think I'll take it." Or "Isn't this pretty? I'll take it along just in case." Pack with a purpose in mind for each item.

This week, you can also share the travel wisdom you learned from last week's exercises with your organizing group or other friends. Go around in a circle and let everyone share their discoveries. As each person finishes speaking, take a few minutes to discuss the merits of these ideas and tips. Take notes and profit from the group experience—the pool of travel knowledge should be amazing. You might also compare your master lists to see whether you left anything off. Perhaps at the end of the year, when you are all basking in the glow of having achieved your lifelong goal of getting organized, you can take a weekend trip together! I wonder who will have the smallest, lightest suitcase?

WEEK THREE

Before You Leave the House

This week, you can

- Identify things to do before you leave home
- Create a home inventory
- Prepare your home for your absence

Time required: Thirty minutes to make specific notes about the upcoming trip; an additional ninety minutes if you stop and create your inventory.

THIS WEEK, WE'RE GOING TO GO through our travel paraphernalia to be sure we're ready to leave home. You don't want to discover the day before your departure that your suitcase no longer serves you. Equally tragic would be the discovery that your favorite piece of carry-on luggage now reeks of the lotion you spilled coming back from your last vacation. We're also going to touch on that thorny issue of the second, or vacation, home. It can get confusing when you have more than one residence and duplicate items. I have a great tool for you to use to keep track of everything you own, especially your valuables. It's called a home inventory. But first, let's examine our gear.

- Check out your suitcase and overnight bag. Do they need to be replaced?

- Do you have a unique ID tag that helps you find your bag on the baggage carousel? (One of my clients ties a tulle bow on the handle.)
- Do you have a sturdy bag that you can fold up and put into your suitcase? If it's about the size of a grocery shopping bag, it can accommodate your souvenirs. In fact, a canvas grocery bag from your local market is ideal because it's lightweight, inexpensive, and sturdy.
- Do you need to purchase any other travel specialty items, such as a travel clock (smartphones usually have an alarm), an inflatable pillow, a jewelry travel case, or a blanket for the plane? (Lots of travelers swear by space-saver bags. These are not the space

bags we used in previous projects. You don't need a vacuum cleaner to get them to work. They are designed specifically for travel. I find them to be more trouble than helpful, but maybe they'll work for you.)

- If you don't mind using the airline pillow, bring your own pillow case. A travel wrap big enough to cover you if you wish to sleep and your own pillowcase will protect you especially during the era of pandemics. You can also carry on an inflatable pillow.

You should check with your cell phone provider before you leave the country. Tell them where you plan to travel and ask for the most cost-effective way to use your phone. You need to do this so that you avoid unexpected and exorbitant charges. If this is your family holiday, do you really want to be making calls home from London or Shanghai? Part of a vacation is leaving behind the constant need to communicate that society imposes on us. Research your options and your needs. And don't forget that if you're staying in a large hotel, you will have access to their business center. Your friends can communicate via email. I talk with a friend in Manchester, England, each week via FaceTime. It's free and we stay connected. When either of us is traveling, our Tuesdays at 10 chat is canceled for the week.

Be sure you appoint one or two ICE (In Case of Emergency) contacts on your phone. Should you be rendered unconscious, you want someone you trust to be guiding your medical treatments.

I have a lot of sympathy for kids who have to travel with their parents on long trips. It's one thing when it's a trip to Disney World and you can't wait to get there. It's another when you want to stay home with your friends or do something entirely different. I'd be asking: "Are we there yet?" myself.

Tell your children that they can't bring every toy they own. Then show them by example what an economical packer *you* are! Take something they love, bring a surprise (something they have been asking for), and promise them a souvenir from the trip. If your child loves to read, you are in the best situation of all. If he or she isn't old enough for a smartphone, you can turn an old one into an e-reader by downloading the app. Wipe it clean of personal info so if it's lost there is no private information to be gleaned.

Decide as a family where your vacation will be. Research together. If you're going to a foreign country, get an app that teaches common everyday phrases. Or find a native speaker on Instagram whose feed offers daily lessons. You'll all feel less lost.

Allow your children to do additional chores around the house as a way to earn extra spending money on the vacation.

Remember that children take their emotional cues from you. If you are happy about this trip, odds are they will be too. Are you traveling with teenagers? Before you go off the deep end, take a minute to remember what it was like. You're stuck in limbo between childhood and adulthood. Your body is a chemistry set of hormones that make you act in ways you don't understand and can barely control. Let some of those holiday outbursts slide. If you are now using aromatherapy, remember you can diffuse at the hotel. You can also make concoctions or purchase pre-made ones to counter stress and have them in a roll-on in your purse. There's a reason I always smell of sandalwood.

As soon as it's age appropriate, let children and teens be responsible for their own suitcases. I guarantee that "less is more" will be learned after one trip!

CREATE A HOME INVENTORY

A home inventory documents the contents of your home and is an invaluable tool for all homeowners, especially those with multiple residences. It's actually a practical tool for any homeowner or renter. If you are ever the victim of theft or a fire or flood, you can show your insurance company the items that have been lost. With very valuable items, you want to set aside the purchase receipt, as well as an appraisal or any provenance documents. You might want the originals in a safety deposit box and copies on hand. Scan those hard copies and pop them onto the cloud as well.

In the old days when I had to create an inventory, it was an arduous process. We used Polaroid snapshots and had to painstakingly document every item. With the advent of smartphones, we're all walking around with a digital camera and a video recorder, so you can easily document a room in minutes. Walk into each room and slowly show all the contents. Work from one end to another. You can make some comments as you do this. Remember that you're documenting large and valuable items as proof of ownership in the event of a disaster. The IKEA lamp you got for your daughter's room is not going to be an issue if you lose everything in a fire.

If you go to the app store you will find—shocker!—that there are several apps that help you create home inventories. They will offer different ways to document the contents and guide you through the process. I would check with your insurance agent and see if they have any specific recommendations. You can elect, for example, to have a blanket replacement amount but carry a rider for jewelry, in which case you would want each piece individually appraised and have purchase receipts.

With a home inventory, you'll always know what you have and where it is. If you do move from residence to residence, you can take all your inventories with you via the cloud or the app you used to create it.

In the case of multiple residences, I would absolutely use an app for a formal approach. I'm certain your insurance agent may recommend a private service that will go to each home and do the documentation needed. I can't imagine the Queen of England wandering around Windsor Castle with a smartphone and an app, can you?

Before we move on, I'd like to share a personal experience from a time when an inventory would have saved me weeks of work. When my parents died, it took three months to sort through their belongings. I vowed that I would live the rest of my life being ready to move at a moment's notice. "If you see it, pack it." This is my mantra! Yes, it takes some time to create a home inventory, but it takes more time to run around looking for things. A lot more!

THE WELCOMING HOME

After a trip, it's wonderful to be home, isn't it? Personally, I see everything in my life with new insight. You will find that coming home to an organized household is a special treat. I'd like to give you some tips on things you can do before you leave to make your reentry as smooth as silk. Are you ready?

Although I don't think you have to do a major cleaning before you leave, it helps if you do all the laundry, toss all the garbage, give any fresh food to a neighbor or friend, and make sure the place is picked up. No piles, please!

Be sure your pantry is stocked with basics. You might be surprised how comforting it is to know you have food in the house. Again, nothing that can spoil; otherwise you'll be greeted by an aroma that will knock you back out the door!

About a week before you leave, set timers so that lights go on and off in the evening. Be sure to use energy-efficient light bulbs. In Los Angeles, our DWP supplies every homeowner with a few long-burning bulbs each year. See if your city has a similar program. Energy-efficient bulbs cost more but last a long time. You can also invest in light bulbs that become flashlights when the power goes off.

Stop your newspaper delivery.

For longer periods of travel you can utilize the USPS's Hold Mail service. Otherwise, have a neighbor bring in your mail each day. Ask him or her to walk through the house to check for leaks, broken windows, and such. Be sure this person has your itinerary so you can be reached in case of an emergency. Leave your homeowner's insurance policy number out as well as the contact information for your agent. In fact, be sure you have that information with you at all times. I have a folder on my phone called "Insurance," and all communications from Geico (my carrier) go into that folder whether it's for renters insurance, automobile insurance, or an umbrella policy I carry. In an emergency, I only have to open one folder.

If you have plants, be sure someone knows how to take care of them. You will want to lower the thermostat, but be careful you don't suffocate or freeze your plants. If your collection is small, perhaps they need to be farmed out while you are away?

Speaking of care while you're gone, have you provided for Fido and Fifi? I prefer to have a pet sitter come and stay in my home rather than board my dogs. If you do board them, be sure to take along their favorite toy, a blanket for their crate, and an article of clothing that has your scent. An old T-shirt will do fine.

Whether it's a boarding situation or a pet sitter coming to your home, check references before you go. Be sure your pet's shots are current and meet the requirements of the boarding facility should an emergency arise. Last but not least, have your itinerary posted in your home or give it to the facility so they can reach you in an emergency.

A detailed itinerary and local emergency contact numbers are also key if you are leaving someone to care for your children!

Choose a good friend or family member who is at a distance and send them the details of your itinerary. In the event of an emergency like a plane crash or a terrorist attack, this adult could help coordinate things at the home front. Better safe than sorry, I say.

If you have a home security system be sure your house, child, or dog sitter knows what to do if the alarm is tripped by accident. Let your home security team know that you will be away and give them the names of those in residence.

If you tend to get homesick, take a favorite photo with you for your hotel room. When you get home, put out one or two souvenirs so that you will be reminded of the wonderful time you had. Speaking of photos, as you walk out the door get a shot of your stove. When you wonder if you turned off the burners, you can instantly literally check.

Unpack your suitcase within twenty-four hours of returning home! When a half-unpacked suitcase sits in the middle of the floor, it looks sloppy. Put your suitcase back where it gets stored.

Do your laundry within two days of returning home. Put everything away so it's there to serve you again. That's what our possessions are meant to do—serve us. In the unorganized home, they run our lives.

Again, be sure you leave a tidy home before you set out on a journey. You don't want to be stimulated mentally, emotionally, and Spiritually on your trip only to be instantly demoralized as you open the front door and realize you left your home a mess. My longtime dog sitter was fabulous taking care of my Golden Retrievers. He wasn't exactly the Tidy King. The day I was to fly home, he'd gather his things and my housekeeper would come by to clean and do laundry. It was worth every penny.

These precautions take a little time to put in place. But they will give you peace of mind and are worth the effort. The minute my plane takes off or my car pulls out of the driveway, I leave my cares and concerns behind. I want to be in the present moment where my journey is taking me, not mentally stuck at home. Having lived through a major earthquake and been in New York on 9/11, I see every physical object as a gift given to me by the Universe. It's all on loan. Put your safeguards in place and then don't look back. Own your stuff. Don't let it own you.

WEEK FOUR

Pack and Bon Voyage!

This week, you can

- Learn how to pack like a pro
- Pick up tips from a busy business traveler
- Get tips on car travel

Time required: Two hours to plan and pack if you're headed out of town.

I N THE BEST OF ALL POSSIBLE WORLDS, your prep work is complete a few days before you leave. There's a lot to do, so you want to schedule all necessary steps on your calendar. Give yourself some wiggle room because you are bound to have a delay or two. Perhaps you can take off this week on a mini-trip and experience the ease all this planning is meant to provide. So first, let's take a look at some basic tips for packing your suitcase.

GENERAL YEAR-ROUND TRIPS

Keep your travel paraphernalia stored in your suitcase. You don't want to have to hunt for the items you use only on vacation!

For example, when I travel abroad, I like to wear my passport and other valuables in a special pouch around my neck. I keep that pouch in my suitcase.

If you are a frequent traveler, have your cosmetics and overnight bag ready to go at all times.

Are you a music buff? Make a playlist just for this trip. In the future every time you hear one of these songs, you will be transported back to a special time.

Do you have any underwear you're ready to toss because you just got a new stash when you organized your closet? Consider taking the old with you and just tossing it as you go! Do the same with socks and bras.

With the ever-changing world of terrorist threats, be sure you check with your airline about the latest regulations for carry-on luggage. As of this writing, if you put all liquids and gels into a one-quart bag and no item is over three ounces, you're safe. But these guidelines can change. If you can't buy travel-size personal items, the dollar store or any chain pharmacy will have small containers so you can make travel sizes of whatever you need. Then you just have to refill the bottles as needed. Regardless of airline rules, you don't need the large economy size of any product you use.

Check the local weather report one last time. If a large storm has moved in, you might have to add a few articles of clothing. It's wise to check with the airline the night before and, as I noted previously, get your boarding pass and seat assignment.

If you are traveling abroad, check the government travel warnings for the country you are headed to visit. If it's a hot spot, check again the day before.

Keep all travel documents in one place, preferably in your home office. Again, you don't want to have to go on a wild goose chase the night before you leave to find your passport. I have a file folder called "Legal Docs." Some of my clients like to use a code name for this file. Call it "I Love Lucy" if you like, but just don't forget the code! You can also use an app like TripIt. It stores all your travel docs and can get flight info for all airlines.

Subscribe to your wireless provider to be sure you have all the latest updates.

Subscribe to your favorite airline's newsletter and collect air miles via their frequent flyer program. You'll find many ways to accrue miles through their site.

Here are two more of my favorite travel apps:

- InsureMyTrip.com will allow you to compare insurance policies for your flight should you decide you want coverage for canceled flights or emergency medical transport home, etc.
- SeatGuru will help you pick the best seat by showing you the configuration of your aircraft and what is available.

THE SUITCASE

When we pack, the suitcase is open and flat. We see a nice square that has to be filled. What we need to remember is that once the suitcase is closed, we pick it up by the handle and the contents of that nice flat world slide into new positions. As you pack, keep in mind where the true bottom is!

Put your heaviest items such as shoes on the bottom. You can keep them in individual shoe bags. Let the shoes create support for your packing tiers. They sell see-through packing cubes so you will always be able to identify which shoes you need.

Why let the inside of those shoes go unused? Fill them with goodies! Socks are the logical item, but feel free to be creative. If you have highly aromatic feet, you might want to skip this tip.

You can avoid wrinkles in many ways. Some people swear by tissue paper; others roll their clothes. The larger the roll, the less likely you'll have wrinkles. However, a big roll is a space hog, so keep it to two items.

Many travelers use cubes or specially designed soft containers to segregate types of clothing. For example, I might have a cube with all my underwear and another with undershirts or tees. I like this method because you are creating categories.

Using the side pouches of your suitcase is tricky. You don't want to store big items that will push into the center of the suit-case floor and essentially rob you of usable space. Use them, by all means, but do so with care. You can have a separate jewelry holder or you might wrap some jewelry in a pair of socks or a soft scarf and make use of those side pouches.

Some people put their toiletries in a special bag. Some of these clever bags can be hung on the bathroom door hook. I worry about forgetting this item like Shay did in China. If you have that master pack-ing list with you that I suggested, you will remember! I have everything in the one-quart Ziploc bag that's allowed by the TSA. Once I arrive at my destination, I switch to a makeup bag. The kind you get with a makeup purchase is perfect.

THE CARRY-ON BAG

Whether you need more than one suitcase depends, I think, on the reason for your trip rather than its length. If you have a lot of formal social engagements, for example, you need a large suitcase. For the rest of us, there's mix-and-match and the wonderful world of accessories.

If your carry-on is merely an adjunct to your suitcase, here are two rules of thumb to guide you. Have a change of underwear and a fresh top with you. If the airline loses your luggage, at least you can feel fresh while you figure out your strategy. Your fellow travelers will thank you. You also want all your legal documents and your toiletries. High altitude does strange things to lotions and potions and the containers that hold them. You want any spills, explosions, or leaks to happen in a small bag, not in your suitcase, where an accident can ruin your clothes.

I use a sneaky trick when I travel. I have a very large purse and one suitcase with me at the airport. My onboard purse is large enough to hold legal docs, my real everyday purse, and toiletries. It's actu-ally an overnight bag. When the airline rep asks to see my purse, I flash this bag. It's a bit of a cheat that will give you extra packing room in your suitcase. Coach makes the overnight bag I use. It's classy and wears well. You can find a version to suit your taste.

The material you have worked on this month should turn you into a champion traveler. Remember that every vacation will impose special demands. The tem-perature is a huge factor. The length of time you'll be away is an important con-sideration. Another big influence is where you are staying and, of course, the purpose of the trip. If you have a large family, create a list for each family member and ask them to check off items as they prepare to go.

HEY! HOW MANY BAGS YA GOT THERE, LADY?

Are you like my client Susann, who likes to check her suitcase? Susann gets on the plane with just her purse. The purse Susann carries is a large one that holds her valuables and important papers for her journey. She sends her personal care products and makeup onto the plane in her large suitcase. I like to have these items with me. There is no right or wrong; do whatever works best for you.

Now for some people and for various reasons (you're traveling with children or you have lots of meetings and formal functions to go to), you may need to check a bag, have a large purse, *and* take a carry-on bag. I would still keep all valuables with you in your purse. For me, the key ingredients

TIPS FROM A BUSINESS TRAVELER

One of my clients is an attorney who travels the globe for business. He came into my life as my client and like many others stayed to become a friend. Joe and I are both competitive personalities. When we get into a room and start organizing, look out. Joe holds the record as the client who worked with me the longest number of continuous hours. We started around 10:00 in the morning and quit at 2:30 the next morning! Joe won that round, however, because while I was traveling the freeways home, he stayed in his office until 5:00 a.m. working. If they ever host an organizing marathon, Joe and I are shoo-ins to win!

I asked him to share some key travel secrets he has learned over the years. Here are his tips:

- Wipe the air vent and serving tray at your airplane seat with a disinfectant wipe
- Have a portable charger even if your suitcase has one built in
- Travel adapter, if going abroad
- Earplugs
- Compression socks
- Noise-canceling headphones

Take a small roll of duct tape. If anything starts to fall apart (like your suitcase after a particularly brutal baggage handler flings it into the hold of the plane), you can secure it with duct tape. There's a reason Joe's nickname is MacGyver!

Call ahead to find out what amenities are provided by the hotels where you're staying.

Use a VPN not public/free Wi-Fi

When you travel for business, be sure to wear business attire on the plane. If your luggage is lost, you'll still be able to attend meetings. Business attire sometimes works wonders for getting upgraded.

Walk from your hotel room to the nearest fire exit and count how many doors you pass to reach the exit. In the event of a fire, even if it is dark and smoky, you'll be able to feel your way to safety. I think this last tip is worth its weight in gold. I've been all over the world and never thought to do this!

are money (cash, credit card, and a debit card), all travel documents (inoculations, tickets, hotel and car confirmations, and so on), sometimes a checkbook, and personal contact information (family and friends). In your carry-on, you can have your snacks and a basic change of clothes for one day in case your suitcase is lost. If you are traveling with children, you might reduce your extra clothing to fresh underwear only and use the extra space for toys. If your child is old enough to manage a small suitcase, have them bring little roller bags as carry-ons. That way they can carry and be responsible for their own plane entertainment, snacks, water bottles, and so on. In the final analysis, you should only have extra luggage if you need it, not simply because you can. And you won't know what you really need until you sit down and make a plan.

TRAVELING BY CAR

Taking a trip in our own vehicle certainly allows us to be more lenient with what we haul to the new location. Did you like my choice of verb? If you are taking too much, you are hauling stuff, not packing what you need. I would still plan carefully and use a checklist. No matter how you get there, why be burdened by too much stuff? After all, someone is going to have to pack it, unpack it, and make sure it gets back home. I want to say, "What a drag!" And that is literally what it is. Excess weight drags down the vehicle and lowers gas mileage efficiency.

Don't put off your car's pre-trip service until the day before you leave. What if you discover your vehicle needs a repair and the mechanic doesn't have the part in stock? If you need a rack or other tools that will enable you to take special equipment, be sure you order them well in advance. Take some time to get to know how to use your new tools quickly and easily.

Check your glove box and trunk before you start packing. Can you leave any items at home? If you travel with office supplies or some portable files, for example, you won't need those at Disney World! My male Golden Retriever was a very old man. I had lots of pillows and blankets in the back seat to keep him comfortable and safe. When I took a road trip without him, however, I transferred all that to my dog sitter's car. If little Spirit had to go to the vet, he still traveled in style and safety. What's in your car that could easily stay home?

After you're on the road, take a few minutes to clean the car out each evening, especially if you're traveling with young children. You'll be amazed what treasures the back seat holds for you!

Be sure you have a spare tire in good condition in your car. It's also nice to have some basic tools, such as jumper cables and a jack in case you have to change your own tire. In that rare emergency when I get a flat, I used to call the Auto Club. Ford is my current lease, and they offer a free tow service. Guess what? Geico offers towing with my automobile insurance! It's good to know you have options. Read the fine print so you are aware how many free miles per tow you get and what the cost per mile is after that. In an emergency, you want no surprises. It's also wise to carry an emergency kit with some dehydrated food or energy bars, a few gallons of water, one pair of exercise shoes, a wind-up radio, a flashlight, and a warm jacket or blanket. I have dogs, so I also carry food and biscuits for them, as well as their own stash of water. I can't tell you how many stray dogs have profited from my supplies over the years.

By the way, ladies, don't forget to have a small makeup kit in the glove compartment of your car. The operative word here is "small." I carry powder, lipstick, my favorite fragrance, a toothbrush, floss, and some toothpaste. Tissues are important to me, and you'll find them in every room in my home and of course in my vehicle.

If you have small children, you'll want a pop-up container of Handi Wipes. I didn't use them often, so my container dried out. Now I carry a spray bottle of hand sanitizer instead. Have fun with your emergency kits. Stock them to suit your personality. And set a reminder on your calendar or computer so that you check your kit every six months. You don't want to be hauling expired, dried-out products around!

THE BOTTOM LINE

We do three kinds of travel in our lives. Travel for pleasure broadens our life experience. I can tell you that standing in the shadow of the Great Wall changed me as a human being forever. A trip like this is worth its weight in gold. Make your pleasure travel a time of renewal. Enjoy it as the truly Spiritual experience it is. Don't let this kind of trip be about how many outfits you brought to wear.

Travel to see family and friends can reconnect us to our roots. Often, we dread these trips because there is so much emotional baggage. Try to rise above the normal family bill of fare. Enjoy the people to whom you are related and with whom you experienced your formative years. It is by understanding and treasuring the past that we sweeten our future experiences. Besides, they won't always be there for us to have this experience.

Business travel is rarely fun, but this time away from home can serve two purposes. First, we can honor the work that has been given to us. No matter what we do, we add to the nobility of life on planet Earth. We are part of a vast interconnected web. Without our contribution, the whole is diminished. Second, travel helps clear our personal mental cobwebs. We return home to view our situations in a new light.

I hope you enjoy all of your travels more now because you have less "baggage" to schlep around. Before we exit travel, let's spend a few minutes considering how we organize photos. We seem to document everything today, even the mundane, but travel offers us the opportunity to record our great adventures.

Documenting Our Lives with Images

There was a time when every home had secret boxes of loose, random photos hidden away waiting for an album. The box elicited feelings of guilt when seen while promises of producing extravagant albums after retirement were made. Travel exacerbated the issue because we all take so many shots. These days those boxes are an anomaly. We're all photographers every day snapping away and sharing our lives instantly on social media. Can you remember a time when you didn't know what your coworker had for lunch? It's a different world. Let's set some guidelines:

- Professional photographers take hundreds of shots to get the one you swoon over in a magazine. When you get home from a photo-worthy day, fearlessly delete the runners up and save the winner.
- Of course you love your child; but they will not be interested in thousands of photos documenting their every move. If they grow into that kind of adult, they will need therapy, not albums.
- Look deep into your heart and know which kind of person you are: the one who makes an album for every occasion or the person who, like me, transfers photos off my phone onto private Pinterest boards. I have them if I need them.
- Regularly sync your phone and your computer so you can remove photos from your phone (to keep space for the next great event that needs documenting). I have an external drive for my computer and just about

everything goes to the cloud and Dropbox as well. I can access either of those from anywhere in the world. Farewell to dragging albums out of a burning home. (It's good to replace your external hard drive every few years.)

- Should you want a formal keepsake for yourself or key attendees, sites like Shutterfly will help you turn your photos into albums.
- If you are the one who loves to scrapbook and make photo albums, set up a workspace in your home so you can make creating these projects a reward, not another item on your to-do list. Check out the (finished) basement, family room, or home office for space.
- Once you have albums, keep them on a prominent bookcase so family and friends can peruse them.
- If you like to see photos printed out, discard duplicates. Keep photos in special photo boxes until you are ready to work with them. Organize by event or individual.
- Photos fade over time, so be sure you have family photos from your grandparents digitized before you lose them.

It's a nonissue for some of us and a source of joy for others. There is no right or wrong. When it comes to whether or not you enjoy working with photos, you know what my favorite advice is: You do you.

SUMMARY

WEEK ONE

Write in your journal about past travel mishaps to learn from your mistakes and avoid repeating them in the future.

WEEK TWO

Create a personal travel checklist.

If you're working with a group, compare travel mishaps.

WEEK THREE

Examine all travel paraphernalia to be sure it's ready to go.

Create a home inventory.

WEEK FOUR

Understand the fundamentals of packing.

BONUS TIP

When I travel, I tuck a few sticks of incense in my suitcase. At each stop, I burn one to release the energy of the previous occupants. Yogis and Feng Shui practitioners do this all the time. Try it. The worst that can happen is that your hotel room will smell good! Do you stay in nonsmoking rooms and can't burn incense? Pull out your portable aromatherapy machine!

Exit Rituals

If you want to save local resources at your hotel, you can hang the "Do Not Disturb" sign out and do without maid service. I don't think you have to be as tidy in a hotel room as you are at home. It's a vacation or a business trip so fun or work activities are the agenda. I would, however, visually scan the room before you leave so you aren't returning to a room that looks like a cyclone blew through in your absence.

If you are a guest in someone's home, you'll also want the freedom to let your organizing hair down. Be conscious, however, that your host might need to enter the room in an emergency, and you don't want to appear like you have no respect for their living quarters. Ask if you can do the bed linens before you go or at the very least strip the bed and bring your sheets and towels to the laundry room. Take a short video of the room before you open your suitcase and be sure the room has been restored before you leave. Some people arrive with a host or hostess gift, while others send one with a thank-you note after they return home. I realize this sounds old fashioned. I think it's just good manners. We don't want to live in a world totally devoid of kindness and appreciation. Okay. I don't. Are you with me?

SURVIVING YOUR MOVE

We've wandered long enough in empty buildings.

I know it's tempting to stay...but I want to go home.

–RUMI

PEOPLE TEND TO THINK OF MOVING as difficult because so much mental, emotional, and physical work is involved. I think it wears on us because we are thrust into chaos and the unknown. We are attached to our things. They are imbued with our energy. Suddenly everything we love and depend on is hidden in boxes. Professional movers may be transporting everything and that means a crew of strangers has our stuff in their hands. And no matter how much you love the new location, you have to take the time to find the exact place where everything should go. A beginning always holds within its reality the end of something else.

As a professional organizer, I love moves. Every box holds mysterious wonders for me to release from the prison of paper and cardboard. I have the fun of finding the perfect place for everything and turning an empty shell of a house into a home; it's like Christmas morning. I probably average six moves a year—that

is, six moves for other people. I haven't moved in over eight years. I'll admit that when it's your own stuff in those boxes, it's no longer Christmas morning! It's hell week.

Your work is made much easier if you are packing an organized home. If you are getting ready to move and have been following along for eight months, you are in the catbird's seat. You have not only whittled down the majority of your stuff from the extraneous to the precious but have also been developing the skill of organizing. You are ready for anything.

Books have been written about how to have a successful move. If you are comfortable using the internet, pages and pages of free material are waiting for your perusal. You'll find tip sheets, references, information about your new city of residence, and more. If you consult with professional movers from large companies, they will offer you reference material as well. My job here is to get you pointed in the right direction. Like a kid in the candy store, I want you to recognize the best when you see it. Let's get started.

If a move isn't in your future or in the life of anyone you care about, feel free to use this month to catch up on previous projects or, if you have children, to take a peek at next month when we deal with children in their rooms and managing school work.

If you have a group, you can read the material and discuss your experiences with moves. You can also discuss the organizing projects you have chosen to tackle this month in lieu of a move. The commonality of all projects should be more obvious by now, as well as the inherent power of the Magic Formula.

HABIT OF THE MONTH

Each day this month, consciously devote five minutes to actions that move your impending relocation forward. Toss some tattered linens, call financial entities, clean out your Tupperware. The action is yours to choose.

If you are not facing a move, learn to devote five minutes a day to maintenance. Pretend you are here for the first time: What's out of place? One of my favorite clients calls this "seeing with fresh eyes." Organization is about creating good systems. And good systems are maintained with regular monitoring.

AFFIRMATION OF THE MONTH

I am guided with ease to my new home. I embrace the life waiting for me. I also bless and thank my current home. I release it to the new occupants. I am thankful for all the participants in this transition.

Self-Care Practice

This may be the most stressful organizing project you can undertake. Moving ranks high on the list of the top ten stressors for a human being. If you feel too frazzled for a quiet meditation break because you can't stop your racing mind, I've got you covered. Many of my clients use meditation apps. These offer guided meditations, which means you focus on the voice of the narrator and what he or she wishes you to consider rather than making an effort to clear your mind of all thought. If this appeals to you, jump on the meditation app bandwagon. Try a few and see which one you relate to the most. In a month filled with the upheaval of moving this might be your best choice, especially if meditation is new to you. You can also find guided meditations from Dr. Jon Kabat-Zinn and Sharon Salzberg on YouTube. They are leaders in the Mindfulness movement and you are safe in their hands. As Vietnamese Buddhist monk Thich Nhat Hanh, known as "the father of Mindfulness," puts it, "To practice Mindfulness is to become alive."

WEEK ONE

Moving Questions

This week, you can

- Answer the four key questions to planning a successful move
- Examine your emotions concerning this move
- Make preparations for the new location

Time required: This depends on the size of your move. Moving the contents of a studio apartment across town requires less planning than moving the contents of a four-story house to a new state. Allow two to four hours to flesh out a detailed plan. It will save you time, money, and energy in the coming weeks.

I'M LATE! I'M LATE! FOR A VERY important date!" The Mad Hatter in *Alice in Wonderland* is running here and there in a fit of frenzy. We all know someone like this, don't we? This person doesn't get much accomplished, but they forever make their days sound dramatic. Sometimes a big job like a move will turn us into a temporary Mad Hatter. Let's not go there!

This week, we need to answer four questions: How much time before the move? What's the budget? Is the new residence bigger or smaller than the current one? And are you moving all your possessions? You can use worksheets for these answers rather than your journal because I'd like you to create a special binder for your move. This way, as with a remodel, you needn't go on a quest for an errant piece of paper. If it relates to your move, it can be in only one place. Remember, if you use your phone for everything, you can scan all documents and have a folder on your phone. I still like the binder because you will surely receive brochures and collect samples if you are working with an architect, interior designer, or contractor. Binders come in all sizes, so secure one that's perfect for your unique situation. You may want a decorative box for swatches.

We're going to work on these questions later this week so that we have the lay of the land. However, should this move not be something you have embraced emotion-ally, I offer some journal prompts to help you come to terms with the experience.

As I wrote these words in 2007, my client Susie was planning to move across the coun-try. She saw this as a great adventure for her and her daughter, a new beginning in a part of the country they had not experienced. Not every move is eagerly anticipated.

When my parents passed away one year apart, I held on to their retirement home in the Allegheny Mountains outside Pittsburgh for five years. I never lived there. I literally visited my stuff. Looking back, it's a mix of the hilarious and the sad; it was the best I could do at the time, when an immediate move was beyond the scope of my emotional or physical well-being. I didn't understand the power of attachment to stuff the way I do now. What twenty-five-year-old does?

However, this experience ultimately created my ability to move with ease for the rest of my life. It also planted the seeds for developing my talent to help others. If you look for the gift sitting in the middle of the sorrow, you will find it's always waiting patiently for you. Sometimes all it takes is a willingness to see things differently. And that's what this week is all about.

Please answer the following questions in your journal if you are facing a move you dread.

- Why are you moving? Please be spe-cific. For example:

    o Is it to care for an older relative?
    o Have you taken a job in another city or state?

    o Has your spouse taken a job that is uprooting the family?
    o If you are a renter, has your build-ing gone condo or been sold?

These are a few of the more common reasons why people leave the homes they love. What is yours? After you note the reason for your move, take some time to write in your journal about it. Here are some ideas to get you started. As always, specifics are golden:

- Are you afraid that you won't be able to adequately care for your elderly parents or relatives?
- Are you one of several children in a large family who has been given the task of caring for a parent or relative?
- Are you angry with siblings and rela-tives for foisting the task of caring for a parent or relative on you?
- Do you feel your career is going to suffer because of this move?
- Are you in any way jealous of your spouse for his or her good fortune?
- Are you leaving behind a strong net-work of friends?
- Is it difficult for you to make friends easily?
- Do you love the home you have now and fear you won't find anything as nice again?

Good old-fashioned fear is usually at the heart of the matter. After you identify yours, you can list some anecdotes. Here are some examples. Let's say I love my home and fear I will never find another like it. A house is brick and mortar. A home is the conscious creation of the inhabitants. And love is the key ingredient. Love isn't packed in a suitcase. It can't be left behind. You take it with you and decide to whom among your new circle you will extend the gift of friendship. You are also in charge of staying in touch with those you are leaving behind. What creative ways will you employ to do just that? The internet has made this step easy, with Facebook and Zoom leading the charge.

Remember that your possessions are traveling with you. Embrace the challenge of decorating the new space. Perhaps this is your opportunity to experiment with bold paint colors. Or perhaps you will sell most of your furniture and start creating a new look for your family. Did anyone say dream/ vision board? I hear Pinterest calling now.

I am not shy in professional or work situations. I am shy in social gatherings. Are you like me? Why not join a church, mosque, or synagogue? What about taking some classes at the local community college? Are you a member of a profession? Attend some meetings sponsored by organizations that cater to your group. When I first moved to California, I was a professional actress. I made lasting bonds in my acting class, in the part-time jobs I held, and at the church I attended at the time.

This is your week to uncover the fear and send it packing with a plan. Whether you are in this group or you just can't wait to move, the next step is to answer the four questions. This is a nonemotional, left-brain assessment of the task at hand. Are you ready?

THE FOUR QUESTIONS

You will be amazed how powerful and in control you will feel after answering the four questions in this section. If you're in panic mode, these questions will restore calm.

Question One: How Much Time Before the Move?

After you have a date set, it pays to break your move into sections and then schedule each related task. Work backward from the move date. For example, it can take up to two weeks for your mail forwarding request to be honored. Ask your regular postal delivery person what he or she recommends. Then schedule your visit to the post office on the day suggested or schedule the change online. You don't want to do this at the last minute and wait for two weeks for your mail to start arriving. This can make you late on some payments, and the last thing you need is to ding your credit report.

Let's take a look at a typical list of vendors and companies you'll need to contact. These include the following:

Animal care providers
Cable or satellite connection
Catalogues
Childcare providers
City services such as trash pickup (in most cities, homeowners get an extra free trash pickup after a move to help get rid of the moving debris)
Doctors and all health-care providers, for medical records and copies of active prescriptions

Financial institutions (If your bank is part of a national chain, check to see if there is a local branch in your new city and submit a change of address request. Alternatively, don't forget to set up a bank account in the new city when you have your new address and to empty any safety deposit boxes if you are leaving the area.)

Friends and family

House of worship

Insurance companies (auto, homeowners, life, disability, and so on)

Magazines

Newspapers

Phone

Post office

Professional and personal clubs and other memberships

Schools

Utilities

What would you need to add to this list?

In this day and age, when customer service reps at most companies can drive you to distraction, you might want to set aside two days for nothing but phone calls. If this is not possible, carve out twenty to thirty minutes each day until each one has been contacted. Remember to get confirmation numbers and the names of those assisting you. Take a deep breath before each call and brace yourself for delays. If you are internet-savvy, see how many items you can cross off your list by going to the company's website or sending an email. We're an automated society now. The trick is to secure that receipt and save it on your computer or phone in a special folder created for this move.

Question Two: What's the Budget?

Your budget is a key consideration because it dictates whether you use professional movers or rent your own truck and call in favors from friends. It will also determine whether you pack or have the movers do it (my choice). A budget will also dictate if you will be unpacking yourself or hiring someone like me to do it for you. I would suggest that you not have the movers unpack you. Movers are not professional organizers. They literally unpack, leaving you with a sea of unwrapped possessions and crowded closets instead of a sea of packed and labeled boxes. With the latter, you can open everything at your discretion and it's all safe and organized until you do unpack. Getting the boxes and furniture into the designated rooms is the main task of your mover.

When you have your budget, be sure it's the amount set aside for the actual move. Moving, even if you do it yourself, is an expensive proposition. The amount of stuff you are transporting, the distance you are traveling, and the amount of packing supplies are key factors. You may have no control over the distance, but you can certainly determine how much you are taking with you. If you have been working for several months now, you have many of your possessions already in plastic containers.

You may need to paint or do some touch-up work at the new residence. You will surely have to leave deposits with new vendors. You want to be sure you know how much money you realistically need for each wave of the operation. A frequent comment I hear in the days following a move is, "Regina, I'm hemorrhaging money!" Establish your budget and be realistic. Don't just wave a credit card at every expense.

Question Three: Is the New Residence Bigger or Smaller Than the Current One?

If your new home is bigger and you have generous funds, you can enjoy the process of decorating and shopping. If funds are tight, just buy the essentials and feather your nest over time. Again, I would set a target date for completion even if it's a year. You'd be surprised how many people can't face moving in and "owning" a space. Walls stay bare. Rooms get used for storage and remain filled with debris. Instead of a home, they camp out for years. Take out your calendar and schedule your goals for the new home.

Question Four: Are You Moving All Your Possessions?

Moving is a great time to downsize. Or should I say, it's a great excuse to downsize! After you have settled on the new location, take a sheet of paper and list all the rooms in your current home. Leave a little space and, under each heading, list the major items from that room. Put a check next to each one that is going with you. If it isn't, make a notation of its fate. For example, "give to Aunt Marie" or "donate to charity" or "sell on eBay or Facebook Marketplace."

Don't worry if you don't know all the answers the day you create the list. This will help you make a plan. When you're finished, you'll know how many items are going to charity, how many will be sold, and which ones are being given to family or friends. Now you can set about scheduling charity pickups and calls to relatives. If you enjoy yard sales, schedule that too. There are detailed instructions in the section on tackling the hidden areas.

ONE-STOP SHOPPING

At the start of the month, create a binder for the move. You can use tabs to separate the sections. I would use sheet protectors rather than three-hole punch original documents. That way, the documents will stay clean and the binder will be more inviting to use. You can, of course, have a digital-only record of important docs. Following are some ideas for the various sections you might need.

Children

I'd put school information here, as well as sports or hobby materials you have researched. A lonely child who misses her friends but loves to horseback ride will be cheered up if you present her with some information about the stable down the street!

New Home

Here you can keep your moving contract, insurance policies, documents from banks and utility companies, and worksheets. If your move involves a purchase of a home, keep key documents here as well.

Our New Hood

If you are moving to an area that is totally new to you, you'll want to do some research on your city. The internet puts the world at your fingertips. Bookmark some basic information to help make your first day run more smoothly or save it in a folder called "New Neighborhood" under the category "Move." Where is the nearest supermarket, cleaners, or Starbucks? It's nice to know, isn't it? You might call this section by the name of your new town to personalize it. The GPS on your phone will help you feel like a native.

Pets

Fido and Fifi may get a little upset with all the changes a new move involves. Be sure to have their immunization records handy and the name and address of their new vet. Be sure you also have any pertinent medical info should either of them have a chronic condition. Don't forget to follow the local ordinances regarding licenses for your furry friends as soon as possible.

Preparation

The first section can house all preliminary materials.

Travel info

This section is for hotel, flights, directions, and so on, if this is needed.

A WORD OF WARNING

This is not the time to fret over organizing projects you didn't complete. It's a waste of time and money to haul belongings with you that should be sold or donated. It's equally a waste of time to sit down and work on a project such as completing your photo albums. Put your photo collection in archival storage boxes and send them off to their new location. If you are not excited about this move, be conscious of the time wasters that will try to draw you away from creating a battle plan. "Oh! There's that needlepoint project I never finished. I think I'll work on that instead of this silly list." No matter what it takes, stay focused!

The Roman Furniture

I spent a day with a client who would let me touch nothing. I gave her instructions and she did whatever I asked her to do. I felt like a puppeteer. Raleigh felt that if she let me do the organizing, somehow she was a failure. This is like hiring a caterer and then saying you need a grocery list and recipes and will do the meal yourself. This was the only time I ever experienced a client with such a specific type of low self-esteem. We weren't together long enough for me to uncover the cause. On the surface she had everything, including a husband who adored her, healthy children, and an ocean of money.

The new home was in a wealthy area in Los Angeles. They shipped everything from their Rome townhouse to Los Angeles. It doesn't take a genius to figure out that what is elegant and appropriate in Rome will look odd in a casual, sunny climate thousands of miles away. With the new furniture put in place, it was instantly clear it should all have been sold in Italy. New furniture was purchased, and the Roman contents wound up in the large garage where they were languishing when I arrived. No decision had been made on their ultimate disposal.

These good folks were fabulously wealthy and the expense meant nothing to them. The average family does not have expendable income on this level. I don't want to see you waste money, because even if you can easily afford it, the money you save can go to a charity. Believe it or not, it's common for folks to assume that what they own will work anywhere. Trust me. Not always.

WEEK TWO

Pack Up

This week, you can

- Meet with professional movers, even if you plan to do your own move, to gather tips and tricks
- Continue to eliminate whatever you can and get it out of the house ASAP
- Start packing if your move is imminent

Time required: Depends on how close you are to the move. If the move is more than six months away, allow two to three hours for research either on foot, by phone, or on the internet. If it's coming up soon, complete your research in a few hours and devote additional time each day to packing, if you are responsible for that.

I F YOU PLAN TO PACK YOURSELF, ASK someone who is experienced at packing breakables for some tips. Some professional organizers pack households. And some organizers like me leave that to professional movers; we do the unpacking. You might call a moving company to see if they have a mover who can give you a few hours. Some moving companies have lots of workers who "job in" on an as-needed basis. You may even have a friend who likes to pack. If my client Susie ever wants to walk away from corporate America, I swear she could be a professional packer. She did her entire house in Burbank without help. When I met her in the South to get her settled, nothing was broken. She's a pro!

If you go to a box store, they will tell you the correct size and type box you need for everything you are packing. They also have tip sheets. Moving truck rental offices, professional movers, and the internet will all give you guidance. You don't have to buy anything or hire anyone. You can go on fact-finding missions. You'll find how-to videos on YouTube and sites like

HOW TO PACK

Here are some key things to remember if you are doing the packing:

- Don't lay dishes flat on the bottom of a box. Stand them up and have one lean against the other, using lots of paper around each plate to cushion movement. If a box gets dropped, dishes that are stacked tend to break in half.
- Remember to cushion the bottom of the box with extra paper. This applies to all boxes with fragile items. Be generous with your paper: Better safe than sorry.
- You may want to invest in special boxes known as dish packs for all your kitchen items. They are made with a thicker cardboard that provides extra protection.
- I would purchase packers paper because the ink from newspaper makes everything you own filthy.
- If you have fragile, valuable, or sentimental items, you may decide to wrap them in bubble wrap, then place them in a moving box with a dense layer of crinkled kraft paper so they get double the cushion.
- There are special boxes geared for all the various items in your home. For example, never put books in a large box. Use small file boxes or purchase special reinforced boxes. You can give yourself a hernia if you use a big box!
- Use soft, unbreakable items such as sheets and towels to cushion fragile, breakable items.
- When you pack items with lots of parts (such as kids' toys), make liberal use of Ziploc bags.

You would be surprised how much time gets wasted looking for the smallest of objects. Label the contents of each bag.

- Be conscious that what goes on the truck last comes off first.
- If you have valuable antiques, hire a dealer or antique shop owner to come in and pack them for you.
- When you pack entertainment items (DVDs, CDs, and VHS tapes), try to use small boxes if your collection is large. You might also be able to keep your categories intact this way, which will make unpacking a breeze! If you have long ago popped your media onto the cloud, pat yourself on the back.
- Leave clothing in dresser drawers. You'll have to refold, but that's not a big deal.
- Purchase special boxes called dress packs for your hanging clothes. The tall box comes with a rod for your hangers. Don't overpack. I've seen clothing arrive so wrinkled it was all unwearable.
- Make use of the space at the bottom of a dress pack. Toss in your shoes and boots or hat boxes. The cardboard ones will survive. Provide cushioning for the acrylic ones and wrap them for safety. Scratched and/or cracked is not the look you seek.
- Sometimes you realize you have some breakables you forgot. If you have a large box, put breakables on top of heavy items. You'd be surprised how many people don't think and put heavy items on top of delicate ones. Don't tempt fate!
- When you rent your truck, rent a dolly or two and lots of movers pads. You want

to protect not only your furniture but the floors at your new location.

- Lots of people are now recycling their boxes online for a fee or free. Some consumers are returning the used boxes to the moving company. If you rent them rather than purchase, you save a little.
- Even if movers are packing you, you might want to save some money on moving day.

How? Save time beforehand: Do some of your own packing! Ask the moving company rep to bring some boxes with him or her. I would pack only nonbreakable items such as towels, linens, books, and any media you own.

- If you have valuable paintings or expensive mirrors, pay to have them professionally crated unless you can hand carry them to the new location.

eHow.com. Remember that moving is a skill, and watching a few videos will either inform you or make you realize you need a pro.

If you are still working or managing your family or both, you must take extra precautions to keep yourself healthy. This is not the time to cheat on your sleep or your food intake or to stop drinking water. It is in fact the time to be hypervigilant about all of them! It is also the time to ask for help. When people tell me they don't want to bother their friends or family members, I have to wonder about the quality of those relationships. Are the connections based solely on sharing the good times? Ask for help. The day is coming when your friend will need you. The self-care practices in every section will also help you when panic starts to rise. It's one of the reasons I focus on them every month and offer a wide variety. I'd do some breath work and then meditate to start. While I did packing or prep work, I would diffuse oils, play music, or plan a break to do some yoga.

Please read through all the material for next week, even if you choose not to use a professional mover. I have tips and tricks you can adapt to your move. For example, I put up signs for my movers to direct them in the new location. You'll want to do that for the family and friends who are helping. After all, they want this to be over quickly more than you do!

WEEK THREE

Deal with the Movers

This week, you can

- Learn how to find a quality mover
- Keep your movers happy
- Welcome the pod people or pack the pod
- Place furniture in advance
- Create mover alerts!

Time required: Three to four hours.

FINDING A GOOD MOVER IS NOT A SIM-
ple task. You want to find a company
with an established history and a set staff
of movers. Why is this important? Because
when a company "jobs in" laborers, you
may not get someone who is as experienced as you might expect or as careful or,
quite frankly, as honest.

Look for a family-run operation and
interview two or three companies. Check
them out with the Better Business Bureau.
A recommendation from a friend or satis-
fied customer is always worth its weight in
gold. A move across town is one animal. A
long-distance move is a horse of a different
color. Here are some questions to ask the
person who comes to your home to give
you a bid.

Don't be afraid to ask about their position with the company. Is he or she the
owner? If he or she is an employee, is
the company so large that this person
never actually meets the moving crew?
Will the truck that pulls up to your home
be the vehicle that transports your
stuff across the country? Or will there
be a stop at a warehouse or a transfer
to another van? Remember: Every time
your things are moved, there is a possibility of breakage or theft.

What is the cost of their insurance? Contact your homeowners insurance and
see if your existing policy will cover
you. Find out the consequences if
something breaks and what happens if
it was in a box that you packed.

Ask about the mover's labor force. Do they job people in or is this a set crew?

Be sure you have finished eliminating items from your home so that the company rep isn't factoring in items destined for a charity or some other destination, such as your Aunt Marie's house. Every time you add or subtract items, you cause a ripple that is reflected in your estimate.

Be sure you understand how the final payment will be made. Usually it's a cashier's check or credit card at the destination. If you show up with a check (especially from an out-of-state bank), they will literally refuse to unpack the truck. Trust me. I've seen it happen.

HANDLE WITH CARE

We all like to be treated with respect. And that applies to your movers. Most of my clients over the years have been generous. Every so often someone balks at the idea of giving a tip or providing some food because the move itself is so expensive. Let's look at it this way: This crew has all your worldly possessions in their care. You want them to be happy campers. Movers are human beings. They'll go the extra mile to grab that falling box if they feel you care.

Have coffee and donuts ready in the morning, provide a few pizzas or sandwiches for lunch, have bottles of cold soda or drinking water on hand, and give a tip. You'll reap a big dividend. When you get to moving day, be sure there's a working bathroom that the movers can use. Have

some soap, paper towels, and toilet paper on hand. Set this up at the new location as well.

In addition to appreciation, movers like clear direction. This little exercise will save you time and energy on moving day. And you know what they say: Time is money. Let's move on and do some additional preparation.

THE KNOW-IT-ALL THAT'S YOU!

"Where does this go?" This is the question of the day when you're dealing with movers. We want to devise a way to make life easier. Remember the pages you wrote designating the destination of the stuff in each room? Take them out this week, because we have part two. Please take a sheet of paper and draw a line down the center. Label the left column "Current Home" and the opposite column "New Home."

Step one is to list the rooms. Under each room indicate only the furniture that's making the journey to the new house. In this exercise, we are not concerned with donations or sales. Use the pages from our previous exercise as your guide. If a room also houses a large collection, make note of it. For example, in the family room you might have your old VHS, DVD, and CD collection. Simply write "Entertainment Collection."

Step two is to write down all the rooms that are the same in both homes. For example, "Kitchen" will be the same. You'll no doubt have at least one bedroom and one bathroom. The contents of these rooms are the easiest to transport.

I like to make signs for my movers. You

can generate them on the computer in a simple Word document. I call them "mover alerts." For example, on the door leading into the kitchen, I would tape a piece of paper with the following instructions:

MOVER ALERT!

Please Label The Boxes From This Room:

KITCHEN

SAVING ON A LONG-DISTANCE MOVE

A few years ago, one of my assistants decided to move from the East Coast to California. As you can imagine, this is an expensive proposition. Linda, however, is full of entrepreneurial spirit and is a master researcher. She decided to whittle her possessions, including furniture, down to what she truly needed and loved. Linda decided to use a portable storage and moving company. She had a pod delivered and, with the help of her sister, packed it over a two-day period. The company picked it up and delivered it to California, where the sisters had hired local movers to unload it.

This type of move requires special skills. First, you have to be a great packer. You're not only packing boxes, you're packing the storage container itself. You need to have a place to park the container and you need to transport your belongings to it. A dolly laden with heavy boxes isn't something everyone can handle. If you have the skill and the patience, a portable storage container is a unique way to go. And there is no question it saves a fortune on long-distance moves. Is there one in your future?

It's obvious, of course. But signs everywhere get the movers into the habit of reading as they enter each room. By the way, don't think because you gave the company representative detailed instructions that all the worker bees are in the know. The instructions were of course recorded. If it's a local move, someone will be in charge, and he or she has probably read the instructions. On a long-distance move, the person in charge is usually the driver of the rig, who will most likely have read everything. You should take the person in charge on a tour of the premises and be sure he or she is privy to and aware of all your instructions. This is one day when overkill is not possible!

WHAT DEN?

Let's say you are moving to a larger house. Until you purchase additional furniture, you are going to distribute what you have a little differently. The movers walk into a room at 7 a.m. and guess it's your den. That's what they label the boxes. Now flash forward in time. You get to your new home and the guys are asking you where the boxes marked "Den" go. You're stumped. You had no idea you had a den! You called that room in your old house the family room. To complicate matters, in the new house there won't be a family room. You're going to be gathering in the living room. There would be no confusion if a simple sign had been attached to the door in your old house that said:

MOVER ALERT!

Please Label The Contents From This Room:

LIVING ROOM

Now take the next step. Generate mover alerts for the new house. You arrive before the movers and hang new signs. As the movers tour the new home, they see that every room is labeled! They see too that you set up a bathroom for them. Everyone is happy and confusion has been reduced. Don't despair, by the way, if your furniture looks a little different than you imagined. I always ask my clients to be there on move-in day just long enough to be sure the furniture is in the perfect position before the movers leave.

Before we abandon this topic, let me say that you can also use large colored dots to identify boxes. You can find them at any chain supply store such as Staples or, of course, Amazon. Add them to your mover alerts and leave a supply of the correct color in each room for use on the boxes in that room. You can also find moving kits with preprinted labels while you're out shopping. Nothing, however, beats moving alerts because they are tailored to your individual needs and situation. And it costs pennies to create them on your computer.

As you can see, whether you are packing the boxes and driving the truck or a bunch of pros are doing the work, moving day requires lots of planning. I promise you it's easier to sit with your journal and work things out now than to frantically run around on moving day shouting: "Why didn't I do anything Regina suggested?" You know what they say? Trust me!

WEEK FOUR

Moving Day

This week, you can

- Have a detailed plan ready for moving day
- Be mindful of "last on, first off"
- Have your "Family Essentials" and, if applicable, "Pet Essentials" boxes ready
- Prep the new home before your arrival
- Set up work conditions that help rather than hinder you

Time required: If you're just reading, allow thirty to sixty minutes to absorb and take notes. If you're moving, you'll be busy every day for the entire week!

OUR GAME THIS WEEK IS TO PRETEND it's moving day. All theatrical plays have dress rehearsals before the show opens. In this case, the dress rehearsal takes place in your head and by reviewing your notes. If you don't have a pending move, you are now in a better position to be helpful to a friend who is on the move, so to speak. Allow me to say that during a move when friends and family members are providing the muscle, one person needs to be in charge. If boxes are being opened in every room with no rhyme or reason or any kind of direction, it's going to take the resident even longer to get settled.

The large wardrobe boxes used to transport hanging clothes are expensive. If you can get them emptied before the movers pull out of your driveway, you won't have to pay full price for them. Sometimes my assistants, in an effort to save our client money, will start taking clothes out of the wardrobes faster than I can organize them. It is at this juncture that we realize that the amount of clothing coming into the home is greater than the closet space provided.

We know something else as well: Not enough elimination occurred at the point of origin. It is cheaper in the long run to set some wardrobe boxes aside and deal with them over the next few days than to smash too much clothing into an inadequate space. Unpacking is like putting together a three-dimensional puzzle. We have to use closets, shelves, dressers, and storage bins to make it all work. We also have to encourage our client to review what was packed in the event too much has been transported to the new location. In this instance, I am the quarterback calling the shots. You'll have to play that role with your friends and family.

WHEN THE BIG DAY ARRIVES

Here are some moving-day tips from the Zen Organizer™.

Keep in mind this phrase: Last on, first off. These are the items you will want to have immediate access to at your new location. They can only get there first if they go on the truck last. Be sure you mark the boxes clearly and communicate your wishes to the movers.

In case of delays or emergencies, you may not get anything unpacked on the first day. Be sure one of the last boxes on the truck is labeled "Family Essentials." Think toothpaste, deodorant, a small first aid kit, prescription meds, and so on. And if everyone has a clean towel and some fresh PJs, they should be okay. Tuck in a fresh T-shirt, clean underwear, and socks for the next day. If you are making this move during the winter months, you'll have to adjust the list to include a few blankets and sweaters.

Another box that should go on last and come off first is "Pet Essentials." This is not a time when Fido and Fifi should be without their favorite beds, dishes, bowls, food, and treats. Set your pets up in a private area in the new home as far away from all the chaos as possible. Be sure they have clean water and food. I like to put a sign on the door that says something like this: "Please Do Not Open: Pets Inside!" If Fido and Fifi are escape artists, one crack of the door and off they'll go. You don't need this drama on moving day.

You also want your dress packs on last and off first if this is a move by professional movers. If this is a family-and-friends affair, it's less critical because you don't have to return these boxes for credit.

Another on last and off first box is one with basic bedding for the family. The goal on the first day is to get linens on the beds, the hanging clothes in the closet, and the essentials unpacked in the bathrooms and kitchen.

Speaking of the kitchen, if you are a person who needs coffee first thing in the morning, have a "Kitchen Essentials" box so you can begin your new life in this home on the right note!

Finally, if this is a long-distance move, you may need to keep the following items in a box you can access immediately: extension cords, light bulbs, phone charger, possibly a landline phone, a few box cutters, and a can opener. What else would you include in this "Emergency Household" box?

Never, under any circumstances, leave valuables unattended. This includes jewelry, small safes, cash, and legal documents with sensitive information, such as your social security number. Your homes at both ends will be open for easy access by the movers. It would not be difficult for someone from the street to gain access to the house. You'll always wonder if your mover pulled a fast one. Don't put them in an awkward position.

THE NEW HOME

If you have access to your new home before move-in day, be sure to schedule as much work as possible. Does your home need new carpet? Should it be painted? It's also important, no matter how tidy the previous tenants, to have your home cleaned before you arrive. Good movers are very careful, but they are human beings. Walls may get a bit dirty, so have some touch-up paint handy. Try a Magic Eraser first and maybe obviate a more formal touch-up.

If you can recycle your packing paper and boxes, make every effort to do so. You can always offer them online either for sale or free pickup. If your neighborhood or building doesn't recycle, be sure you call for that extra trash pickup. Ask if there are any special directions for preparation of the materials. You will surely have to cut the boxes down. Tie them together, keeping sizes in specific groups. The packing paper is always a problem. Stuffing it into boxes is easier than into huge trash bags. One of my assistants once got herself stuck in a room because her trash bags of packing paper were too fat to get through the doorway. I swear. We rescued her and had a good laugh.

As you unpack, it's important to get empty boxes out of the way. I have a guy who sweeps through the house every hour to take away whatever boxes my assistant and I have unpacked. He cuts them down. He also checks the paper to be sure we didn't miss any small items. This is great work for any strong teenagers you might have at home—not to mention a great way to earn a little extra money and help the family get settled.

Do you like music? I find that putting on upbeat music makes the moving and unpacking process go faster. Speaking of happy movers, if you decide to tip them, use cash. If their tips go into the check you write, they may never see the money. You can give all the tips to the supervisor and ask him or her to distribute them. He does get a bit more than the others.

You have to base your tip on several factors. Here are some of the things I take into account: How much stuff was moved? Did these guys pack *and* move? How long did the move take? Were there circumstances (a flight of stairs, a broken elevator) that made it more complicated for them? How polite were they—that is, do they deserve a tip? Did they seem to take care of your things during transport? In other words, were boxes placed on the truck with care or hurled on with great abandon? Were they mindful of the fresh paint at the new location? Did they damage any furniture? Your tip represents a thank-you for good service.

Let me give you an example of a move where I urged my clients *not* to tip anyone. These guys showed up late. One had clearly been out all night: He had blood-shot eyes and was still in his party clothes. They didn't have any packing paper, so most of the boxes were inadequately lined, and we had breakage. They dented furniture, took paint off the walls, and were rude to me and my clients. They treated us as if we should be grateful they decided to show up. When you do that, you don't deserve a tip!

Finally, your mover will present you with a manifest. As he or she packs every single box and piece of furniture, it is assigned a number. At the new location, you should cross off items as they exit the truck. If an item is missing, your lead person will give you a form to fill out. Every large moving company is different when it comes to how well they respond to loss and damage. You have to do the paperwork and stay on top of your claim. If your move is local and the truck moves immediately from one location to the next, it's highly unlikely anything will get lost. There's no opportunity. As I mentioned earlier, loss most often occurs during the long hauls, where the truck may get repacked at the warehouse.

Let me add one caveat: If you are working with a company that either you know or perhaps your professional organizer works with on a regular basis, you don't need to cross off each item as it exits the truck. I've never had a single case of loss with my favorite mover, nor has anything been broken. If you're working with a professional like me, you can be sure we recommend only the best. After all, our reputations are on the line.

When you move into a new home, it's nice to do an unofficial ceremony to clear out the previous owner's energy and declare the space your own. Ancient philosophies like Vastu from India and Feng Shui from China offer lots of possibilities. You can also go to your Spiritual home and ask for assistance. A Catholic priest, for example, could come to the home and offer a blessing with holy water.

A favorite of mine is from a Native American tradition. Pick up a sage stick (a bundle of dried sage) and light it with a match. The fire goes out rather quickly. Within seconds, the stick begins to emit a highly aromatic plume of sage smoke. Walk from room to room asking that the energies of all previous residents and their experiences leave this space. You can trace the outline of all doors and windows as a way of sealing in the good energy you are creating with this ceremony. You'll want a shell or small dish to catch the embers and ash. After all, our goal is to bless your new home, not burn it down.

Don't forget you can devise your own ceremony. The power lies in your belief and your intent.

SUMMARY

WEEK ONE

Examine the practical aspects of a move, including the four key questions.

If this is an emotionally difficult move, answer the journal questions to help uncover the fear lurking at the heart of the matter.

If you do not have a move in your future, use the extra time to get caught up with previous projects, such as scrapbooking.

WEEK TWO

Eliminate excess and start packing.

WEEK THREE

Learn how to find a good mover.

Plan for placement of your furniture in your new space.

Discover the value of mover alerts!

WEEK FOUR

Create a moving day binder.

BONUS TIP

This may be a great time to ask how you are doing in the Rewards department. Most adults can't come up with a reward and feel guilty if they do schedule one. Here is a list of fifteen fabulous rewards to get you started. Some are pricey; others cost a song. I hope you try all of them over time.

- Take a bath (diffuse incense, burn a candle, dim the lights, and play your favorite music)
- Book a massage
- Go to a new coffee shop, tea room, or hotel and read a book for an hour over your favorite beverage
- Go on a hike
- Crank up the music and dance!
- Go to a park, sit on a bench, and people watch
- Find a Sound Bath
- Take a class in something that intrigues you
- Have lunch with a friend
- Book a weekend getaway without the kids
- Wander around a museum
- See a new release at the local movie theater and indulge in a snack
- Go for a walk in a different neighborhood
- Binge-watch a series you have heard great things about
- Buy something beautiful (that you can afford)
- Tour some homes for sale if you love design and architecture

Rewards are important, varied, and creative. What are your choices? Find me on social media and let me know what you are doing to say "Job well done!" to you and that all-important inner child.

BACK-TO-SCHOOL BUSY SEASON

Everybody today seems to be in such a terrible rush, anxious for greater developments and greater riches and so on, so that children have very little time for their parents. Parents have very little time for each other, and in the home begins the disruption of peace in the world.

—MOTHER TERESA

HABIT OF THE MONTH

This month, the habit we're cultivating is positive self-talk. Every time you hear one of those negative phrases repeating in your head, stop and recognize what is happening. And then immediately replace it with a dose of reality. Do you hear, "What am I doing? I can't succeed at organizing. I'm too stupid." Stop that tape. Recognize who deposited that negative image into your experience. Forgive them. Release any anger or resentment. And then quietly say something like this: "I am doing the best job I can to get my life organized. Every day I see myself moving forward. I am proud of myself. I recognize my accomplishments. I let nothing stand in my way. I am organized!"

AFFIRMATION OF THE MONTH

As I move into the busy fall season, I embrace the challenges before me. I see myself successful in all my endeavors. I guide my family by example. I give thanks for the opportunities before me.

Self-Care Practice

Everybody dreams about having a superpower. If I could pick one, I would be able to fly. There is something, however, that I do ace that is my real-life superpower. Can you guess what it is? I can sleep soundly anywhere and stay asleep for hours. If there is a noise, I will incorporate it into my dream. My mother always said that one day the world would come to an end and I would sleep right through it. I never knew this was a superpower until I went through chemo-therapy and my doctors were amazed the drugs didn't upset my ability to fall asleep in a matter of minutes. What can I say? Flying would be fun, but sleep is more practical.

Sleep allows the body to restore itself. The brain gets a rest from the constant chatter. And guess what? The rested body and brain make decision-making easier, and that totally affects your ability to get and stay organized. I know nothing about sleeping pills and other drugs meant to alleviate insomnia. I do have some suggestions to help you and some will be familiar to you. Ready? Okay. Let's get ready to fall asleep:

- Get up and go to bed at the same time every day. Routine causes the body to get sleepy out of habit.
- Check the condition of your bed linens and sleepwear. Is it time to replace them? If you feel good in your night garments, it helps to set up sleep as a pleasurable experience.
- How old is your mattress? If it's time, go for a natural fiber one.
- No electronics in the bedroom. Remember, it's a room for sex, fun, and rest, not TV consumption, laptop excursions, or gaming.
- Be sure the bedroom is picked up and everything has been returned to its designated spot. Waking up to a mess is a downer mentally.
- If you are sensitive to sound, try noise-canceling headphones until you establish a habit of sleep or use earplugs or a noise-canceling machine.
- Secure your windows with blackout drapes because the darkness encourages the production of melatonin.
- Try a weighted blanket and/or an eye mask.
- Warm your bedroom; then, as you get into bed, lower the thermostat.
- Stop liquid consumption two hours before you get into bed.
- Do the pranayama 4-7-8 for a few rounds, then meditate for five minutes to relax your mind. I suggest five minutes as a short time frame for beginners. The ideal would be thirty minutes first thing upon awakening and another thirty minutes around 7 p.m. or before bed. These are goals you can build up to as you enjoy the practice. It's a lot to demand of a beginner. The true benefits of meditation kick in around minute twelve.
- I take calcium and magnesium supplements daily for bone health. I also take Formula 303 (over the counter, available on Amazon) before bed to help with leg cramps. It's magnesium and homeopathic remedies meant to help muscles relax. They can also induce sleep. Unlike a prescription medication, there is no grogginess the next day. Check with your doctor if you take prescription meds in general or have specific health conditions.
- Do you like to take a nap in the afternoon? Sleep experts suggest ten to twenty minutes max is perfect and do it between 2 and 4 p.m. There is one caveat: Skip the nap if you have insomnia. It can throw off your sleep cycle and work against you.

WEEK ONE

School Year Questions

This week, you can

- Look at your past experiences of the school year
- See what you are creating for your children
- Discover the genius of routines
- Learn how to create a positive outlook

Time required: One to two hours of journal work.

I WANT YOU TO CONSCIOUSLY CRAFT your path through the demands of this month. It's okay to put new expectations into place. Let me share a personal example. A decade ago, as I lay in bed with the flu, I suddenly realized that I got sick every January like clockwork. I made a decision that I would reverse this unconsciously driven trend. I started saying the following affirmation: "The new year is a time of perfect health for me. Illness is in the past. I am now open to receiving the life lessons I need to learn without getting the flu." I haven't experienced a cold or the flu as a New Year's present since that time. I actually expect to be healthy! Let's see if we can't uncover some of the negative trends that drive you this season.

Please answer the following questions in your journal:

1. Do you remember your school days? Some adults remember very little while others remember them in vivid detail. Which category are you in?
2. Was this a happy time for you? Be specific.
3. If this was an unhappy time for you, can you be specific as to why?
4. If you have siblings, did they experience childhood and school in the same way you did? If you have no idea, give them a call. How did the similarities and differences affect you?
5. Write a brief summary of your school experience.

WHAT ABOUT TODAY?

Do you have school-age children? If you look objectively at their experience to date, do you think you are unconsciously trying to replicate your childhood? Or are you trying to live a new and improved version of it through them?

During a typical school year, what causes you the most problems? Are there issues with your children's teachers, the school's distance from your home, or the amount of homework? Are you active in the PTA? Do your children engage in after-school activities or shun them?

It's one thing to wax poetic about what we remember about the past or how we wish life to be now. It's another to put pen to paper and record our thoughts. We don't always write down what we assume will be our answer. The discoveries are frequently surprising and amazing.

I see parents on the news and on television talk shows complain about the state of their homes during the school year. It makes for great entertainment, doesn't it? I sit back and wonder "What is fueling this drama?" It's different for everyone. There is no one reason why the school year puts your home in turmoil. This discovery is a lot more interesting than putting the entire contents of a room on someone's lawn. That's not healing; that's high TV ratings.

Take the time to dig deep. Offer yourself the chance to release these thorny issues of the past and effect lasting change. Remember too that all the tips and tricks in the world can't permanently change the outer environment until the inner one changes as well. No tool is more powerful in this arena than answering a few thoughtful journal questions.

FAMILY ROUTINES

What concrete things can you do to make this a better year for you and your children? Here are some ideas to jump-start the problem-solving part of your brain.

- Plan food menus a week in advance and schedule time to shop for or order the ingredients.
- Be sure the pantry is always stocked with basic supplies.
- Get up fifteen minutes earlier to make breakfast.
- Get everyone in the family set up the night before: make lunches, lay out vitamins, plan wardrobes, know what breakfast will be, check homework assignments, and so on. Doing all these things in advance makes the morning less stressful, and your morning experience sets the tone for the day.
- Research food delivery services that can deliver meals a few times a week. You keep them in your freezer. These are not processed meals loaded with sodium in the frozen foods section of your local market but healthy meals made fresh expressly for you. As a vegan, I always have Daily Harvest or Splendid Spoon meals ready to supplement whatever I plan to cook. I'll provide links in the Resources section.

Establish routines for the household including chores for everyone.

Call other mothers and fathers in your circle to create carpool duties.

Decide which activities must be dropped from this year's schedule.

What's on your personal list?

CREATE A POSITIVE OUTLOOK

I'd like you to do something for me this week. Carry your journal or a small notebook with you everywhere you go. Listen to yourself speak. Every time you begin a sentence with a negative preface, write it down. They usually sound something like this: "Why should I bother, that never works out!" "I can't bear the thought that…" or "That just makes me sick!" We all have these destructive thought patterns. This week, identify yours. Stay on the lookout for them until you realize they are gone. It probably took some well-meaning adult, parent, coworker, friend, or teacher quite some time to infect your thought patterns. It may take some time to expunge them.

As you key in to your subconscious thought patterns with this exercise, also be on the lookout for the things you say to your children. Are you passing along an army of negative self-esteem beliefs? Listen to how your children speak to you and to others. What do you hear? It's probably you!

You can hammer away at your children and make them feel self-conscious

or guilty for how they express themselves. Or you can change the way you speak to them. Where there has been unconscious negativity, there can now be conscious deposits of love and healthy self-esteem poured into their very Souls.

Write three positive ways to begin your sentences. And then think of three compliments you can pay your children. It must come from the heart to be effective. At the top of the page, write this quote from Gandhi: "Be the change you want to see in the world."

Getting organized is about clearing away the clutter. Zen Organizing™ is also about going deep to clear out the debris in your mind. A calm, well-organized environment will nurture and support everyone present. It's equally true, however, that negative, destructive, unloving comments will wash away any good that has been established in the physical. We are creatures of body, mind, and Soul. This month, as the world celebrates the harvest and prepares for the calm of winter, we begin to integrate and organize on all levels.

FORGET PERFECTION

Perfection in your home is not an achievable goal. Read that sentence again. Tattoo it on your heart. As a parent, you can count on your children having daily arguments. You can be assured of homework wars. You or your children will oversleep and breakfast will be a battlefield. The flu will grab you in its clutches, and the house will fall into chaos. These upsets are part of life. Life is perfect only on television.

What is within your reach is a commitment to moving forward in a positive manner day by day. In fact, a day is too great a span of time. Live breath to breath. As you establish order in your home, don't let chores or rewards become a battlefield. This is especially true if these are new concepts.

Have you been the mom who did everything? Why do you think you chose to do that in your home? Are there things you do for your children that they should be doing for themselves? It may be a shock to your children's system when you suddenly ask them to be responsible. Give them time to adjust. We all dislike change, don't we? Did you do everything because it would get done better or faster? How will your children know how to take care of themselves when they go out into the world if you do everything for them?

I once heard journalist Christiane Amanpour tell a wonderful anecdote on *60 Minutes* about one of her college friends with whom she shared a house. It seems that each member of the household took a turn cleaning up. One of those roommates was John F. Kennedy Jr., and, yes, even he took his turn cleaning the toilet. Need I say more?

Fear of failure might be the culprit. "If my home isn't perfect, what will people think?" Or perhaps you use the environment as one of the areas of life over which you can exert control. Or maybe you are a perfectionist who feels that no help will ever live up to your standards. Or just maybe you are a martyr who secretly feeds off the chaotic appearance of your home and the fact that no one ever helps you.

Here we are, once again back at square one. Change happens within. If you heal your emotional wounds, you will automatically deal differently with your environment and all those with whom you share it. You can fill your journey with more sorrow, or you can spend your time healing, growing, and being an example to all those with whom you share your life.

As we head into the second week, be sure you have a list of changes you intend to implement that will make this month run more smoothly than previous ones. If you come up with a long list, prioritize it and then start with the first few items. Make this a game for yourself and your family rather than boot camp. You don't want to overwhelm everyone and set yourself up for failure. As the changes are implemented, ask for feedback. You know what they say: "Out of the mouths of babes." Be armed as well with a list of age-appropriate chores for your children. In week three, I will share mine.

WEEK TWO

Kids' Rooms

This week, you can

- Bring order to your child's bedroom
- Calm the elements in your child's bedroom: books, toys, and so on
- Introduce "paper problem" solutions to your kids

Time required: Thirty minutes for journal work; one hour to shop if supplies are needed; one to two hours to organize the bathroom; three to five hours to do the bedroom.

THIS WEEK IS THE IDEAL TIME TO organize your child's bedroom and bath, if he or she has a separate bathroom. If you started the program with the first section and followed the other sections consecutively you are by now an experienced organizer and your own room offers a wonderful example to your child. If not, take the time this week to work on your room first. If your children are older, tell them that you want to help them have a more successful school year. Then surprise them by saying that before you can help them, you have to help yourself, so you'll be working on your bedroom too. I was the resident organizer at iVillage for five years, and the ladies were always skeptical

about this plan of action. Over the years, however, I repeatedly gathered testimonials from women who were shocked when their husbands and children started to pitch in without being asked. Trust me, it works. Teaching by example is powerful.

LAY THE GROUNDWORK

What is the purpose of your child's room? You need to know before you add or subtract furniture, toys, clothing, or any decorative items. Do you want it to be exclusively a place of rest? If so, where will he or she do homework? I have friends who have their child do homework in the kitchen. Is your kitchen quiet enough for homework time? Where will your child play? Is your living room or finished basement set up to be a playroom? Will friends be invited to the bedroom? All households are different. Just remember that every activity you eliminate from this room has to be set up elsewhere.

Keep in mind that the way an area is set up does more than make performing a particular activity easier. It gives your child the unspoken message that it's desirable to complete projects with ease. Very often we get quite the opposite message.

child can easily access them. You also want to introduce the concept of categories. Think Barbies in one bin, Legos in another, and soft, cuddly toys in a third. Next month, I'll help you organize the family room as the center of home relaxation and toy central. Lacking this room, you may need to have your child's toys kept in his or her room. Of course, toys will migrate out into the rest of the home, won't they? As long as they have a designated place to return to, there's no problem. If you make your child responsible for restoring order, less will migrate outside the bedroom!

PRACTICE FIFTEEN-MINUTE ELIMINATION

Toys scattered all over the room are overwhelming, not inviting. Who could pick and choose the treasures scattered throughout the debris? If your child is a toddler, it might behoove you while the child is away to eliminate the toys that can be tossed, given to a friend, or donated. As they get older, invite them into the process. Ask what they would like to share with a less fortunate child. Or perhaps you'd like to share these toys with the children of family members or friends? Some parents follow the "one toy comes in, one toy goes out" rule. You'll have to decide when and how you will eliminate. It's a crucial step, and your child needs to be guided in the way that best suits his or her personality and your home life.

After you whittle down your possessions to the gold, store items so that the

SETUP AND STORAGE TIPS

These days, children have a wealth of possessions. You want to keep their room inviting rather than looking, as my mom would have said, like a bomb just went off.

Reading and Learning
Every child's room needs a bookcase and a comfortable chair with a good light source. Cultivating the habit of reading is essential for success in school. It also provides enjoyment throughout one's life. It's great to have a desk and a chair in your child's room. Most children have their own computers.

Children can also learn a great deal from educational video programs. I am not suggesting, by the way, that the privilege of a computer in your child's room include an internet connection! I think it's safer if children surf the internet for school using a computer under your tutelage and supervision. You may want to have a computer in your family room expressly for this purpose or have a laptop available. When you feel your children are mature enough, which is fifteen to eighteen years old for most of my clients who are parents, you can allow them to have a private internet connection in their room. Teaching your child to be a savvy surfer of the internet is important because you have no control over what other parents allow in their child's room. Here are some additional guidelines: always insist that parental controls are turned on; never allow secret memberships or passwords; do random checks of sites recently visited. The internet has an astonishing wealth of information. Sadly, it is also populated by predators who seek to exploit a child's innocence and inexperience.

Clothing

You'll want to have a stepstool so items in the closet and drawers are accessible. Put a low clothing bar in the closet so that little children can reach some of their own clothes. Learning how to dress yourself like a big boy or girl is a game in itself, isn't it? It's also a great self-esteem builder.

Another way to make everyday clothes such as underwear and T-shirts available to tiny folks is to create instant shelves using your closet rod. You'll find products that attach with Velcro strips over the rod in the closet section of most large stores. We first considered their usefulness in the Bedroom section. They are designed for adult sweaters and shoes, but you can use them to store kids' clothing.

Toys

There are many ways to creatively store toys. A toy chest is a favorite solution. My only caution would be the lid. Will it hold in place wherever it's stopped? Is it lightweight? A heavy lid that crashes down on little fingers will cause unnecessary pain.

Storage containers on wheels are my favorite. They can be used for toy categories. Later you can use them elsewhere in the home. I like their endless versatility. In addition to The Container Store, check out the children's section of large stores such as Target, IKEA, and Walmart.

Wicker bins may suit your décor better. I like the ones with canvas inserts. You can wash them periodically and keep them clean.

Don't forget that you can store soft toys in a hammock made for this purpose. It will get stuffed animals off the floor at bedtime. You can also rotate your child's selection. When they grow too old for stuffed animals but aren't yet ready to part with them, a few friendly faces can smile down on them until the day arrives to find their toys a new home.

You can easily find multi-tiered, lightweight toy storage units with different size bins. It's so easy to grab what you need and still create categories. Not only do you have different bins for specific types of toys, the bins come in different colors.

If you have the space, you could have a storage bench or a seating unit against a wall with bins underneath. The Pottery Barn excels in carrying items like this. Try their main catalogue, as well as the ones they produce for kids and teens.

Remember the hanging bags you attach to a closet rod that I mentioned in the "Clothing" section? You might be able to store toys in the narrow bags designed for shoes.

Make use of colors to teach little ones about categories. You can say that all the Barbies for example need to be picked up and returned to the yellow bin. Or you can make use of the designs some containers have and suggest that all the Legos go into the dinosaur bins. You are teaching categories without making it into a thing.

Large Toys

If you have generous grandparents and friends who like to send gigantic stuffed animals or toys, ask them to please stop until you live in larger quarters. Suggest that they hold on to them. When your children come for a visit, they will have something special to play with. Communicate clearly and lovingly that you just don't have the storage space. This is especially true for apartments in large cities such as New York, Chicago, or San Francisco. If the message isn't received, donate the items to a charity. I've seen large toys take over the living room. The unspoken message is that the children rule. There is no longer any room for your partner or any adult friends. The home is then out of balance.

Art Projects

Some projects are messy by nature, and carpets, walls, and linens can be stained by their various parts (such as markers, crayons, paints, and glue). Keep those stored

outside your child's room or on a high shelf. The house rule is that an adult has to be supervising when those are in use.

At the appropriate time, you will relax the rules and allow your children to access these on their own. Accidents are bound to happen, which is why I advocate using easy-to-clean materials and waiting until later to purchase heirloom quality furniture. Give your children a break. They're not coordinated adults in pint-size bodies. They're kids!

The Bed

Although I follow the principles of Feng Shui and prefer to see nothing under the bed, I realize that sometimes that space must be utilized. If your child doesn't have room for a dresser, try a bed with built-in storage drawers.

If storage isn't an issue but the room is small and you'd like to have little guests sleep over, try a trundle bed. However, don't forget the beauty of a simple air mattress that pops up in seconds and comes with its own motor.

Kids' Bathrooms

Splish splash, I was takin' a bath! If your children have their own bathroom, here are some tips to keep it organized.

Add another stepstool to make the sink more accessible.

You can use drawer liners and acrylic organizers in this room just as you did in your own bathroom.

Keep counter debris to a minimum and store needed products in containers, again just like you did in your bathroom. Choose items that are easy to clean and that make organization easy, logical, and inviting, and keep everything accessible.

The Entry to the Home

If your children explode into your home wildly tossing books, coats, and sports paraphernalia everywhere, "something is rotten in the state of Denmark," to quote Shakespeare.

Coats and all clothing should have a designated spot. Your children need to hang up their coats, not toss them on a chair or the floor, waiting for you to put them away.

If they're very tiny, put a small clothes tree or series of hooks by the front door. You can mix and match benches, mirrors, baskets, and hooks to find the solution that works for your family.

During inclement weather, put out a boot tray and an umbrella stand.

THE HOMEWORK WARS

If you just purchased this book and have decided to start with your child's room, you'll want to get your paper wars under control before you try to teach him or her. In the end, enforcing a code you've read about is less effective and less likely to be successful than teaching the elements of a system you use.

As your children grow older and have homework, you may want to introduce a file cabinet or a file box just for their use.

Why not organize and store homework for your child in the same way you keep your bills and work papers? What a great skill to learn at a young age! Full instructions are in the "Organizing the Business of Life" section. You'll find these elements are easier to teach if you are making use of them too. Needless to say, if you want your child to go digital, the instructions will easily adapt to that format. Learning how to assess and manage is the key common denominator. The ultimate resting place can be a file cabinet, a computer, the cloud, or the moon. Ease of retrieval is what we are after.

If your children fall into the category of "if I don't see it, I forget it's there," have no fear. I offer other ways to keep track of paper (besides the traditional file system) in "Organizing the Business of Life." Decorative boxes and binders, for example, can easily house school and project papers. Like I do with my adult clients, I encourage a mixture of solutions. Teach your children how getting organized really is creative and they'll pass these skills on to their kids. Getting organized—the gift that keeps on giving!

Establish rules for when homework and chores in the home are to be done. For example, do you have a studious child who likes to get homework out of the way the minute he or she gets home? Or is your child athletic with a need to blow off some physical steam right after school? You can't mandate personality. You can create schedules that are productive and harness those natural tendencies.

My mother had a pet peeve that drove me crazy as a kid. Now I see what she was trying to teach me. My mother checked my homework. It had to be done correctly, but it also had to look good. My writing had to be neat. The paper had to be clean. My mother was teaching me to have respect for the physical objects in my life, for the way I presented myself, and for the recipient.

When your children bring home notes for you from teachers, school flyers, homework assignments, or whatever you can add to this list, has it been stuffed into their backpacks and turned into trash? Give them a zippered pouch (all stationary stores have them) and teach them to put *everything* here as they acquire it during the school day. At night, you can sort those papers together.

As your children get older, they can be responsible for putting the papers they have gathered into a file with their name on it. Have a small portable file container in the entry or on the kitchen counter. Wherever your children first enter the home is where these files should be. In this case use special files with accordion sides so no slips of paper can go astray. You might even give each child a separate file color to make the folder more enticing to use.

In the evening after dinner, take a minute to check what's there. It's a great way to stay on top of a child's schedule and what is being requested of you from school. Do a little product research using the Resources section at my website. Choose something functional, sturdy, and attractive.

Put anything you need to sign back into the zippered pouch. Put that into the backpack. Finally, remember to periodically check your child's schoolbag or backpack. You want to be sure he or she is being thorough!

I realize that most school communications these days will come to you via email. You'll be using DocuSign for forms that need to be returned and most likely dealing directly with the teacher. The above instructions are great for teaching your children to have communication without words by sharing paper and placement. Guess what? That's what happens in an office with in- and out-boxes or now via email. If you can see the bigger picture, you won't resent these setups. You will see them as life strategy moments.

You may also need to factor in elements that may apply only to one child. Does your child have ADHD? Is he physically handicapped? Do allergies plague him? Whatever the special challenges, get help and tailor your children's routine to their abilities.

Barbara Corcoran is a true real estate mogul. You probably know her from the TV show *Shark Tank*. She is also the author of one of the funniest and wisest books on growing up in an organized household. It's called: *If You Don't Have Big Breasts, Put Ribbons on Your Pigtails: And Other Lessons I Learned from My Mom*. Barbara's mom ran a tight ship. But then you have to if you're raising ten kids! In every chapter, Barbara tells funny stories about her childhood and her rise in the real estate world. Each chapter closes with how she took her mother's skills as a mom and used those principles in business, obviously with great success.

●●●
●●●
●●●

If you've been reading these suggestions and thinking that they wouldn't fly in your house, ask yourself when you decided to let your children run the show and what you get out of that experience. Children and animals want someone to be in charge. They crave order and discipline because those are manifestations of being loved. You won't lose your children's love if you impose rules. You'll be gaining their respect. Not to mention teaching them how to parent!

WEEK THREE

Get Your Kids to Stay Organized

This week, you can

- Choose some chores: the lifeblood of household maintenance

Time required: Sixty to ninety minutes to create a system and a chore chart.

IT'S ONE THING TO ORGANIZE A ROOM. It's another to maintain it—especially when it's your child's room. Help your family continuously keep the goal in mind. Guess what? The maintenance required to stay organized is really a series of chores. Here are my suggestions for children's chores and routines. Look them over and use whatever is right for the children in your home.

BEDROOM

Make the bed every morning. Even a young child can smooth a sheet and toss the comforter over a pillow. No military corners required!

Put away all toys and media. Your child's room is not a war zone. At the end of the day it has to be picked up. Chaos in your environment makes it more difficult to sleep well, think clearly, and function in an organized manner.

Put dirty clothes in the hamper, not on the floor!

Children can learn how to do laundry and put it away. At your favorite organizing store, you will find a "folding board." It will help you and your children learn to fold like pros. Forget perfect origami folds and go for consistency.

Older children can vacuum.

BATHROOM

If your children have their own bathroom, as they get older they need to keep it stocked with items such as toothpaste, shampoo, and toilet paper. You need a central storage area to serve as the source.

Every time they leave the bathroom, the

244

One day the Closet Factory asked me to organize a new closet installation in the home of an influencer. Just because you are increasing the space you have doesn't mean you can be sure everything you own will find a home. I spent a day eliminating items with the client. On shoot day, the closet looked fabulous. I decided to organize the drawers in case we needed an interior shot.

Her then-boyfriend had a ton of T-shirts that filled a deep drawer. The closet designer showed up and asked if she could help me. "Well," I replied, "I've got a ton of T-shirts to fold." She watched me as I turned each garment into a perfect department store fold. Suddenly she stopped me and said: "Regina, he's a guy. He's not going to appreciate this or maintain it." We folded every tee in half and then half again and placed them in the drawer.

What is the bottom line? Know your audience. Understand what is important to them and how much energy they are going to put into maintenance. Don't waste your time or put unrealistic demands on them. Let your children experience the creativity, ease, and joy that organizing brings. Don't make the process distasteful.

This young man loved his setup. In fact, he went from boyfriend to husband and now father. The video is online if you want to see it. You'll find the link on my website. And we didn't shoot the interior of that drawer after all!

counter should be wiped off and towels refolded. The floor is not a storage facility.

KITCHEN

Meals present several chore possibilities: put away groceries; make dinner or help with prep; set the table and then clear it; wash the dishes and then put them away. Learn how the family loads a dishwasher if you have one. And practice the art of putting things away when dry.

MISCELLANEOUS

Water the plants.

Empty the trash from all receptacles in the home.

If you have a pet, he needs fresh water and food every day. Birdcages need to be cleaned. Dogs need to go for a walk and their poop has to be picked up. Every pet has its own special maintenance routine.

Do you have a backyard? Older children can cut the grass.

DR. TAYLOR'S CHORE GUIDE FOR CHILDREN

When is a child old enough to do chores? I have met many wonderful mothers over the years. One, however, stands out. My client, Dr. Taylor, is an obstetrician/gynecologist with a large practice, and she and her husband are the hands-on, loving parents of seven. I worked at this home over the course of one summer. My client and I talked many times about the importance of chores. Her children have chores starting at eighteen months! I thought you might like to see how Dr. Taylor teaches home management and self-reliance to her children. As she said to me, "By the time my children are eighteen, they can run a home, manage their finances, and take care of themselves." How many parents can say that?

Eighteen Months Old

Give your children a squirt bottle of water and let them wipe surfaces in the kitchen at their eye level. The lower half of your refrigerator will get very clean!

Three Years Old

Children can learn to pick up items in their room and return everything to its proper place. Gradually, they can start to pick up all the rooms in the home.

Five Years Old

As they get older, children gain coordination and strength. Their chores can therefore increase in difficulty. Around this age, teach them how to vacuum, dust, and straighten a room.

Eight Years Old

Full kitchen duty is now assumed. This includes the following chores: wash dirty dishes, load and then empty the dishwasher; put clean dishes away; put food away when groceries come into the house; clean all surfaces, sinks, and the floor.

Twelve Years Old

At this age, children learn how to do laundry for the family, including sorting, washing, folding, and putting it away.

Fourteen Years Old

Now they learn how to create menus, manage a food budget, and cook the family evening meal.

Sixteen Years Old

At this age, they are ready to do the family grocery shopping, as well as shop for their personal wardrobe.

Are mistakes made? You bet! However, as Dr. Taylor shared, ruined clothes, a bare pantry, and dreadful meals were great teachers. "Chores are a responsibility for all people living in the household. If the children needed money, they had to work for it. I hired them to do extra household chores. As they got older, they could work for me or my husband." I was touched to learn that each child was required to tithe 10 percent of these extra funds to charity.

Has Dr. Taylor inspired you to integrate chores into your household routine?

ENFORCING ROUTINES

After you have your list, you'll need to enforce it. The best-run homes employ a strategy dividing chores into two categories: those required as a contributing member of the family versus those that help a child earn a little extra money. You'll need to create a personal solution that takes into account the following elements: the number of children, how many chores you have to assign, and, of course, the amount of money you have to dispense.

Money isn't the only reward you can offer. Most children are motivated by privileges. Let your child earn special time alone with mom or dad. Maybe a Saturday at the zoo without little brother? I remember earning horseback riding lessons, movie passes, record albums, and tickets to the theater when I was in school. Rewards need not be given after each chore is completed. Develop a rating or point system so that consistency of performance is established.

When children are little, many parents use a chore chart and display it prominently as a way to motivate. They use stickers and stars to note chores completed. You could also use a blackboard and use hatch marks to keep tabs. Perhaps you can even foster a little healthy competition to see who earns the most rewards first? If you go that route, handle that element with care. Competition can be inspiring; comparisons are demeaning.

If there is a reward for performing one's chores, there must also be consequences when the work isn't done. The loss of highly prized privileges is probably your best source of motivation. In today's world, the easy punishment is loss of media privileges: no TV, no music, no video games. And who hasn't regretted his actions when he hears those immortal words: "You're grounded!"

The loss needs to be commensurate with the negligence. Remember that this isn't really about punishment. It's about teaching cause and effect. We all suffer consequences as adults when we do not deliver what we have promised or been paid for. How else will a child learn these concepts?

A lot of modern families live like tenants in a rooming house. There is so much attention paid to individual schedules and achievements that any kind of family life vanishes.

- Drag your kids away from screens and take them on nature walks.
- Volunteer with them at food pantries or animal shelters.
- Take them to protests so they learn the value of participating in democracy.
- Rethink the value of a packed calendar.

Learning how to get out of boredom or depression and back into a productive state is a life skill we all need. Screen time doesn't offer that dividend.

Even if it's only Sunday dinner, be sure you put family time on your calendar!

Most of this year you will be working on projects that make your physical space more organized. Now more than any other time you will be directly drawing in the members of your family to carry their fair share. At the beginning of the calendar year or your personal journey into Zen Organizing™, you're asking to have your work respected. Now you're saying, "You too have to learn how to do this." If you started with the first section, you have already been a remarkable teacher, example, and mentor—what every good parent hopes to be!

WEEK FOUR

Handle Obligations

This week, you can

- Learn how and when to volunteer
- Learn step-by-step tips for successful projects

Time required: Sixty to ninety minutes for journal work.

VOLUNTEERING IS A GREAT WAY TO play a more active role at your children's school. Inside or outside the school environment, it has a wonderful extra benefit—your children see you extend yourself on behalf of others. They experience the true meaning of community. It's a win-win for everyone involved.

Most of the time.

Some people should hold off on volunteering because they are overextended. There are those who use being a volunteer as another way to demonstrate how busy they are and by extension how important. This week, we're going to look at how to decide whether you can take on a project and how to make it work if you do.

HOW TO HANDLE A VOLUNTEERING REQUEST

At the start of our journey, I told you that the whole of anything is overwhelming. You get control over a task when you break it down into smaller increments that you deal with one at a time. From the beginning we've been doing just that as we brought physical order to the various rooms in our homes. Now we're moving from the world of the physical to the world of projects and homework.

Let's say you are asked to organize a fund-raising event for your child's school. Your knee-jerk reaction is to say "yes." You want to be helpful and involved. As the details come in, you try to handle them. You start to feel pressured and overwhelmed. You were promised help but no one steps forward. Everyone knows they don't have to because you are responsible. You start to burn the midnight oil. You hate yourself for agreeing to do this. You hate the school and everyone on the committee. Finally, the day of the event arrives. It passes in a whirl and then it's finished. You are hailed as a great parent who saved the day. Does this sound at all familiar? Let's replay this event with a little Zen Organizing™ magic, shall we?

Step One

Thank the representative of the school who requests your help. If you are truly and sincerely interested in helping out, say that you need to find out all the particulars before you commit yourself. If you are not remotely interested and want to run screaming from the room, politely decline. Remember that you don't owe anyone an explanation when they make a request of your time. "Yes" or "no" with a warm smile is all that is required.

Step Two

The particulars are the basic facts of the operation: the date, the budget, the committee, and the goal. I want as much information about past events as possible. Were they successful? Why? What worked? If they were not successful, have someone spell out exactly why and how they missed the mark.

Step Three

Having a committee is vital. However, it can't be just a collection of bodies. It must be populated by members who have the time to produce the results you need. You are the captain of the team, not the troops. Are any of your volunteers experienced? For example, do they do PR for a living or have they been the go-to person for PR at all school events?

Step Four

You say "yes." Now you need to break the event into the steps that will produce the result you are seeking. This list is your action plan. Leave nothing to the imagination. The world will always toss in a monkey wrench, no matter how organized you are. If you don't understand what you are faced with in terms of detail, everything becomes a monkey wrench.

Step Five

Your list of steps should be put into chronological order. Now you know when the event is and what it will take to make it happen. Counting backward from the event, schedule every single step in your day planner. Assign committee members to handle each detail. Give yourself wiggle room for delivery of the biggest components, just in case.

BREAK EVERYTHING DOWN INTO STEPS

The time comes when you hear a request and you automatically start to break things down in your head. Let me give you an example. When Molly had to have a science project for her fifth grade class, the first thing her mom, Susie, had her do was research. What were the possible projects? Which interested her the most? Which ones did she feel most confident tackling? After she chose the experiment, Susie and Molly sat down and broke the project into sections. Each one had a target completion date marked on a big calendar.

Each section was then further broken down into the steps that would make it happen. Susie, like me, loves this kind of planning. She also created checklists to keep Molly on track. I am delighted to report that Miss Molly received the highest mark possible for her project. If you can teach your children how to break homework assignments into their components, you will be giving them a gift they can use throughout their lives.

Your assignment this week is to take a project you have due this fall and handle it in this way. Break it down into steps. Schedule deadlines on the road toward the due date. Ask your team members for help if you need it. If you are without a team, I bet you have an organized friend who could help you. Learning how to tackle simple projects will help you achieve all your goals. A goal is really a project! It has components and due dates. You can

achieve it after you take it out of the realm of wishful thinking.

GUIDED IMAGERY

You can put one more tool into your Zen Organizer™ arsenal: guided imagery. We've been working all year with positive affirmations. Positive actions will be sabotaged by negative thoughts. Our affirmations are the antidote. Guided imagery is another way to reprogram yourself. Although you can find many sources of books and tapes on guided imagery, I'd have to say that Belleruth Naparstek stands head and shoulders above everyone else in the field. She has recorded material for all areas of life. I hope you'll check out her work and consider one that feels tailored to your needs. I'm not sure I could have made it through chemotherapy without her guided imagery for that experience.

When you understand the simple concept of breaking the entire project down and then working the Magic Formula (eliminate, categorize, organize), nothing can stop you. Your fears may rise up and you'll find yourself suddenly stuck in a drama or feeling overextended. We can sabotage ourselves in lots of ways. Recognize your fears and then breathe your way through them. Remind yourself it's just one step at a time. See the end result in your mind. Repeat your affirmation. Reprogram yourself for success! And if you love using apps for to-do lists and projects, be my guest.

SUMMARY

WEEK ONE

Use journal exercises to investigate your school experience to see how it affects you today.

Uncover your destructive thought patterns.

Make a plan for positive change this fall.

WEEK TWO

Organize your child's room and bath.

WEEK THREE

Create chores and consider consequences.

WEEK FOUR

Revisit the concepts of time and goal setting as they apply to the busy school and holiday season.

Meet with the Zen Organizers™ to compare notes.

Learn how to break projects into their components.

Reprogram yourself for success.

Consider the power of guided imagery.

BONUS TIP

Working on our children's rooms seems most appropriate as the school year begins. If that's when you have chosen to read this section the end of September is in sight and it's wise to start thinking ahead to the holidays. Where do you want to celebrate them? If it's with loved ones who live far way, make your travel reservations now. If you are staying home and want to show off your newly organized space, we'll be using the Magic Formula to get a better grasp of worry-free, stress-free entertaining and decorating in the "Entertaining with Joy!" and "Creating a Festive Holiday Atmosphere" sections. Don't forget to check your finances so you'll know your budget as we enter the last phase of the year. This holiday season your celebration will be based on reality, not the pull of emotion. The great thing about numbers is that they never lie.

Exit Rituals

As you organize your home and master exit rituals, you can tailor them for your child. Be sure you teach them the benefits of the ritual to their emotional and physical well-being. It will be an epic fail if it's all about duty, perfection, or parent-pleasing.

RELAXING IN THE COMMON ROOMS

And the day came when the risk to remain tight in a bud was more
painful than the risk it took to blossom.

—ANAÏS NIN

A FEW YEARS AGO I WAS TRAINING A new assistant and took her with me to a first-time client's home. As it turned out this was not an ordinary session. This was baptism by fire!

When we walked into the house, I had a hard time not reacting outwardly. I prayed that my assistant would take her cue from me. Bless her, she did. She told me later that a character in a recurring *Saturday Night Live* skit would walk into a room and exclaim, "Holy Mother of God!" She said she had to swallow those words as they leapt into her throat the minute we entered the house.

This situation was close to the worst I had ever seen. The living room looked like a bomb had gone off. There wasn't a clear space anywhere. Unpacked boxes from the last move were stacked in the kitchen area. They were being used as makeshift tables. Stacks of magazines, newspapers, and unopened mail languished on the tops. You had to walk around the boxes to make your way inside.

We guessed the kitchen hadn't been cleaned since the last tenant moved out. Children's toys were everywhere, and I mean that literally. I couldn't single out anything because it was an overwhelming jumble. It didn't look like a collection of toys. It all looked like debris. The hall closet was spacious but emitted a strong odor. I opened the door and knew instantly: They had mold!

As we walked through the home, chaotic energy swirled around our heads. The beds weren't made. The closets held more than clothing; they were like big storage bins. There was so much clothing it poured out of the dresser drawers. In fact, you had to step over it as you walked around the bedroom. Suitcases from the last trip were scattered about and were now being used as adjunct dressers. Folding and organizing are great, but it was clear that more clothing was here than the space could accommodate. The bathroom too had a product explosion that looked like they had hit dollar day at the local drugstore. In each room, the mess reared its head. It was overwhelming.

We assured the family that their home was average. "I've seen this situation many times," I said. In truth I had not, but adding shame to the mix would have prevented any progress.

The wife shared with me that while being organized had never been her strong suit, things had become out of control after the recent birth of her third child. That day, we strove to make a difference. We dove into the primary suite, the playroom, the living room, and the kitchen, working like demons over an eight-hour period. Our goal was to uplift the household's day-to-day experience.

The point of this story is a simple one: What reaction do people have when they enter your home? We want family members to be proud of their home. We want guests to feel welcome the minute they cross the threshold. The sweetest time of the year is upon us—the world celebrates one holiday after another from October to the end of the year. Let's get ready to join in by having a home that is a celebration of life 365 days a year.

HABIT OF THE MONTH

Here are some ideas that can be assigned to all family members this month. The family room gets used every day, and the chores it provides create habits that go far beyond the simple actions they represent. They ingrain the habit of *completion*.

> If an afghan or throw blanket gets used, it will be folded when the user is finished.
> When a toy is taken out, it is put back when playtime ends.
> If a board game is taken out, the pieces are gathered when it's time to put the game away.

What will you add to my suggestions?

AFFIRMATION OF THE MONTH

I honor the Souls of all who enter my home. The environment welcomes those who live here, those who visit, and those who come to help my family. May everyone who enters feel blessed.

Mother Earth, aka Grounding

Remove your shoes and socks and walk on the earth. A forest would be a lovely spot to practice this ancient technique, as would a sandy beach. Some of you no doubt have huge backyards, while others live near a big city park. I love the ocean because the sound of waves lapping the shore combines with the smell of the salt air and the feel of wet sand on my feet. I am instantly at peace.

Grounding sounds somewhat goofy; however, it has a scientific basis. In brief, our bodies become charged with the electrons on the surface of the earth when we come in contact with our bare skin. Grounding is reported to improve the quality of sleep, boost your immune system, relieve stress, and promote healing. I know from personal experience that it feels fabulous. If you are a bit fastidious and can only focus on the fact that if you go to a public park there will no doubt be dog urine on the grass, this practice is not for you.

The Yogi Tweak

I take off my shoes the second I am inside the front door. I love feeling my feet connect with the wood floor. This is an ancient practice from yoga. The goal was not to bring in the energy from the world outside to your personal sanctuary. In modern times it serves to keep your home cleaner! I am on my feet for hours every workday due to my profession, and I see a soft tissue expert who works on my feet periodically. He likes to call shoes "leather coffins."

Think of that the next time you enter your home, and your shoes will fly off.

I think it's important for you to know that I respect science and am floored by all the things modern surgery can do. Three generations ago a broken hip was a life sentence to live in bed and risk death due to infection. Today we routinely replace hip joints. A miracle has become commonplace.

I also have a deep respect for ancient healing modalities. I think we are most powerful when we combine our knowledge rather than tossing out wisdom because it isn't modern. "Better living through chemistry" was well intentioned in its time, but it has polluted the air and the waterways. Today we embrace Grandma's cleaning formulas, seeing the power of vinegar, lemon juice, and baking soda. This book seeks to find the most conscious choice for all that ails us, whether that's a titanium hip or walking barefoot in a forest.

WEEK ONE

Home Questions

This week, you can

- Take a tour of the rooms you share with others
- Make a quick diagnosis of the story these common rooms tell friends and family
- Develop specific goals for each room

Time required: Thirty to ninety minutes, depending on the size of your home, the condition of the rooms, and how many people live there.

THIS FIRST WEEK, TRY SEEING YOUR home's common rooms through new eyes. Begin by leaving the house. Take a short walk around the block, hang out in your backyard and toss the ball with your dog, or drive to the store to get some oat milk. When you come back home, walk in and pretend you're somewhere you've never been before. Walk first into the dining room, next into the living room, and finally into the family room. Look around and take it all in.

Now sit quietly for a few minutes in each room and answer the following questions in your journal. When you are finished in one room, move to the next room and begin again.

1. What is your first impression of this room? Are the people who live here tidy? Do you think they do much entertaining?

2. Does the room feel infused with energy or is it lifeless? Does it feel loved and used or abandoned like a movie set?

3. Do you find the room invites you to stay or do you feel like you want to run away? Is there a comfortable place to sit?

4. Is the room cluttered? If your answer is "yes," what gives you that feeling? Are there too many decorative items? Too many photos? Do you see piles everywhere? Perhaps the room is filled with too much furniture. Be specific.

5. Is no one picking up the room or do you think storage is inadequate?

6. What would you like to add, subtract, or do in this room to get it ready to serve your family more efficiently?

7. How would you like to see the room used? Be specific. For example, something like "I want the family room to be a place where we can crash and be comfortable" is a bit nebulous. You might say, "While the rest of the family is watching a football game, I'd like to have an area to scrapbook or needle-point." Or if you want an area for small children to play alongside a space that adults can enjoy too, that requires a different set of solutions, doesn't it?

You may think this exercise sounds silly, but I assure you, you have done part of it many times before! Every time the phone rings and a friend or family member asks if he or she can come right over, I bet you tear through the house seeing it with fresh eyes, don't you? Maybe you were sitting in a comfortable chair enjoying the Sunday paper when the call came. Now you see that your comfort zone is really a bit chaotic with newspaper sections strewn about your chair. You start picking up in a race with time. This exercise just builds on that common experience.

Take a few minutes after you write in your journal to reflect on your responses. You might check your vision board or Pinterest to see what images you chose for these areas. Let this week be about developing the mental blueprint for what you are going to create. Savor these ideas. This is not a homework assignment. If you feel pressure, you aren't doing it right!

This is another month that requires a little more elbow grease than others, but the rewards will be long term and, for some of you, astonishing. Spontaneous guests will no longer strike fear in your heart. You'll greet anyone who shows up at your door with ease. Remember that regular family Sunday dinner I suggested you schedule last month? Now you won't have to clear off the dining room table. It will always be waiting to serve you! And if you notice the family gathering more often and having more fun in the family room, well, that's what it was designed for! Let's get started, shall we? Holidays, birthdays, and anniversaries are around the corner and we want to be ready to party.

A Soldier's Story

In the spring of 2020, I was contacted by the Wounded Warrior Project and asked to run an organizing challenge based on Zen Organizing™. We only had a month but we did several sessions a week. I was grateful to be able to help men and women who had sacrificed so much for my country. I remember giving instructions one day for a different exercise, and a soldier raised her hand. "Could you explain that another way?" she asked. "I've had multiple brain injuries in combat and I'm having trouble following you." I have never been so humbled in my life. When I asked everyone to do the exercise I just shared with you, I feared I might be met with resistance. To combat veterans, walking into your home with what I refer to as fresh eyes might seem silly, I thought. How wrong I was.

Everyone did the exercise and had amazing discoveries. The group was mostly women. Our regular gentleman was older and very quiet. He didn't share much, but he always came to class with a twinkle in his eye and a gentle demeanor. I asked if he had done the exercise. "Oh, yes!" he replied. When I asked if he could share what he had learned, his response floored me. He said quietly: "Now I know why everyone complains. I saw what they see." I thought that was a very brave admission to a group of strangers. I asked if he had shared his discovery with his wife and children. "Oh, yes!" he responded enthusiastically. I then asked if he had any plans to change his ways and again he was all in with whatever needed to be done. He just had one request. He wanted to clean up his mess while the family was away the next weekend. He didn't want any input. He wanted to do it all on his own. I will carry this man and his story in my heart forever. If he can do the exercise, share the outcome, and be motivated to change, so can you!

WEEK TWO

Has Anyone Seen the Dining Room Table?

This week, you can

- Declutter your dining room table
- Create a room that is inviting as well as organized
- Find creative ways to enjoy the dining room if your dinner party days are over

Time required: Two to five hours, depending on your situation.

IF YOU HAVE BEEN FOLLOWING THE program from the beginning, I have a wonderful surprise for you: Your dining room should snap to attention with very little work. Why? Because your kitchen works in concert with this room, and by now, it's already organized. In addition, your dining room table should be paper-free because you've already organized your home office. However, if you are jumping into organizing at this point, let's try to make some dramatic progress. I presume your dining room table is buried under paper, children's homework, or your craft projects. Here are fifteen easy steps to a beautiful, inviting dining room.

1. If you have a home office, your papers need to be boxed up and taken there.

Rather than tossing everything into boxes with wild abandon, however, I want you to quickly look through each pile before it gets packed. Why? Because I would bet money that there are outdated items here you simply do not need. Here's a primer of items that can be tossed immediately: old newspapers and magazines; invitations to parties that you missed; flyers for sales that have passed; catalogues from companies that keep you regularly supplied; children's art projects (you can't save them all!); and junk mail. Try a quick fifteen-minute elimination round!

2. If you have no room dedicated as a home office, take these boxes to the room that functions as a part-time

office. For most people, that's the guest room. Or perhaps you have a kitchen nook designed as a work area. Those spaces usually have one file drawer. On the other hand, if you live in a tiny apartment with no office area whatsoever, I suggest you purchase a few decorative file boxes in wicker, rattan, or faux leather. They will blend into your décor and be functional. For now, tuck the boxes of miscellaneous paper into a corner. Don't put them into the back of a closet where they will be forgotten.

3. In today's world, everyone is so frantically busy that an evening meal as a family unit has become a rarity. If you can't sit at this table every night as a family due to conflicting schedules, do plan on at least one meal a week. This is a wonderful tradition that gives everyone a chance to stay current with all the members of the family. I also think inviting friends over for dinner is a capital idea. It fills the dining room with energy. What's the point of having a room that gets used once a year and is otherwise a dump site?

4. In addition to a table and chairs, most dining rooms have a sideboard or hutch. Here decorative serving items are displayed and stored. When it comes time to celebrate Thanksgiving dinner, you know where to find everything. Or do you? Clean out these drawers or cupboards of any extraneous items that may have settled here.

5. Be sure that your good dishes, silverware (wrap in special cloth to prevent tarnishing), decorative pieces, cloth napkins, and such are housed in the sideboard or hutch. See whether you can use some decorative or serving pieces in an artful display.

6. If items in the dining room belong in other rooms, now is the perfect time to return them. Did you leave a sweater here that belongs in your closet? Is the floor littered with toys that belong in your child's room or the family room? You get the idea.

7. If the room appears bare and you have an overcrowded living or family room, why not see whether something could successfully migrate here?

8. If you have a special collection you'd like to display, would a curio cabinet fit in this room? This is a good time to say a word about collections. No matter how beautiful, rare, or expensive your collection is, remember that less is more. The eye can take in five or six beautiful objects; after that it starts to feel like browsing through a shop. Rotate what's on display. People will think you redecorated.

9. Sometimes you get a bonus and the dining room has a closet. This is the ideal place to hang linens after they are cleaned. As with your clothes closet, remove the dry cleaner's plastic bags and, if necessary, store the linens in canvas. If your collection is large, line up in the same color order you used in your closet and keep holidays just behind, preferably in the order in which they occur.

10. If your dining room has a closet, check to see if there is room to add an extra

shelf. If your kitchen is overcrowded and you have no garage, the turkey roaster might just find a home up there! Perhaps you use your grandmother's dishes for holidays while your spouse's heirloom dishes are kept for sentimental value only. Store them in padded holders made for this purpose. They too might live on that top shelf.

11. Take a look at the room itself. Is it time to freshen the window coverings? Do you need to hang something on the walls or perhaps replace what has been there since Noah built the Ark? I often find that people neglect to update their dining rooms.

12. Color is a wonderful tool to bring new life to any room. Red stimulates the senses. If the idea of a red dining room strikes fear in your heart, what about one red wall? When you were noodling around Pinterest to refine your style, you may have noticed that one or two designers seem to speak to your Soul. Check out their Pinterest boards or Instagram feeds and see what they do to jazz up a dining room. Kelly Wearstler is one of my favorite designers. She does daring things I might not want to try, but in her fearless approach, I often see possibilities. "Adapt, not adopt" should be needlepointed on a pillow. If you make one, send me a photo. If I receive enough, I'll make a Pinterest board just for those pillows!

13. If you have never been a candle person, try some scented ones in this room. Citrus stimulates the appetite. You can also burn dessert-scented candles. Fresh apple pie may not be on the menu, but your family and guests will believe it is!

14. Consider a pretty vase in the center of the table with fresh flowers each week. Supermarket chains carry inexpensive bouquets that put fresh flowers within everyone's reach. Or support your local farmers' market.

15. If you have a green thumb and there's a window, put some dramatic plants in this room. If you feel you have a black thumb, trust me, there is no such thing. Go to a nursery and describe the lighting the room gets. You'll be directed to the plants that will thrive in this atmosphere. There are plants you would be hard-pressed to kill and others it takes a village to help thrive. Be sure your nursery understands your skill level. Be sure to schedule watering day on your calendar. Yes, I did just say that!

By completing these steps, you will have created a dining room that is inviting and ready to serve your family and friends at a moment's notice. If you have a group that meets in person rather than over Zoom, I hope your Zen Organizers™ will have even more fun in this room the next time you gather!

DO I *HAVE* TO ENTERTAIN?

Everyone's life is different, and every life has stages. When it comes to organizing or celebrating holidays, one size doesn't fit all. If your dining room is gathering dust, let's consider a few alternative ways to use this room.

If you have been hosting holiday dinners and throwing parties for decades, you can officially retire. Pass the torch—and your favorite china for festive occasions. Do you have a hobby? Perhaps you long to scrapbook, quilt, or needlepoint here. No law says you can't turn your hutch or sideboard into storage for your hobby supplies.

If you are the mother of young ones and they have no place to do their homework, by all means, use this table. Perhaps you can use a storage container with multiple drawers to house some of their homework supplies. If you have that closet, you can wheel the unit in and out at will. If not, tuck it into a corner. Table pads, which protect the wood, are a wonderful investment. Simply place a vinyl tablecloth over them.

If you are a couple and both work at home since the pandemic, this room may need to function as an office for the immediate future. You'll need an internet connection, ergonomic chair, great lighting, and a place to store your work supplies. If entertaining is off the table due to a combination of work schedules and young children, keep the room tidy but fearlessly use it daily as a work space. You can rotate hours in this room and share the table with your kids when they do homework. When you have Zoom meetings, set up the background to look less like a dining room or use a pop up screen. Tell everyone this is your conference room.

You need to assess your needs and your dreams and use the space accordingly. Just remember that no matter what creative use you have invented for your dining room, it can be tidy and inviting. It should also be easy to convert it to family meal time if you need to. Organizing gives you options and should open the world of possibilities. It shouldn't lock you into what everyone else is doing.

WEEK THREE

Put Some Life in Your Living Room

This week, you can

- Clear the clutter and put life back in the living room
- Learn what to store in this room
- Declutter your piano

Time required: Varies.

WHEN I WAS GROWING UP IN BROOK-lyn, our living room was rarely used. In time, I realized that this didn't pertain just to our house. If I visited a friend, everyone relaxed in the furnished basement. If that didn't exist, we sat around the dining room table over coffee to chat. The living room would be decorated with the best a family could afford, but the family hardly ever used it. Lots of things were saved for special occasions.

Our living room was dear to my mother's heart. She selected every piece of furniture with care and displayed many of her antiques. Behind the long couch, however, was a small area that was hidden from view. The family's record player was there along with a tape recorder and my record collection. I would come home from school and sing my heart out for about an hour before I did my homework. This hidden area was where I dreamed about my future.

I was the only one in my family who regularly entered this room. It was misnamed, as most living rooms were. They should have been called "the frozen room." My mother actually had plastic flowers in a vase. Can you imagine? She kept them covered with a piece of plastic so they wouldn't get dirty. Now, there's nothing wrong with having a more formal space in your house, but if you have a room stuck in the deep freeze, let's thaw it. At the end of the calender year you can enjoy the fruits of your labors with a holiday party. If you happen to have anything covered in plastic, start there. Ditch it!

If you have a formal living room and use it for entertaining, do you like the way the room looks? If the décor bothers you, can you do any quick fixes until you have the funds to redecorate? Remember that a coat of fresh paint or one dramatic wall, a few green plants, and some new artwork on the walls will transform any room. Perhaps

---

NEVER GET DISORGANIZED AGAIN

My former assistant Lynn is very organized. She once demonstrated something that I teach my clients and students: The secret of being organized is having a good system.

Tidying up is different than getting organized. If I tidy a room, I'll have to do it often because there is no rhyme or reason to where I put things to make the room appear welcoming. When clients lament to me that they are always getting organized because it doesn't last more than two weeks, I know instantly that they have simply tidied up. Your grandmother was right: There should be a place for everything and everything must be in its place. The next time you need it, you'll know just where to look. In other words, create a system!

One day I stopped by Lynn's house before we were to go out. The night before, her three then teenage children had entertained friends, and as a result the living room/family room looked like a bomb went off. While I freshened up in the bathroom, Lynn said she would straighten up the room. I said nothing but thought, "Good luck!" Well, believe it or not, less than ten minutes later that room could have been photographed for a magazine. How? She knew where every displaced item in that room belonged. I was impressed, and then said to myself, "Here is what I teach being put to work!" And work it does. You will tweak your system over time as circumstances change, but a good system will always make life easier. That's my money-back guarantee!

---

it's a simple fix like sending the rug out to be cleaned. Even new throw pillows on the couch will make visitors think you did some serious redecorating!

If you have a piano, be careful not to have clutter on top. Once again, too many photos or too many decorative items and the eye can't focus. If you have a lot, divide them into categories and rotate them with the change in seasons. Organize your sheet music and keep it in the piano bench.

Often formal living rooms have storage areas that don't get used. Is this the case with your home? When we organize the family room, you may be in need of storage for less frequently used items. Perhaps they can migrate here because these rooms are usually fairly close together. Cupboards, for example, can hold board games you want to hold on to but rarely use now that the kids are gone. You'll find permanent game boxes online to house your collection once the cardboard starts to crumble. This is especially useful because it's best to store games on their side rather than stacked. You simply pull out the game you want rather than tackling an entire stack. If the kids are still home, it's much easier for them to help themselves and then restore order.

You might want to have a shelf on a bookcase devoted to photo albums you have completed. If you need to leave your guests for a bit, they can get to know your family better by looking at an old album. Now that you've taken the time to scrapbook or put your photos in albums, why not share them with others?

Perhaps you can fill a cupboard or some drawers with your overflow candles. You might even want to store less frequently used sheet music in one of these cupboards. Take a few minutes to sort it by category so that in the middle of a party you can easily come up with the song you need.

I'm not suggesting that the living room be a secret dumping ground for clutter you can't part with! I am suggesting that storage in any home should not be wasted. This room is related to the dining room and the family room. Guests usually relax here before and after a meal. It seems the appropriate place to house overflow items from these other rooms. What will you store in your living room?

The Pandemic Push

We seem to be moving out of the era of the great room and once again embracing walls. I love huge rooms, but are they practical? Without sound absorbers like rugs, drapes, room dividers, and big furniture, it's going to be noisy. What if you now work exclusively from home and need to carve out a workspace in the great room? Let's consider a few key items:

- Remember in the kitchen how we created zones for particular activities and placed the related tools in their designated locations? Do the same in the great room.
- Carving out an area to work doesn't mean it has to look like an office all the time. Use a laptop instead of a desk model computer for one. If you

have a Wi-Fi hookup, each person needing the area just has to log in and start work.

- If you are using a desk with no drawers, place a decorative box on it and keep office supplies inside when you aren't working. Small pouches with zippers can keep those supplies separated. You'll be able to grab what you need without having to dig through a treasure trove of paper clips and staples.
- Be sure you have adequate lighting and—can I say this too often?—an ergonomic chair.
- How big is your family and how social are you? In a large family with children, friends will be dropping in after school while extended family may fill the space on weekends. Carve out areas for them as well.
- Are there hidden areas in the home like an infrequently used guest room that are better suited for transformations to work zones? Last week we considered the dining room as an option.
- You can carve a great room into zones with portable screens, large pieces of furniture like bookcases, hang a beaded curtain, use color or rugs, raise the floor in one area, or use different types of flooring. Pinterest has a plethora of images to inspire you.

Remember these suggestions provide visual separation. Noise is your real challenge. In a pinch, throw on noise-canceling headphones and dive into that laptop! The

COVID era ushered in a heightened need to share space. There are no solutions that provide a seamless transition—human beings are involved. You have to consider all the factors, from the limitations and possibilities of the space to the personalities involved and their needs as far as timing and function. Resolution is possible. Compromise is the currency that leads to a successful outcome.

WEEK FOUR

The Family Room

This week, you can

- Make the family room more fun to be in
- Share the fun: assign a chore!
- Learn how to organize the most common items stored in the family room, including family photos, media collections, and books

Time required: Four to six hours to organize; one to two hours to shop for supplies, if you need them.

I T'S IMPORTANT TO HAVE A ROOM where everyone can kick back and enjoy the TV, play games, watch a favorite movie, or listen to some music. I also think it's great to have a space where children don't have to be worried that one spill will cause Mom to explode. Formal entertaining is reserved for the living room. The family gathers here.

With that said, furniture in this room should be treated for easy cleanup and stain protection. Removable covers that are easily washed or dry cleaned are another boon for those prone to spill or who have pets. I am in this category. The coffee table and worktable in this room should either be treated or have the tops covered to prevent damage. If you can, have easy-to-wipe-off surfaces instead of wood. If it's not prohibitively expensive, you might have a glass top cut to fit the table. Make sure to have the corners rounded off to make them less sharp.

The freedom to enjoy, however, comes with a price. And that is the need for maintenance. Mom frequently becomes the sheriff who polices the mess in this room, but no one over the age of two should walk out of this room without having a hand in restoring order! Remind your family of these rules: If you take a toy out to play with it, return it. If you open the doors to a cupboard, pull open a drawer, or take the lid off a storage unit to get something, close it before you leave. If you brought something here from another room, return it when you're done. You get the idea. If you have a large family, responsibility for this room can rotate on a monthly or weekly basis.

IS THE ROOM FUNCTIONAL?

When you wrote about this room earlier this month in your journal, were you happy with it? What can you do to make it a more inviting space? This room takes a lot of wear and tear. With your goals in mind, the following tips should get you on the road to fulfillment.

Are some items ready to be trashed or donated? Let's remove them.

Would you like to see some items in other locations? Take them there now. As an example, perhaps you want your children to do their homework in their rooms and you see notebooks left scattered in the family room. Or maybe you were paying bills here instead of your home office and you see those papers were left on the coffee table. You may also see mundane items such as glasses, cups, and plates that need to be returned to the kitchen.

Now that the room is less crowded, let's survey it again. After you fold the cozy weighted blankets and plump the pillows, close the cupboard and cabinet doors, and empty the trash can, is the room the way you'd like to see it? If the culprit is a need to redecorate, make a wish list and check your budget to see when you can replace items. For example, does the room need a fresh coat of paint or a new sofa? If you're going to scrapbook (or do any hobby, really) here,

do you have a worktable for that purpose? Is the trash can adequate for the room? Draw up your design plan and divide it into two groups: the items you can purchase immediately versus the things you'll do in the future as funds allow.

I recently worked with a woman who showed me a great table for scrapbooking that was stored in her guesthouse. When her husband saw that we had brought it into her office, he wasn't happy. "It's so ugly!" he said. I assured him that it could be revived. Sometimes a high-quality furniture polish will do the trick. Or you might want to sand it down and paint it a festive color. There are all sorts of special paints and application techniques. This seemingly simple fix can actually be quite creative. Since this was in her private home office and out of sight, it would also be easy to simply have a piece of glass cut to fit the top. Look at old furniture in a different light. A new slipcover will revive a couch that is in good condition but stained or faded. You may not need to purchase new furniture after all.

DISPLAYING PHOTOS

Another big chaos culprit in family rooms is a glut of photos on display. If your children are in college, ten photos of them as toddlers will be of interest only to you! Take those photos out of their frames and store them in an album. Put your current life on prominent display. Remember: Less is more in this situation. If you have a lot of photos framed, rotate them.

Teens often complain to me about photos of themselves that their parents have prominently placed in the family's common rooms. A word to the wise: If your child struggled with weight or acne and is now slim with alabaster skin, he or she doesn't want the photos of a painful past on display for their friends, dates, or anyone else visiting the home to see. Be sensitive to these unspoken issues.

ORGANIZING SOLUTIONS

Let's look at some organizing solutions and products that will help out the family room.

Collections

CDs, DVDs, records, cassettes, and VHS tapes used to occupy much of our personal storage space. In today's world streaming and cloud storage capabilities are causing physical collections to wane in popularity. Thank goodness because their absence frees up so much space in the home (usually the family room). I am leaving the original instructions intact in case either you or perhaps someone in your family needs a little assistance in the form of ideas. You can put a lot of unconscious emotional attachment onto a collection by associating it with a time in your life that has now passed. Or you may justify these space takers by saying you spent good money acquiring them. Be compassionate.

Feel free to organize the old collections and go all streaming into the future. One day you will look at these relics and suddenly be ready to toss. Don't fret. In one way or another it happens to everyone. I've had several clients who had a death grip on the original boxes their electronic equipment came in. I'm talking about a glut of boxes! In one case, we put a loft in the garage so these empty boxes had a carved out space to live. In another instance, we put a prefab shed on the property. Now you see how after three decades I am never bored by this work.

Solutions

If you have cupboards with deep drawers, you can purchase inserts to store your collections in an orderly fashion. These holders are usually in acrylic and lay flat. You put your VHS tape or disc in a slot to keep it in place. If you want, you could also have a carpenter put in custom-designed slots in wood.

If you are willing to part with your jewel cases or store them in the garage or attic, purchase binders and special inserts to hold the discs. This is an incredible space saver! Break your collections down into categories and store individual binders on a shelf or outside this room if it's crowded. If your son is an avid gamer, for example, he can keep his album in his room. If you and your spouse enjoy music that drives your teenagers up the wall, you can store your music in the primary suite. If you have a CD player in your bedroom, you can enjoy your music without comment.

There are also towers for CDs and DVDs. I've seen some that mount on the wall. You might want something whimsical that fits in with the décor of the room.

Or you might want to store them by category on the shelves of a bookcase. You can get inexpensive bookcases at stores such as IKEA or the local home store. If you like, add a coat of paint. They may not be fine furniture, but who can tell when they are filled with media?

Hardly anyone plays records or cassettes anymore. (Most people reading this won't know what a cassette is!) Transfer your all-time favorites to the cloud and donate the rest. Current and detailed instructions for how to transfer are best found on Google. It will depend on the service you use, such as YouTube, Amazon Music, or Google. Did you know that they make special display frames for record albums? You might want to display that Beatles album you got when it first came out. That's a great example of something that will be a conversation piece for all music lovers. What's your favorite album?

If you do store your albums, purchase special record boxes. And don't place heavy items on top. You run the risk of warping your treasures.

Everyone in the family needs to sit down and go through their personal entertainment/media collection. The goal is to eliminate the items they no longer enjoy. Donate these to a charity. Or you can go to www .cashforcds.com if you'd like to make some money to replenish your favorite category.

As everyone weeds out their collection to get down to what is really listened to or viewed, divide what you are keeping by type. This is the best way to store multiple items in rapidly expanding categories rather than organizing them by strict alphabetical order. Here's an example of categories: divide movies into action, comedy, and drama rather than lumping them all into one huge alphabetical grouping of every movie you own. (You'll notice I did alphabetize my categories!) After you cull and sort, you're ready to decide how to store. Do you need drawer inserts, binders, bookcases, containers, or another type of holder? Add these items to your shopping list.

Books

So many books, so little time. If you have a large collection of books, be sure you pull some for charity or donation to your local library. Yes, I know. Books are like children or old friends. But some need to be passed on to others. For example, your high school and college textbooks need to go. If you have paperbacks that are mysteries or self-help (once you know who did it and how to fix it, let someone else enjoy the process), give them to a charity or retirement home.

Perhaps you once enjoyed a hobby that no longer interests you. Give those books away and make room for the hobby that has captured your fancy today. You get the idea. Your first task is to whittle down your collection. As you're doing that, you can start creating your categories: biographies, novels, self-help, and special interest, for example. Next, we'll talk about organizing your book categories. The Magic Formula comes to our rescue again, as it has throughout this book.

Keep in mind that your entire book collection doesn't have to be housed in a single room. Your book categories can be placed in specific and special places around your home. I used to keep my Spiritual books in my bedroom. After I redecorated last winter, that bookcase moved to my office. Now those books live there along with the ones that relate to business or my profession. My office is in my home and neither my FedEx guy nor my best friend enters it. It's my sanctuary. What books would you put in your sanctuary?

Next to my love seat in the living room, I have the current books I want to read. They sit on a side table and I use bookends to keep them upright. As I finish each one, I decide if it's going to stay with me or be passed on to a friend or charity. When I had a house, I kept novels in the guest room and coffee table books in the living room.

Keep a selection of general favorites in the family room. Cookbooks belong in the kitchen. Let little ones have books of their own in their rooms. I hope you read to them each night. Consider the size and scope of your collection as well as the size of your living space and divide your books accordingly.

After you distribute your "whittled down to the gold" collection, you may find you need some bookcases. Portable bookcases that fold open (the shelves drop down) are great for small collections in tight spaces. Whatever style décor you have and whatever your budget, the perfect bookcase is waiting for you!

In your quest, don't ignore the world of bookends because they are invaluable. There are fun ones, ornate ones, ones for children, and utilitarian ones that do the job and offer no beauty. Again, match your bookends to the décor in your room. Nothing looks sloppier than books falling all over a shelf. Try not to line them up like soldiers. Instead, have a row lined up on one shelf and on the others try different visual designs. You might have a stack on the left side of the shelf and on the next, a straight line of books held to attention with bookends. The next shelf up could reverse the pattern, and so on. Artful placement is part of your décor.

Magazines, Catalogues, and Newspapers

I want to give you a present. It's worth the price of this book. Will you accept it? Here it comes: You do not have to save every magazine and newspaper that comes into your home. You do not have to hold on to these items because something important might be in there! You don't have to feel guilty when they hit the recycle pile. There, I said it. Now you have to believe me. Did you just feel a pang of pride and think: "I don't subscribe to any physical magazines, catalogues, or newspapers. I am all digital." Well, that is a step in the right direction but consider canceling those that no longer interest you or have a "Miscellaneous Subscription" file on your computer. If you want to peruse the list from time to time to see if a reactivation is called for, you have one place to look. See "Organizing the Business of Life" for more info.

Toys

It's never too early for kids to learn about putting items in categories. Toys can be your first teachers. Divide your child's collection as you see fit. Groupings like the following might work: stuffed animals; franchises (think G.I. Joe or Barbie); Legos; puzzles; and board games. You want your children to be able to reach toys so that they can help themselves and also return them easily. Use bags that zip to help keep small board game pieces together. At arts and craft stores such as Michaels, you can find bags in a wide variety of sizes. You don't have to use the ones in the grocery store, because they are probably a bit too big for the pieces of most board game collections.

Remember those plastic containers on wheels that I love so much for storage? You can store the lids and use them in the family room for toy categories. This works well because young children can pull an entire group of toys over to their designated play area. When your children are older and these containers have outlived their usefulness, they can store other items throughout the house.

I like toy chests, provided the lid stays put whenever you open it. A heavy lid crashing down on a small hand or head is a painful experience. Wicker, rattan, and other natural products provide us with baskets you may like better than plastic containers because they blend with your décor. Just be sure they are smooth (and preferably come with pull-out washable liners). You don't want anyone getting scratched as they set out to have a good time!

As with displaying your book collection, displaying toys depends on the amount you have and the space available. I have lots of clients who ask their children to eliminate toys periodically so that underprivileged children can have them to play with. I think this plants a seed of generosity in your child that will flower in ways you cannot imagine.

A small table and chairs are wonderful if you have the space. A surface that is easy to wipe off and resists being stained by crayons and markers is best. Stores such as Target have a wide selection. Why pay a fortune for items that are meant to take a beating? Besides, you won't feel so bad when the children grow up and it's time to donate the furniture to charity.

And let's not forget that the family room is also the perfect place for adults to play. This room is a great place to work on the family photo albums or make quilts or do needlepoint. Maybe that table can be cleared periodically so that Dad can have a poker game with the guys.

This week it's time to start using those wonderful organizing tools in the rooms you share with others. As with all organizing, some hard, physical work is involved. However, think ahead to the reward that awaits you. Your family will have comfortable places to gather in the home. Your friends will feel more welcome. And perhaps best of all, spontaneous visitors will no longer fill you with dread. This month you're more than a Zen Organizer™. You're a Soul Nurturer!

SUMMARY

WEEK ONE

Develop a mental blueprint for the way you want your dining room, living room, and family room to look and function.

WEEK TWO

Pick and choose from the organizing solutions offered for the dining room.

Think outside the box when deciding how this room will be used.

WEEK THREE

Rescue the living room from a dead zone to a room filled with vital energy.

Learn to use all the storage available in the living room.

Start your shopping list.

If you're part of a group, you might shop with your fellow Zen Organizers™.

WEEK FOUR

With tools in hand and a well-designed plan of attack, bring order to the rooms shared with family and friends.

Move on to organizing the all-important family room and decide how books, media, and toys will be housed here.

BONUS TIP

Gardening is hard work (hello, weeds, I'm talkin' to you) but it can bring incredible peace and fulfillment to the practitioner. If you have a lawn, does all of it need to be a vast expanse of water-guzzling green grass? Why not try a few raised beds and grow some of your own food? If you have a deep kitchen window, why not grow herbs? Snipping your own bounty to flavor a home-cooked meal is a special kind of high. If you are an apartment dweller with an avowed black thumb, why not get one almost-impossible-to-kill plant and see how it brightens a room and brings life into the equation. Every time I have planted seeds, when that first green sprout appears, I want to run around showing it to everyone as if I just had a baby. Life is a miracle and we have the privilege of bearing witness.

Here are some additional benefits of gardening:

- Gardening can relieve stress.
- You can make it a Mindful practice.
- Gardening provides an opportunity for children to learn where food literally comes from.
- Moving about your garden is good for your heart and builds hand strength.
- Join a community garden and foster feeling connected (something the post-pandemic world needs).

Exit rituals can be created for each of these rooms, but they will be unique to your family and how each is used. Think of the steps you create as a way to bless the next user of the space, even if that happens to be you. We want others to love and respect us, but we sometimes forget that first we have to give those gifts to ourselves.

ENTERTAINING WITH JOY!

Wear gratitude like a cloak and it will feed every corner of your life.

–RUMI

IF YOU'VE BEEN BUSY GETTING ORGA-nized all year, I have some wonderful news for you: The holiday season should be like no other. Not only is your home ready to receive guests, it now supports rather than sabotages you. About this time I am sure you feel special gratitude for all that you have accomplished. Thanksgiving is *your* holiday! I use this holiday as the standard-bearer. If you can organize a big holiday celebration, you can ace smaller gatherings with aplomb.

Don't panic if you have just started the program. With this section you will have the tools to plan a lovely holiday gathering. I'm also going to help you do a quick fix to make your home look like you've been organizing all year. End-of-the-year festivities are always associated with a lot of work. A good plan, however, will allow something else to sneak into the picture: joy.

Well, we don't have a minute to lose. Let's get ready to give thanks, shall we?

HABIT OF THE MONTH

As each day of this month draws to a close, write in your journal one thing for which you are grateful. It might be something like the health of your children. Or it could be gratitude for something that happened that day. Nothing is too insignificant to count, even something as simple as being waved into busy traffic by a smiling motorist qualifies as an experience for which you are grateful. Don't forget to take a turn being that generous motorist. You can note you were "Grateful this day for the opportunity to be kind to another human being."

AFFIRMATION OF THE MONTH

As the challenges of this month come to me, I greet them with a smile and a positive, can-do attitude. I do the best I can each day. I am filled with the joy that permeates this holiday season.

Self-Care Practice

During the holidays it is common to increase alcohol consumption that in turn dehydrates our bodies and robs us of the extra energy we need in exchange for a bit of euphoria. I'm going to suggest that during these busy times we become vigilant about pure water consumption. I'm not suggesting you totally eschew alcohol! I just want you to be mindful about water consumption. Your body has no clue what Christmas or any other holiday means. It's a machine. Help it function.

WEEK ONE

Holiday Stress Questions

This week, you can

- Look back to your childhood Thanksgiving experiences
- Decide what kind of holiday you will create this year

Time required: Thirty to sixty minutes.

WHEN YOU HEAR THE WORD *Thanksgiving*, do you have a knee-jerk reaction? Did you have the kind of holiday you see on TV and in the movies? Or was it a sad time of year? TV and movie images can really do a number on us. They are idealized versions of reality. I think this is a great holiday because we don't have to worry about presents. All we have to do is count our blessings and...oh yes, eat!

Sometimes, however, that's where this holiday causes us trouble. Maybe you're the designated host or hostess for the family and, while you love having everyone over, you struggle with that big meal. Getting all those dishes to the table at the same time isn't easy. I think it's silly to spoil the holiday with concerns about food, so I have some fabulous guidelines for organizing the day.

For too many of us, entertaining, especially for the holidays, adds pressure rather than joy to an already overloaded schedule. As a society we don't just celebrate the holidays, we seek to achieve an unrealistic level of perfection. I encourage you to write in your journal about your holiday experiences, especially those of your childhood. Let's take some time this week to figure out what would make you happy this season.

Please answer the following questions in your journal:

1. On a scale of one to ten, how would you rate your childhood Thanksgiving experiences? Whether your score was low or high, what factors did you take into consideration to arrive at your score?

2. Was there a particular holiday that stands out as being the best? What details can you list that made it so special? Be specific.

3. On the other hand, was there a holiday that you remember as a very sad time? Was it due to something that happened that year, such as a death in the family? Or perhaps a divorce that forever changed the landscape of your life?

4. List five things you experienced growing up that you feel are essential ingredients of a really great Thanksgiving celebration. Why?

5. Now list five things you experienced growing up that you absolutely avoid at all costs. Why?

6. Have these questions brought up anything else about the holiday that you'd like to write about in your journal? Please do so now. Set your timer for five minutes. When you have completed all the questions, you are free to return at your leisure and write until you find resolution.

7. These questions are designed to remove forever any knee-jerk reactions that have their origins in the past. It's over. You need to acknowledge what happened and then make the decision to learn from it and let go. For example, look at those five things that you feel are essential to this holiday. How are you going to bring all of them to this year's celebration? And what about the things you never want to repeat again? How will you avoid those? Plan this holiday. Don't just let it happen to you. That's why we take the time to write in our journal.

Now let's skip to the present:

1. Do you enjoy Thanksgiving? If yes, what delights you? If not, when and where were the seeds of your discontent sowed?

2. Do you always have a large group over to your home? Or are you a sought-after guest?

3. Would you like to do something different this year? Perhaps you love family gatherings but you'd like to see another family member step up to the plate and host the festivities? Or maybe you'd like to skip Thanksgiving this year and go to a warm Caribbean beach for the long weekend? Be specific and then ask yourself, "How can I make my dream a reality?"

If you are harboring a dream Thanksgiving, when are you going to make it a reality? It might not live up to your expectations, but at least you won't die wondering! I had a client who decided one year she didn't want to be with her family. She loved them dearly but she wanted an adventure. A few days before Turkey Day, she got an invitation to go to dinner at the home of someone she didn't know. Ordinarily she wouldn't have considered this invitation. Would you want to go to a Thanksgiving celebration where you knew only the person who had invited you? Of course not!

But this invitation had a catch. It was the home of a famous movie star. There would be about thirty people, with two chefs preparing a fabulous meal. She went. Wouldn't you? Her family still teases her about the year she threw them over for a famous actor. I asked my client if she would do it again. She told me she had a lovely time but realized that of all the holidays in the calendar year, this is the one to spend with family. By the way, she says it was the best meal she's ever had on Thanksgiving!

And, yes, the movie star was gracious and kind. And, no, I can't tell you who it was!

Every time anyone shifts the relationships in a group dynamic, it creates the opportunity for everyone to experience something new. Be as loving and direct as you can if you decide to make an announcement that's going to rock the boat. A change in tradition must come from a place of love and not be an opportunity to punish a family member for past hurts. Make peace with your plans for this Thanksgiving.

WEEK TWO

Make a Clean Sweep

This week, you can

- Sweep through the home to make sure it's ready for guests
- Plan your day, from the food to the table settings

Time required: The sweep depends on the size of your home and the state it's in when you begin; the planning depends on the extravagance of your goals. Be generous and allow two to three hours for the sweep and one to two hours for the planning.

IF YOU BEGAN THIS PROGRAM ELEVEN months ago or if you just organized the kitchen, you know where your holiday serving pieces, china, and crystal are stored. You still have a lot of planning to do, but you are ahead of the game. If you haven't done that work, let's start the week with some emergency measures designed to get you ready for company.

Most families gather in the dining room to eat and then, stuffed, lie like beached whales on the comfortable furniture in the family room. So let's start in these rooms. The work we do now will help you down the line when you are ready to spend some time in these rooms getting organized. For now, we want to make space for your guests. Please get some heavy-duty trash bags and a timer. You may need a file folder and a few boxes.

Give yourself thirty minutes in each room for speed elimination. During this time, you need to move as quickly as possible. No stopping to swoon over the photograph of a loved one. No time to spend a few minutes complaining about the stack of magazines or newspapers you never get to read. Your goal is to be in perpetual motion!

What are you looking for? Here are your guidelines:

1. Toss the obvious debris. Empty the trash cans.

2. Return items that don't belong in these rooms to their rightful home. For example, has a cup, glass, or plate been languishing here for a few days?

3. If your dining room table has been used as an office, put papers into a box. Instead of dumping everything, go through the papers quickly, a stack at a time, before they get placed into the box. Toss old sale flyers and catalogues, invitations that have passed, menus for restaurants you have no interest in, catalogues you receive all the time, and so on. Store only the papers you need to keep.

4. Be on the lookout for items that need your attention before Thanksgiving. Keep those in a file folder. This is your temporary "Action" folder. You don't want to miss an important payment such as your mortgage because you tidied up the dining room for Thanksgiving. This is a time to consider automatic payments for set monthly amounts. Store your box out of the view of guests. The more digital you are, the smaller the box!

5. When you get to the family room, you probably won't be confronted with papers. Here the culprits are usually those newspapers and magazines that never get read. Recycle all but the most current.

6. Return toys to your child's room. If the family room is where they normally reside, box up the overflow until after the holiday.

7. Fido and Fifi may have their own explosion of toys. Keep them contained in one area. A nice basket for pet toys is always welcome.

8. Take a minute to make a list of products you need such as magazine holders, containers for toys, and a nice holder for all the remotes. You can shop for these online before Thanksgiving.

9. Take a look around after your big sweep. If you were to plump the pillows, fold the afghan, run the vacuum, and dust, would you be good to go? If not, what else is there for you to do? If you have things in mind such as painting, new wallpaper, or refinishing the wood floor, ask yourself if you can realistically get this finished in time for Turkey Day. If you can't, be sure to tell everyone at dinner how excited you are about your upcoming plans to refresh the look of your home.

10. Is your kitchen organized? If not, we can do some things to make working here a lot more convenient and comfortable. Let's begin with your counters. Do you have too many gadgets and canisters out? Let's move all the items you no longer want on display to the nearest table. You need your counter space for prep work and cooking.

11. Open each cupboard and drawer in turn and fearlessly gather the items you can toss or donate. Does this open a space for those counter items you don't use that often? By the way, as you locate all the items you need for your holiday table during this expedition, pull them out. You need to get them ready for Thanksgiving.

12. If you didn't remove enough items to make room for your counter overflow treasures, let's find a place to store

them until you organize the kitchen. There is usually a cavernous space above the refrigerator. Is that available to you? What about the smaller space above the stove? Do you have a garage, a basement, or an attic with some open space? Do you have a walk-in pantry with floor or shelf space? If you come up dry, keep the items on a back counter. Thanksgiving dinner requires lots of pots, pans, cooking tools—and space. I suggest in the Kitchen section that you serve your family from the kitchen and eat in the dining room. For this holiday you might serve from a sideboard in the dining room if using the kitchen isn't practical. Why? If people have to get up to get seconds (or thirds), they hesitate. Thanksgiving doesn't have to be about eating yourself into a coma.

SUCCESS IS IN THE DETAILS

Whether you are already organized or you've just completed tidying up for the big day, we're ready to move forward. This is a busy week! If you can host Thanksgiving, you can do dinner parties all year long with your eyes closed. This day is the big test. You'll need to make several decisions, beginning with your budget.

1. Take a sheet of paper or work in your journal. At the top of the page, write down the amount of money you can comfortably spend to produce your ideal Thanksgiving holiday. Keep in mind that the gift-giving season starts next month and you don't want to blow your entire holiday budget on this one meal. We're going to work out the details to be sure you can honor this figure. Let's begin by creating your guest list.

2. The next order of business is to decide whether you are going to have a sit-down dinner or a buffet. The latter is the easiest way to serve a large group.

3. You want to create an elegant and inviting table setting. Will you be using your good china for this holiday? Do you have enough place settings for everyone? If you have several sets, are you comfortable mixing and matching your pieces? You can mix and match for the main course or use one set for the main course and another for dessert. Take a minute to decide how the table will be set. Tablescaping ideas abound on Pinterest.

4. Will you have wine with your meal? How many bottles will you need? What other drinks do you want to offer your guests? Whatever beverages you serve, do you have the requisite crystal and glasses? Do you have an icemaker or ice cube trays or will you have to purchase ice that day?

5. Do you want to have a fresh flower arrangement or do you have a traditional decorative piece you use?

6. Would you like music in the background or will you be eating to the strains of football?

7. Do you want candles for the table? Will you use scented or plain; traditional,

dripless, soy, or beeswax? Do you have candlestick holders?

8. Do you use a special holiday tablecloth? Does it need to be cleaned? If it has been hanging for the past year, it may need to be pressed.

9. Do you have enough cutlery? If you are using real silver, does it need to be polished?

10. If you aren't serving buffet style, will everyone be at one table? Or will you have several seating areas set up? In either case, do you have enough chairs?

11. Do you want the little ones at a special table? Will they be using the everyday dishes instead of real china?

Your Thanksgiving holiday is taking shape. Next week we'll finalize our plan.

WEEK THREE

Plan the Menu

This week, you can

- Create your to-do list and shopping list
- Design your menu
- Try the menu provided here from a professional chef

Time required: Varies.

AT THIS JUNCTURE, YOU HAVE AN-swered the questions that will shape your celebration. First, create two lists. The first will be your to-do list of all the things you need to prepare at home and the other will be a shopping list. For example, on one list I would note that I have to borrow some serving dishes and clean the good china and crystal. On another I would note that I have to pick up wine, a fresh flower arrangement, and paper place settings for the children. Take a minute to do this. Don't forget, a list is only productive if you actually use it! You'll want to set aside the time to take care of the tasks indicated. Take out your calendar and start scheduling!

Remember the story of Molly, and how her mom had target dates for the completion of her science project on a big

calendar? Well, in essence, we are counting back from our target date and scheduling the steps that will carry us to our goal. Organizing is simple and has many applications throughout life. Since the first edition, Molly has become a nurse and started a fitness business. Her organizing skills shine. Her wise mom fostered them in her childhood.

WHAT'S FOR DINNER?

This week, you'll need to design your menu. From this menu, you will create a food shopping list. If you have relatives or friends who love to cook, check to see what they are bringing this year. This way, you'll have one or two fewer dishes to prepare. If some of your guests aren't the best cooks in the world, consider what item you can ask them to bring. Is there a wonderful bakery in your neighborhood? Let someone pick up the pies. Is there a fabulous florist nearby? Ask a guest to provide the centerpiece.

The tips in this section on preparing the meal come from a professional chef, my dear friend Tanya Russell. She has retired now but spent several years cooking for a Hollywood power couple and created special events for clients of her Los Angeles–based catering company. A great chef has to be organized and have a keen understanding of time management.

PARTY PLANNING 101

This section is meant as a primer for those who find entertaining a daunting task. What did we learn at the beginning? The whole of anything is overwhelming. You need to break down projects into manageable chunks. Let's apply that bit of wisdom to planning a party.

What Is the Purpose of the Party?

Are you celebrating a birthday, a graduation, or a promotion? Would you like to impress someone you work for, are in love with, or newly related to through marriage? Is it a major holiday, a wedding, or a funeral?

After you answer this question, you'll be amazed how much you automatically know about your event.

For example, a graduation is traditionally in June, right? You will want a filling but light menu. People don't want turkey, yams, mashed potatoes, and gravy when it's one hundred degrees in the shade!

If it's a holiday meal, certain dishes will be expected, won't they?

You might be further guided by your ethnic heritage. When Italians are invited for a traditional Sunday family meal, for example, they are expecting pasta, not haggis!

How Many Guests?

What is the best format for the number of people you will be entertaining? You probably can't seat thirty at your dining room table. Do you want a buffet or a cocktail party?

At this point you have the reason for the party, an idea what type of food will be served, the number of guests, and the format. See how easy that was?

What Is the Budget?

You want to design your party as artfully as you would your home. What do you want for your guests? Champagne, multiple courses, a sparkling array of hors d'oeuvres? And what about the centerpiece, flowers, and music? Will you do all the cooking and the serving or will you hire a caterer?

Price your elements and see if you came in on budget. If not, start eliminating or find cost-effective ways to provide the same amenities with a lower price tag. Wine is a good example of an item with a wide price range.

And don't forget that you can always eliminate a guest or two!

Could friends contribute a dish or a dessert? This is especially helpful on a day such as Thanksgiving when the meal is large and takes a lot of preparation.

Perhaps you'll cut flowers from a friend's garden rather than order a centerpiece this year. (In Los Angeles, for example, roses bloom all year long.)

Why don't you cross candles off your list and create a mood by installing a dimmer switch instead?

Plan the Specifics of Your Menu

For your menu, here are some considerations to guide you:

- If it's going to be a cold winter night, you probably want to have a nice hearty soup to start the meal.
- If it's summer, a light salad would be a refreshing choice for after the main course, European style.
- Decide what the focal point is for the meal and design around it. For example, Thanksgiving is a big meal with lots of heavy food. Everyone arrives hungry for traditional fare. If you fill them up with hors d'oeuvres, they won't have any room for turkey! If kids are in the house or guests come from a long distance, tide them over with cheese and crackers or a nice platter of fresh crudités and some dip. Keep it simple. You want them to be seduced by the incredible aromas wafting from your kitchen!

TAMING THE TURMOIL OF TURKEY DAY

At this point, I think we should look at Thanksgiving. As the mother of all dinner parties, it's all gravy after you have this meal under your belt! Let's pretend the big day is next week. What are you going to do?

Perhaps the biggest detail of the Thanksgiving meal is the star attraction: the turkey. One of your most important decisions will be to choose a fresh or frozen bird. A frozen bird can be picked up on Monday with your other ingredients. A fresh bird will need to be ordered this week. Pick it up next Tuesday because the stores are a zoo the day before Thanksgiving. If you have vegetarian or vegan guests, add some sides and get a smaller bird. This vegan thinks Tofurky is dreadful, so you needn't consider it a replacement food for all your nonmeat consumers. Check out Chefs Chad and Derek Sarno's website, Wicked Kitchen, and the book they cowrote with David Joachim, *The Wicked Healthy Cookbook*, for inspiration. We vegans are happy with sides and a salad.

The following is a sample Thanksgiving menu from Chef Tanya.

THANKSGIVING DAY MENU

At the Table with Family and Friends
Hors d'Oeuvres (optional: two choices maximum)
    Stuffed celery with goat cheese and fresh herbs
    Crudités platter with buttermilk ranch dressing
    Cheese and crackers

Main Meal
  Roast turkey with gravy
  Cornbread dressing
  Baked macaroni and cheese
  Candied yams with golden apples
  Herb mashed potatoes
  Cranberry and orange chutney
  Green beans with roasted shallots
  Yeast rolls
  Squash soup (optional)

Desserts
  Sweet potato, pumpkin, apple, or
    pecan pie
  Ice cream or whipped cream or both
    (optional)

Beverages
  Wine or champagne
  Sodas
  Water (sparkling and flat)
  Cocktails (optional)
  Coffee and tea with milk or half-and-
    half; sugar and artificial sweeteners

DON'T FORGET YOUR
SHOPPING LIST

Don't go to the store without a shopping
list this week. And before you go, check
your pantry and refrigerator to see what
you have in stock. If you see an ingredient,
be sure it's fresh and you have enough.
This is not a week to make assumptions!
The market is too crowded this time of
year for repeat visits.

At the same time, you might consider
having groceries delivered, especially if
you are in a big city and walk everywhere.
With the price of gas, it's often cheaper to
tip the delivery person than to drive your
own car. Give yourself a break and conserve your energy for cooking. You don't
want to be an exhausted host who can't
wait for everyone to leave!

A STRESS-FREE ENVIRONMENT

Although the process of preparing a huge
meal can be stressful because it's a lot of
work, try to stay positive. The holidays are
about families celebrating together—the
holiday is not supposed to be perfect. If
you have vowed to make this a memorable
Thanksgiving for your loved ones, you are
now armed with the wisdom to carry you
through the day.

DELEGATE!

This is one of the biggest meals of the year. Don't be a martyr! After all, this isn't your boss you are entertaining, it's your family and closest friends! Assign chores to those living in the home. Ask everyone to help after the meal is over. Cleaning up after this meal is usually a social time for the family and their guests. You'll have lots of volunteers because they all want leftovers!

Tanya feels strongly that the post-Thanksgiving cleanup is part of the holiday. Guests may want to swap recipes with you. People may have another glass of wine as they clean up the kitchen and get ready for dessert. If you see that the pots and pans will take extra effort to clean, just let them soak until everyone has gone. Everything else will be put away.

One word of caution from your Zen Organizer™: Don't let people do whatever they please. Assign tasks and give specific instructions! You don't want the order you created in your kitchen destroyed by Aunt Tilly, who believes she knows everything about kitchen placement. She can take care of her own space. This is yours!

At the close of this week, you need to know that your home is ready for guests and that all elements (dishes, candles, crystal, and so on) are ready for Thanksgiving. The more time you spend planning and making notes, the smoother the day will run. If you have family members at home, be generous with the chores you assign. This isn't a one-person operation. Besides, how will children learn how to host their own parties if you don't involve them?

Be creative.

WEEK FOUR

Countdown to T-Day

This week, you can

- Create a step-by-step guide to Turkey Day
- Set the stage
- Clean up the kitchen and restore the house

Time required: Varies, depending on how elaborate your meal is and how many people are at the table.

O UR GOAL THIS WEEK IS TO ORGA-nize our time, conserve our energy, and have fun! Here is an outline for a meal made from scratch with all fresh ingredients. My goal is to help you see how activities are scheduled over the four days. Please adjust to suit your schedule and taste. Whether you baste your turkey or put it in a cooking bag, whether you make stuffing from a box or prepare dressing from scratch, these are your decisions. These detailed notes are to help you understand how to plan and manage your time.

Monday

- Complete all food shopping by the end of the day (except for any forgotten emergency items).

- If you plan on making the stuffing from scratch, make the bread for it today.

Tuesday

- Assemble all the ingredients for the stuffing in a Ziploc bag and then store it in the refrigerator. (Casserole dishes are okay, but they take up too much space on a day when you have so many things to store.) On Thursday, you can add broth and cook.
- Make homemade yeast rolls today. Store in a Ziploc bag or an air-tight glass container. If you prefer, you can purchase ready-to-heat rolls. They can be heated and served on Thursday. Tanya's favorites come from a company

called Bridgford. I've included their website in the Resources section at my website.

- Do all your sauté work. Refrigerate.

Wednesday

- Make the desserts. Sweet potato pie and pumpkin pie can be served at room temperature. Do you want a topping for these pies, such as ice cream or whipped cream? Be sure those items are on your shopping list!
- Make the cranberry sauce today so the gel has time to set by dinner tomorrow.
- Clean and prep the turkey. Keep it covered in the refrigerator until tomorrow.
- Peel and slice the yams.
- Parboil the green beans today and store them in a plastic bag in the refrigerator until tomorrow.
- Assemble the macaroni and cheese or other casseroles.

> The best stuffing is cooked inside the bird. Put it inside a special bag made for this purpose. It's much easier to remove a bag than to scoop out stuffing! Stuffing bags are available in all supermarkets. It also keeps the turkey moist!
>
> Note that cooking stuffing inside the turkey adds thirty to sixty minutes to the cooking time.

Thanksgiving Day

- Set the table in the morning while the bird is cooking.
- Cook the turkey starting at 5 a.m. Wait at least an hour until the coating starts to turn brown and then baste approximately every thirty minutes. If you start basting too soon, you'll be washing off the seasoning you applied at the start. The average-size family bird will be ready by 10 a.m. Let it cool before you cover it. A cooked bird can stay out until the meal is served. For our purposes, the meal will be served at 3 p.m. Please adjust all times to suit your family and the size of your bird. (Putting the turkey in the oven at 5 a.m. means you can have your oven free to cook the rest of the meal by midmorning.)
- Cook the yams you prepared yesterday.
- Whip the eggs and milk to pour over your macaroni and cheese, and bake.
- Peel, boil, and mash the potatoes today because they are so easy to prepare.
- Add shallots and finish cooking your green beans.
- If you have die-hard salad lovers who must have their greens on this day, toss a fresh salad (add ingredients to your shopping list).
- Today, with your prep work behind you, all you have to do is literally cook and serve the meal. This planning will allow you to enjoy your guests.

THE AFTERMATH

Doing your prep work the day before means you will have fewer pots and pans to wash after the meal. For the most part, the dishes will be served in the containers in which they were cooked, particularly casseroles, such as the macaroni and cheese. When the meal is finished, scrape the debris from everyone's plates, rinse the dishes, and pop them into the dishwasher. If you don't have a dishwasher, stack your rinsed dishes to be cleaned after everyone has left. Your fine china and crystal should always be washed by hand.

If your turkey was bigger than your group needed, you can send everyone home with leftovers. This is also an opportunity to off-load Tupperware if you have gone all glass. Even your family will have turkey sandwiches for a few days. This gives you a break from the kitchen the rest of the weekend.

● ● ●
● ● ●
● ● ●

Is your home the designated house for the December festivities? You might want to keep your china and crystal handy. You can pack it all away next month. If your entertaining is over for the year, store your fine china with an eye to protecting it for generations to come or to sell it when you retire from entertaining. Read more about this in the second section, where we organize the kitchen.

Life is always changing and so can we. Don't let your experience today be limited by yesterday. Discovering your perfect Thanksgiving is what this section is all about.

GREAT GRAVY

Good gravy garners raves for the cook, doesn't it? Our chef has a secret weapon in her arsenal: Toss the giblets you remove from the turkey. A week before Thanksgiving, purchase extra necks and cook with celery, carrots, onion, and water. The juices from this concoction will not only give you a fabulous turkey stock, you can freeze it. Use this base to make your gravy.

You can also use this stock to make your stuffing. Our chef keeps homemade chicken stock in her freezer at all times. You could use that on your stuffing or dressing as well.

If you cook your stuffing inside the bird, you need to add time to the cooking process. My chef suggests that you cook the dressing outside the bird. To add flavor, however, she fills the cavity with cut up carrots, onion, and celery. Throw away these ingredients before you serve the bird. Also, use only fresh spices, especially fresh sage.

SUMMARY

WEEK ONE

Write in your journal about the kinds of holidays you have experienced in the past.

Find out what Thanksgiving experience you want to create this year.

WEEK TWO

Get your home ready for company.

Create a budget, guest list, menu, and shopping list.

WEEK THREE

Success is in the menu you create and the schedule you plan. Learn from the sample provided by a professional chef.

WEEK FOUR

Finalize the plan for Turkey Day.

BONUS TIP

When you enter a home on Thanksgiving Day, the heavenly smells of the meal make us all salivate and want to start eating immediately! At this time of year, it's easy to find candles that emit the aroma of apple pie and other mouthwatering foods. Stock up and have them entice your guests at dinner parties you'll be hosting all year long. Try to purchase nonparaffin candles made of beeswax or soy with natural cotton wicks. It's amazing the ways we can find to spare the environment. By the way, the home is more often than not polluted by many things including toxic cleaning agents, paraffin wicks, smoking, inspect sprays, and volatile organic compounds (VOCs), so this might be an opportune time to consider an air purifier.

CREATING A FESTIVE HOLIDAY ATMOSPHERE

To be what we are, and to become what we are capable of
becoming, is the only end of life.

—ROBERT LOUIS STEVENSON

CHARLES DICKENS WAS RIGHT: "IT was the best of times. It was the worst of times." I would guess that's how most of us would describe every holiday season we've ever experienced. Some moments are so delicious and full of joy, we can barely contain ourselves. And then there are those moments when we are Soul weary and in need of a week in the tropics.

When you hear the first Christmas carol, does your stomach do a belly flop? Suddenly you realize that there is a laundry list of things everyone *expects* you to do this time of year. Aunt Jane and Uncle Bert will be looking for a holiday card, your sister hopes to get something other than a one-size-fits-all item tossed into a box at the last minute, and your kids expect Santa to bring them the latest toy craze. And that's just the tip of the iceberg. It doesn't take into account that mountain of work on your desk or the everyday

demands on your time when it's not a major holiday. Take a deep breath. The Zen Organizer™ is here to help you make your way through the maze. One step and one decision at a time.

We're going to systematically examine all the parts that make up this holiday. You'll have instructions to help make it easier to accomplish each step (sending cards, planning your gift-giving strategy, hosting a holiday party, and so on). I even asked a world-famous party planner to contribute some direction so your holiday display will be especially effective this year. We'll consider ways to celebrate the holiday season that involve giving back—to your community, to a cause that's dear to your heart, or even to people half a world away. We end the month with a look at productive things you can do to get ready for the New Year—in addition, of course, to tossing or attending a fabulous party!

I honor Christmas, Chanukah, Kwanzaa, and any other holidays that occur in December, but for ease of reading I use the example of Christmas throughout this part.

HABIT OF THE MONTH

This month your schedule will be frantic. Rather than take on the additional stress of acquiring a new habit, please make a list of the habits you have acquired this year. Be vigilant about performing them each day. Don't let them become casualties of the holiday. Here again are my all-time daily favorites: make your bed, wash dishes and put them away, check trash cans daily, and put your keys in the same place the minute you enter your home. (Eyeglasses or remotes can be substituted for keys should you have that habit nailed.)

AFFIRMATION OF THE MONTH

I stand in the center of the storm known as end-of-the-year madness. I am an oasis of calm. I release to the past all the sad, unhappy, or angry memories that have filled my mind. The past is over. I learn from it. I do not hold on to it. This month is rich with opportunities to create new, positive, happy memories for me to savor. I open myself to receiving my good.

The Art of Placement

Clients frequently ask me if I like the layout of furniture in the room we're organizing. I'm pretty good at moving things around for a better experience, and I inevitably hear: "Regina, you should add decorator to your services!" I love design but don't have the time or the energy to do the deep dive necessary to join the ranks of the pros. (I will list my favorites in the expanded Resources section on my website.) What, then, is my secret? I move furniture in accordance with the basic tenets of Feng Shui, or "The Art of Placement." It's a philosophy that originated in China thousands of years ago and may have grown out of a similar system from India called Vastu Shastra.

Feng Shui's ancient roots use the compass and an eight-sided diagram called the Bagua. In the last century a man named Professor Lin developed a system that required no compass and worked solely off the Bagua. You can do a deep dive and see if The Compass School or The Intuitive School (aka Black Hat) is right for you. I am a longtime student of the latter.

Feng Shui seeks to remove blockages in the physical space to allow for the free flow of energy. Using the Bagua we know which aspect of life is affected by those physical blockages. The areas are career, health, relationships, children/creativity, helpful people, skill and knowledge, family and wealth, prosperity, and fame and reputation. Each area has a corresponding color and element. Don't worry about a deep dive right now. I am suggesting you might want to do a little investigating and see how Feng Shui can help you with your furniture layouts and the flow of energy, aka chi, in your home. Maybe you will shift some things for the holiday celebrations? If you are adding a tree or other decorative items, it's the perfect time to play with these ideas. Don't be surprised if your guests ask if you redecorated!

A New Year beckons and offers the optimal time to refresh your space. Shift furniture and you feel like you moved into a new space. The same is true when we move decorative items. Until your investigation begins, here are some basic tips you can apply immediately.

- Have a water element at the entrance to your home and/or your home office. This can be literal water (usually a water fountain), a mirror, or an image that includes water like a photograph or painting.

    In traditional Chinese restaurants you usually see a fish tank near the entrance, right? The water represents money and the fish keep it moving, i.e., keep the money flowing. We're dealing in symbolic language, so relax and have fun with this.
- Never sit with your back to the door. It's a weak position energetically. Where does the godfather sit in an Italian restaurant in Little Italy? In the back facing into the restaurant so he can see who enters, who exits, and what's happening.

    You don't want anyone sneaking up on you. My clients tell me no one

in their family is into pranks. Again this is symbolic language: you don't want anyone doing sneaky things behind your back in life.
- Don't sit directly facing a window. Why? Your ideas are apt to fly out the window. In other words, it may be difficult to concentrate. No choice? Get window coverings and hang a beautiful crystal. At the very least, you'll have an occasional rainbow in your office.
- The optimum is with a wall at your back for support in a position where you can look up and see both the entry and the window. Move a light chair into different positions and see where you feel most powerful.
- Looking for a relationship? Check out your bedroom and see if you have lots of images of single people. Invite coupling by having twos in abundance: two candles, two people in paintings or photos, and two chairs. You get the idea.
- You can use countermeasures to Feng Shui rules to your advantage. Let's say you work in a corporate setting and you are at the end of a hallway. You would not want to sit in line with the door. In Feng Shui, as everyone walked down the hall you would be impacted by their energy. But you could place two chairs in that position so that no visitors stayed too long. In a guest room place the bed in line with the door so your guests won't settle in and overstay their welcome! My Feng Shui master teacher had a wicked sense of humor.

WEEK ONE

Time to Make a Holiday Plan: Cards, Gifts, and More

This week, you can

- Do journal exercises to help you trace the wounds as well as the joys of past celebrations that you have unconsciously brought with you
- Check your calendar to see what you can reasonably add to your schedule
- Plan a party, create a gift-giving guide, or send out snail mail or electronic holiday cards (or any combination of these)
- Consider the tools that lighten your load

Time required: Thirty to ninety minutes of journal work, and at least three to five hours to create your gift-giving guide, plan a party, and get your card list ready. Shorten the time if you remove an activity.

WE'RE ALL OVERBOOKED AND BUSY as it is, and then December comes along. Now we have a schedule that is nothing short of Herculean. Without a plan, it's also easy to go overboard, and you may find yourself walking through department stores like a zombie on Christmas Eve with your credit card in your hand. (One year I entered the New Year with a bloated credit card bill. That experience is how I became an apostle for financial responsibility!)

This time of year takes an investment of time, energy, and finances. Let's work our way through the month and see if we can't craft a personal expression of the holiday that meets our emotional needs but doesn't break our bank account. Real estate agents have a universal slogan: location, location, location. Zen Organizers™ at this time of year especially need to shout out: budget, budget, budget.

This is a busy week in terms of journal work and planning, but I have designed it this way to give you a much deserved break at the end of the month. My vision is for you to work hard but with focused rather than scattered energy. I want you to be like a laser beam when you're in the mall, at the supermarket, or surfing the internet for gifts. You'll find that the energy you save is energy you can pour into the time you spend with family and friends.

Our journal work this month is going to be abbreviated because we have so much to accomplish. By now, you know the drill. The seeds of yesterday's negative experiences grow like weeds today unless we rid our mental garden of debris. These seeds are expressed in our actions, our beliefs, and most especially our expectations. Here are your journal questions:

1. In the past, was this a happy time of year or did you dread it? Or both?
2. If you were filled with dread, how different are your present circumstances? Is it possible that you are unconsciously carrying negative expectations that could be put to rest?
3. How can you release the tight grip these memories have on you? Will forgiveness heal the wounds? Has enough time passed for you to have clarity?
4. Please list three positive holiday memories. What elements could you repeat?
5. Moving into your adult life, have your expectations and experiences changed over the years? Could you be specific?
6. Do you think you have a good time now because of your childhood or in spite of it?
7. Very often we remain loyal to our parents by replicating what we experienced as children. Are you a slave to the past? Have you ever viewed your holiday experience from this perspective? What

revelations come to you as a result of this particular exploration?
8. If you could have, be, or do anything this holiday, describe in detail what would transpire. When you are finished, ask yourself how close you can come to giving yourself the ultimate gift of making your vision a reality.
9. Jesus, if I may quote him here as a great teacher, said: "It shall be done unto you according to your word." We create and draw to us exactly what we believe. In many ways, that's the real secret, isn't it? In this season of magic when everything seems possible, when the birth of a new year is on the horizon, what words will you speak about this holiday and how you plan to celebrate it?

THINGS TO DO: TAKE YOUR PICK

This season has many elements, and I think most of us have a guilt response that impels us to either do it all or judge ourselves if we don't. What constitutes doing it all? Let's see if I can cover it in one list: send out holiday cards, buy a great gift for everyone (teachers, postal carriers, coworkers, and so on), decorate to the nines, attend your children's school events, host a family holiday dinner, throw a party, go to as many as you can yourself, have a romantic Christmas, and enjoy an out-of-this-world New Year's Eve while giving some thought to New Year's resolutions. Whew! I don't know about you, but now I need a nap.

Let's take these one at a time. Feel free to design a personal response. If the truth were told, I would hope no one was trying to do everything on this list! There isn't any month quite like December in terms of obligations to oneself, family, and friends. Take a deep breath. Remember to relax, remember to focus on enjoying your time with loved ones, and remember that no one can please everyone all the time.

CHECK YOUR CALENDAR

Your calendar—whether it's the one on your computer, your phone, an app, an AT-A-GLANCE or similar system from the stationery store, or the one with Golden Retrievers on it that's hanging on the wall—needs to be your new best friend. You can't survive the holiday season with ease without it. If this is new for you, watch your calendar become a key part of your newly organized life 365 days of the year.

Here are some ways to integrate your calendar into your holiday preparations:

- When you receive an invitation to an event you want to attend, RSVP as soon as possible and note the event in your calendar.
- As you decide what activities will be part of your holiday, mark on your calendar when certain things must be accomplished. For example: "send all out-of-town gifts," "mail Christmas cards," "stop at the mall on the way home from work," or "schedule time to cyber-shop." You don't want to miss "Johnny's school recital

tonight!" You surely don't want to be a no-show at the "company holiday party."

Have you ever heard yourself say: "Oh, no! Is *that* tonight?" or "What do you mean we missed it? I was sure that was *next* week!" With a calendar, those days are over. Nothing is as valuable as a calendar to the organized person. If you're just starting to get organized, you will immediately experience how the season's demands are suddenly easier to handle. By the way, I always buy myself a present at Christmas. Why not splurge a little and buy a calendar system that makes you feel good when you use it? If you like it, you're more likely to use it. I can't think of a nicer gift to buy yourself!

PLAN YOUR PARTY

Using the material from the Thanksgiving celebration last month, you are truly armed with the tools you need to make your family holiday dinner or a party for friends a success. You will have to tweak the guidelines to suit your event, but you have the basics. The first steps are universal: establish a budget, decide what kind of event you want, create a guest list, plan your menu, create a shopping list, and make decisions about the extras, such as decorations and music.

If you are hosting a party, you'd better get the invitations out as soon as possible. Perhaps phone everyone rather than send invitations via snail mail, or do an online invitation blast. The reason I suggest this is that this month is a busy social time for everyone. You want to be sure you'll have enough "yes" responses to make a party worthwhile. The holiday family gathering on Christmas, on the other hand, will be similar to that outlined in "Entertaining with Joy!" And let's face it, that's a captive audience, isn't it?

I am by nature an introvert, and large gatherings were torture for me until I came up with an exercise I do now before I enter the festivities. I stop outside the door and give myself an assignment: I must find at least three people who need a little TLC. I trust my gut and seek out the person who feels insecure about their appearance. A heartfelt compliment goes a long way to building their self-esteem. I look for the person who just suffered a breakup, was laid off from work, or lost a loved one. I offer an ear. I find the person who wants to start a business but needs encouragement. You get the idea. It isn't calculated or phony. I am on a mission to be of service, and that takes the onus off me. Give it a try. This practice signaled the death of my social anxiety.

START GIFT SHOPPING

This week would be an ideal time to prepare your gift list. If you walk through the mall or scroll through sites like Amazon without any guidelines, you'll get into

---

I'd like to help you craft a plan to avoid overindulging at parties and the big home-based meals this month ushers in. We want to enter the New Year with happy memories, not an extra five pounds in our midsection. It takes a little mental and physical organizing, but here's my list:

- On the day of the gathering be mindful about what you will consume. Have a nutrient-dense breakfast and lunch. Arriving at a party ready to eat everything in sight will tempt you to overeat.
- Nurse one or two drinks rather than downing several with great speed.
- If you feel anxious, go into the bathroom for a few rounds of your favorite pranayama.

- Save room for dinner by going easy on the hors d'oeuvres. Have one of each of the most interesting or unusual choices as a sampler.
- Eat your main course slowly and wait twenty minutes before you make the decision to have seconds. If you feel full, stop. Aunt Helen won't die if you skip seconds of her amazing casserole.
- Take two bites of dessert rather than a full slice of cake or pie.
- Keep up your exercise routine all month.
- If your holiday brings up painful memories, journal about your feelings. Don't stuff them down with excess food, alcohol, shopping, or sex.
- Be vigilant about adequate sleep and water consumption.

financial trouble. And as those bloated credit card bills arrive in January, it will be anything but a happy New Year. In the next section is a guide for you to follow. I do all my shopping on the internet. It's equally important to have a budget even if you do all your shopping from your couch. It's all too easy to get carried away and overspend when you don't have the reality of goods in hand.

First, however, I have some words for those of you who say, "I have no idea what to get anyone!" I know two solutions to this dilemma. The first is to learn to listen. People show and tell you all the time what they like, need, and want but would never buy themselves.

If you are still racking your brain but coming up dry, do the next best thing: call that person's best friend, especially if it's a woman you are trying to shop for. After all, wouldn't Robin know what you could get Batman?

If you can't remember a single hint from a conversation this past year, call a mutual friend for help. If you are buying a gift for a business acquaintance, ask his or her assistant for guidance. Does the person have a hobby, such as playing golf? Go to a pro shop and ask for help in finding a useful gift. A favorite place in the world? A beautiful coffee table book about that country or area would be an appreciated gesture. Remember too that every interest spawns magazines.

Every year some toy breaks away from the pack as the must-have toy on every child's list. Shopping early is your safest bet. If you run into trouble, try eBay or Facebook Marketplace or call the manufacturer directly. When work demands are such that you can't shop early in the season, ask another parent to pick one up for you. Should you come up dry, perhaps Santa can leave a note explaining that he left the gift at the North Pole and Mrs. Claus is popping it in the mail. You'll buy a little time with that one!

Another trick is to have a file that holds gift ideas. I save items from magazines and department store catalogues all year long. You can have a file on your computer called "Gifts of Interest." That way, you can gather ideas without having to print them. You'll save not only paper but time. And if there's a link to the website, you can click and shop there directly! I have a Pinterest board devoted to fun gifts so if you get truly stuck check out my ideas. Do you have a favorite influencer? They will surely guide you to great gifts. (Since this is a pay to play world, be sure you follow ethical individuals, not folks who would sell you swamp land if the recommendation made them a buck.)

Remember too the safe gifts that you can give just about anyone in a pinch: fine wine or champagne, flowers, food, candy, or candles. Get a gold pen and write a message on the bottle. If the tag gets separated, the recipient won't be left to guess who the generous person was who got that great champagne.

Finally, it won't help you this year, but consider starting your gift list early and doing your gift shopping all year long. You can take advantage of sales this way. When December arrives, you can skate to the head of the class with perhaps the biggest headache handled in advance. Just don't tell your friends what you did—they might hoodwink you into helping with *their* Christmas shopping!

Creating Your Gift List

Let's start work on our gift list. In the upper-right corner of a large sheet of paper (or on a computer), note the amount of money you can comfortably spend on gifts this year. For many of you, that total may be a holiday bonus. Remember to factor in any traveling you may be doing to visit relatives, any parties you want to host, and the family Christmas supper if it will be at your home. You must subtract every additional expenditure you incur this month from the total available.

Haven't we all forgotten a big-ticket item and then said, "That's okay. That's what credit cards are for"? In the world of Zen Organizing™, debt is the four-letter word we dare not speak. If you have high credit card bills, that's really another type of clutter, isn't it? Our goal this year has been to streamline your life. Your finances are a huge part of the equation.

If you have a computer, it might be wise to create your gift list as a Word or Excel document. This way, you can cut and paste at will. You'll also be able to print a shopping list that's easy to read. If you shop over several days, you can cross off items and leave home each morning with a revised list. All year long we've been paying attention to the importance of the visual appearance of our homes. As you get organized, you will want beauty,

peace, and calm in all aspects of your life. Yes, even your lowly shopping list can be visually inviting.

On the left side of the page, leaving a space equal to three or four lines, list everyone for whom you want to purchase a gift. In parentheses after each name, note the amount of money you are willing to spend on that person. Add those individual amounts and see if the total exceeds your budget. No problem if it does. Just reduce the amounts until you're in the black again. You can also decide to eliminate one or two people. Very often, our desires are bigger than our wallets.

When you have completed your list, go back and note one, two, or three possible items that fall within the price range indicated. When you go to the store, you won't be flying blind. You'll be headed for specific departments. Indeed, you can choose the ideal store for the gift in question. And if you are really lucky, you can score multiple gifts in one store or, at the very least, do all your shopping at one mall. I call this "geographical intelligence." It means grouping your errands so that you don't backtrack throughout the week. Don't abandon this practice when the holidays are over.

Time and Money Savers

If you can shop online, you will save wear and tear on your body and your schedule. You can have the merchant gift wrap and mail the item for you. What could be better? Add up how much your time is worth by the hour, the cost of gas or public transportation, and possibly a babysitter, and

When you look at your list be sure to remember the current life circumstance of each person. Instead of asking "What can I get so-and-so?," ask "How can I help so-and-so?" You'll come up with completely different ideas. A new mom doesn't need another sweater, but she would love a few hours to take a bath and rest. Make that a reality for her. Someone going through chemotherapy doesn't need a new tie. He'd probably love having some errands crossed off his to-do list. You get the idea.

Here are some ideas to fire your creativity:

- Offer to babysit or hire someone
- Pay for a family membership in the local zoo, children's museum, or amusement park
- Get a gift certificate for the hottest restaurant in town for the foodie on your list

- Gift someone a few hours with a professional organizer, house cleaner, personal trainer, therapist, or gardener
- Offer to run errands
- What about a spa day, haircut, mani-pedi, or massage appointment?
- Offer theater or concert tickets
- Purchase an online meditation class or yoga postures series
- Get a gift certificate to the new Pilates studio
- Buy some high-quality oils and a decorative diffuser
- Gift a Himalayan salt lamp in a shape that has meaning to the recipient (round, jagged, lotus, pyramid). Everybody can use a little magic. Be sure yours has a dimmer switch.

online gift-wrapping is suddenly the bargain of the century. At the very least, early in the month order all gifts going out of town. You will save more than gas. You'll save time by avoiding at least one trip to the post office. If you are not comfortable shopping online, search for your dream gifts in the pages of catalogues you know and trust.

Sometimes a friend or relative has a dream gift outside our financial means. With a little imagination, we can contribute something related. Here are two examples. Let's say that Mom and Dad are celebrating their twenty-fifth wedding anniversary. They want to sail from New York to London on the *Queen Elizabeth*

II. You'd love to pay their passage, but you can't begin to afford such an exorbitant gift. However, you can buy them a series of dancing lessons at the local community college. When they go on their dream voyage, they will have a blast.

One of my clients needed to get her brother-in-law a Christmas gift. She knows he likes to try different types of beer and, as it happens, she prepares his expense reports for business travel. She put together a Christmas gift basket filled with beer from all the countries he visited that year. She called it "Your Year in Beer & Cheer!" See how easy it is to put together a memorable, creative, and unique gift that won't break the bank?

Everyone is stressed to the max this season, so why not give some folks on your list the gift of self-care? Check out the local spa and see how much a massage or facial costs. Go to the local beauty salon and check the price of a manicure and pedicure combination. And remember: these treats can delight men, women, and children. Finally, don't forget to treat yourself for all your hard work.

Prepare your list this week and see how many gifts you can send from the privacy of your own home. Next week you can hit the mall if necessary.

PURCHASE GIFT WRAP AND SUPPLIES

If you are getting ready to shop next week, make sure you have gift wrap, gift bags, tape, and ribbon. You may also need sturdy boxes for mailing and approved packing tape from the post office. You want to be sure you have gift tags. Have you ever wrapped a large number of packages for family members and had the tags fall off? It's no fun trying to remember your gifts by the size of the box!

You'll also need stamps and perhaps some priority mailing boxes. If your local post office is a zoo this time of year, handle a lot of your business online. You can have the tools you need delivered at no charge to you. In addition, you can have your packages picked up by your mail carrier when he or she delivers your mail. However, you must schedule this in advance. Need a zip code? Don't fret. You can find it in seconds at the official post office website, www.usps.com.

HOLIDAY HELP

If you have a lot on your plate, consider hiring a part-time assistant for the holiday season. If you live near a large university or college, they probably have an employment office for their students. Are you active at your house of worship? The pastor might know of a retired person who could use a few extra dollars this season. Young or old, help is available.

RE-GIFTING

This is a touchy subject, isn't it? Oprah and I don't see eye to eye on this one. If someone gives you a gift and you don't like it, don't want it, and won't ever use it, I say pass it on. I tell my clients it's nice to have some space on an out-of-the-way closet shelf that holds these items. Here's the trick: Never pass this gift on to someone who has a relationship with the person who gave you the gift. I'm suggesting recycling. I would never advocate hurting the feelings of another human being who was kind enough to get you a gift.

Some parents whose children are fortunate enough to be invited to lots of parties take some of the smaller gifts away when they get home. They know their young children don't need these items and won't miss them. Have you ever had a crying child at your front door? You know, the one who simply refuses to go home? One of my clients pulls down "The Magic Box." It's filled with these miscellaneous party gifts. The child gets to reach in like a grab bag and take something. The catch is that the child must first agree that once they have the gift, it's time to go home and enjoy it!

By the end of this week, I predict that you are going to feel differently about the holiday. Take time to do the journal work and make plans. This will allow you to experience the idea that attention to detail makes things possible to achieve with ease. Spread your assignments out over the month. And remember: You don't have to do it all. You can, however, give your all to the things that bring you the joy of the season.

Craft a Sustainable Holiday

Here are some ways to make your holiday kinder to the environment:

- Be sure any holiday cards you purchase are made from recycled stock.
- A fake tree sounds like a good idea, but it's actually not great for the environment because it can't be recycled. You'd be better off buying a live tree, getting one in a planter so it can move outside in January, or finding one you can rent from a sustainable tree farm. Some rental farms will let you have the same tree every year. Talk about a beautiful family tradition!
- If you need to replace your holiday lights or add to your collection, find LED lights. They use less electricity and last longer. Set a timer so you don't fall asleep and forget the tree and outside lights are still on.

- Instead of buying new ornaments, go to Pinterest and find instructions for making them. If you have children, this is a great way to create memories and establish new traditions.
- Tossing a party? Use your china and glassware. You'll save money not buying the disposable versions. I know they come festooned with holiday images, but ultimately they are just ugly additions to the local landfill.
- Skip the big box stores and supermarkets and shop at your local farmers' market. You can find handmade gifts in addition to homegrown (organic) food. Support your local farmer and the local economy.
- Have you scheduled a fun outing with family or friends? Instead of meeting there, why not carpool? Better yet, try public transportation or (dare I suggest it?) walk to the event.
- Building on the fun outing theme, why not buy a few museum memberships so that throughout the year you and your friends or family members can meet up for special events?
- Do you have a smart home controlled by a system you operate from your phone? You can set routines and have safety measures and energy-saving steps done with the press of a button. Label them something simple like "Leaving" for your daily home exit. If you plan to visit Grandma's home for the holidays and will be gone for a week, set a "Vacation" routine.
- Don't fret if you are not in a smart home. You can set routines and have

the list on your phone to remind you what to do until the steps are an ingrained habit. I might suggest you put those lists in the shared family app you use or print them out and put them on the refrigerator. A lot will depend on the ages of your family members and how responsible they are by nature. Another factor will be if you employ people like a housekeeper or babysitter who will also need to know how to leave the home in a safe fashion.

- If you decided against composting when we organized your kitchen, now is a great time to revisit the enormous about of waste composting saves from a landfill. Your solution will depend on the size of your home or apartment and any outside space you have access to. If you live on a farm or have a big lot, an outside compost unit is a no-brainer. If you are in a small big-city apartment, the electric countertop version is genius. Many big cities have composting programs and would be delighted to guide you and share resources.

- Finally, let's consider the enormous waste of wrapping paper. Be sure you purchase recycled products going forward. As much fun as tearing through the wrap might be, how about asking the family to unwrap gently so that paper can be reused? Or make the switch to gift bags and use them for years to come. I had a client who used newspaper to wrap gifts. Last but not least, cut open paper sacks from the grocery store and decorate them. Think outside the box.

Finally, a word about children and what sponges they are for emotional energy. If they see you enjoy implementing planet-saving measures, they will grow up naturally looking for ways to add to the childhood measures they experienced at home. If, on the other hand, you complain about recycling, composting, or any other measure to save resources, they will be inculcated in that value system. What we say and what we do are powerful teachers. The watchword for Zen Organizing™ is apt here: be Mindful.

WEEK TWO

Get Your Home Holiday-Ready

This week, you can

- Tune up your home for guests
- Bring out the decorations
- Hit the cyber stores and brick-and-mortar stores

Time required: Varies.

LAST WEEK YOU DID A LOT OF PLAN-ning. This week you'll put the pedal to the metal and get out there. Now is the time to get your home tuned up for the holiday onslaught of family and friends. Some of you will also be busy shopping, others will delight in planning a great party, and still others will have cards to complete. What-ever needs to be done from the items we dis-cussed, this is your week to complete these tasks. It's better to push a little this week so you can relax for the rest of the month. Of course I use the term "relax" a bit loosely. It's in short supply during December!

DECLUTTER BEFORE YOU DECORATE

If you have been following along for the course of this year, your home is ready for anything. If you need a crash course in decluttering your environment, you can see the notes at the beginning of "Enter-taining with Joy!" and quickly make the kitchen, dining room, and living room pre-sentable for family and friends. The New Year is on the horizon—I trust that getting organized will be one of your resolutions.

Get the decluttering out of the way this week, especially if you are going to bring out decorations. Think of your home as an artist's palette. See your decorations as colors you are adding to this palette. If there is no room for them, your beautiful things will simply clutter the canvas.

I sometimes visit a post office near my acupuncturist's office. One of the postal clerks goes all out for every holiday. It's hard to describe what she does except to say that every single vestige of space is filled with a decoration for that holiday.

This includes her desk, her counter, and the walls at her end of the long counter she shares with two other employees. It doesn't stop here, however, because she decorates herself as well. The result is that you can't see or appreciate any of the decorations because the eye registers it all as clutter. As a balance, no one else has a single decorative item on display. Think about your home in years past. Have you gone overboard? Just as you can rotate your decorative items, you can rotate your holiday items, saving some for next year.

UNTANGLING THE DECORATIONS

Decorating is one huge project during this season. What will you do for this holiday? Will you get a tree? Will it be fresh or do you have an artificial one waiting to make its annual appearance? Do you have a stash of decorations? If you need to start over, add decorations to your holiday shopping list. I like to add one new ornament a year.

Will you have live plants around the house? A client told me that after one Christmas, he planted his poinsettia. Guess what? It grew like wildfire. Now he takes cuttings from his own poinsettia and decorates the whole house. The small houseplant poinsettia turns into a nice green plant after Christmas. They may no longer be festive, but they still clean the air in your home.

This is a good week to take out your decorations. If you haven't been working the program all year, this is probably your first encounter with these items since last Christmas. Are the boxes worn and weary? Consider purchasing heavy-duty containers when the time comes to repack everything. This time of year, they come in green and red, and while this makes them easy to identify from a distance, I would stick to clear or off-white containers with wheels. Down the line, you can recycle these containers for other types of product storage. A computer label or one made with your personal label maker will reveal the contents. Search Etsy to find specialty labels for every part of your home. Or bite the bullet and purchase a top-of-the-line Brother P-Touch that can handle one-inch tape. Once again we see choices abound for a simple thing. Are you having fun yet?

I keep lights in one container, decorations in a second, and ornaments wrapped in tissue paper in a third. You can also get section dividers to keep your ornaments safe and separate. To keep your light strings untangled, you want to wrap them around something. A sturdy piece of cardboard works well. It's not unlike unwinding the garden hose.

DECORATING TIPS

My client and frequent collaborator Shay Watson is the founder and creative force behind Aesthetica Events. Shay plans elaborate parties for the rich and famous. He also does interior design. Although he is based in Los Angeles, his clients take him all over the world. Shay takes a space and transforms it in creative and imaginative ways that would take your breath away.

Here are some holiday decorating tips Shay wanted to share with you.

1. Take a few minutes to sit quietly and think about your individual decorating style. Which of the following would you use to describe yourself and the way you express yourself in your home: simple and modern; over the top; or elegant and chic? What color choices predominate? Do you like matching or contrasting patterns in a room? Work with that, not against it, this season.

2. Consider a theme for this holiday. Perhaps each room will have a different theme? What will be the connecting link? For example, imagine you love neutral tones. The bright red and deep greens of Christmas are foreign to your everyday color scheme. Instead of overwhelming your home and your senses with traditional Christmas colors, you could use gold as your base color and carefully use red and green as the colors that pop.

3. Have you ever had a print framed? If so, you understand the concept of using a color in the matte or the frame that will make something in the print pop out. Decorating is the three-dimensional version of that process!

4. A little glitz or sparkle is part and parcel of the season. Use this element as an accent. Once again, you don't want tinsel to overwhelm. Perhaps the glitz is used to draw the eye to a collection you treasure, such as antique angels in a centerpiece?

5. Lay out all of your holiday decorations and place similar items together. You want to know on sight how many candles, angels, or snowmen you really have. If you can, place everything on a large surface such as the dining room table. Remember, the goal is to choose what you are going to use as you create your holiday design. Most people allow every single ornament to explode into their environment. It can be overwhelming and nothing is really seen or appreciated. You don't have to use it all.

6. Balance your arrangements by grouping items in odd numbers rather than even. Think one big, medium, and small item per group. You can easily imagine three red candles in descending size to see how this would work. When you are placing your items, have a common element that connects them. This could be the item itself (all angels or candles, for example) or a common color or tone.

By the end of this week, you will have used the canvas of your home to create a personal expression of the holiday. I hope you take the motto "Less is more" to heart. The key is not to allow every trinket you own to explode into the environment. Follow Shay's advice and your friends will be astonished at how inviting your home looks this year. Remember to enjoy everything you tackle this month.

The Blue Zone

You know by now my passion for nutrient-dense eating. You have probably heard of Dan Beuttner, who researched and wrote about groups of people around the world who traditionally live to one hundred years.

They are vital, alive, and active, not in nursing homes or taking copious amounts of prescription drugs. Here are some tips from those communities about celebrating the holidays in a more conscious way.

- Gifts are lovely, but the holidays are about connecting and celebrating in person for these groups. They prefer to celebrate accomplishments over a big communal meal than spend money on grandiose gifts.
- Blue Zone people love to gather around and share a holiday meal. They are vocal about expressing gratitude, and when the meal has been consumed, they don't trundle off to watch football. They go for a long walk or turn on some music and dance!
- Blue Zone residents see a Spiritual component to the holidays. If your family isn't the type to go off to midnight mass (as an example), you could easily teach them a simple pranayama and meditation technique from this book and do it as a family. I can't imagine introducing a more meaningful tradition.
- Long-living residents in the Blue Zones tend to be plant based but do eat meat sparingly throughout the year. Special meat-centric dishes appear during the holidays. These folks remain conscious of portion size and the meal continues to be predominately plant based. This makes the meat a treat, not the focus.

Here's my Zen Organizing™ tip: If you can't get home for the celebration, set up a Zoom chat and establish a format. Allow everyone to share in turn for a few minutes before you go to the free-for-all. Record it all and edit together highlights that you can email to everyone who participated. If video editing is beyond you, just record the structured part of the gathering and email that to the participants. This will be THE best gift of the season.

WEEK THREE

Volunteer with Good Cheer

This week, you can

- Find ways to give back
- Complete any holiday details left undone

Time required: Because there are so many variables, this week is left for you to plan as you feel you need to.

THE GOAL REMAINS TO BE ABLE TO celebrate the holiday next week with a sense of accomplishment and joy. If you can steal a few hours from all the card writing, gift buying, and party going, I suggest getting in the holiday spirit and doing some volunteer work. It will add something to the season that I cannot capture in words. Here are some ideas to get you thinking about how to offer your talents and time where they will be most needed this season:

- Contact your house of worship and see if they have any holiday programs that need volunteers. Perhaps a family needs help this season, and you could donate a few gifts to the children, or drive a sick parent to a doctor's visit,

or run errands for the family. One of my Zen Tribe members asked her entire family to donate whatever they had earmarked for gifts to a house of worship that used the funds to provide Christmas gifts and food for several families. As my Tribe member said: "We all have enough stuff."

- Check your local newspaper. Organizations that need help are always featured this time of year.
- Many groups dedicated to helping the homeless will sponsor a holiday meal program. See if your services are needed for food prep or serving.
- Has a particular disease touched your family? There are organizations devoted to every major illness; contact them to see if they need your help

at any holiday fund-raisers. If you don't know of any organizations, call your local hospital for guidance.

- The internet offers a wealth of opportunities. You can start with www.volunteermatch.org or www.sixdegrees.org.

- Do you play an instrument or sing? Why not offer to entertain at a long-term care facility or retirement home? When I was an actress, I wrote a short holiday play each year and a group of us performed at schools for the mentally and physically handicapped. You won't find a warmer, more appreciative audience anywhere!

- Call your local chamber of commerce and see if a community project needs your gift of time. You might find yourself using your gardening skills to beautify your neighborhood.

- Would you like to volunteer on a long-term basis? Why not become a Big Brother or a Big Sister? You can begin by making a child's holiday special.

- Is there a hospice in your community? Perhaps you could sit for a few hours with someone who has no family members present.

- Even if you can't donate your time, you can donate through what I call "conscious giving." So many organizations will help the less fortunate in the world for a small donation. They give you a certificate to present as a gift. Last Christmas I made several donations in the names of those I wanted to honor during the holiday

season. They were touched to know that in their name school children in Afghanistan would have books for the year. On my website you'll find my favorite charities in the expanded Resources section.

- A special group that needs extra TLC this month are the sweet creatures who find themselves in animal rescue facilities. You might be able to walk a dog that hasn't had a special human in months or bottle-feed a kitten abandoned by its mom. If you have pets at home, remember that this time of year can be stressful for them. Their environment is changing and more people are coming to the house. Give them a few extra treats throughout the month, such as an extra walk in the park or a new toy. It's pretty easy to make your own treats or provide healthy items like fresh or dried blueberries. You don't want to ply Fido with supermarket treats and have him start the year a little thick around the middle.

You may find that your volunteer experience touches you in unpredictable ways. Don't be surprised if it becomes a regular part of your life. The key, I think, is to help others using a talent you already have. You don't have to be an actor or a musician! If you are a hairdresser, a manicurist, or a coach for a sport, if you love kids, or if you are just a good listener, someone in your community needs you. The great thing, of course, is that you need them just as much.

WEEK FOUR

Here's to a Happy New Year!

This week, you can

- Make a list of all last-minute details
- Create a holiday checklist for the big day
- Stock up using after-holiday sales
- Make use of the week between Christmas and New Year's

Time required: Varies.

THIS IS IT. TAKE A DEEP BREATH AND make a list of everything you have to do before the holiday. Eliminate whatever you can; delegate like crazy; schedule all remaining details in your planner. Remember the first thing you learned: The whole of anything is overwhelming. It's one step at a time to the finish.

If you didn't get your cards out on time, be happy that they are going out at all. Take guilt off the table. Behind on your shopping? Do as much as you possibly can at this point online or by phone, realizing that some gifts just won't arrive in time for Christmas. However, never underestimate your power to think creatively! Here are some ideas to inspire you:

- If your loved ones are far way, call a local store and see if they can make a timely delivery. Perhaps your friend or relative would appreciate some champagne for their holiday meal or a beautiful floral centerpiece?
- Is there someone on your list who likes the theater or concerts? Call the local theater or concert hall and see if you can buy tickets for a performance you know they will love during the New Year. Order a subscription! You can of course use a ticket service.
- What about the guys on your list who love sports? I bet tickets to a hockey, football, or soccer game would make you a hero.
- Do you have a relative or friend who has wanted to take up a sport or learn a new hobby? Buy them a series of

lessons! Your local community college will have courses at a reasonable price. If you have young girls in your life, I bet they love horses, right? Ask if they like to hang out at the barn; if so, give them their own grooming kit.

- Don't forget the beauty of useful products. Give a Red Cross Emergency Kit to everyone on your staff—along with their bonus, of course. One year a dear friend of mine left the room in tears on Christmas Eve. Her husband gave her the biggest, fanciest, most outrageous vacuum cleaner on the market! Gentlemen, she doesn't want a household cleaning appliance. Trust me. And remember: Young children and teens don't want useful products either!

Once you open your mind to possibilities outside the box, you will be amazed what happens. And if you wind up at the local mall on Christmas Eve, take a deep breath. Be grateful you have the means to shop and loved ones to shop for! It sounds corny, but you're going to need to shift your attitude. You'll also want to eat before you go. What is worse than greasy, unhealthy mall food?

Before I went shopping, I'd think long and hard about how I might be creative. I just know you can make someone happy with a unique gift. And let's face it, we all have enough generic gifts to last forever.

And finally, if you haven't bought a single gift because you had the flu, tell your loved ones what happened. Say you'd like to exchange gifts after Christmas, because you don't have the time or the strength to make the December deadline. Take care of yourself emotionally and physically.

THE DAY ARRIVES

Every family and culture has its own traditions. Some families celebrate with a big meal on Christmas Eve while others have their big holiday celebration on Christmas Day. You can tweak the guidelines (and the menu) presented last month and be ready for family and friends to arrive.

Don't burden yourself with a deep cleaning and organization of the environment. Do a quick sweep again this week if your home needs it. Everything will look great. If you've been organizing all year, you have no piles. If you're new to the program, they will be your focus shortly. Right now you have gifts to wrap!

If small children in the home believe in Santa Claus, you'll need to hide your purchases and put them out when the children go to sleep. If they are older, I hope you've been wrapping and placing beautiful packages under the tree for a while.

Getting the tree is also governed by family and cultural traditions. In Brooklyn we got our tree right after Thanksgiving. My mother used to say that it took so much work to decorate it, we might as well enjoy it right up to the New Year. In Los Angeles, it's usually so warm that keeping a tree for that length of time is tricky. I buy late and leave it up until the Epiphany in January, which I believe is the European tradition. What works for you?

Try to balance your celebration so that you aren't exhausted. Here are some ideas for you to consider:

- If you hosted Thanksgiving, let someone else in the family host Christmas.
- Don't be shy about giving assignments to family and friends who are coming over to celebrate with you. Let them contribute to the meal—and to the cleanup!
- As you enter the last week, if you are feeling stressed and overbooked, take some things off your calendar. If that means you miss a party or two, it will be far superior to spending the big day in bed with a cold.
- Watch your eating habits all month but be especially vigilant this week.

Eat before you go to a party. Eat before you shop. Stock up on healthy snacks and don't allow candy, cakes, pies, or donuts into the house.

- Above all else, don't lose sight of the deeper meaning of the holiday. When you feel yourself rushing, rushing, rushing, make yourself slow down. I can't tell you how many years I got lost in the *shoulds* of this holiday only to wake up on January 1 wondering where it all went. I have a great button I like to take out this time of year. It says it all: "This is not a dress rehearsal." Indeed. It's the real thing. And we don't get a repeat opportunity to experience it in a different way.

The sight of discarded Christmas trees on the sidewalk has always filled me with sadness. Here are a few Mindful ways to dispose of them:

- Check with your local municipality. Most have a special pickup service for Christmas trees and will recycle them.
- Chop up your tree and add it to your composting pile.
- Know any woodworkers? They might turn your discard into some creative items. Who knows? Maybe even Christmas ornaments for next year's tree!
- If you live in a country or suburban area, you can drop your tree in a field or in a pond. Once you have a spot in mind, if it isn't your property, check with local authorities. It's great for the environment but may not be allowed due to volume. If you live in NYC, don't head to Central Park! Can you imagine thousands of trees being dumped in Sheep's Meadow?!
- Does your climate support pine trees? You could keep your living tree until next year or even plant it in the earth. I once owned a house in the country that sat on three acres. There was a small zone of pine trees and I used to wonder how they formed that cluster. I have my suspicions that a previous owner planted their Christmas trees.

The New Year Beckons

After Christmas, some details will need our attention. Gifts may have to be returned or exchanged. Post-Christmas is a great time to stock up on recycled wrapping paper and holiday cards for next year. Perhaps you want to take the decorations down early so you can take a quick trip out of town to celebrate the New Year. Do you need to tidy up and get ready for a New Year's party? We've covered all these areas this year, so you know how to proceed. One more item, however, begs for your attention. Can you guess what it is?

You want to enter the New Year with a plan. Those wonderful days between Christmas and New Year's are ripe for sweeping out the old and making way for the new. Many cultures honor this week as the perfect time to literally and emotionally do a clean sweep. New Year's resolutions often stay in the realm of wishful thinking, but they don't have to. A New Year is an offering of opportunities. Make way for the new and chart your course with a series of well-thought-out and executed goals. Don't be afraid to take the next step—you can always take it one week at a time.

Perhaps before you look into the future, it would be powerful and healing to take a few minutes to list five things you are grateful for this year. If we look on social media at the lives of famous influencers, actors, politicians, and the rich and famous, we can feel small and unaccomplished. Trust me. Those portraits are filtered—literally and figuratively. No one has a perfect life. No one.

If you learned to make your bed every day and love the way your room looks and feels, list and celebrate that. If you took a long-dreamed-for trip to Bali and were inspired to start a blog, add that to the list. If you discovered you love meditation, I say: "Way to go!" And if you find that being in the present moment is now how you roll, my work is done here. Everything counts is the point. No effort or accomplishment is ever wasted. The world is waiting for the gift you came to give. Being organized makes it easier to fulfill this gift called your Life Purpose. The late, great Sidney Poitier said it best: *Be useful to the journey.*

SUMMARY

WEEK ONE

Write in your journal to examine how past holidays have influenced the way you celebrate.

Examine the various elements of the holiday (cards, decorations, parties, and so on).

Learn how to prepare a holiday gift guide.

Create a shopping list for mundane items such as cards, wrapping paper, and tape.

Tidy the house.

WEEK TWO

Set your individual plan into motion.

Decorate your home.

WEEK THREE

Get caught up on all unfinished details.

Consider holiday volunteer opportunities.

Celebrate with your fellow Zen Organizers™.

WEEK FOUR

Celebrate!

Consciously prepare for the New Year.

BONUS TIP

As the current year draws to a close, I thought you might enjoy doing a practice done for thousands of years by people the world over to consciously release the old. You can use your fireplace if you have one or have a fire with candles in a container you designate for this purpose each year. This is a wonderful family tradition.

Sit in a meditative state and quietly think of things you want to release. Here are some examples to fire your contemplation (pun intended): judgment, hair-trigger temper, laziness, depression, gossiping, or lack of motivation.

About twenty minutes before midnight begin a meditation and as the clock approaches midnight, hold uncooked rice in your hand. Infuse it with all the things you no longer need. Toss it into the fire and say this ancient mantra: "Om Swaha." This signifies joyously releasing what you wish to toss into the flame. Return to your seat and enter the New Year in peace and meditation, embracing the opportunity to have a fresh start.

If you have a party planned, you can of course do this fire ceremony the next morning. If you imbibed a wee bit too much, do the ceremony when you are clearheaded. "Om Swaha" can be done anytime you have a new beginning to embrace and want to release habits or qualities that no longer support your new circumstance.

Some of my clients eschew rice and just burn slips of paper with the unwanted qualities written down into the fire. It's your intention that matters. But then that's true of every single action you take, isn't it?

IN CLOSING, THE BEST IS YET TO BE

Some of you began this program one year ago and your lives are transformed. Others are at the start of the adventure. People with a vested interest in organizing their lives and clearing the clutter are headed for change. Sometimes it's clear what that is when they call me. A baby is about to be born or a new job has been accepted. Perhaps a new home has been purchased or a disease has been beaten. Your life is changing and your level of organization must change as well to support the new reality. If the change isn't known when we meet, it will make itself known in short order. It's an amazing process to watch unfold. This happens with my clients, and it will happen with you.

At the end of a year, you will feel as if we know each other. I have certainly shared a large part of my personal history with you. I invite you to write to me from my website, www.ReginaLeeds.com. If you'd like help creating your Zen Organizer™ group, I'd be delighted to assist you. You are welcome to join my private group of Zen Organizers™ known as Regina's Zen Organizing™ Tribe. Check the Resources section for details.

In airport lounges and hotel lobbies, on the street or in a restaurant, please come and tell me your story. Getting organized is going to make your life easier and your life experience richer and deeper. Come over and tell me all about it!

I want to end our year with a quote from the great Indian yogi Paramahansa Yogananda, the author of *Autobiography of a Yogi*.

Feel the hidden waters of Spirit trickling through all material life...feel the divine bliss of Spirit within you and all things.

Namaste,
Regina

Acknowledgments

Everything is energy....Match the frequency of the reality you want
and you cannot help but get that reality....It can be no other way.

−ALBERT EINSTEIN

One Year to an Organized Life was first acquired by editor Katie McHugh. The concept of a year devoted to getting organized had frightened other editors. Katie, however, is a visionary who instantly understood the scope, the audience, and the goal of the book. She never once interfered in the creative process. Her directives were concise, powerful, to the point, and minimal. Katie raises the process of editing to an art form. There is no doubt in my mind that she made the original *One Year to an Organized Life* a better book. I am forever in her debt. I can in no way adequately express my gratitude to her and the team she assembled.

Fast-forward over a decade after its publication and enter another team of angels led by editor Dan Ambrosio, assistant editor Alison Dalafave, production editor Sean Moreau, designer Kevin Gilmartin, copy editor Mike McConnell, and proofreaders Annie Chatham and Susie Pitzen. Not only did they allow me to update the material, they respected and supported the new vision I had for it. *One Year* is still a hands-on guide with step-by-step organizing instruction. With the addition of new material from the worlds of yoga and meditation, recycling as it relates to fashion, and conscious eating (to name a few), it has become a guide to a Mindful lifestyle. Zen Organizing™ has evolved in ways I could not have imagined over three decades ago when I coined the phrase and set out to organize physical environments. I am forever in this team's debt as well.

Writers and their agents usually part company faster than celebrity marriages crash and burn in Los Angeles. As of this writing, agent Marilyn Allen and I are moving past a twenty-year collaboration. I was blessed the day this kind, intelligent, talented, and dedicated woman entered my life. Thank you for everything you do, Marilyn.

Kudos to the first brave souls who joined the Zen Organizing™ Tribe. They humble me with their fearless dedication. The original group is now called the Tribal Council, and they jump in to inspire and advise all the newbies who join the Tribe. Special thanks to Marlene Sohl, Joan Von Weien, Chris Rowley, Frankie Snell Villar, Toni Lawrence, Susanna Miller, Kiaran Weil, and our intrepid moderator Arisa Takahashi.

The material in *One Year* takes the serious reader on a voyage of discovery that requires a combination of old-fashioned elbow grease, mental commitment, and emotional courage.

One Year to an Organized Life has been blessed by everyone who touched it. It is my hope it will now bless you, your life, and your journey.

Resources

To be of value this section can't be static. It needs to be a vibrant guide to all the latest in the world of organizing and related disciplines. With that in mind, what follows is a *brief* introduction to some of my favorite resources. I invite you to visit my website, www.ReginaLeeds.com, for a comprehensive list of the latest companies, products, books, and other discoveries to help you on your journey to a Zen Organized lifestyle.

REGINA'S ZEN ORGANIZING™ TRIBE

A Lifetime Membership is $300 and includes the following benefits:

- Private Facebook group
- Weekly Zoom meeting (Saturdays, 10 a.m. PST, for thirty minutes; recording is available until the next meeting begins)
- Weekly video pep talk to inspire your week
- Weekly resource tip
- Weekly meditation class taught by one of our members who is a certified meditation teacher

We follow *One Year to an Organized Life*; however, members are free to work on any area of concern in their home or workspace. If you'd like to experiment to see if we're right for your journey, you can have a one-month membership for $25 and apply that payment to the Lifetime fee should you decide to join us. You can also purchase Lifetime memberships as gifts for family, friends, and coworkers.

Please write to me for payment details:

Regina Leeds
ZenOrg1@gmail.com
www.ReginaLeeds.com

CHARITIES I ADMIRE

Brides Across America
Free wedding dresses for military and first responders: www.bridesacrossamerica.com

Dress for Success
Helps women dress professionally for job interviews and the first days of employment: https://dressforsuccess.org/about-us/

Hope in a Suitcase
They provide foster kids with suitcases and basic supplies to restore dignity to their lives: www.hopeinasuitcase.org

Operation Prom
Provides free prom dresses and tuxedos to low-income students: www.promnationalnetwork.org

The Angel Gowns Project
They turn donated wedding dresses into burial gowns for babies who never go home, and they ship around the world: theangelgownsproject.org/about-us

World Central Kitchen
Founded by celebrity chef José Andrés, the organization goes to the sites of natural disasters and war to feed those in need. In addition to money, you can donate your time: worldcentralkitchen.org

CREDIT REPORTS AND IDENTITY THEFT

Free Annual Credit Report: www.annualcreditreport.com or call (877) 322-8228 (created by the three nationwide consumer credit reporting agencies [Equifax, Experian, and TransUnion], this centralized service allows consumers to request free annual credit reports)

Equifax: www.equifax.com or call (877) 576-5734

Experian: www.experian.com/fraud or call (888) 397-3742

TransUnion: www.transunion.com or call (800) 680-7289

Federal Trade Commission: https://consumer.gov/section/scams-identity-theft (for detailed information about identity theft reports)

DESIGN

Annie Sloan: www.anniesloan.com (paint expert)

Athena Calderone: www.athenacalderone.com (designer and author)

Beata Heuman: www.beataheuman.com (designer and author)

Kelly Wearstler: www.kellywearstler.com (designer and author)

Linda Applewhite: www.lindaapplewhite.com (designer and author)

DONATIONS

Clothing and Household Items
Career Gear: www.careergear.org (provides professional attire for job interviews to disadvantaged men)

Goodwill Industries International: www.goodwill.org (sells donated clothing and household goods)

One Warm Coat: www.onewarmcoat.org (collects and distributes coats for free to those in need)

Salvation Army: www.salvationarmy.com (sells donated clothing and household goods)

Computer Technology

The following sites refurbish and distribute computer technology (laptops, desktops, printers) to economically disadvantaged youth in the United States and around the world.

Computers 4 Kids: www.c4k.org

National Cristina Foundation: www.cristina.org

World Computer Exchange: www.world computerexchange.org

Miscellaneous Items

Hungry for Music: www.hungryformusic.org (distributes used musical instruments to underprivileged children)

OneSight: www.onesight.org (check their website to find out where to donate your old prescription eyeglasses or sunglasses; or contact your local Lions Club)

Reader to Reader: www.readertoreader.org (accepts books for children and teens and distributes to school libraries nationwide)

Suitcases for Kids: www.suitcasesforkids.org (provides luggage for foster children who move from home to home)

FOOD

Bridgford: www.bridgford.com (Tanya's favorite rolls)

Wicked Healthy: www.wickedhealthyfood.com (vegan chefs Chad and Derek Sarno)

Daily Harvest: www.daily-harvest.com (vegan food delivery)

Splendid Spoon: www.splendidspoon.com (vegan food delivery)

HELP WITH ORGANIZING

Bublup
An app to help with organizing home and office projects

Cozi
Family organizer for all aspects of your modern life

Evernote
Bring your notes, to-dos, and schedule together to tame life's distractions and accomplish more

Google Docs
Part of a suite of offerings from Google with special applications for projects from the office to home remodeling. You can create, edit, and share web-based documents, spreadsheets, and presentations. Store documents online and access them from any computer: docs.google.com

Pinterest

A great place to store memories, search for new ideas and recipes, or build your brand: www.pinterest.com

MIND, BODY, AND SPIRIT

Anima Mundi: www.animamundiherbals .com (herbal resource)

Belleruth Naparstek: www.health journeys.com (guided imagery and meditation)

Elena Brower: www.elenabrower.com (aromatherapy and yoga)

Jo Bregnard: www.jobregnard.com (yoga and self-care expert for caretakers)

Jon Kabat-Zinn, founder of Mindfulness-Based Stress Reduction and author: mindfulnesscds.com

Marlene Sohl: www.shinewithcolor .com (Aura-Soma registered practitioner products and consultation)

Mysteries.Net: www.mysteries.net (meditation and yoga site)

Pamela Miles: www.pamelamiles.com (reiki master and spiritual healer)

Self-Realization Fellowship: www .selfrealizationfellowship.org (meditation and yoga site)

Sharon Salzberg, author and cofounder of Insight Meditation Society with Jack Kornfield and Joseph Goldstein: www .sharonsalzberg.com

NATURAL CLEANING

Mrs. Meyer's Clean Day: www.mrsmeyers .com

Naturally Clean: The Seventh Generation Guide to Safe & Healthy, Non-Toxic Cleaning, by Jeffrey Hollender and Geoff Davis, with Meika Hollender and Reed Doyle (British Columbia, Canada: New Society Publishers, 2006)

Seventh Generation products: www .seventhgeneration.com

Tom's of Maine products: www .tomsofmaine.com

OFFICE AND FILING SUPPLIES

AT-A-GLANCE: www.ataglance.com

FLAX Art & Design: www.flaxart.com

Gubb: www.gubb.net (helps you make and store lists)

Office Depot/OfficeMax: www .officedepot.com

See Jane Work: www.seejanework.com

Staples: www.staples.com

ONLINE AUCTION AND SALE SITES

Cash for CDs: www.cashforcds.com

eBay: www.ebay.com

PROFESSIONAL ASSOCIATIONS

Clutterers Anonymous: www.clutterers
anonymous.org

Codependents Anonymous: www.co
dependents.org

Messies Anonymous: www.messies.com

National Association of Productivity &
Organizing Professionals (NAPO):
www.napo.net

RECYCLE

1-800-GOT-JUNK?: www.1800gotjunk
.com or call (800) 468-5865 (removes
just about anything [furniture, appliances,
electronics, yard waste, and renovation
debris] and makes every effort to recycle
or donate items)

PaperBackSwap: www.paperbackswap
.com

Rechargeable Battery Recycling
Corporation (RBRC): www.call2recycle
.org or call (877) 273-2925 (recycles used
portable rechargeable batteries and old
cell phones)

REDUCE AND STOP UNWANTED MAIL

DMAchoice: www.dmachoice.org (online
tool to manage your mail)

Opt Out of Preapproved Credit Card and
Insurance Offers: www.optoutprescreen

.com or call (888) 567-8688 (official
website of the consumer credit
reporting industry to accept and process
consumer requests to opt in or opt out
of prescreened credit card and insurance
offers)

TRAVEL

Flight, Hotel, and Car Reservations
Cheap Tickets: www.cheaptickets.com

Expedia: www.expedia.com

Hotwire: www.hotwire.com

KAYAK: www.kayak.com

Orbitz: www.orbitz.com

Travelocity: www.travelocity.com

General Travel Information
AccuWeather: www.accuweather.com
(provides weather forecasts for locations
in the US and abroad)

Automobile Association of America:
www.aaa.com

Centers for Disease Control and
Prevention: wwwnc.cdc.gov/travel
(provides travel health information)

Department of Homeland Security: www
.travel.state.gov/passport (to apply for a
passport or get information on traveling
abroad)

National Oceanic and Atmospheric
Administration: www.noaa.gov (provides

information on daily weather forecasts, severe storm warnings, and climate monitoring within the United States)

National Weather Service: www.weather .gov (provides weather reports on specific locations within the United States)

Transportation Security Administration: www.tsa.gov/travel (provides updated information on security screening and items allowed on an airplane)

Weather Channel: www.weather.com (provides weather forecasts for locations in the US and abroad)

Weather Underground: www.wunder ground.com (provides weather forecasts for locations in the US and abroad)

Index